Relays

WRITING SCIENCE

EDITORS Timothy Lenoir and Hans Ulrich Gumbrecht

Weimar, 30tᵉⁿ April 1829.

v. Goethe.

An Herrn

Carl Jügel
angesehenen Buch= und Kunsthändler
Wohlgeb.
in
Frankfurt a/M.

fr.

Relays

LITERATURE AS AN EPOCH OF THE POSTAL SYSTEM

Bernhard Siegert

TRANSLATED BY *Kevin Repp*

STANFORD UNIVERSITY PRESS
STANFORD, CALIFORNIA
1999

Relays: Literature as an Epoch of the Postal System was originally published in German in 1993 as *Relais: Geschicke der Literatur als Epoche der Post,* 1751–1913, ©1993 Verlag Brinkmann & Bose, Berlin.

Stanford University Press
Stanford, California

Printed in the United States of America

CIP data appear at the end of the book

CONTENTS

Part Three

Mail Beyond Human Communication

TABLES AND FIGURES

Table

Figures

Relays

Introduction

Noise and wrangling on all channels: that was the situation to begin with. Language was a pipeline that constantly was clogged with the ambiguities of rhetoric. Philosophers were its plumbers. Thus began an epoch of the postal system that equated transmission channels with language, language with communication, communication with understanding, and understanding with the salvation of humanity: "For language being the great conduit whereby men convey their discoveries, reasonings, and knowledge, from one to another, he that makes an ill use of it, though he does not corrupt the fountains of knowledge, which are in things themselves, yet he does, as much as in him lies, break or stop the pipes whereby it is distributed to the public use and advantage of mankind."[1] After Locke, it was supposed to hold true that words could claim to represent things only when they were preceded by communication. After all, before language set about the task of representing the ideas of things, it was a "common tie" or the "bond of society."[2] What is, therefore, is posted. The world was the legacy of sites of transmission, of halts, relays, switches. The truth of knowledge thus demanded a postal hygiene that ushered the philosophers of language into office and prestige. From Locke to Wittgenstein I— or from the beginning of British sea power to its zenith—it was their mission to build an empire of semiotic Puritanism, a world that was everything that was the case, or everything that was passed along. It was no accident that the crowning achievement in the suppression of interference in communication—the Morse Code, which first made the deep-sea cables praised by Kipling effective—was the work of American Puritanism.

The author wishes to thank first of all Sepp Gumbrecht, who first had the idea of an American translation of *Relays*; Bud Bynack, who did a great job editing the translation; and Stanford University Press for making the book a reality.

The philosophers had to keep silent on one point alone. On whose behalf were they keeping the pipes clean? If pushed on the matter, they claimed that their discourses were issued in the name of a Supreme Commander, whom Locke called God. What they did not give were the names of the commanders or generals who had issued the orders for constructing empirical systems of communication.

Today, the mathematical theory of communication deals with codes that have nothing to do with understanding, in contrast to everyday language and its philosophers, but that (in their cryptological origins) have much to do with an ambiguity that remains constant, no matter how long one might listen or write it down. Today, there is also the prospect of writing the history of communication as human intercourse from the perspective of postal strategies, if only by way of experiment. The following pages deal with such a history. If the world is a legacy, or everything that is the case, then the knowledge of things, which according to Locke must perforce be the entire purpose of language, depends on eternal peace. An eternal postal peace ensures that everything that is the case will be delivered without "noise and wrangling"[3] and without distortion. Eternal peace, of course, is merely a metonymic euphemism for empire, and empire—in Latin *imperium*—is just a word for chains of command, for the postal frame of fate. Yet the metaphor of language as a pipeline subject to clogging,[4] which slips past the plumbers in order to represent the channel within the channel itself, shows that figuration and confusion already are present whenever there is communication. As the site of all transmission, the postal system is the possibility for every possible kind of rhetoric.[5] Clogging is unavoidable.

Someone who knew that America is a legacy, something to be passed along, has written this all down much better than the writer of these pages might have done; hence, *The Crying of Lot 49* could not possibly become the object of this study. Literary scholarship conducted as the analysis of media and discourse must come to a halt before the researches of Oedipa Maas because those researches are its own. The empire is a postal system, and the postal system is war. It follows that things, their presence, what they are, all of it therefore is open to doubt. An enemy resides in technology, which alone is what makes things into objects in the first place. The empire of posted objects, the world that is everything that is the case, is distorted, interrupted, irreducibly nonactual: it is metaphorical. The name of the "metaphoric catastrophe"[6] is Tristero. The beginning of eternal peace, which is just another name for the *renovatio imperii*, continues to be an idealistic dream of pure power—as it was at the end of the Thirty Years' War and at the end of the *horrendum bellum grammaticale*[7] that Locke so dearly wished to inaugurate:

> "The salvation of Europe," Konrad says, "depends on communication, right? We face this anarchy of jealous German princes, hundreds of them scheming, counter-scheming, infighting, dissipating all of the Empire's strength in their useless bickering. But whoever could control the lines of communication, among all these princes, would control them. That network someday could unify the Continent. So I propose that we merge with our old enemy Thurn and Taxis. . . . Together," Konrad is saying, "our two systems are invincible. We could refuse service on any but an Imperial basis. Nobody could move troops, farm produce, anything, without us. Any prince tries to start his own courier system, we suppress it. We, who have so long been disinherited, could be the heirs of Europe!" Prolonged cheering.[8]

Yet, as Oedipa Maas promptly objects and with good reason, they had not spared the empire from collapse. Nor have Konrad's confederates—from Locke to Habermas—saved the empire of language from "useless bickering." Eternal peace, the realm of angels, always fails to appear in the end. Disorder grows, entropy increases, and with it the level of uncertainty about whether everything is what it pretends to be.

But what does it matter? Indeed, one must not believe what the plumbers say: "When a man speaks to another, it is that he may be understood."[9] Those who question the Powers that Be and the media that have implanted a need such as this in our bodies, those who study the circuit diagrams of the postal system on the basis of which letters and printed matter develop their powers, have made a deal with the opposing side. From the very start, they will not share this need for harmony, the need that gives philosophers the opinion that all texts are grounded in understanding and all relays in human communication. They will be ready for the wily disguises of the will to power, and not for the fulfillment of the divine will to truth.

> No hallowed skein of stars can ward, I trow,
> Who's once been set his tryst with Trystero.[10]

CHAPTER ONE

An Epoch of the Postal System

We speak of the delivery of mail.
—*Martin Heidegger*

After he had spent a lifetime writing letters and piling up grievance upon grievance, the moment came when the words ceased lamenting in order to become "generally instructive" remarks[1]—when the love letters stopped in order to make room for a theory of the postal system. This theory, too, was delivered by the postman. The moment at which, or in which, there was a theory of the postal system was itself already intercepted or delivered by the mail; a theory of the postal system always is a theory in the postal system, as well.

It was delivered [*zugestellt*][2] sometime in March 1922 to a woman journalist in Vienna, Lerchenfelderstrasse 113. A phantom letter. In sheer paradox, it unmasked a gang of phantoms as the agent of every exchange of symbols, a gang that had wrested from people the control over their discourse in letters. Then the people perished, as if what they appeared to be depended on the absence of the postal system and technical media. "The easy possibility of letter writing must—seen merely theoretically— have brought into the world a terrible disintegration of souls. It is, in fact, an intercourse with ghosts, and not only with the ghost of the recipient but also with one's own ghost which develops between the lines of the letter one is writing."[3] Everything here is open to doubt: the person sending the letter, Dr. Franz Kafka, insurance agent and phantom of himself, the paradoxical sense of a letter reflecting on the (im)possibility of writing letters, the man or the woman addressed, Mrs. Milena Jesenská, on whom the letter bestows its greeting, but from whom it at the same time seems to turn away in order to address a third person, who always reads the letter too (it is obviously the deceived husband, Ernst Pollak)—which is why the recipient, at the moment the letter begins to speak *of* her, changes gender and becomes an absent person ("a friend," in German, a masculine noun). The disintegration of souls (or the possibility of viewing the possibility of writing letters theoretically) is (also) the disintegration of the sexes. So quickly does a theoretical discussion of the postal system as a theory fall prey to the imponderable when its condition is itself a dispatch of the mail.

The imponderable or impassable[4] aspect of the moment in which letters were promoted to theoretical opinions about their own impossibility results from the mutual implication of theory and history. Inasmuch as Kafka's theory existed as a historical effect of what it viewed as its subject matter, it implied its own historical specificity. History—as the unity of events and their narration (*res gestae* and *res narratae*)—is subject to a postal a priori in the modern era. According to Heidegger, this a priori became explicit at the moment Leibniz made the claim that *ratio*, without which there is of course nothing (and thus nothing in history, either), had to be *ratio reddenda*. That is: "reason is what must be delivered [*zu-gestellt*] to the representing, thinking person."[5] Since Leibniz, there has been no representation without delivery; and that means without delivery, there is no "objectiveness of the object." Thus, only what can be posted exists at all. Heidegger, who worked on the postal control board at the Freiburg post office during the First World War,[6] must have known. It is therefore no coincidence that he heard the "delivery of mail" in Leibniz's *principium reddendae rationis*—and probably with good reason. Leibniz's rationalism, after all, coincided exactly with the emergence of the very same territorial state postal systems in whose carriages he likely spent most of his life and whose radically new principle was precisely to make people the subjects of postal deliveries. The historical a priori of the principle of *ratio reddenda* was the idea that appeared so abstruse to Kafka in 1922, that is, "the idea that people"—people in general, without further classification—"can communicate with one another by letter."[7] This idea surfaced relatively late in the history of communications systems, as even a brief glance at the communications technologies of the centuries before Leibniz suffices to show.

The five thousand clay tablets of the letter archives founded in the city of Mari around 1750 B.C., for example, which came to light in the desert sands on the banks of the Euphrates in 1935, do not bear witness to the communication of "people," but instead to the scriptural power of Shamshi-Adad and Zimrilim, the despots called to power by Enlil. Since the ability to write existed only as a function of the royal "information service," all writing posted nothing but the power of the royal name. The letters deal with the death, wedding, war, and greatness of a single person.[8] The same is true of the letter archives of Amenhotep IV (Akhenaten) from the fourteenth century B.C., the tablets of which survived undamaged for thirty-two hundred years, until they were destroyed at the end of the nineteenth century by the residents of El-Amarna, who were illiterate, but good at business.[9]

But a postal system that used clay tablets to carry information was a medium with a very limited rate and speed of transmission. The *angaréion* of the Achamenidian Empire, which according to Xenophon was founded by Cyrus in the sixth century B.C. (the first known postal relay system), thus probably contributed to the shift from cuneiform to Aramaic in the writing of Persian by scribes under Darius, a transition that allowed the introduction of light papyrus or parchment.[10] This light and easy possibility of letter writing served exclusively as a medium of control and command between the king and his satraps. Control had to be exercised not only over the peoples who had been subjugated by the Persians and were prone to rebellion, but over the satraps themselves, as well.[11] The *angaréion* posted the empire as the royal word, which transcended the regional living space of ethnic groups.

It was in this form that the Persian Empire came to the Romans. After Persian communications technology was adopted, first by the Seleucids and then by Alexander the Great, its Egyptian version finally provided Augustus with a model for the *cursus publicus*—that is, for a postal system that served to transmit the *imperiums* or imperial *oraculums* and military communications, as well as to transport high-level functionaries. As the name itself indicates, the use of the *cursus publicus* was reserved exclusively for the emperor and the provincial governors. And even these officials had to present a certificate issued by the emperor or the praetorian prefect (later also by the *magister officiorum*) in order to gain access to the medium of the empire.[12] "People" did not communicate through the postal system; on the contrary, the postal system communicated through people, who had to perform angarias, that is, compulsory services or

liturgies for the maintenance of the postal system. In order to curb extensive corruption in the imperial postal system, which always was tanta-
mount to a conspiracy against the empire, Diocletian created an imperial
secret service, the *schola agentum in rebus*, and placed the postal administration under its authority.[13] Eventually, under Theodosius and Hono-
rius, the use of the postal system by private persons was even punished by
death.[14] Since the network of the *cursus publicus* was coextensive with
the *orbis terrarum*, banishment to Pontus meant being transported beyond the *limes* of the world for Ovid. While the *Tristia* are laments over
the loss of postal connections, the *Epistulae ex Ponto* use the medium of
literature to decry the catastrophe in the postal system.

Postal systems are *instrumenta regni*. Until well into the early modern
period, that was blatantly obvious. Thus, the famous edict of Louis XI by
which the French state postal system replaced the courier system of the
University of Paris decreed that all those who dared to submit private letters to the postal system were sent to Hades, just as they had been in the
last phase of the western Roman Empire.[15] Initially—between 1490 and
1516—the Taxis Post did not consist of permanent routes, but of varying
connections between the emperor's current location and his court
chancery, since, as Maximilian I let it be known, the postal system had
been established "for our well-being and our honor."[16] For this reason, the
postal services established according to a 1516 treaty that Franz and Baptista de Tassis concluded with Charles I (after 1519, Emperor Charles V),
were "not to be sent out at all, except for the letters of the king."[17] Postal
routes were to connect the cornerstones of the Habsburg Empire in Spain,
the Netherlands, Rome, Naples, and Germany in order to arrange the
marriage politics and diplomatic alliances in which the empire manifested
itself. In an imperial postal system such as this one, a "message" did not
mean "communicating with one another," but was instead a notification
to "act in accordance," *Danachrichten* in the Middle High German meaning of the word. In 1496, Maximilian also set up the first field post on
German soil—obviously not for reasons of psychological warfare, since
his mercenaries were illiterate, but instead, for the purpose of transferring
orders to "act in accordance" to the army command.[18]

Like the state postal systems, the courier services that came into being
during the Middle Ages formed closed systems: they posted only their

own respective institutions. The university post circulated students and scholars, along with knowledge, the communal courier systems circulated the business of the magistrate, the butcher post that of businessmen, the princely couriers that of the princes. The couriers of the monasteries, in fact, transferred only a single message: the death of brothers in their order.[19]

In the seventeenth century—in the context of the so-called postal reformation at the end of the sixteenth—the situation changed. Exactly in 1600, Cardinal Duke Albrecht VII, viceroy of the Netherlands, granted the Taxis formal permission to charge postage for private letters,[20] thus legitimizing an abuse of the postal system they long had been practicing. Supported by an imperial communications technology that was misused for the general communication of "people" and that thereby lost the definition applied to it since the sixth century B.C., the absolutist state invented the uniformly ruled space, the territory. Within this space, the people were subjects, pure and simple, and therefore vassals of the monarch, insofar as a general postal system provided the opportunity for words to circulate beneath all the discursive barriers of guild and estate. The only prerequisite for this was a redefinition of the postal raison d'être: postal systems no longer existed for the well-being and the honor of the emperor or the king, but for the well-being of a population of subjects.

Insofar as the existence of objects is bound to reason's delivery to cognition, the power of the state grounded itself in the establishment and monopolization of that delivery. The state produced "subjects" in both senses of the word by inventing the general post, the postal monopoly, and the usefulness of the postal system. By means of titularies, registers containing correct modes of address according to social status or rank, every subject gained access to a discursive authority in the postal realm that allowed him to determine his own affairs and at the same time forced him, with each determination (destination), to register his affairs with the state. The ubiquity and invisibility of the state were thus to be found in the representation of the postal system as a medium for private correspondence between cognitive subjects.[21] Between objects and the modern subject with true cognition, the commands of royal, electoral, or ducal postmasters reigned supreme. In 1649, Frederick William the Elector founded the Prussian state postal system. The post was dispatched twice a week and, since it also moved by night, it attained speeds that had been unknown until that time. Absolutism made words available to the people, and a medium available to the words, in order to make the people speak about themselves, to control their speech, and to finance the state's expenditures for such control with the postage charged for that speech. If the basic element of the imperial postal system had been the route, for the territorial state postal system it became the relay[22]—a site where the people became entangled in the discourse. As postal systems became a technology of the government with the invention of postage and the monopolization of service, the people likewise came to believe they were capable of determining their own affairs postally. Institutionally, this meant that the postal system fell under police jurisdiction.

"What empowers in the principle of reason" was the postal system. Once the *principe postale* provided for the delivery of cognition, the objects' mode of being was a monopoly of the state. The interpretation of *principium rationis* as *principium reddendae rationis* thus described precisely the transition from the old imperial postal systems—in which the delivery of being constantly transcended the people—to the new absolutist postal systems and their new vassals, or subjects. In other words, that reason must be delivered implied the governmentalist "idea that people can communicate with one other by letter."

Like Heidegger's lecture, Kafka's theory of the postal system recited the end of the ability to think that thought. This end, as it immediately became apparent, had reigned over the possibility of letter writing from the beginning: the possibility of a postal system merely had been a configuration of its impossibility, insofar as the subjects who imagined themselves to be in communication with each other had been nothing more than unconscious agents of power politics. But the theory itself did not escape this end. As a theory, it still belonged to the epoch of the postal system it declared to be over. At the moment that the subject perceived the true principles and objects of cognition as historically specific principles of power, the solidity of that subject dissolved. It became a phantom. Only phantoms can advance theories about the postal-historical a priori of the subject and its communicative structure.[23] The impassability of the thought that the possibility of letter writing is unthinkable is suspended by the delivery [*Zugestelltsein*] of representation and cognition and the objectness

of the entity. To deliver, indeed, means to make arrive, to bring to appearance (this being the predominant meaning in *reddere*, which, after all,
also includes the delivery of letters). At the same time, in German, the
same word, *zustellen*, means to withdraw. Delivered to the human senses,
the reason for what exists always is the reason already withdrawn from
them. This means that the history of the postal system, which appointed
Leibniz as the postmaster of modern ontology and the people as the subjects of letter exchange, is itself an epoch of the postal system—"epoch,"
that is, understood in the Greek meaning of the word, which Heidegger
brought to language, as restraint: "Epoch does not mean here a span of
time in occurrence, but rather the fundamental characteristic of sending,
the actual holding-back of itself in favor of the discernibility of the gift,
that is, of Being with regard to the grounding of beings."[24]

It is the withdrawal that gives. Stated differently and more technically:
the epoch is a relay that is necessary so that something arrives and comes
to be known. "To post is to send by 'counting' with a halt, a relay, or a
suspensive delay, the place of a mailman, the possibility of going astray
and of forgetting. . . . The *epokhé* and the *Ansichhalten* . . . is the place of
the postal."[25] Epochs precede history as its postal a priori. This has important consequences for the historiography of the postal system. The
ideas of epoch, halt, withdrawal are "immediately homogenized with
postal discourse."[26] If the "epoch of the postal system" in *genitivus sub-
iectivus* means that the epoch is a delay and a halt belonging to the postal
realm, how can it still be possible to speak of an "epoch of the postal system" in *genitivus obiectivus*, how can the postal system itself be epochal?
How, then, can there be a history of the postal system? The postal system
would have to precede the postal system, or: "The post is an epoch of the
post."[27] The postal system—and this remains the horizon of any attempt
to analyze literature as an epoch of the postal system—is thinkable only
by taking into account the withdrawal of the postal system.

There is more at stake in this than the reflections of a philosophical
discourse on the relationship between the theory and history of the postal
system. The issue is instead the relationship between the two fundamental functions fulfilled by the media: recording and transmission. After all,
what is holding back, other than recording in relation to transmission? As
the unity of *res gestae* and *res narratae*, history is a dependent variable of

the grand epoch of the postal system, the technology of which is characterized by clay tablets, papyrus, parchment, paper, books, and postcards. The epochs of history are recording technologies. They are the immediate object of sub-epochs of the postal epoch such as those of the imperial postal systems, the state monopoly, the principle of reason as *principium reddendae rationis*, the subject as individual recipient, or the world postal union. But these recording technologies, these material conditions of history, are in turn just as many sites of withdrawal, postal halts—sites, that is, at which sending is detained: *mutationes, mansiones*, relays. What is recorded is the necessary trace of posting, provided there are a postal system and its dispensations. Archives are the trace that is the epoch of the postal system.

Strictly speaking, there are in fact no sources for the history of the postal system (and therefore no such history either) in the sense that books, let us say, are sources for a history of the book. After all, documents themselves merely bear witness to historical means of recording: at best—as letters and so on—they were the object of a dispatching to which their margins (addresses, seals, stamps) still testify. But dispatching cannot testify for itself the way recording can. Outside the archives, one can at most dig up a few archeological finds, the names of French towns such as Mudaison, Musizon, or Mudahon, which betray the previous existence of a Roman *mutatio*,[28] and the innumerable inns "Zur Post." Seen from this perspective, the object of this study might be said not to exist at all, since this object is the principle that gives existence to begin with.

For the time being, however, it seems more fruitful to consign positivity—that characteristic feature of sending, which is the principle for everything that exists—to the epoch of the postal system, if only on the basis of the margins of delivery to be seen in archival materials. In its positive sense, *epoché* means nothing but interception. Every delay of the dispatch as a necessary interruption of the transmission process for the purposes of sending is a type of interception. "The relay is not only the nexus of power in the economies of transport and circulation, but also potentially the least secure point in the entire communications system."[29] Insofar as recording is a form of conveyance that counts with this halt or relay, that is, a *poste restante*, it is a phenomenon of interception. That a letter always can also not arrive—can be intercepted, purloined—is nothing less than the condition allowing it always to reach its destination.[30] Such a destination can bear the name "human" as long as the data of interception take the postal halts of the senses and of the mind into account. Here lies the site of aesthetics. In the context of a theory of the general post, aesthetics is a datum of interception. It corresponds to, and emerges from, the particular state of technology and of the media within the epochs (in every sense of the word "epochs"). The impossibility of technologically processing data in real time is the possibility of art. Literature, as an art of human beings, is a gift of interception, which operates on the basis of feedback loops between human senses and the postal materiality of data processing known as the alphabet. As long as processing in real time was not available, data always had to be stored intermediately somewhere—on skin, wax, clay, stone, papyrus, linen, paper, wood, or the cerebral cortex—in order to be transmitted or otherwise processed. It was in precisely this way that data became something palpable for human beings, that it opened up the field of art. Conversely, it is nonsensical to speak of the availability of real-time processing (as we just have), insofar as the concept of availability implies the human being as subject. After all, real-time processing is the exact opposite of being available. It is not available to the feedback loops of the human senses, but instead to the standards of signal processors, since real-time processing is defined precisely as the evasion of the senses.

Literature is implied in the postponement of sending as the possibility for interception by the senses. In 1776, D'Alembert defined literature precisely and only in this way in a letter to Frederick II:

> Sire! I received, almost at the same time, the two letters with which your
> majesty has been pleased to honor me, dated the twenty-second, and the
> twenty-sixth, of October. Those letters and that which I had the honour to
> write to your majesty, about six weeks ago, have been longer on the road
> than usual. The worthy clerks of the post-offices, receiving orders which, no
> doubt, are highly respectable, but which I should rather any person should
> execute than myself, who open letters on their route *through Germany* (for I
> dare not say *through France*) have apparently been more eager than usual to
> read for their instruction, or rather for their melancholy amusement, what a
> great king is pleased to write to an afflicted philosopher, and the answers of
> the poor philosopher to the great king. It cannot be denied, sire, but that

these clerks are, in every sense of the word, *men of letters*, and have vast curiosity to examine the beautiful.[31]

The beautiful owed its existence to the postal epoch. It was in the (self-) restraint and prolongation of the mail that literature existed. D'Alembert's metaphor merely had to be inverted and the principle of classical authorship was securely in hand. *"Men of letters"* were *Postbediente* in every sense of the word—both postal servants and people served by the post.

This was the beginning of a sub-epoch of the postal system that was literature itself. But if literature, as a work of art, as the creation of "the individual,"[32] was to appear in the truth of its concept—instead of as merely the state of technology and of the media in a postal epoch—the genealogy of literary knowledge had to be both delivered and blocked. Classical/Romantic authorship was established by anthropomorphizing the seventeenth-century postal *raison d'état*. Eighteenth-century poetry was simultaneously a cover-up of the postal service and a delivery of the mail in the production and communication of knowledge. The transference of the "idea that people can communicate with one other by letter" from the discourse of the police to the discourse of eternal and inalienable natural rights produced literature as an epoch of the postal system. The origin of this "idea" in the *raison d'état* was concealed to the extent that the postal medium was depoliticized, while at the same time the postal institution became a police institution, and the dispatch of private letters came to be the policy of enlightened despotism.

In media-historical terms, the line separating politics from morality—from which Hobbes derived absolutist sovereignty and in which the demise of that sovereignty already resided—ran between the postal system and letters. As Reinhart Koselleck has shown in his analysis of eighteenth-century lodges, the role of secrets was to mark the boundaries between morals and politics and to define the internal social space in which morals were to be realized: the space of the soul.[33] The postal counterpart of the lodge secret was the confidentiality of the letter. In the *Theresiana* of 1786, violations of this confidentiality still showed up only as "roguish, fraudulent actions" with "almost no names of their own."[34] The Universal Prussian Common Law established the bourgeois individual as a postal concept only in 1794. Advocates of Enlightenment, by contrast, already in earlier times had agitated in favor of a *raison d'état* that transcended *raisons d'état*, specifically defending the confidentiality of the letter, which they derived from natural law, against all such state policies and defining it as the private space of bourgeois freedom.[35]

Within the space of secrecy thus erected, men of letters—literati, moral philosophers, and professors of rhetoric—established "the idea that people can communicate with one other" as a power and a right that comprised "the individual" in general, while at the same time the architects of this space, who had been the proponents of *raisons d'état*, fell into oblivion. In the course of this discursive transformation, the machinations of the Black Cabinet—which still had fed directly into literary production at the court of Louis XV[36]—became postal practice for Classical authors in Germany at the end of the eighteenth century. An unpolitical will to truth stepped in to take the place of power politics' will to knowledge. To the extent that literary works were linked to a logistics of intimate confession, they became individual. Consequently, the eighteenth century no longer defined the practice of letter writing in terms of the *ars dictamini*, but in terms of intimate confessions. The private did not precede the private letter in the process of this transformation—in either a chronological or a causal sense. On the contrary: the private medium was defined as the medium for the definition of the private.

The sub-epoch within the grand epoch of the postal system, when "people can communicate with each other through letters," was relatively short-lived. It lasted as long as literature existed in the form of a private letter to a feminine reader who could be designated by a variable and as long as private letters existed in the form of feminine "nonsense" that a poet like Goethe was able to put into rhyme. Gellert's epistolographic works mark its beginning, Keller's *Misused Love Letters* its end. Even today, this sub-epoch continues to deliver a conception of the subject to literary scholars that apparently curses them with the inability to think of letter writing as anything but a means for the expression and communication of people. Only because of this has it been possible that this sub-epoch continues to be confused with the "essence" of the postal system. Precisely one hundred years ago, Georg Steinhausen initiated the misidentification of this sub-epoch of the postal system as the history of the exchange of letters in which "man" is both subject and object: the *History of the German Letter*, in which the only process at work between the Middle Ages and the end of the eighteenth century was the self-actualization of human communication.

In drawing his well-known line beneath the sub-epoch of the postal system known as "human communication," Kafka counted only the technical inventions of bodily transportation among the measures humanity had taken in the struggle against its metamorphosis into an army of phantoms:

> Humanity . . . in order to eliminate as far as possible the ghostly element between people and to create a natural communication, the peace of souls, . . . has invented the railway, the motor car, the aeroplane. But it's no longer any good, these are evidently inventions being made at the moment of crashing. The opposing side is much calmer and stronger; after the postal service it has invented the telegraph, the telephone, the radiograph. The ghosts won't starve, but we will perish.[37]

For Kafka, the postal system did not count as one of the "natural" means of communication, but instead as one of the inventions of an opposing side called "communications technology." This view resulted from a rupture that separated the conveyance of persons and information, bursting the seams of the sub-epoch of human communication and along with them the seams of literature as an epoch of the postal system. Kafka's perspective on these matters corresponded precisely to the state of affairs in 1871. On principle—and that means as the legal right of monopoly—the dispatch of information and persons previously had been the concern of one and the same institution, that is, the postal system. From the seventeenth century until the mid-nineteenth, postage for the transportation of symbols was economically assessed according to geography in the same way as the transportation of bodies for the simple reason that both were accomplished by the same means of transportation. The same postal carriage could convey both a letter and its writer. The subject of the letter's text (Todorov's *sujet d'énoncé*) and the subject of the letter's speech act (Todorov's *sujet d'énonciation*) fell under the jurisdiction of one and the same institution of exchange. The postage for a letter thus had to represent the amount of distance to be covered and the weight of the letter as precisely as possible, as if handling the letter involved the actual person.

Consequently, symbols could hold forth as a replacement for bodies; letters could be imagined as the proxies of an absent body. This, of course, was the foundation of humanity's postal peace of mind, the ineradicable axiom in the theory of letters and the premise taken a priori as given in Steinhausen's *History of the German Letter*. Not until the Postal Law of October 28, 1871, were the last remnants of royal prerogative in the conveyance of persons relinquished—and thus peace of mind as well[38]—after the railroad network had been developed to the point that not even an ecological niche remained for postal carriages in the dimension of space. (They had had no chance from the start in the dimension of speed, at 8 kilometers per hour as opposed to the subsequent 50 (1840), 65 (1860), and 80 (1880) kilometers per hour of the railroad.)[39] For the postal system, information therefore was all that was left, and thus the phantoms came, after "natural" railroad traffic—accompanied by shocks, "railway spine," and traumatic neuroses—had crushed unified postal control of letters and persons under its wheels.

Once writing letters came to involve partisanship for the revolution in communications technology and against the revolution in transport technology, the substitution of symbols for bodies was a thing of the past. Bodies and symbols were in a state of war. As a result, the "naturalness" of writing, which—as the imperative of all men of letters since Gellert—had ruled over the discourse of letters, came to an end. Around 1900, the descendants of the poets became the agents of phantoms. There could be no doubt, at least for the Reichstag deputy von Arnim in a parliamentary speech, "that the transportation interests involved in the rapid communications system definitely deserve priority over the other interests. . . . The traffic of the rapid communications system . . . is much more important than the question of whether persons travel by horse or by electricity (From the right: Very true!). I need only point out that our political, our commercial, our social life in general is not possible without telegraphic communication."[40]

The diagnosis in Kafka's theory of the media matched Reichstag speeches aimed at integrating telephony into the postal system with this much precision. Once social life itself came to depend on systems for the transmission of information—systems that claimed a monopoly on long-distance discourses, both written and oral—love did not dream of interpreting the soul of the man or woman who had written the text of the letter it was reading, but dreamed instead of calculating postal modalities. "Written kisses don't reach their destination," Kafka declared,[41] simply because the postal detour no longer led them to literature, but to the power of the media themselves. Once the postage stamp canceled authorship as an invitation to discourse, and the postcard—the stamp you can write on—had done the same for the confidentiality of letters and so for human communication, love was a matter for transport firms, or no matter at all. Based on this historical premise, a media and human experiment would run its course in 1912 under the title *Letters to Felice*.

Yet for all that, there *is* a theory of the postal system, now that there are postmodernism and its disintegrated souls. Insofar as the mass media's standards of transmission and the technical media have put an end to the sub-epoch of human communication, the authors of letters become theoreticians of the postal system—at the expense of humanity's peace of mind. This development can be understood, as Kafka and the psychiatry of his time understood it, in a technical sense—that is, in terms of neurophysiology: the armies of neurotics produced by the First World War were a mass symptom of the spiritual media's failure when confronted by a reality that exploded into an emergency. When the restraint or withdrawal of the postal system, upon which peace of mind had been grounded, was itself withdrawn, a "war of nerves"[42] was underway in the form of correspondence that simulated this emergency and as the world war that was the emergency itself. Yet the theory of the postal system still belonged to the postal epoch. Thus, Kafka's phantom letter continued to be literature (that is, without consequences), instead of putting literary studies on the right track for a "communications" theory that would start with the media and its wars rather than with humanity's peace of mind. In Germany, literary studies had no need to venture into the impassabilities [*Unwegbarkeiten*] of such a theory. The impassabilities of postal history and theory are certainly not very surprising, since passability [*Wegbarkeit*]—forming a way and keeping it ready—is just another word for a historical state of the postal system. As an aporia in the Greek sense of the word, however, impassability appears in the discourse of deconstruction only as a hysteron proteron—which suggests that the postal system is concealed even in a thinking that ultimately seeks to deconstruct history in favor of an interminable *theoréo*. This is in accordance with Foucault's insight that Derrida's postulate of the endless indeterminacy of meaning belongs to pedagogical discourse, and thus to the sub-epoch of the postal system that puts humanity's peace of mind to rest in the discourse of philosophy. As far as the pedagogical postulate of interpretation's impassability is concerned, the epoch of the postal system still is concealed, even in the aporia itself. Aporia therefore appears only as an aporia in causality. Rather than reflecting its basis in media, the thinking of aporia merely leads before the tribunal of a philosophical category.[43]

Topographical concept that it is, however, aporia itself already states that meaning is not indeterminate, but confined. The passable postal routes (or discourses) of its deliveries were opened up only by the impassable in the first place. Aporia thus attains the positivity of a margin that makes it possible to analyze a discourse on the end of the possibility of humanity's postal peace of mind. Such analysis can be performed using postal-historical a prioris that establish meaning without being meaningful themselves.

But discourses must have become *things* that can be assigned specific dates in history,[44] if we, as the phantoms of this history, are to decipher the command that led Kafka to the question of just how one could come up with the idea "that people can communicate with one another by letter." This means that testimony such as Kafka's frequently cited question—*before* it is a statement that can be either true or false—is a thing worth noting for the fact that it is, rather than is not.[45] The readings presented here are thus aimed at finding what provides information on the brink about the gift of simply giving: commands, addresses, dates, storage, feedback—in short, the postal discourse, which is hardly a discourse at all, but still determines the fate of literature. The aporias of a history or theory of the postal system are united with history itself as an epoch of the postal system—with the status of books as technical media, that is, and of letters and any other documents that are registered in archives and upon which books depend. The passabilities of such materials hardly can take us beyond the impassabilities in a history of the postal system, but then again, such impassabilities will last only as long as books do. For the moment, books still can take into account a stage in the postal system at which machines take control—as Alan Turing has said.[46] The analog media disclose the end of the sub-epoch of human communication in the ground and the groundlessness of communication, the noise of the channels. The digitalization of analogs, by contrast, makes the object of the postal system itself—transmission—disappear into universal signal processing. This means nothing other than that Leibniz's principle of reason as *principium reddendae rationis* can be fulfilled via something other than *cognitionis* since the Second World War. Once human beings no longer are the relay and ground for what is, an epoch attains self-actualization and a history reaches its end.

Human beings have ceased to be the relays of history. And since only what can be posted exists at all, from now on, only the gods or the machines "know" what is. What is in store for us is a delivery of the mail that forgets about us and builds empires—beyond the brink.

PART ONE

The Logistics of the Poet's Dream

CHAPTER TWO

On Time (Registered Letter I)

On the threshold of modern authorship, the body of a scholar intercon-
nected with the postal system dreamed of optimizing its interconnection.
As in all visitations, the medium it dreamed up was a medium of dreams:
a commercial mailing for the postal system. As an ideal, it both failed to
recognize and camouflaged the situation: it displayed perfection in the
form of obsolescence. The failure to recognize perfection in the perfection
of the failure to recognize nonetheless was significant: it was the test pattern for a historical rupture. The scholarly body bore the name Lichtenberg,[1] and therefore wrote in fragments:

> This will be a letter I deliver myself. This manner of delivering one's own
> letters does involve some inconvenience, but certainly has great advantages
> as well. The letter can be opened at every station, things can be crossed out,
> added, or even suppressed entirely—which postal servants do not normally
> allow. And a major advantage, and indisputably the greatest of all, is that
> it can be delivered on time, or left in the [mail] bag when the auspices are
> unfavorable. If the post also held this advantage, it would be one of the most
> perfect inventions the human mind ever has stumbled upon. I always have
> envied authors who become very old, such as e.g. His Excellence von Haller
> and Voltaire, because they can deliver their works to posterity themselves,
> and observe the face it makes upon delivery, and thus can take back the
> entire letter as a result, and our finest intellects, who write so terribly
> indiscriminately, are to be excused in this much.[2]

Optimal exchange of information amounted to maximum solidarity in the
exchange of mail and travelers—and thus to the elimination of the postal
system as an institution. Lichtenberg united sender, courier, and secret-
service agent in his own person. An attack of this sort upon the state's

monopoly on the post and upon the police annulled the venerable theorem—which dated back to Artemon and was first given its classical formulation by Philostrat—that the letter was *sermo absentis ad absentem*.[3] The letter, after all, does not just supplement the presence of the voice, it supplements supplementation itself. But the absence of absence does not allow any signified to arrive—only the silent moment of a delivery that does not take place. Lichtenberg questioned the very use of symbols by subjecting them to an impossible test: the attempt to write what cannot be written—the distance between bodies, or the "rapport sexuel."[4]

As long as letters and the mail continued to map the distance to a place where symbols might be translated into bodies, what was written perforce was something interminable. Because the relationship of bodies does not cease to be unwritten, letters do not cease to be written. Writing, which could not eliminate itself by anything other than manipulations of writing—such as crossing out and adding—never came to an end, unless it was a contingent one. After all, it is the contingency involved in the delivery of letters that denies the postal system the honor of being known as "one of the most perfect inventions." Writing and bodies never come together "on time." Everything revolves around this "on time," and not just the perfection of the postal system. Because what could it be, this "on time," except for the Eucharistic moment when the symbol's *différance* would be blotted out—the sacred moment of the symbol's transsubstantiation into what it had signified only a moment before: the body? And that would not come to pass because a master once had demonstrated the trick and then ordered its repetition for all eternity. It would happen only if writing qua writing abbreviated the distance between signifier and signified in successive stages, from postal station to postal station, until the designated moment and the moment of designation coincided. Symbol processing would mean giving Adamic commands. Contingency would be banished from the world by a qualitative leap in the structure of symbols.

But Lichtenberg's postal system foundered on precisely that point: the crisis of command in the world of words. Without orders from a higher authority,[5] nothing arrives on time, because contingency—or the fall from grace—dwells within the signifiers themselves. Further still, if a symbol is to arrive at all, it cannot arrive "on time": "you understand, within every sign already, every mark or every trait, there is distancing, the post, what there has to be so that it is legible for another, another than you or me, and everything is messed up in advance, cards on the table. The condition for it to arrive is that it ends up and even that it begins by not arriving."[6] In practice, this meant that the letter is "left in the bag." The crisis of command was followed by the crisis of connection.

Because there is post in every symbol, no letter arrives at a time common to symbols and bodies; it gets stuck, or continues to be written asymptotically, endlessly approaching the absence of absence. If the *limes* of difference between symbol and body approaches zero, the production of text escalates toward infinity.

Whoever makes propaganda for the optimization of literary media according to the principle of such a letter does not accomplish anything of the kind—Lichtenberg did not produce finished works, but merely "Waste books."[7] Or perhaps he instead becomes addicted to criticizing editions of his own works—as happened in the not unwarranted example of Albrecht von Haller. The professor of botany, anatomy, and surgery in Lichtenberg's Göttingen—the great reviewer and literary critic—not only reviewed his own publications and even his own life anonymously from time to time,[8] but also delivered eleven editions of his *Alps* to "posterity" over the course of forty years in order to open them at every station and cross out or add words, in answer to the criticism of scholarly readers. Haller's self-criticism went something like this, for example. A verse from the *Alps* read as follows in the first two editions of 1732 and 1734: "Astonished, the goats see streams in the heavens flowing, / That flee from the clouds, and into clouds themselves are pouring."[9] In the third edition of 1743, the astonished goats were cut, now replaced by "a stranger," who in turn already was replaced by a "wanderer" in Haller's personal copy of that edition. The wanderer appeared in print in 1748 and continued to do so thereafter, but not without the accompaniment of the following footnote: "My own patrons have found fault with these two rhymes. They are thus probably difficult to excuse. For all that, I ask the reader to consider the fact that the goats of the first edition, had they already been people, would not have admired a daily spectacle."[10] The editions that followed banished the continual omissions and additions to the realm of this footnote, until the last edition finally provided a more extensive an-notation from Haller's hand in 1772. In the form of a naturalist's eyewitness account of the high-alpine waterfall in the Lauterbrunnen Valley, the footnote now contributed the *verba propria* for the metaphors mentioned above.[11]

Documentation such as this was not included without reason. Poeticized Alps, after all, were caught in a deep crisis of legitimation. Before Goethe bound nature lyrics to the truth of a transcendental signified known as The Woman and sexualized all waterfalls, everyone—including Haller—was asking if poeticized nature was not pure nonsense. The suspicion ran as follows: either its phrases meant nothing at all, or they merely duplicated the discourses of natural science. Haller therefore provided two types of annotations in addition to critical footnotes: the first type (often including eyewitness testimony from Swiss peasants) assured that Haller's rhetorical figures did not come from the usual stock phrases of rhetoric, the *copia verborum*, but instead actually were to be found in nature. The second type were of the "Lohensteinian"[12] variety and demonstrated that such things *were* to be found in the literary storehouse of the *copia rerum*: in botanical atlases. Words and things were no longer stored in the same medium, and because of this, words needed a referential discourse that previously had been an authority only for things in nature. By the time scholars began to leave their libraries for a stroll in the country, Haller already was near death and in the delirium brought on by eight grains of opium a day.[13] But by that time, no one became an author who could not believe that words said what they said without the referential discourse of science: two years before his death, Haller had to defend himself from the accusation that he had done nothing but plagiarize his whole life long.[14] The postmaster's letter, by the time he delivered it, was no longer his own letter at all.

Lichtenberg's fantasy of authorship as the ability to equate a letter with a literary work foundered at both ends of the metaphor. Either the letter stayed in the bag, as in the case of Lichtenberg's "work,"[15] or it arrived without a legitimate claim to ownership, as in the case of Haller's. The fragment was thus a text that fell between two historical stools. On the one hand, it already contained the seeds of modern authorship, in which books were understood as intimate letters from authors to readers, especially feminine readers; on the other, it was as yet unable to relate to words in anything but a purely philological context. Crossing out and adding were techniques that achieved nothing with words except more or fewer words, techniques that indeed actually found application in Lichtenberg's own letters.[16] Haller's name, moreover, was a hallmark for the very flaw that made the postal system just as imperfect an invention as Lichtenberg's aphorisms were imperfect literary works. The misfortune of it all was that the truths of nature were not a matter for the discourse of poetry to decide. What was lacking here was something imaginary: a nature identified with the soul as the origin of pure and purely hallucinatory signifieds. When the intimate media of the private letter and the diary finally had sexualized the exchange of symbols, the endless administration of words in the Republic of Scholars would come to a standstill, and the copyist would come to nature and authorship. Once a higher authority declared Mother Nature to be the only guidebook for letter writers, a soul would be heard speaking and its appearance seen when in fact nothing but symbols were being read. Bodies and symbols always were "on time" when they came to an end in the voice of such a soul.

What was transmitted by Lichtenberg's metaphor of the letter as a literary work, by contrast, did not arrive (there): since the postal technology of metaphors was nothing but a metaphor for postal technology, the former failed, just like the latter. But Lichtenberg did not invent this postal technology; he merely discovered it—as a postal standard that was very widespread at the end of the eighteenth century. A so-called "enchartment," or registration, ensured the individuality of every letter.

> In the postal systems of Prussia, Saxony, and many other states, the instance of a letter being lost can occur even less frequently, because here every letter is specially registered on the post card, specifically the name of the recipient and the place to which the letter is destined, by means of series of numbers immediately affixed to the letters. Here, when a letter turns up missing at a postal station, it soon becomes apparent where it is to be sought, since every letter can be traced from the site of its registration to the site of its destination.[17]

From around 1800 until Heinrich von Stephan's "General Disposition" in the ninety-ninth issue of the post-office paper on December 18, 1874, every letter was something for which there was no official terminology:[18] a registered letter. In postal systems that did not register letters as a general rule, "registering" simply meant treating oneself to the private luxury of enchartment. What Lichtenberg announced for his letter was an everyday postal practice: registering the distance between bodies on a post card that provided records and surveillance. At every station, the card was opened and the place name, date, and postal servant's signature were entered. Every letter thus received a biography that was inscribed along with the geography and recorded its *Wanderjahre*. The postal system wrote the "annals" of every letter, transforming each into a unique individual so the institution that guided it to its goal—like the psychology of the time—could use a complete biography in the case of deviance in order to identify the moment and place at which the individual had strayed from the true path.

As long as letters had a personal history at the post offices, they could serve as metaphors for the individuality of the people who wrote them. By identifying the history of the letter with the history of the writing self, Lichtenberg's registered letter moreover unified the rhetorical and postal meanings of the metaphor and thus provided a general model for the letter in 1800. Only inasmuch as the letter had an individual history could it be the transmission/metaphor of the individual self and thus (according to the classical definition) what it always had been:

> Letters are among the most important monuments the individual man can leave behind. Lively people imagine even in talking to themselves that an absent friend is present, to whom they confide their innermost thoughts; and so, too, the letter is a kind of talking to oneself. . . . What makes us happy or brings us pain, presses upon or occupies us, frees itself from the heart, and, as lasting traces of an existence, of a condition, such pages always are more important to posterity, more so when the writer was absorbed by the moment alone, less when the future came to his mind.[19]

Enchartment, as the biography of the letter, was the postal a priori for the existence of letters as the transmitters (or bearers) of individuality grounded in the biographical. Because the letter itself was only what it was within a historiography, it was serviceable both as a medium for securing the traces of individual history and as a means for recalling those who were absent. It *was* what it transmitted—an individual, that is, and could therefore answer for that individual.

Nevertheless, Lichtenberg's model—the individualization of the postal system as a postal epoch of literature around 1800—was realized only in conjunction with another invention the human (or the masculine) mind has stumbled upon: The Woman or Nature as the *oikos* of the letter's text. In other words: the invention of the private letter.

CHAPTER THREE

Gellert's Coup: Folding the Private Letter

In their monastic existence, a scattering of local memory caches, the Middle Ages inscribed, and above all transcribed. The monastic rule of Monte Cassino, founded around 520, demanded that every monk spend a certain amount of time each day reading. Cassiodor complemented the Rule of the Holy Benedict by making it a sacred duty of monastic inmates to copy books.[1] They wrote—after Alexandria and its papyrus fields fell into the hands of the Emir Amr ibn al-As in 642—*in membrana*, which means on parchment. And as long as animal skins were the writing materials of agrarian Europe, all sending was a dispatch of postcards, and therefore fundamentally public. Parchment, after all, could be rolled up with some difficulty, but was practically impossible to fold, and because of this, letters and documents were one and the same in both concept and fact. Both were called *dictamina*, and the technology for producing them bore the title of *ars dictandi*.[2] Not until Europe had shifted over to the domestic production of paper (the first European paper mill began operation in Fabriano around the middle of the thirteenth century) did the characteristics of parchment—durability and publicity as opposed to transience and the ability to fold—become significant. The capability of distinguishing between documents and (sealed) letters did not mean the postal system already had transcended the realm of juridico-political codes and was moving in the direction of textual intimacy. The "privacy" of folded paper instead appears to have given kings the opportunity to engage in secret politics behind the backs of the chanceries—the hour of courtly intrigues had arrived. The king, after all, did not have to hand such letters over to the Lord Privy Seal as in earlier times, but sealed them instead with the mark of a personal signet.[3]

At the beginning of the modern period, Gutenberg's invention, which became a major success only on the basis of paper, finally unfolded the paper again and relegated the future distinction between "public" and "private" to the realm of the text, which was no longer divided into parchment and paper, but instead into typography and chirography. Yet as long as no one was able to call the discourse his or her own, since discourses of every kind were stored at the site of an Other or in the system of *ars dictandi*, there could not possibly be any question of private letters. "Wilt thou know," a sixteenth-century *formulari* asked neophytes in the art of writing letters, "wherebye one learns to compose letters? Then I tell thee it happens bye the rhetoric art."[4] This art or technology demanded extensive studies of the classics on the part of the letter writer, even in the sixteenth century, and thus, it goes without saying, knowledge of Latin and Greek. As a result, Erasmus conceded the right of letter writing only to scholars.[5] *Exercitatio* and *imitatio*, the foundations of the scholarly letter, merely occupied the space opened up for them by the lack of institutional postal access to any pragmatic relations to singular addresses— whether individual persons or events. An intimate discourse, which could have reached only them, only here, and only now, was not available. In 1522 the Taxis's system of imperial communications, which was exclusively at the state's disposal, was only beginning to be infiltrated by businessmen. And it was the letters of these very businessmen, which were constricting the space of scholarship, that Erasmus attacked in his polemic. Under the restrictions of humanistic rhetoric, on the other hand, senders and recipients were nothing more than etho-poietically produced imitations of the heroes from ancient mythology and history, and the *narratio* of letters was merely a collage of classical quotations. The illusion of "individual" authorship in letters thus was merely the result of a trick, the double application of the principle of imitation. After the imitation of classical topoi came the imitation of classical imitation itself: "All of these [borrowings] must be adapted with appropriate changes . . . so that the theft is not given away by the very fact that they are so ill assorted, like a bit of bad patching or faulty soldering. In borrowing foreign material let us imitate Virgil's skill, so that it appears not to have been borrowed from other sources, but to be original with ourselves."[6]

According to the law stated by a communications technician who haunts the pages of Thomas Pynchon's novels, "personal density . . . is directly proportional to temporal bandwidth."[7] If speaking that is addressed unequivocally is to be possible, the temporal bandwidth of a "self" must be at least equal to twice the time separating sender and recipient. Under conditions in which imitation extended to nearly all the external references in the letter, the temporal bandwidth between recipient and sender was exactly as large as the time required to read the corresponding classical passage(s). The range of persons and random access to them were accordingly large: an effect of the differentiation of postal institutions that posted nothing but their own conditions or standards. Thus, Erasmus's *ars dictaminis* posted not the person Desiderius, but the *memoria* of Erasmus Roterodamus. And it did so in a completely historical sense: *De conscribendis epistolis* was written and sent as a letter and received and printed (or pirated) as a book apparently without any singular references standing in the way that bind discourses to unrepeatable times, places, and people. Letters were recyclable discourse.

Territorial or absolutist postal systems, by contrast, defined a new and different situation. Speaking with Foucault: a new type of rationality called the *raison d'état* transformed everyone into subjects of the modern state. The governmental technology of such centralized political and administrative power was a comprehensive police system—the knowledge and practice of establishing order and regulating all relationships: between the people and the state, the people and things, the people and the people, and the people and discourses. In 1611, this passed for *monarchie aristodémocratique*: "the police must, in the broadest meaning of the term, secure 'traffic' among men. Otherwise, men would not be able to live, or their lives would be insecure, plagued by poverty and threatened continuously."[8] In the aristodemocratic police state, the gazetteers for this traffic were Baroque letter-writing guides. Instead of alluding exclusively to a classical library, the letter's external references were now replaced by tables classifying the possible ways to produce letters. The grammar-school rule of "practice and imitation" now made way for the art of bringing different registers into alignment so that the guidebook produced precisely the letter demanded in a given communicative situation. The rule of *aptum*, after all, demanded that "the letter" "duly / be written according to the usual customs of the court / that the word be disposed in accordance with the persons and the matters. One writes differently to a prince / differently to a citizen / and differently again to a peasant."[9]

In order to allow for the seemly disposition or rhetorical combination of words, persons, and matters, Georg Philipp Harsdörffer's *Teutscher Secretarius* first provided a titular grid that represented both sender and recipient and placed them in relation to one another—which had a decisive impact on the letter's stylistic stratum and topology. Second, it provided a grid of situations or—in pragmatic terms—illocutions. Third, the *Secretarius* divided all "greeting-friend-enemy-instruction-complaint-consolation-bequest-chancery-love-exchange-business" letters not as the humanistic guidebooks had done, into rhetorical genres of discourse usually expanded to include a *genus familiale*, but instead into a thematic grid that in itself represented a system of knowledge. In Harsdörffer's system, every part of the *formula-historia-formula* schema could be addressed in every conceivable letter. But that was not all. On the basis of the representational interrelationship of all the grids, each part of the letter—title plus *salutatio, causa, historia, conclusio,* or signature—also offered a feasible way into the letter to be written. As an application of the rules, a letter always would be a manifestation of the exemplary nature of the rules and therefore never would be a private letter.[10] The rules were exhausted in the rhetorical combination of the application grids intersecting in a given letter, and every letter was part of the system of rules. The possibility of representing the rules by usage was given quite simply by the finite number of applications: provided that a certain number of letters had been written since the Beginning—in which, of course, there was the postal system[11]—all usage always was reusage. And because it was Baroque, such reuse could be calculated. With n titles and a situations, the number of possible letters was always $a(n^2-n)$. In the case of the *Teutscher Secretarius*, this came to exactly 1,221,990 possible letters.

Such calculability, based on the representation of external references, was an abomination to the eighteenth century, insofar as it ordered innovations in the symbolic and media technologies of individualization to the front lines in the war for universal alphabetization[12] in Central Europe. Not quite a hundred years after Harsdörffer, Christian Gellert, a Leipzig professor of rhetoric, systematically trimmed away all representative (and thus public) external references in order to transform each and every one of them into characteristic (and thus private) internal references. Gellert's coup and the invention of subjectivity in general were not based on something entirely new, but on a systematic transvaluation of all the values of Baroque discursive practice by way of implosion. First, the site of the titular table, which classified recipients and senders according to status, birth, possessions, dominions, honorary offices, duties, and gender,[13] and which represented their position in relation to one another and to all other possible senders and recipients, now was occupied by a universal address called "The Individual" that could produce contact between all letter writers. Then, chattering away about the intimate confessions of the soul, nature stepped in to take the place of art, which had affected and animated bodies. And in the process, the very same rhetorical figures that had demonstrated the skill of oratorical artifice since Cicero now bespoke naturalness for Gellert. This began with basic rules such as the *perspicuitas* and the *brevitas*—an etymological necessity—and continued as far as artistic devices such as the *apostrophe* or the *percontatio*.[14] A third replacement involved the table of occasions [*Kasualraster*]—the pragmatics that were given prior to all content and that had structured guidebooks more or less the same way from the Middle Ages until well into the eighteenth century. The letter eliminated occasion from the guidebook in order to generate it internally as a fictional situation. Such was the program in Gellert's sixteenth *Letter*. As if it were describing the obliteration of occasion's a priori as far as the letter's text was concerned, Gellert's letter set up a situation in sheer autoreferentiality that was not to be found in any of the old European guidebooks: the scene of writing.

> Madam,
>   Last night I had an unhappy dream. You were sitting and writing, and even if you were nearly sixteen miles away from me, with the help of the dream I could still see that you were writing to a good friend. Who was happier than I? Every moment I looked to see if you might soon be through with the letter, since I thought nothing with more certainty than that you were writing to me. Indeed, many a time I was already reaching out to take the letter away from you. Then your little son came in and bumped into the table so carelessly that the ink spilled. In my anxiety, I wanted to reach for either the letter or the ink, and thereupon I awakened. I told my old aunt about my dream. She told me ink meant quarrel and strife with absent ones. Oh Madam! But not with you! The heavens would not permit it! No, I will give you no opportunity, I will

gladly not ask why you do not answer me. Grant me only permission that I may continue . . . to write to you every post day.[15]

Lichtenberg might have been saved. Rather than obliterating the difference between absence and presence (and that means writing itself) with ink, Gellert traveled in the medium of dreams or fantasy to a presence that preceded the post, and as soon as the letter threatened to be finished, he spilled the ink. After all, according to the wise woman's clairvoyant interpretation of the dream, ink meant nothing but writing—writing in the language of difference or of the postal principle. What was at stake was the classical definition of the letter itself. Instead of being promulgated as a discourse between absentees alone, the letter created the presence of an absent person's doppelgänger for all those who were not present. From then on, letters were reflections of glances—glances that at once found the glance of the Other, inasmuch as writing was dreaming, and lost it, inasmuch as dreaming was writing. Because of this, writing henceforth was performed only in the trope of the *praeteritio* that what was written did not exist at all. After all, the answer to the question Gellert did not *not* ask—"Why don't you answer me?"—was the sole content of his letter, a content invoking the obliteration of the text itself because it threatened to expel the doppelgänger from his dream existence and dream presence. Such an existence was merely appearance, and thus identical to narcissism, as a letter addressed to Gellert explained. "But how should I reward you for all the entertainment your letters have given me?" the jubilant young Count Moritz von Brühl responded. "Your power of imagination shows me to you from such a lovely angle!"[16] Catching oneself in the glance of the Other promptly invoked the literary in the second half of the eighteenth century: in Brühl's imagination, he and Gellert were transfigured into the hommo-sexual couple of classical letter writing *kat exochen*: Cicero and Atticus.[17]

Less than half a century later, Ludwig Tieck's *William Lovell* would popularize Gellert's system, which set up an opposition between absence/writing/strife and presence/hallucination/love, in the radicalized form of the epistolary novel's discourse about itself:

I always want to start a letter to you, take the quill and write down all sorts of things, and in doing so forget about you. Then suddenly you occur to me once more, the entire letter is interrupted by some coincidence, and it is impossible for me to find the thread again. . . . —When I close my eyes, I converse with you and tell you of all my grief and cares. I find nothing comical about this; what else do our letters do? Perhaps in a different life, distant thoughts will come together more quickly and nobly than happens with language and dead symbols; perhaps it is only then that we will own what we have only been granted now to hold.[18]

The ideal Romantic letter writer practiced and internalized Gellert's lesson that writing letters was dreaming about the letter writing of the Other, and in the ideal case was thus dreaming about the dreaming of the Other, to the point that letter writing, paradoxically enough, began to get in the way of letters. Writing, scratching on paper with a quill, was synonymous with forgetting the Other; only hallucinating with one's eyes closed was allowed to be called communicating—letters were a communion such as this in the state of Original Sin. The conquest of death would at once be the conquest of writing; it was not for nothing that in many places Thot, the inventor of writing, was also the ferryman of the dead.[19] Letter writing after death would be telepathy—or telephony. As a result, Lovell mistook the mail for a (not yet invented) telephone even while still on earth when he wrote to his beloved: "o how do I thank you, happy genius who first invented the means for sharing thoughts and feelings with dead masses, and thus for speaking unto lands afar."[20]

This sort of communication between angels and the redeemed also could be pure insanity (and heaven a madhouse), as James Tilly Matthews, a former tea broker and patient at Bedlam Hospital, demonstrated in London at exactly the same time that Tieck was writing his novel. "Brain-saying,"[21] magnetically induced telepathic communications, was Matthews's name for Lovell's heavenly communications technology, which drove him to madness rather than bliss (because obviously there were a couple of criminals or doctors at the other end of the line who would not stop talking gibberish). Assuming Lovell's letters, like Werther's—none of which ever was sent—were addressed to the reader of the novel via general delivery, instructions for reading the epistolary novel itself can be discovered in Lovell's hallucinatory technology of communicating. Gellert's dream post would become Romanticism's—not undangerous—aesthetic of reception. No wonder Matthews's paranoia spread like an epidemic over Central Europe after 1800.

The replacement of the external references of the table of occasions with the process of imagining the occasion into the letter produced a fundamental fictionality. The letter's transformation into literature was due to a further substitution: "phantasma," as a rhetorical figure representing the absent or dead, was replaced by the "power of imagination" as a capacity of the soul.[22] The creation of literature as the process of "imagining" into the letter external references that previously had been separate and distinct coincided with the intimacy of the letter and the preservation of its confidentiality. The meaning and purpose of such confidentiality was to produce immediately the possibility for betrayal of a truth the production of which was itself an effect of this confidentiality: the feigned truth of The Individual. That very sleight of hand was performed by Gellert's justification for the fact that nearly all margins were trimmed from his letters: since "the world" does not normally think of The Individual in general, but instead of "such and such man, who has this or that service, this or that serious office, this or that age; . . . his affairs, his writings, his friends,"[23] all of the titles, once so dear to the Baroque, had to be cut out. After all, "certain circumstances constantly get mixed in with them, which we do not want to be known. Yet who is a more loyal traitor than a letter?"[24] After the withdrawal of the titular grid, intimate secrets went to press. The secret was a technology of denunciation and power that was developed and tested by the secret societies of the eighteenth century, as Reinhart Koselleck has shown: "The secret became a control mechanism consistently wielded by the Order of Illuminati, for example. The priestly regents of that order began by . . . introducing an accurate secret reporting system. Brethren were obliged to file sealed monthly reports about themselves—in moral candour—and about their fellow brethren. 'Thus he must necessarily decipher and compromise himself and others, in writing.'"[25] In other words: he must create a modern subject. The private letter systematically identified the confidentiality of the letter, self-reflection, and the power of control, and therefore—in still other words—was synonymous with the education of civil servants.

CHAPTER FOUR

Post Day in Wahlheim

The private letter, a compromising of oneself in writing, was the medium of transmission that, alongside the recording media of diaries and auto-biographies, assumed the function in an alphabetized Central Europe that confession previously had carried out as the old religious means of control. Ministerial officials like Cabinet Councilor Johann Ludwig Klüber could point proudly to the fact that the postal technology of private letters was far more efficient than the postal technology of confession ever had been: "What is locked up most carefully in the heart, in one's own living room, is entrusted without hesitation to the postal service by everyone, by hundreds of thousands every day. The postman's satchel thus holds incomparably more secrets, and no less securely under proper administration, than the seal of confession, and the symbol of discretion is none other than that of the postal service."[1] This did not count out, but counted on the fact that the text of the heart, the secret truth of the individual, always had circulated as public discourse: connected to the archives and their mounds of paper, which laid the foundation for human sciences such as psychology. "On his deathbed, an invalid writes down an observation about himself, mails it, and dies";[2] and Karl Philipp Moritz's *Magazine for Empirical Psychology* publishes it. The post-office window replaced the ears of the priest.

In 1774, another invalid also made confessions of his introspections that lasted for weeks in letters to a friend, committed suicide, and an editor put his letters in print: Goethe's success as an author was perfect. That the letters of a dead man named Werther exhibit none of the characteristics of a letter (before the age of envelopes) other than the date— no address or salutation or sender—makes them suspect. And indeed, whoever takes the trouble to work out the days of the week for the dates on these letters with the help of a calendar will find something remarkable. What distinguishes Werther's packet of letters from all the others of his day is the completely even distribution of the letters' dates—with a single exception—over the days of the week: Werther wrote fifteen times on a Monday, fourteen times on Tuesday, nine on Wednesday, eleven on Thursday, eleven on Friday, thirteen on Saturday, and thirteen again on Sunday. By contrast, letters that actually circulated at the time indicate that a maximum number was written either just before or on a certain day of the week: the so-called post day, when the weekly *Ordinari-Post* was sent. "Letters could not be sent as often as desired, as they can today, but had to wait instead for the 'post day.' . . . On post day, everyone sat down to write. . . . Thus it was often said: 'I have post day,' or 'I dispatched post day to N'; one did not forget to write 'daily,' but missed a few post days, or had wanted to write from post day to post day, or postdaily, just as one expected mail every post day."[3]

In *Werther*, by contrast, there is no trace of writing from "post day to post day." The conclusion to be reached from this is obvious: either Werther's letters never were sent or—which amounts to the same thing—they were not letters at all, but a diary: a dead man's letter to the reading public, general delivery. There are several indications for the accuracy of this hypothesis. First, Werther kept a diary,[4] as the reader is told on a single occasion, but one never finds out when he was keeping it; nor is it to be found among his private papers. This suggests that the diary and the letters were identical. Second, the letters Goethe wrote to Auguste Countess zu Stolberg after the publication of *Werther* in 1775—which conform to the novel like a program—explicitly called for the transformation of letters into diaries: "Good night. Want to write you a sort of diary, that's the best thing. Do the same for me, I hate letters. . . . "[5] The reason: if writing was to be the confession of the soul's intimate secrets, it was possible only "from moment to moment."[6] In other words, it could not be subjected to the regimentation of "postdaily" communication. The soul needed a medium that was accessible to it at all times. For this reason, and because authors could not exist without intimate knowledge of women's hearts, Auguste was supposed to write a diary as well: "Dear, I'm asking you to write me a sort of diary too. It's the only thing that vanquishes the permanent distance."[7] The third indication for the accuracy of the hypothesis that Werther's letters were never sent is the Count's letter, which the editor discovered in his posthumous collection of letters.[8] Since it hardly can be assumed that Werther sent this letter to Wilhelm, it follows that the entire collection was found in Werther's possession. Finally, while the distribution of the letters' dates over the days of the week does not indicate a maximum, it does indeed indicate a minimum. This fact becomes especially significant when the division of the novel into two parts is taken into account: the last letter of the novel, which was written on a Wednesday, was Werther's first letter after his return to Wahlheim. A solution to the Wednesday riddle might be that Wednesday was post day in Wahlheim. Since none of the letters were sent, none were written on the only day when they could have been mailed. Because confessions had to flow when they wanted to, they did not so much as trickle at the very time they were supposed to flow according to a schedule.[9]

Letters sent to posterity via general delivery are testaments. And testaments, on the level of the novel, regulate the relationships between all persons. Yet while Werther's general-delivery letters, including his testament, reached their readers under cover of the authorial name of Goethe in a manner that never had existed before, the opposite was true of the general-delivery letters of the dead in the novel. Things never arrive at the destinations given in such letters. Since the letters of the dead are dead letters, they continuously require travel on the part of the surviving dependents. In fact, the dysfunctionality of testaments is the reason for all of the journeys undertaken in *Werther*. At the beginning of the novel, Albert is on the way to settle his inheritance after the death of his father.[10] The husband of the young lady in Wahlheim is on the road because an inheritance is being withheld from him in Switzerland.[11] Werther himself travels on account of such matters on behalf of his mother; it seems his aunt is trying to deprive her of her inheritance.[12]

The writing of the dead, which had been entrusted to the law and the church as the scriptural powers of old Europe, is intercepted. The oral testament of Lotte's mother, by contrast, is all the more effective (after all, it bequeaths Lotte to Albert). And Werther's testament also functions for precisely that reason—because it transcends the end of the novel in a direction leading to the holy site of orality, which is designated by her mother. In the great beyond, where Lotte would reunite with her archetype as her mother's proxy, the love story of Lotte and Werther would have a "happy ending." In life after death, as life after the end of the novel, this happy ending could only be the novel's eternal resurrection in the reading of (feminine) readers. And Lotte and Werther could become the hero/ines of the novel because they foreshadowed this identifying act. Lotte became her mother, to whom, in the hour of death, she had given the promise that she would be a mother to her brothers and sisters.[13] Werther, as a translator who identifies himself with the author of the translation, became a poet. *Werther*'s author thus was in reality his hero's executor, insofar as he carried out his last will and testament, or his incestuous wish, by transforming it into the promise that a love like Werther's would mean the identification of women with The Woman, and therefore the promise that all masculine readers, provided they became Werther or poets, could sleep with The Woman.

It was no accident that testaments structured what is presumably the most successful epistolary novel of all time, especially if the letters were diary entries—that is, archived intimate confessions of the soul. As far as the preservation of confidentiality was concerned, all letters were testaments in Werther's time insofar as the safeguard against premature disclosure of testaments provided the legal basis for the confidentiality of the letter. In A.D. 68, state sanction for the testament's confidentiality first had been established in writing by the *Lex Cornelia de falsis*.[14] Until the end of the eighteenth century, violations of the confidentiality of the letter thus were classified together with disclosures of testaments as *crimen falsi*. Even the *Theresiana* of 1768 still knew of no specific designation as such for the will to knowledge aimed at intimate confession that would sustain the *Werther* novel four years later: "Within its broad scope, this depravity includes all manner of evil advantages . . . of which some . . . are treated as special topics by this meticulous legal codex; others, however, and indeed the more vulgar, are presented here. The rest, to which, because of the variety of such roguish, fraudulent actions, one can give almost no names of their own, are included under the general category of *falsus*."[15]

Only after the General Prussian Common Law of 1794 were violations of the letter's confidentiality prosecuted as "invasion of privacy" and no longer as the intent to commit fraud.[16] From then on, the letter was primarily a confession, even in the eyes of the law. In this sense, *Werther* functioned like a bill the lawyer Goethe had presented to the legislature of readers. The Werther Bill proposed that letters no longer be viewed as testaments, which allowed only for fraudulent interests and therefore not for reader identification or the epistolary novel, but as diary entries, and therefore as intimate knowledge. As knowledge, they would be assigned a special criminal motive—the desire of Goethe's (female) readers. Viewed from this perspective, the novel's success was nothing but the legislature's approval of this new definition and desire for letters. *The Sorrows of the Young Werther* was the letter's passage into law as literature.

CHAPTER FIVE

Set the Controls for the Heart of the Night

But the bill's passage and the transformation of the confidentiality of the letter into literature obeyed a supreme pedagogical command: think for yourself. The *ars dictaminis* was a scandal because the rules for ordering words were nothing but words themselves. Since Adalbertus Samaritanus and the *Rationes dictandi* in the first half of the twelfth century, "epistolic" *dispositio* was achieved by the succession of five epistolary components: *salutatio, exordium, narratio, petitio, conclusio*. The letter, as Steinhausen complains, thus became a "form that can be easily filled out"[1]— or in more technical terms, it was addressed at all points. In the Baroque Age, after all, the connection between these individual components had been produced by specific conjunctions, "for the *exordium* 'while,' for the *narratio* 'when,' for the *petitio* 'thus.'"[2] For the reader, all of these conjunctions were addresses that enabled direct access to individual parts of the letter, just as the corresponding grids in the letter-writing guide did for the writer in turn. By contrast, in the dispositive of pedagogy and psychology, the possibility of addressing individuals was worth more than the possibility of addressing words: "All the letter-writing guides in the world will not teach us to think. Skillful reasoning, a lively power of imagination, knowledge about the things of which one wishes to speak accomplish the most here. Reflect upon what you want to write. Order your sentences in your thoughts. Do not always look for the connection in words, but rather in the succession, in the similarity and dissimilarity of your thoughts."[3]

Gellert's mail—like that of the secret societies—arrived. From 1770 on, the wind was blowing from a new direction in German schools. The boys' bodies were refitted with the armor of a new mnemonic technique.

Instead of making verses according to the rules of the *ars poetica*, students now had to fill pages with their own ideas about the works of famous writers. Instead of words, meaning was recorded. One stopped enlisting armies of nameless poem writers and started to introduce the business of interpretation. The new technology of individualization, the German essay, did not keep tabs on whether a poet could be recited and imitated, but instead on whether he had been understood.[4] The concept of "understanding," which had made a new career for itself after the reception of Klopstock's works, designated an empathic process; the degree of its success was a moral criterion of evaluation and was measured by sentimental bodily secretions [*empfindsamen Körperabsonderungen*].[5] On the reception end, "understanding" complemented Gellert's order to think on the production end. The avalanche of letters set off by Gellert's *Letters* threw up the bridge that linked Klopstock to modern readership, reading aloud in a small circle of initiates to silent reading in one's own chambers, the secret society to the literary market.

As a function of deregionalized reading, Gellert's command to think controlled and verified Klopstock's command to understand. He thus gave a definition of the letter that departed from the classical definition in a small, but decisive way: "It [the letter] is a free imitation of good conversation."[6] Freedom here was the command to subjugate words to the power of thought so that neither the rhetorical combination of words nor the emotional state and desire of bodies, but instead the text of the heart was written in letters. This double bind nonetheless made it possible to monitor the performance of understanding by mail. It was no accident that the letter was the only independent form of development promoted in the schools after the pedagogical reforms.[7]

From then on, words had an individual origin in thought, and discourse meant translation. Words were metaphors for ideas formed by the soul—every self thus became the subject of its own discourse, a priori. Words now were the subject's private property: the precondition necessary for the existence of private letters. The symbols in the treasure chest of signifiers became provisions for the reader's nourishment.[8] This was precisely what was at stake in Gellert's criticism of a thank-you note in Neukirch's *Gallant Letters*. "I am thus being far more sensible," Neukirch had written to Herr von Rauter, "when I remain silent. Your Excellency knows my heart and finds within it all the letters that are needed for a speech. You yourself shall make your own hymn of praise and be satisfied."[9] With keen insight, Gellert immediately recognized the point being raised:

> It is nearly impossible that a letter case should not come to mind when one reads of the heart, and a typesetter in the case of Herr von Rauter, who makes his hymn of praise for himself. . . . What are letters in the heart? How can you see them? If this idea is to make any sense, it can only mean as much as: You know my heart and know that I have all the feelings necessary for sincere thanksgiving, but not for any speech whatsoever.[10]

So precise was the function performed by the replacement of the Baroque *ars poetica*'s battery of signifiers, for which Gutenberg's invention was indeed the a priori,[11] with the knowledge of a soul police who apprehended intimate thoughts or feelings instead of a universal code. Neukirch's unreasonable demand upon Herr von Rauter was called "the poetry of occasion"; Gellert's was called "interpretation." And since signifieds subsumed vast quantities of signifiers, mnemonic technique no longer was tortuous training in an art requiring the memorization of thousands upon thousands of letter combinations, but instead was a natural ability. *Terminus ad quem* was to implant an authorship *en miniature* inside every letter writer so that "I think" could accompany all of his reading.[12]

In the epoch of the postal system known as literature, the private letter's most important function was to act as a medium for controlling the deregionalized market for books. Even the *Messia* was enlisted as a love letter and read out loud: Wieland read it with Sophie Gutermann (who later became Sophie de La Roche), Lavater with Barbara Schulthess, Herder with Caroline Flachsland, Voß with Ernestine Boie, Miller and later Sprickmann with Charlotte von Einem. The poet's text, as Alewyn recognized, became nothing more than a medium for communication.[13] With universal alphabetization and Gellert's *Letters*, this medium's confinement to face-to-face circumstances became obsolete. After all, Romantic authors were not the first to use the postal system as a communications technology for the purposes of educational strategy; Gellert already had done so. "I know that you read," he wrote to the "best feminine correspondent in the world,"[14] the sixteen-year-old Johanna Erdmuth von Schönfeld. "Couldn't you tell me from time to time about the books you read, the ones in which you found something to your liking or your disliking?"[15] At first, Gellert recommended such books individually and sent them by mail. Soon, however, Schönfeld received an annotated catalog of Gellert's private library, and along with it systematic access to an entire program for girls' education. Gellert inaugurated the first long-distance lending library. Its holdings, of course, contained Gellert's own works— including the *Letters*.[16]

Gellert's use of the mail as a remote control for hermeneutics found imitators, one after the other. In 1765, for example, Goethe, then a student in Leipzig, not only repeated to his sister the epistolographic theories he had heard or read the day before in Gellert's class on "German and Latin methods for the formation of understanding and style,"[17] but also prescribed or prohibited the reading of certain works: "But take note of it, you shouldn't read any more novels than I allow. . . . But don't be afraid lest Grand[ison] Cl[arissa] and Pa[mela] might perchance be excluded. You should not lack in good reading entertainment. I will write to Papa on account of this."[18] Just as Goethe imitated Gellert, Clemens Brentano, who also had a sister he wanted to hook up to a telepedagogical system of control, imitated Goethe after 1800.

> I've commissioned the book dealer *Guilhomman* to send you the Homer.
> Did you receive it? You should furthermore read the travels of the young
> Anarchasis next, and very carefully. These will instruct and amuse you. But
> you must not restrain such reading in any way; you must honor it by loving
> it. . . . When it's possible, write down your sentiments during or after your
> reading and send me something of the sort.[19]

Brentano's long-distance lending library posted educational programs for budding women readers purely in accordance with Gellert's command to think, if an individual was to write back at all: "Consider, dearest child, that thinking is the homeland of soul, and don't look in foreign regions where your guardian angel did not set out to find you."[20]

Since an angel is simply a courier in ancient Greek, and "angelos" originally derived from the Persian word *angaréion*, in just so many words, Clemens Brentano's command meant that his sister was only to be in places where she could receive mail: "since culture lies in chaotic night, where there is no post."[21] Dark continents like Africa, where there is "no postilion,"[22] were to be found everywhere that discourse followed the syntax of the body (in Bettina Brentano's case) or the syntax of a battery of signifiers (which amounts to the same thing). Working with the pedagogical requirement that discourses can be addressed individually, the colonial soldier Brentano strove to reduce the vacuum of leadership in Central Europe. "Set the controls for the heart of the sun," a command or a title by Pink Floyd once read. In Brentano's case, however, it was the heart of the night, and the controls were not on a panel, but a desk. It was not Romanticism that first located the chaotic night or *tohu wabohu* before the beginning of the bourgeois world in the soul of a woman who is not at home in thinking. To the extent that the *ars oratoria* were separated from aesthetics, the critique of the scholarly right of disposition over the pragmatic dimension of discourse recruited talented people from beyond the Scholars' Republic—talent that had no pragmatic skills, it was true, but that was all the better equipped with Truth. Since women were excluded from the universities, and thus from poetry as well, they were a fortiori uneducated;[23] the discourse of the soul police transformed such exclusion into the gift of women for handwriting and reading, which was at one with nature. Alphabetized women took up positions at the input of handwritten script for letters: "I know ladies who write the most beautiful letters . . . who are lively by nature, but certainly not educated. They knew nothing of Menantes or Weis or Neukirch, and yet still they wrote well."[24] And they also took positions at the output of typescript for poetry:

> The Pharisees, textual scholars, and the nation's supreme commanders do not believe in him [the *Messiah*], but I am happy to see that this superb poem has found enormous applause among those who are brilliant only for their own sake, and not for the sake of the Fatherland. Our ladies avenge the author for the indifference of our highly educated men and for the tasteless prejudices of our professional critics of art.[25]

There was a single criterion of classification from the Baroque sender/recipient grid that was not erased in the new order of things, but instead was actually universalized: sex. After the middle of the eighteenth cen-

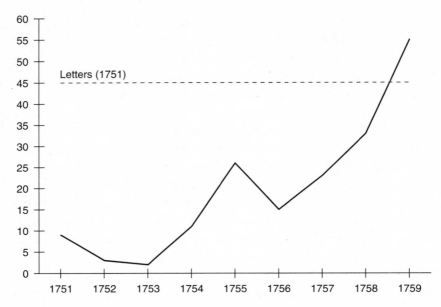

FIGURE I. The outstripping of hommo-sexual letter writing: Percentage of women in Gellert's correspondence.

tury, reading and writing consequently became transitive with regard to the sexes. For the purpose of recruiting female letter writers, Gellert issued an executive announcement in 1751: "It is quite certain, gracious lady, that your sex excels in correspondence, and in a short time you will be new evidence of this."[26] Gellert's appeal announced a program for outstripping hommo-sexual correspondence not only qualitatively, but quantitatively as well. That program also included his own correspondence, since the percentage of women recipients and senders in Gellert's *Letters*—a proud 44 percent—in no way corresponded to the reality of Gellert's letters. The complete edition of his correspondence records the women's share as barely 11 percent for the years 1750–55. In 1756, that share became 15 percent; by 1758, it had reached 34 percent, and in 1759, with 54 percent of his letters sent by or received from women, Gellert actually had beaten the mark set in his letter-writing guide by 10 percent [see Figure 1]. This practically exponential rate of increasing connections was something for a postal minister to write home about. Gellert no longer wanted to write to men. "Nor should he expect an answer from me," Gellert let Rabener know via the young Schönfeld, "because when I have time to write, I write to the ladies and not to him."[27]

There was a historical-postal a priori for the establishment of private lending libraries à la Gellert and thus for the private letter's function as the medium of control in hermeneutics, as well. As far as Gellert was concerned, this a priori was established by the events following August 28, 1756. On that day, the Prussian regiments of Frederick II marched into Saxony. The Saxon army confined itself to holding the "dung heap" (Brühl) of the base at Pirna and laid down its arms on October 26.[28] Saxon post offices continued to be administrated by Saxon officials, but for the Prussians; the long-standing bickering between the two postal districts—one can assume—was forced to arbitration in the Prussians' favor.[29] The result was that Saxony, and thus Leipzig, and thus Gellert as a citizen of Saxony and Leipzig, now had the benefit of enjoying the Prussian rate for printed matter, which was reduced to one and one-half-pence a pound for four miles—"in the interests of literature and the book trade."[30] Such rates were a stimulus for the export of silent reading, the mnemonic technology of understanding, the culture of the norm and individualization, into the countryside. The postal system—long before the establishment of "printed matter" as a full-fledged category, by the way—began to establish the first economic preconditions for the deregionalization of the literary market. The library catalogue went out to Schönfeld three years later. The bourgeois program of education reached nobles like Countess Vitzthum von Eckstädt and her daughter, who then became subjects—something that could hardly have been financed without the rate for "printed matter" enjoyed by poorly paid bourgeois professors. This act of the postal system "in the interests of literature" was the first step in the direction of a German state constituted entirely of education officials in the nineteenth century. But that was not all. The very same year, in 1759, Gellert's eldest brother, Friedrich Leberecht, was promoted from master of fencing and written homework at the University of Leipzig to postmaster general at the main post office in Leipzig.[31] And what is more, his second-eldest brother, Christlieb Ehregott, held the position of chief foundry director and professor of metallurgical chemistry at the mining academy in Freiberg—a post in which he was succeeded by a certain Friedrich von Hardenberg, alias Novalis. The Gellerts held all of the strategic launching points for the modern bourgeois state: the corps of education officials, and German poetry, heavy industry, and the postal system.

The postal system's interest in literature, however, was not confined to printed matter alone. It also concerned handwriting, but with a reversed policy on rates. Except for the "*trial records* of advocates, courts and parties"—as Heinrich August Raabe revealed in his *Postal Secrets*—"the *manuscripts* of scholars and book dealers must bear *higher* rates at many post offices."[32] While Raabe denied any legal authority or competence on the part of the postal system, he did not deny its competence in matters of literary criticism:

> The *manuscripts* of scholars, as the most precious products of mankind, must indeed form an exception, and in some ways it would truly be desirable if, just for the sake of making criticism easier, the differences in the value of these manuscripts were assessed by the postal service, or if it at least suppressed the bad products of a few quill drivers in order to protect book dealers and the public from larger losses. This could be counted among good deeds of the postal system that as yet remain unknown.[33]

The fee structure of the postal system in 1800—low postage for printed matter and high postage for manuscripts—set the pattern for the Romantic literary criticism of the time. A year after Raabe's *Postal Secrets*, Friedrich Schlegel considered it to be the mission of such criticism—as "thorough understanding,"[34] which meant "reading that is constantly repeated over and over again"[35]—to check the harmful effects of the postal rate for printed matter. Romantic criticism, that is, was to control the way in which, "since the invention of book printing and the spread of the book trade, a massive amount of thoroughly bad and completely unsuitable texts has flooded the minds of modern people, overwhelming, confusing, and misleading them."[36] This involved nothing less than propagating the education of a readership consisting entirely of interpreters. Yet such a readership could be brought about only on the condition that massive amounts of books were in circulation. Novalis already had said as much in 1798: "For me, book making is not being expanded on anything close to the proper scale."[37] Only then would it be possible for all people to become men and women readers and for all such readers to be equipped to become little authors: "Wilhelm Meister's apprenticeship— it is all we have now.—We should have as many apprenticeships as at all possible, written in the same spirit—all the apprenticeships of all the people who have ever lived."[38]

The *Bildungsroman* was the specialized literary genre capable of suspending the harmful effects of the flood of books by means of a flood of books because it was a novel about not only the hero's education, but the reader's as well. Confronted by "massive amounts" of text, the reader was given the lesson that "memorizing is of no use at all unless the actor"—who was also a reader[39]—"has not first thought his way into the spirit and intentions of the author; the letter is nothing without the spirit."[40] Because *Wilhelm Meister's Apprenticeship* was the first novel to prescribe its own method of interpretation, it was "the absolutely new and unique book that one can learn to understand only by itself"[41]—a book that was the opposite of the masses—and was what its reader should become: a "personality and living individuality."[42]

Since the hero of the novel also was the ideal reader, every reader of the novel could become at once both the hero and the reader, raised to the second power. As reader of his own reading, every male reader recognized himself as the mirror image of Wilhelm Meister and in reading thus became the author of his own apprenticeship. And that apprenticeship was written nowhere but in diaries and private letters that demonstrated the "fundamental understanding" "known as characterization,"[43] an understanding that thus transformed all readers into the "senders and authors of their own intimate symbols/characters."[44] Things worked out as Novalis had wanted: the private letter posted character as a function of the flood of books. (Feminine) readership was authorship at a reduced rate.

CHAPTER SIX

Postage

In the seventeenth century, a letter had represented one of x possible applications of the rhetorical rules for letters. It existed only as a case of congruity between different classificational systems and rubrics in the letter-writer's guide that were to be observed in each and every case. In this sense, medieval guidebooks already had defined the letter as *oratio congrua*.[1] As such, its existence was grounded in the *techné* of this congruity. After Gellert's coup, the letter no longer was a more or less two-dimensional congruity of this sort, situated horizontally on the level of *connexio verbalis*, but instead was a congruity standing in a vertical relationship to the text. The individual letter thus attained a completely new form of being. It ceased to be an example or a case of application and became an individual, the fruit of a writing that could not be represented, rather than that of readings and combinations (*inventio* and *dispositio*).

Thus, the letter became the site of production for a new form of truth: a three-dimensional truth that no longer existed in the authority of the topoi, and therefore in the text's references to another text, but instead in the folding back of what was written onto writing. The insinuation of an authorship for letters, the letter's ability to be interpreted as the expression of intimate thoughts, resided in this folding back of circulating matter onto production. In this respect, the letter's transformation into literature via the elimination of all the external references represented in the letter-writing guide was not an event in the history of literature, but instead the occurrence of a shift in the universal *episteme*.[2] What caused such folding back, however, can be seen only with regard to the nondiscursive practices of the symbol, which opened up the horizon within which the letter's transformation into literature could become an event in the history of literature. This means that the folding back of the letter's text onto an original act of writing was a response to the postal supplementation of its references, which were fictionalized and pulled back inside the letter. The letter's transformation into literature as a function of hermeneutic spiritual guidance therefore was determined by a transformation of the postal dispositive. The question is thus quite simply this: what was the postal principle that allowed the letter's transformation into literature to make its appearance?

The answer is to be found in the vicinity of an event marking the anthropological foundation of knowledge about the exchange of words. When Prussia (as the first state to do so) introduced legislation compelling the use of the postal system in 1715,[3] The Individual became the definitive ground for the exchange of information/people/goods. Unlike the postal monopoly of the seventeenth century, which merely had rooted out competitors in the struggle for state power (e.g., the cities), compulsory use of the mail [*Postzwang*], as the "obligation of the public to avail itself of the postal services of the State or the Empire for travel or the dispatch of materials,"[4] resulted from concerns about the behavior of a population that was participating in exchange. Compulsory use was among the measures taken by a power that had placed life under its directorial management: exchange became a matter for the bio-politics of population.[5] This bio-political turn alone, which for the first time forced people to ignore completely the corporatively organized courier services that remorselessly diversified human beings into businessmen, scholars, clerics, and nobles, first brought the face of humanity to light as the meaning and purpose of the postal system. Once compulsory use of the mail had defined the state's monopoly on power over discourse, every letter writer was a subject of posting. Further still, by compelling the use of the same medium for the transportation of one's own person as was used for the transportation of letters, compulsory use was able to link the exchange of symbols and bodies in an institutional manner. This monopoly turned the state into the reason and guarantor that bodies and symbols could be reciprocally translated and sent. Both aspects of compulsory use—relating to the mail as to oneself, and the institutional linking of metaphors in the exchange of texts and glances—were preconditions for the letter's transformation into literature that began with Gellert.

Yet the introduction of compulsory use of the mail that reformulated discourse at the beginning of the eighteenth century merely marked a consequential transformation in bio-politics itself. Generally speaking, the will to monopolize the means of discourse processing was one of the phenomena called forth by a particular innovation near the end of the sixteenth century. That innovation, after which the postal system began to exist only in the form of bio-politics, marked the beginning of the modern period itself in terms of information economy: the invention of postage. Once the loss of the Netherlands and the bankruptcy of the Spanish state had plunged the empire into a financial and postal crisis, Rudolf II decided to place the postal system in the service of "private" exchange, establish fixed postal rates, remove its revenues from the postmaster's private purse, and use those revenues to pay for its expenditures.[6] *Emergentia regni*: for once, at least—here—it was a matter of the postal system.

On the surface, the invention of postage seems merely to have legalized the Taxis's misuse of an instrument of state. But postage was in fact one of the innovations by means of which the old empire had transcended itself. After all, it was here that a new type of power became visible. Using postage as a means to finance the imperium's power over communications technology—and thus, in its Latin meaning, the power of command—meant abandoning a Machiavellian view of the population as one resource among the many to be exploited. As one of the "forces of the state"[7] that did not just come about on its own, the population now had to be governed skillfully and in a way that completely redefined the relationship between the postal system and the people: usefulness to the population became the raison d'être of the postal system, from which the state's benefit now was only secondarily derived.

Such a definition of the postal service was unprecedented in the history of the Western world. The new form of being for the state postal system transformed all other postal institutions into competitors for revenue from postage: a state power depending upon the welfare of the population had to monopolize the postal system.[8]

The directorial management under which power had placed life was, of course, the police. Its subject matter was (and is) the network of relationships between people and between people and things. "That is to say, the things for which the government must take responsibility are people, but people in their relationships, their ties, their intricate entanglements with the things that are riches, the resources, the basics of living . . . it is people in their relationships with these other things that comprise the costumes, the habits, the particular forms of doing and thinking."[9] After the linkage between state power and the behavior of the population had been established in matters of postage, the postal system could be understood only as a subsystem within such a network of relations. It therefore became obvious that the postal system was an institution of the police—as one of the groundbreaking works on police science in the eighteenth century, Johann Heinrich Gottlob von Justi's *Foundations for the Power and Well-Being of the State*, explained:

> The postal systems are a police institution for the convenience of the *publici* and the promotion of commerce and industry, by means of which letters, goods, and persons are quickly and safely transported at certain and designated times, for a certain amount of post money. . . . They are a police institution, however; since they are directed by the authorities for the convenience of the *publici* and the promotion of the best interests of the community.[10]

Convenience—the ultimate purpose from which the postal system derived meaning in the order of the police state—was not merely *commoditas* or *expedire* in the sense of "being conducive," but also *opportunitas*, being opportune, or at hand. "A good continuity of the mail" thus "required that the mail's arrival and renewed departure be established on major routes, and especially on those leading to major trade centers, in such a way that correspondents have time to answer the letters received."[11] The goal of the postal system was to ensnare people in discourse, and the technology used to accomplish that goal was the relay and its attunement to the entire network—timing. Only after the calculating convenience of corresponding posts did correspondence exist in word and deed.[12] And not until the police duties of a model postal system included the production of the expectation that letters should be answered could novels begin with the line "How on earth does it come about that you don't write?"—and immediately go on to reject the possibility that the "letters [had been] lost in the mail."[13] Not until the gaps in the net were closed could they open up between letters.

Only mail that arrived opportunely was a real opportunity for the state to make the income it needed "for its self-preservation and the promotion of its prosperity."[14] *Raisons d'état* would have it so, and so it came to pass. In the Prussia of Frederick II, "French management" saw to it that the mail brought in nearly twenty million talers in state revenue between 1741 and 1786.[15] The amount of income, however, had ceased to speak the transparent language of political wisdom. In the police state, such revenue had to be interpreted in terms of its origin by a financial science dedicated to the best interests of the community. The state's revenue bespoke the *prudentia civilis* of its sovereign only if it was the natural expression of a situation where things—as concerns for the art of governing—reached their destination. The business of governing is itself therefore a matter of postal system: making sure that things reach their destination, that they correspond to it—that they do not lose their meaning. In 1755, when Frederick decided (despite the reservations of Postmaster General von Gotter) that Prussian postmasters were to be paid exclusively on a commission basis from a percentage of the fees—so that they might contribute even more to the well-being of the state[16]—the art of governing itself had strayed from its destination. "On the whole," Heinrich von Stephan wrote in his laconic commentary, "the mail was a good source of revenue for the state."[17] In the theory of police science, however, the mail could be a good source of revenue only in the precise case that it was not. After Justi's extremely successful theory of postage, high levels of state revenue no longer were defined as the representations of high postal rates, but exclusively as a function of the quantity of dispatches in circulation, and the postal rate's most important mission was seen as regulating the growth of that quantity. With a single stroke, the old ratio between profit and postage became reciprocal.[18] "One easily sees," Justi stated boldly in his *System of Finance*, "that these rates must be very reasonable. . . . If high rates are established, one is fooling himself badly in thinking this will increase post revenue." "If post rates are reasonable," he continued in the following paragraph, "no one thinks a thing about the postage. Hence, several hundred thousand letters are written that contain no serious business, but consist instead merely of novelties, demonstrations of courtesy, and assurances of friendship. Only when postage is high does one refrain from these types of correspondence."[19]

Postage thus assumed a radically new status. Instead of being primarily a state levy (as it had been in the seventeenth century), from now on postage would be a technology of existence above all else. On the basis of the rapidly advancing alphabetization of Central Europe, it no longer would be the role of postage to achieve maximum utility from an established and unquestionable circulation of discourses, but instead to produce these discourses in the first place: "And henceforth the theory of production must always precede that of circulation."[20]

Postage had the poietic power to make a "foundation of existences"[21] visible just below the threshold of history, as the *Foundations of the Power of States*—if only in the quantitative material of police-science statistics.

Forty-five years later, Justi's theory of postage as a technology of existence assumed the guise of a pedagogical theory with concerns that went far beyond the "promotion of commerce" and clearing the way for writing as a luxury that was economically opportune for the state. The situation was grave in 1811, when Johann Ludwig Klüber, a cabinet and privy councilor in the service of Karl Friedrich of Baden, published his first treatise on the postal system. The empire had fallen; no less than forty-three different territorial postal systems divided the area it once had occupied.[22] Prussian post offices either had been annexed by the French, as in Hamburg, or were under French control, as in Berlin. On account of the transit postage that each territorial ruler charged for letters passing through his district, postal rates were in some instances four or five times higher than before 1806.[23] In this state of affairs, the level of postage did not measure the bad judgment of a single prince so much as it reflected the state of the empire's collapse. Klüber's treatise—in accordance with the theory that postage was responsible for the existence of what it measured—drew from this the conclusion that the postal system had to become a "*national and state institution,*"[24] inasmuch as it had to rebuild the nation itself by way of rate reductions. The birth of the nation from the spirit of reduced postal rates? This idea was a double-edged sword as far as Klüber was concerned; as the loyal servant of a prince in the Rhenish League, he hardly can be suspected of harboring the sentiments of a Prussian patriot—despite his friendship with Hardenberg.[25] Klüber's unconcealed sympathy for the idea of a national mission for the Thurn and Taxis Post,[26] which he wished to see rise "as a phoenix from the ashes of the Rhenish League" to become "a new and beneficial bond for the re-unification of the Germans,"[27] seems to suggest that he had not quite seen the writing on the wall. Napoleon was anything but graciously disposed toward the princely badgers,[28] after all—to say nothing of the permanent war Prussia was waging against the Imperial Post.

But Klüber's empire was not of *this* world at all. Conceived from the perspective of border crossings, of transit, his theory of postage was pre-scribed for the parousia of an empire no longer governed by absolutist *raison d'état*, but by the absolute "World Spirit."[29] It therefore tran-scended police science, which started with the *territorium* as a matter of principle and viewed its boundaries as those of bio-politics as well.[30] That is: only in the event of a *translatio imperii* could the badger make his return as a phoenix. Command—the Latin meaning of the word *im-perium*—no longer issued from the Viennese Hofburg, the court of the Habsburgs and the courts of *x* number of German princes. Instead, it em-anated from institutions within the new educational state, where the World Spirit already was preparing for self-actualization in 1810—the crucial date in Klüber's appraisal of the empire's ruins: with the introduc-tion of essays on qualifying exams in the new *Gymnasien* (approved by the expert appraisal of Schleiermacher), with the reorganization of the scholarly exam committee responsible for these essays (begun by Hum-boldt), to which Hegel was appointed in 1820,[31] and with the introduc-tion of the state exam *pro facultate docendi*.[32] In accordance with the new situation of command, postage in the new empire did not regulate the mere appearance of existences as police statistics, but instead the produc-tion of The Individual. "An institution for public instruction and the for-mative education of individuals may not be treated as an immediate source of finance for the state, and this should be no less true of the postal system."[33]

In its true calling (or command), the postal system was not a transport institute at all, Klüber instructed, but a pedagogical institution, and the well-being of the state was a variable dependent on pedagogy. The state thus had a profound interest in promoting "universal exchange among men . . . as much as possible,"[34] not because educated individuals were "also more lucrative for the state treasuries"[35]—something Klüber never completely lost sight of—but because both the productive writing "of men in general," as it had first been posted by compulsory use of the mail at the beginning of the eighteenth century, and compulsory school attendance were derived from the "ultimate purpose of the state," which (in the words of Niethammer, an education official and patron of Hegel, three years before Klüber) demanded that every *"citizen of state . . . be an individual."*[36]

The essential characteristic of this "World Institute,"[37] which posted individuals in order to transcend the territorial state, set the pattern for a "spatial revolution" in the determination of postage for letters: *territorium*, with borders that became increasingly impermeable the greater the distance crossed by the letter, was replaced by an infinite geography that became increasingly permeable the farther the letter was sent. In the ratio of postage (which included not only the factor of distance, but also that of weight) to distance, an increasing scale created proximity and emphasized the center (the rate at which the letter became more expensive increased progressively with the distance crossed), while a decreasing scale created distance and emphasized the periphery: the (colonial) empire. "A letter should become increasingly inexpensive the farther it travels in the same post. . . . In due consideration, this principle was put in practice on the post routes of the Taxis, which were once very extensive."[38]

In terms of administrative and therefore postal technology, the transition from the police state to the education state was the invention of a new geographical signworld. Yet geography itself still remained the historical a priori for everything the post could mean around 1800. Postal roads in Prussia were geometrically surveyed in 1801, and the scale of distance was literally inscribed onto the earth with milestones. The distances to be read on these milestones regulated both the time and the fees for the conveyance of persons and packages, while the scale for letter postage already had been established in 1766 on the basis of mapping surveys.[39]

The linkage of circulation to the same geographical grid in the case of information, persons, and things—and the metaphoricity provided by this *tertium comparationis*—formed the pedestal of the postal system as the quintessence of exchange in symbols *and* bodies. Geography was the surface on which compulsory use of the mail was inscribed in the form of the institutional and metaphorical linking of the exchange of persons and letters. The establishment of "men in general" as the subject of post qua compulsory use necessarily encompassed the existence of a common ground for words and people, which in turn was bound to an age of the "metabolic vehicle" (in Virilio's words) that was reaching its end.[40] The rule of the educational state therefore meant that the creature of compulsory postal use—"The Individual"—was preparing to transcend every territorial principle within the space of an infinite geography. Thus, the space had been technically constructed in which the old travel novel could become the *Bildungsroman*. Goethe's *Wilhelm Meister's Apprenticeship* and a fortiori *Wilhelm Meister's Journeyman Years* could do without the names of almost any specific territories. The earth was assuming a human face.

In the wake of the transformations of postage into a means for the production of discourse and the postal district into a pedagogical province, the dispatch's form of being was penetrated by a historicity that practically demanded a new theory of the letter. The folding back of the letter's text onto the act of production invented a historical depth for the letter that accounted for the poietic theory of postage. Words thus took a turn that led to the rapid disappearance of the *ars dictaminis* in the first half of the eighteenth century. After all, the Baroque letter-writing guide had administered a circulation that was basically ahistorical. The grid of occasions and titles, the rubrics of *captatio* and *conclusio*, established a system of discourse that antedated every individual letter, a system in which every type of production had always had its site. The taxonomic order of discourse conflicts with original production in both conception and fact: it merely realizes the repetition of a store of applications that remain eternally unchanged.

The transition from word processing to an economy of proliferation thus could be accomplished only by individualizing and historicizing the external references of the letter. In the future, the letter would submit every inventive art and every skill in making connections to a function that previously had been unknown: the confession of individual origins. The self's confession thus became the occasion of occasions.[41] Not until the letter—like the Fichtean self—posited itself and produced the occasion that made it necessary in itself could it exist in proliferation. The letter received its truth only by being folded back onto itself, and therefore

could not cease to acknowledge its origin, the soul. The "irresistible desire to communicate oneself" that Steinhausen documented for the eighteenth century had conducted the business of a state and an educational
system that operated in the same medium. It was the determination or the
command of their medium of control—the postal system—that first led
people like Caroline Schlegel to be overcome by "a frenzy of writing
fever . . . in which she dispatches letters by the dozens"[42] to state officials,
philosophers, and poets. In short: the transformation of the letter into literature was among the media prerequisites for the genesis of the modern
education state. From this transformation, literature—the medium of
command that took the place of the princely order in the new empire of
the World Spirit—claimed the privilege "that a very large part of correspondence, such as the literary . . . merits complete or partial exemption
from taxes, just as all correspondence generally merits encouragement
through low postal rates."[43]

Amid all the ruins of the Imperial Postal Service, Klüber discerned the
situation. After all, there was at the same time another (grand) duchy
with the same Rhenish League policies and the same relation to the Thurn
and Taxis Post as Baden, a place where Klüber's claim had been honored.

CHAPTER SEVEN

Goethe's Postal Empire

The name of that duchy, as the reader will have guessed, was Saxony-Weimar. The epoch of the postal system known as literature, which had dawned in the name of individual education, found its master signifier in the name it still bears today in Germany: Goethe. The reasons for this hallmark are not entirely a matter of everyday knowledge. After all, the name of Goethe was invested with the extraordinary right, as a postage stamp, to put the discourse of an author and most especially the discourse of his readers in circulation. In fact, the story is still rather unclear. What appears certain, however, is what Heinrich von Stephan learned in 1874 from a Baltic historian in the rooms of the Imperial Postal Museum:[1] "that Goethe had received from the princes [of Thurn and Taxis] the privilege of sending his letters free of charge in the entire Thurn and Taxis postal district, and that these letters always were sealed with black wax and authorized by Goethe's initials"[2] [see Figure 2]. Now this in itself would not be anything unusual, insofar as Goethe, like all members of the court, obviously enjoyed exemption from postage as a privy councilor in the service of Duke August. But that exemption applied only to the state mail Goethe sent, that is, only to letters that bore the duke's seal. What the historian was pointing out, by contrast, was the exceptional extension of this privilege to include Privy Councilor Goethe's private letters:[3] the letters of Goethe the author.

The elevation of the name Goethe to the rank of postage stamp most likely occurred in the year 1806, when the fiefdom of the postal system in Saxony-Weimar and everywhere else was transferred into the hands of the sovereign princes after the dissolution of the Holy Roman Empire of the German Nation. But as a provincial postal system, the Thurn and Taxis

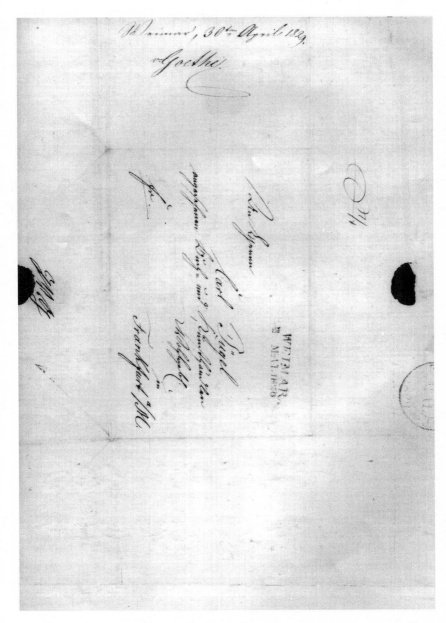

FIGURE 2. A postage-exempt letter sent by Goethe, sealed with black wax and authorized by the writer's initials.

Post was then handed over again by the duke to the prince as a feudal tenure—just as it was in Klüber's Baden.[4] There is admittedly no evidence to document Goethe's acquaintance with Prince Karl Alexander von Thurn und Taxis before the letters subsequently written after the prince took an interest in Goethe's geological collection at Carlsbad.[5] Nevertheless—and despite what was not and could not be said—this acquaintance dated all the way back to Goethe's earliest childhood. After all, Goethe's ancestral home in Frankfurt was in the immediate vicinity of the Taxis palace.[6] By granting the privilege of exemption to his onetime neighbor, the postal prince merely lent truth to what the latter would write about the Taxis Post in *Poetry and Truth*. Goethe assessed the "widespread" expansion of "moral and literary exchange" as the establishment of a police of the heart ("A person would spy on his own and others' hearts"), in the same way Klüber did—as a result of the fact that "the Taxis postal system was reliably swift, the seal secure, and the postage reasonable."[7]

That was an easy thing for Goethe to say, since—with the most affordable postage imaginable for letters bearing the name Goethe—the Taxis indeed had promoted an expansion of literary exchange with no other purpose than deifying the author and constructing an Age of Goethe. In the days before Rowland Hill, it was general practice that recipients paid the postage, rather than senders, in order to make sure they actually received the letter, and consequently it was not just Goethe's letters that were free of postage, but also the letters of Goethe's friends, Goethe's readers, and Goethe's admirers of every possible description. Only a year after the privilege was granted, this postal a priori already was sustaining *Goethe's Correspondence with a Child* and the epistolary novel that came out of it. Bettina Brentano was permitted to write letters without end—and that means love letters—to Weimar every post day because the postal system had set aside a postage-free channel for just such a relationship between feminine readers and the author. Otherwise—especially when postage fees rose so dramatically after 1806—nothing might have been sent at all, certainly not Bettina's love, which could exist only in long letters full of beautiful but weighty nonsense. Bettina said so herself. "Adieu. I am ashamed of my bulky letter, in which there may be much nonsense. If you were not exempt from postage, I would not send it."[8]

Prior to every discourse there was an invitation to discourse, thanks to Thurn and Taxis, an invitation to write letters that never had to end, like love, that could babble on without saying anything, and that incidentally conveyed in addition Mrs. Rat's memories about Goethe's childhood, still remembered faithfully by Bettina, so that he might write the opening chapter of his "confessions" entitled *Poetry and Truth*.[9] Such a fan-mail promotion made it almost inevitable that a star would be born at the receiving end. The recurring conclusion of Goethe's letters, which came instead of a reply to Bettina's endless ones, thus merely expressed a message that was the nondiscursive invitation of a postage-free channel: "Write to me every day, even if it were foliantos [volumes in folio format] it will not be too much for me";[10] "write to me soon, and love me";[11] "write me as much as possible";[12] "To your delightful habit of writing and loving, from day to day, remain constant";[13] "write me all that passes in your mind; it will at all times be most heartily received";[14] or "Farewell, dearest child, continue to live with me, and do not let me miss your dear and ample letters."[15] It was someone else who spoke like this, specifically Karl Alexander von Thurn und Taxis. His incentives to speak kept a discourse of love letters from ceasing at one end while keeping the production of sonnets going at the other, sonnets that were nothing but translations of those love letters. What sustained the author was a woman's postally promoted lust. Poetry or rhymes are the translation of things that do not rhyme, of the confused letter writing or prose of a woman's soul. "The poet is often so happy as to be able to rhyme that which is unrhymed, and so it may be granted you, dear child, to send him without consideration everything of this kind, which you have to communicate."[16]

Because Bettina's letters came to an end in literature, they remained unanswered. And when once a poem did come back to the loving woman, it was a "Charade" that—luckily for her—she did not guess. But that was precisely the secret of literature around 1800. Sustained by the love of women readers that the postal system had called to life, the author could circulate poems in the form of a riddle with a private address (Minna Herzlieb) so that all other feminine readers (like Bettina) could "guess to satisfy themselves,"[17] that is, could guess themselves as the poem's address. Literature as an epoch of the postal system *was* such a charade; it allowed poetry, which was addressed to innumerable women, to function in the eyes of every feminine reader as though it were a private letter written to her and her alone.

Established by the Taxis Post's invitation for all women to post their readerly love, Goethe's empire stretched beyond the Free City of Frankfurt, where Bettina wrote her letters, and Saxony-Weimar, where his postage-free address had created the center of attraction for all letters. In addition, Goethe's empire also encompassed the following cities and states: Württemberg, Kurhessen, the Grand Duchy of Hessen, Hessen-Nassau, Saxony-Meiningen, Saxony-Coburg-Gotha, the principalities of Reuß and Schwarzburg, the Hanseatic cities of Hamburg, Bremen, and Lübeck, the Hohenzollern principality, the principalities of Lippe-Detmold and Schaumburg-Lippe, and to top it all off, the canton of Schaffhausen.[18]

Goethe ruled over the ruins of the crumbled German Empire as no one had in the days of its existence except for the emperor and his royal household. In return for Emperor Matthias's grant of the imperial postmaster generalship as hereditary tenure in 1615, Lamoral von Taxis had pledged "to convey the outgoing dispatches of the Emperor, Imperial Chancellor, Imperial Vice-Chancellor, Imperial and Privy Councilors of the Court, and *other such high officers* without tax or letter fees."[19] After the empire had crumbled and the hard fate of mediatization had befallen the Thurn and Taxis, an imperial postmaster general without empire transferred this direct privilege, which was vacant now, to the ruler of another empire. How could the scandal of the former principal commissary's mediatization be more effectively mitigated than by a *translatio imperii* in Klüber's sense: by replacing what had been lost, self-government under the Kaiser, with self-government under the German Spirit? Fearing for the future of his postal dominion, the prince thus placed his postal routes in the service of the author who was quintessentially The Individual himself by elevating him to the center of attraction for feedback from feminine readers who had fallen in love.

Long before this promotion, both Goethe and the Taxis postal routes already had been hard at work in the secret service of The Individual's formative education. Like Goethe, Karl Alexander von Thurn und Taxis was a Freemason. Goethe had joined the Weimar lodge "Amalia" in 1780[20] and was promoted to master (together with Duke Karl August, incidentally) after only two short years. In December 1782, after the Johannis lodge already had closed its doors, Goethe was received into the "inner and high order."[21] The lodge did not reopen until 1808. The postal prince, by contrast, laid his bricks on very different floors inside the Mystery. In 1799, he became grand master of the Regensburg lodge, "The Thriving at the Three Keys," which was renamed "Carl at the Three Keys" in 1804. Consequently, the Taxis Post obeyed a secret, secondary power in Bavaria and Württemberg. Even if the Taxis Post was superficially under the authority of the emperor (before 1806) or the provincial ruler as feudal sovereign (after 1806), it was in fact secretly in the service of the Regensburg lodge—and that means in the service of an internal state founded purely on the education of man. No fewer than one-third of all the members of the lodge, after all, were also members of the Thurn and Taxis imperium. The imperial postmasters of Regensburg, Munich, Ulm, and Stuttgart belonged to the lodge, as did seven Thurn and Taxis councilors, three cavaliers of the court, three valets, and some members of the Thurn and Taxis territorial administration in Swabia.[22] The Taxis thus did not merely operate an imperial postal system or a network of provincial posts; it simultaneously ran the postal system of a "state within the state," which "Freemasonry definitely amounts to," in Goethe's own words.[23]

If the leader of the Regensburg lodge thus established a postal network that invited all feminine and masculine readers to send a feedback of love and learning to Master Goethe—who named the hero of his *Bildungsroman* after his title in the Weimar lodge[24]—then this was perfectly consistent with the Freemasons' plans for the improvement of Central Europe. As the destination of mail prior to all sending, Goethe became postmaster and "master of instruction" in the "art of being human."[25] The Taxis postal district came to be a pedagogical province *avant la lettre*; indeed, its doctrine of the three reverences merely modified the Masonic doctrine of the three oaths to God, neighbor, and oneself.[26] But the "pedagogical province" itself was merely one station in Wilhelm's *Journeyman* travels through a succession of "zones," which—as Scott Abbot plausibly argued—appear to reproduce the ritual path through the different rooms of the lodge that symbolized progressive degrees of education.[27] The space of the *Journeyman Years* had a postal structure insofar as the postal system was a Masonic state within the state with the purpose of the pervasive pedagogical organization of space. When Goethe expanded the pedagogical architecture of the lodge, where spatial succession was analogous to the stages of life, to include the space of entire landscapes,[28] he merely was identifying the two functions of Karl Alexander von Thurn und Taxis.

Once the postal invitation for all letter writers to address their intimate confessions to the author of the epoch had become a positive fact, everything that was sent on its way as a letter in the postal system was subordinated to the formative education of individuals. Everyone was what Goethe was above all—an individual—and because of this, the postal system, which was organized around the author Goethe as the center of attraction, established the general pattern for individual letter writing around 1800. The invitation to write Goethe was initially an invitation to read Goethe, to understand and to feed what was understood back to oneself in letters. Everyone who wrote letters was at the same time writing to a Goethe *en miniature* within, to a Self, postage free. That, at least, was the opinion of Clemens Brentano, a postal official by the grace of Goethe:

> The writer must at the same time write to himself, since he must become acquainted with himself through the letter. You told me, after all, that the world seemed so infinitely vast to you and you felt lost within it. . . . All of this comes from the fact that you are not yet acquainted with the person inside yourself. You do not yet comprehend yourself, but in letters you look into the mirror of your soul; this is why the deepest truth vis-à-vis yourself is such an urgent need if you are not to fall into error regarding yourself. Because the noble soul has a higher destination [*Bestimmung*]! To obey this is its entire mission; the world is so full of events, it's like a fabric in which the harmonious education of every individual must serve as a necessary and sturdy thread.[29]

In Goethe's postal empire, letters passed at once through a route of transmission and a route of feedback. The problem of correct address, to which the *ars dictaminis* had dedicated extensive titularies and lengthy treatises on the *salutatio*, thus was banished from the face of the earth. If Romanticism answered the question "Where are we going?" with "Home, all the time,"[30] it answered the question "Where are we writing?" with "To Goethe, all the time." In a system that posted The Author, all letters unerringly arrived at a universal address: the Inner Person. This address corresponded to the horizon of a worldwide postal empire as it was established by postage measured on a scale that decreased as distance increased—or by the *Journeyman* travels. And because of this, a world that seemed infinitely vast, a world in which one felt lost, became obsolete a priori. Only because Bettina did not know her own address (the above-mentioned Inner Person) and would much rather write to Goethe himself, was she lost in the wide world: a letter that could not be delivered. In Goethe's epoch, sealed like a letter in black, Clemens Brentano's pedagogical discourse continuously produced postal metaphors: the noble soul had a higher destination, and its entire mission was to arrive at it, so the world could become a fabric or a text that spoke only of the harmonious education of individuals; in other words, so the world could become a *Bildungsroman*. The Novalis program was running, and kept on running. Bettina Brentano's *Apprenticeship* was under way on the self-governing mail routes of German Poetry.

Inasmuch as letter writing meant accepting an invitation from the postal system to write to an internal author, every letter writer was assigned an authorship *en miniature*. Under a postal dominion that promised communication with Goethe by writing letters, all writing—insofar as it involved letters to one's Self—was held captive by the form of being of the discursive group containing the function "author."[31] Authorship was subjected to the command of the Primal Author's postal dominion, and everyone who wrote letters to himself or herself was the Primal Author's subject or his vassal. When someone like Bettina wanted to avoid paying the price for addressing oneself postage-free (which according to what was then the most recent theory of police science was what produced discourse), a postal official of the empire of education was on hand right away to demand in the name of Goethe that she pay the penalty: "I would be pleased if you read some history and otherwise mostly Göthe, always Göthe, especially volume seven of his new works; his poems are a virtual antidote for sentimentality."[32] Reading works that—in Schlegel's words—"one can learn to understand only by itself" charged the reader the same amount of postage in "personality and individuality" that was stamped on the works themselves. To the extent that letters were postage-free reflections of the soul, they were an exercise in this kind of "understanding by oneself" as the understanding of oneself.

That letters in circulation became mirrors of the soul via feedback from an Inner Author was confirmed by the imperial postmaster Goethe himself, whose postal privilege had programmed this feedback. He did so—how could it be otherwise?—in the *Journeyman Years*. The confused text of the novella "The Man of Fifty Years" becomes clear and harmonious only when "that admirable woman [Makarie] held up a magic mirror of morality to some unhappy person and show[ed] him the true, resplendent inner form behind his outward, confused one."[33] The mirror of the soul is in this case nothing other than the correspondence circulating between the Baroness and Makarie in which, first of all, the beautiful widow spies on her own inner self (in Goethe's words) and, second, the major catches sight of the widow's glance in that mirror. There are a total of three different glances, which together constitute a *politique de l'autruiche* that makes it easy to recognize the correspondence as a trial run for the famous *Purloined Letter*. The first glance is the one that sees nothing: it is the Baroness's glance, which is documented in the letters themselves. "In fact, only outward appearances and utterances are discussed; no thought is given to inner feelings."[34] The second glance is the one that sees that the first glance sees nothing, and thus sees what it conceals: it is the widow's glance into her inner self. The third glance sees that "these two glances leave what is to be hidden open for discovery by anyone who wishes to seize hold of it":[35] it is the Major's glance. This last is the glance of knowledge, of power (as Lacan made clear)—the glance that men, postmasters, and authors from Gellert to Brentano (not to mention Goethe) cast upon the letters of women. The site at which these letters surrender to the glance of knowledge needs to be called to mind: it is a posting house,[36] and there is no need to wonder about its coat of arms.

It makes a difference that for Goethe the structure of intersubjectivity depended on letters that were not purloined, but instead were delivered by a central exchange office (Makarie). The subjects attributed to these glances were distributed to the persons who embodied them, not according to a logic of signifiers inherent in the wandering path of the correspondence, but according to the pedagogical policy of an authority outside the game that held the reins and directed all mail routes as if she were at once both lodge leader and postal princess. That what was to be concealed in letters always was something to be revealed (a confession) is thus indicative of the discursive order that was embossed by the logic of the letter's confidentiality. At the middle of the nineteenth century, that discursive order would be pushed aside by a new historical a priori that by introducing postage stamps and mailboxes would enable not only a new logic of subjectivity, but the post-structural psychoanalysis of prolonged letters as well. In Goethe's postal empire, letters and souls (which were more or less the same thing in the delivery area of German Poetry) could reach their destinations only if they were addressed to an Inner Author, and because of this, literary works, which were joined inseparably to the author on a conceptual level,[37] could assume the role of mail. The epoch of the postal system known as literature did not just reveal itself in the letter's transformation into literature, but in the "postalization" of fiction as well. And no novel celebrates that epoch with more exuberance than Stifter's *Indian Summer*.

Gustav grows up in a family where all masculine power is excluded, an exclusion that might have gained legitimacy from generational succession, and his mother Mathilda gives him the works of Goethe as a present once he is old enough for such an educational program. After leafing through one of the volumes for a while, he discovers traces of "personality" and "individuality" on its pages: "But Mother, you can see that there are many passages underlined by a finepointed pencil, and with the same pencil there are words written in the margins; these are from your own hand. These are your property, they are not contained in any newly bought books."[38] Hermeneutic reading made a virtue even out of scribbling in valuable books. The marks of thorough understanding in a mother's handwriting beside an author's printed text transformed printed matter, which was circulated on a massive scale, first into an individual and unmistakably unique document, and second into a love letter from a mother to her child.

> Whenever you read these books, you will be reading the heart of the author as well as the heart of your mother which, even if it is far below the author's in value, has for you the incomparable worth of being the heart of your mother. In the future when I read passages I have underlined [in her newly bought edition of Goethe's works], I shall think: here he will remember his mother; when my eyes look over the pages where I had made comments in the margin, your eyes will hover before me, looking from the printed words to the written in the full knowledge that you have before you the handwriting of the person who is your best friend in the world. Thus, the books will always be a bond between us wherever we may be.[39]

Souls communicate through the medium of fiction. The familial constellation of poet, mother, and child transformed the empirical plurality of printed books into the normative singularity of the one volume and bond that represents exactly the postal epoch of literature. The ideal Father introduced his volume into the nuclear family only in order to bind a mother to her child.[40] The poet's text appeared, only to disappear again immediately afterward and to produce the presence of an absent person's doppelgänger for all those who were not present. Goethe's works became the reflections of glances that functioned in exactly the same way as Gellert's program in Model Letter No. 16.

In the exchange of souls between Heinrich von Kleist and Wilhelmine von Zenge, the role of the mail admittedly was not assumed by one of Goethe's works. One of Schiller's did the job. But otherwise, everything went just like it did for Mathilde and Gustav. "My third [errand] was at the book store, where I bought you Schiller's *Wallenstein*—are you pleased? Read it, dear girl; I will read it too. Thus our souls shall meet even in a third object. Have it bound at your whim and my expense, and on the inside page of the volume write the familiar formula: H. v. K. to W. v. Z."[41] The binding of souls was inscribed in the poet's volume. Since the postal system was an institution for the education of individuals, education became the principle of the post. The epoch of Goethe was distinguished by its use of discursive proliferation to define the well-being of the state as something that depended on feedback between the circulating text and an individual origin. The transformation of the postal system into literature with the invention of a miniature authorship for letters— the postage-free education of mankind—bespoke the postal system's integration into the general discursive practice of a state constituted by educational officials.

At the middle of the nineteenth century, the need for posts in the service of the German Spirit and self-government disappeared. Once postage stamps were issued, uniform minimal postage, formerly bestowed on the poet as a privilege, became a universal standard. From then on, the desire to write no longer was heated by the release of intimate confessions into postage-free feedback channels. Such heat was generated instead by the simple possibility of "attaching a stamp" to send letters everywhere nearly postage-free: "No longer does any political, physical, cultural, economic, or linguistic boundary obstruct the course of such a letter in the channels of the World Postal Service."[42] The dark continents had disappeared from a map on which politics, culture, economics—or indeed anything else besides simple topology—were not seen as worthy of indication. The media technology for controlling the Heart of Darkness was installed, but colonial officials for German Poetry like Clemens Brentano would not enlist in its service. Nor would Thurn and Taxis, which survived for only fifteen years after their own postage stamps were issued in 1 8 5 2. The introduction of stamps inflated Goethe's discursive function. At the expense of the epoch of the postal system known as literature, the postage stamp transformed every letter writer into a miniature Goethe by democratizing both the privilege of uniform postage and that of being a center of attraction for letters. Discursive dominion devolved upon a standard price for signifiers via a token that was placed in circulation in that it was withdrawn.

The end of the postal sub-epoch "literature" had necessary consequences for the relevance of a theory of the letter rooted in literary theory. Transformation into literature was a prerequisite for the very fact that the letter could become an object of literary theory, and this transformation had its origins in the anthropological foundation of information exchange. An anthropocentric theory of the letter ensued upon the command that everything circulating as writing had to find its truth in the ineluctable production of human beings (in more than one sense). For precisely this reason, however, it was impossible for such a theory to reflect the postal condition of its own possibility. The "idea that people can communicate by letter" was an idea that excluded a theory of the letter as a dispatch of the postal system. But if the transformation of the letter into literature was rooted in a sub-epoch of the postal system that dawned under the auspices of The Individual, then the relevance of a purely literary theory of the letter was confined to the duration of that epoch. A theory of the letter grounded in the methodology of literary theory therefore lived—in the fine language of Michel Foucault—"in nineteenth-century thought like a fish in water: that is, it is unable to breathe anywhere else."[43]

CHAPTER EIGHT

The Timbre of a Calling (Attunement)

There is thus a debt that the writing of letters has to pay to the history of postage: letters bear the inescapable postage (Foucault's historical a priori) of the postal dispositive, which determined the fate of symbols even before the first character was written. Because the historical function of postage affected the way in which letters existed, a historicity of circulation showed up in economic knowledge, together with the discovery of postage's Promethean power (it created persons by bringing people into postal existence), and the individual letter appeared in Romantic knowledge as the motivating force of a story. The logic of address in the Baroque *ars dictaminis* had stumbled into crisis once the letter writer came to be what he or she truly was only in the process of writing—the ground was pulled out from under the dictates of the *aptum*: the ability to classify and plan the writer in advance. Letter writing meant that the body was swallowed whole by a teleological definition of the subject: from then on, its calling would befall it as what it always had been in its misty origins. Postal service no longer was a technology of existence, but instead a technology of history. Letters were mirrors of the soul, the optical trap entangling the feminine writer in her "deepest truth." Clemens Brentano said so. Just as letters came to be feedback loops in the self-becoming of an individual history (the postal implementation of the movement of the Hegelian concept),[1] "the world" became a fabric that rid itself of all contingency and that was woven from the educational histories of individuals. The *techné* of this fabric was the postal network, and because of this, "the world" and the postal net could become nearly coextensive in Goethe's *Wilhelm Meister* novels—which indeed were the only ones to realize the genre of the *Bildungsroman*, according to the verdicts of literary scholars[2]—and the *Journeyman* travels in particular could amount to the circulation of paper.

If the fabric of "the world" merged with the text of the novel, this came about for only two reasons. First, an art of governing that was essentially postal in nature became complete and perfect: everything was delivered to its true destination, which previously had been deduced from the system of police science. Second, the Romantic identification of "the world" with the novel documented a state of affairs in which the art of governing—which had been revolutionized primarily by the optimizing strategies of absolute idealism—had surpassed and dismissed its old absolutist forms and its traditional domains of knowledge. A technology of governing that had become self-conscious allowed the police—the complicated governmental instrument of capitals or crowned heads—to be replaced by self-regulating/ruling structures that made police science so irrelevant that not even its decapitation mattered anymore.[3] The old command medium of the postal service thus entered the epoch of control engineering via the media practices of pedagogical-psychological discourse, and it was the business of Poetry in 1800 to sustain that discourse. The letter therefore existed as a reflection or a mirror of the true self: hence the principle that "the writer [must] at the same time write to himself,"[4] a demand that would have been complete nonsense in the eyes of a police scientist.

The control engineering that defined literature and the exchange of letters around 1800 (and linked them in this definition) was a short circuit in interpretations. Writing circulated for a single and strange reason: to pile interpretation upon interpretation in order to tease a confession of truth from the letter's text—a confession by means of which an individual had to prove his or her identity.[5] The role of the circulating letter thus was not to produce communication, but instead to assign positions to the sexes, positions inside an organization of knowledge. Women read books by men and postally replied to these men with understanding, which the men in turn answered with a philosophy of understanding, which the women read in order to understand their understanding and to report such understanding, raised to the second power, back to the author, and so forth and so on: a circuit of interpretations that literally revolved around nothing, since it did not convey information, but merely was the "site" where subjects are made to exist via their function in the discourse. Such exchange amounted to the circulation of interpretations that were opportunities for interpretation. The individual thus was legitimated by a discourse it could sustain about itself—but (and here a new dimension was reached by the discourse of confession, which, according to Foucault, had been a major ritual for the production of truth since the Middle Ages)[6] only by way of a detour through the exegesis of others.

Klüber's diagnosis that the confidentiality of the letter had replaced, yet preserved, the seal of confession could not have been more precise. That the confession of truth was produced only in the process of reading, interpretation, and involution meant that the power of individualization resided only in postal data processing, the fluctuations of which processed an unconscious. In correspondences of letters a truth was written that from the very beginning crossed writers instead of merely being stated by them. Once the invention of bio-political discourse, which found the essence of postage in its ability to disappear at the first opportunity, transformed letter writing into an affair of the unconscious, an unconscious became legible. Justi's claim that "no one thinks anything of postage" when low rates prevailed merely meant that the materiality of postal service could remain beneath the threshold of consciousness. The debt the writer owed to the postal service became an unconscious debt, and because of this, writing could elude the grids that had defined obligations in Baroque, case-oriented letter-writing guides, where the possibility of unconscious writing had been ruled out from the start.

If postage became unconscious, however, the unconscious could become an occasion to write, and the interpretability of letters could come into play for the very first time. The letter's text came to be a symptom— the symptom of a measurable and potentially individualized deviance from the reference input or the norm, and therefore a semiotic prerequisite for medical-moral knowledge of sex. The (at least theoretical) tendency of postage to disappear was the prerequisite for a hermeneutics of the private letter that effected the psychologicization of its author. The possibility of confirming a soul (an unconscious) for the letter writer was determined by postage. Once this possibility had set the psychological machine of interpretation in motion, it became impossible for any letter not to reveal its secrets—or those of the soul—to the disciplined eye of its

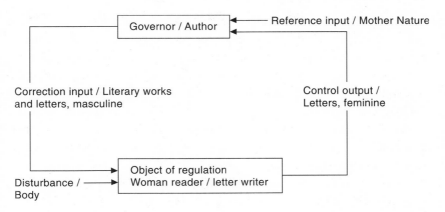

FIGURE 3. The distribution of gender among discursive functions by the control engineering of the postal system.

pedagogical recipients. Brentano thus could counter the symptom in his sister's writing with a diagnosis of hysteria—a classical diagnosis in the dispositive of sexuality.[7]

The distribution of gender among discursive functions that were defined by the control engineering of the postal service resided within the medium of correspondence itself. The private letter, after all, which first posted the intimate as an exclusive site for the production of truth, was grounded in the institutionalization of gender difference within the realm of the post. For Gellert, women's nature was the authentic nature of letter writing, just as it had been the true nature of understanding for Klopstock. As something women did not just have, but actually were—once the extended patriarchal family had disintegrated into the nuclear, Oedipal family—Nature appeared in Classical-Romantic discourse as a phantasm of the loving and alphabetizing Mother. On the basis of the media logic of intimacy, which was indeed nothing more than the modus allowing the phantasm of Nature to be translated into discourse, Nature sustained the regulatory postal circuit as its reference input or its telos. With regard to this designation as origin (or dependent on this "prescribed function"),[8] the Romantic author (or governor) interpreted (or varied) a control output known as the woman's letter—the output of the object of regulation between woman reader and woman writer [see Figure 3].

The interpretation of women's letters scanned and controlled a nominal value that was equal to the resonance between the text of the feminine letter and the reference input The Woman. Once women's souls were correctly tuned by literary works written especially for them—such as *Elective Affinities* (according to Goethe's own testimony)[9]—the timbre[10] of a calling vibrated in the epistolary record of sentiments that had accompanied their reading. Romantic correspondence set free the attunement that this stamp struck. All writing of letters and diaries was aimed at it: to display the Goethe stamp. Here lies the answer to the question of the site of knowledge inscribed by a novel like *Elective Affinities*:[11] that is, how did Goethe the poet know what was in a woman's diary, Ottilia's? As a center of attraction for private records, Goethe was indeed master of all timbres: intimate confessions bore his postage-free address a priori and vibrated to the frequency of his tympani. If they circulated at all, such confessions circulated in the empire of his postal system. No matter what was described in diaries in terms of trembling or timbre, it always is addressed to a will to knowledge that mandates eavesdropping intimately on one's own calling—reading one's own writing. Things did not go much better for Ulrike von Kleist with her brother than they had for Bettina Brentano with hers, or with Goethe. Women like Ulrike, who thought little of the "sacred duty of becoming mothers and educators of mankind"[12]—but were all the more enchanted with the idea of traveling around in men's clothes—immediately received feedback from their high command by return post: "What! Never wish to be wife and mother, to accomplish your highest calling, to fulfill your most sacred duty? . . . Abandon such an intention if you have formed it in your mind. You forsake thereby your highest calling, your most sacred duty, the most sublimely noble state to which a woman might rise, and the one happiness that awaits you."[13]

The relationship to the phantasm of ~~The~~ Woman,[14] into which Ulrike was placed postally, appeared to be as indissoluble as no other at the time, except for the one between words and ideas in the minds of authors. And that was no accident: the blessing of children that supposedly awaited Ulrike was—as Kleist himself made clear in a letter to his fiancée, Wilhelmine von Zenge—above all a blessing promised to budding poets, who hallucinated a Mother's voice at the ground of all language, a murmuring spring of pure meaning. Once the "highest calling" of mothers was found in the adoption of elementary techniques for acculturization,[15] the topos of anthropogenesis was a child's birthday.

> Yes, today is my birthday, and it is as though I heard the good wishes that you conceive for me in the quiet of your heart. . . . And they shall indeed be fulfilled, all your good wishes, you may be assured of it, as I am sure. . . . All that I might call *happiness* can come to me only from your hand, and if *you* wish me such happiness, well then, I can face the future with absolute calm, for that prize will be mine. *Love*, and the cultivation of oneself through *education*—I desire nothing more, and how glad I am that the fulfillment of these wants, without which I could not find happiness *now*, depends not on the will of Heaven, which as we well know leaves the wishes of poor mortals so often *un*fulfilled, but *on you alone.*[16]

Women assume a function in *rapport sexuel* only *quoad matrem.*[17] And therefore the secret of motherly reading lessons was everything a budding citizen of the state[18] or a state official (which amounted to the same thing in Novalis's dictum)[19] could wish for in the year 1800. "Doubly honor the mother who at once loves and instructs [*bildet*] you,"[20] the caption read under the frontispiece of Stephani's *Description of My Simple Reading Method for Mothers.*

Once pedagogical propaganda had succeeded in making alphabetization an affair for mothers, learning to read—on the basis of phonetic methods like Stephani's—no longer was a matter of characters, but of the voice alone. It was for this reason that Kleist, instead of putting letters down on paper, pressed his ear to William Lovell's telephone[21] and *heard* the wishes of a mother's heart—and in the same breath condemned the heavens and their God, the principle of paternal authority itself, which was based on the power of writing and on the distribution of lack. Thus Wilhelmine von Zenge was programmed with the phantasm of the Mother as an elementary teacher in the same letter: "O lay this thought to your breast like a shield of adamant: *I was born to motherhood!* Let every other thought, every other wish be deflected from this impenetrable armor. What other purpose offered by the world could not deserve your contempt. You can achieve no higher merit than by *educating a nobler mankind.*"[22] With regard to such a function as transcendental signifier, woman could act only in the manner of confession. It was impossible to mean nothing in a relationship that meant meaning. Every word written by a woman became interpretable, and therefore as talkative as Mother Nature was silent.

In the postal system of inquisitional[23] interpretation, women would register themselves as individuals in relation to the norm one way or another. Since genders are functions of discursive authorities within an organization of knowledge, the gender of women like Ulrike von Kleist, who fell out of the role this organization assigned to them by mail, becomes dubious: "She is a feminine hero figure, who has nothing of her sex except the hips, a girl who writes with orthographic correctness, plays and thinks strictly to measure."[24] Gender was an effect of interpretations that circulated in the postal regulatory circuit, or of the positions they assigned. The interpretation of interpretation is philosophy. If women were not to lose the timbre of their calling—and thus the stamp of their gender—they could not do without such philosophy, according to the postmaster's testimony: "This [thinking about our life's calling], I said, would be the whole Enlightenment of women and the only philosophy that is suitable for them. Your calling, dear friend, or the calling of women in general, is surely beyond doubt and unmistakable; what else could it be, after all, besides this: *to become a mother and to raise virtuous men for the world?*"[25] Because the discourse of life's calling was capable of truth only when its testimony was gained from the process of interpretation, philosophizing citizens were needed on the one hand—who explained women's nature—and a philosophy for women on the other, so they could understand the deep meaning of The Woman posted by their lovers. "Fine, then!" Friedrich Schlegel had written to his beloved only a year before Kleist; "Philosophy is indispensable to women."[26]

Clemens Brentano's emphatic declaration that the noble soul had a calling was the founding statute for a new generation of authorial postmasters of the soul. Since the individual could speak his truth—which he needed to do in order to prove his identity—only when he subjected his speech to the interpretation of others, the exchange of letters established the conditions for the existence of poet-officials whose job it was to control timbre and deliver souls to their destinations (or callings). The Romantic author, like the subject of postal service in general, was therefore a relay. He existed only as the holder of the postal horses, as the authority of a transition. Crossed by a postal unconscious, the subject could establish itself as a speaker only by interpreting. Because it always had to be supposed that Truth existed at the site of the Other if it was to become speakable, interpretation was the discursive mode that allowed for the production of Truth. Discursive power did not mean asserting one's self at the site of Truth, but rather at the site of its relay. Hence the Romantic authors' insistence that they had nothing to say (to themselves): "Since indeed I can give you nothing, and must expressly demand that you expect nothing but *words* from me from now on, expressions of what you have long felt and known, but not so clearly or well ordered."[27]

Because knowledge always was shifted—elsewhere—the subject of knowledge and the subject of speech never coincided. Instead, they exchanged places in the same way letters and interpretations circulated. "The novelty lies no longer in what is said, but in its reappearance":[28] "I have surprised myself, and become aware that it's *you* who are initiating *me* in philosophy."[29] Provided that knowledge was knowledge of the Other, commentator and author coincided. The author Schlegel only repeated in disguised form (i.e., he commented upon) what Dorothea already knew, no differently than the author Brentano repeated knowledge imputed to Bettina. "Forgive me if I try to tell you things that reside much more purely in your soul, things I actually perceive within you, in order to say them to you out loud."[30] Kleist, too, said nothing but that he could say nothing to Wilhelmine; instead, he could only interpret: "I cannot add to your soul, only develop what nature has put there. Nor even so much, for *you alone* can . . . and if I set a goal for you now, it is only with the conviction that you have long known it. I wish only to make clear what perhaps slumbers darkly in your soul."[31]

The ground of their being continued to be withheld from Romantic love letters. Feverishly, they ran in circles around the pit of a groundless speaking. What was driving them on and preying on them here, paradoxically enough, was the ground of groundlessness: the phantasm of a knowledge of the soul that was as natural as it was entropic, knowledge that had its origin in Mother Nature. The ground of groundlessness was a glimmer: because The Woman had told ALL, she at once tore open and mended the groundlessness of speaking. But natural and authentic knowledge of the soul, if it was to be the glimmering ground of groundless speaking, could not speak of itself. The more silent it was, the more true it became. The ENTIRE truth, phantasmic knowledge as—or of—the ground of letter writing, was of necessity *obscura et confusa*, as Kleist said. It needed others who echoed it: poets as citizens. Its discourse, which was encompassed by a silence that was and told ALL, was promulgated in the clear and distinct form of an unending *praeteritio*. In order to supplement the pit in the ground of groundless speaking, Romanticism—Kleist included—transformed the concepts of the Cartesian/Leibnizian system of knowledge into the predicates of gender.

Kleist had learned it from Fichte:

> Man reduces all that is in and for him to clear conceptions, and discovers it only through reasoning. . . . Woman, on the other hand, has a natural sentiment of what is good, true, and proper. Not as if this were given her through mere feeling, for that is impossible; but when it is externally given to her, she has the faculty of judging quickly through her feelings, and without clear insight into the grounds of such judgment, whether it be good, or not. It may be said, that man must first make himself rational; whereas, woman is already rational by nature.[32]

It may be said that the ground of knowledge was delivered to women— that is, made inaccessible to them. It was thus the task of the author to translate the nondiscursive knowledge residing obscurely in women's souls (that is, an unconscious) into distinct concepts for them. Goethe said so quite bluntly when he told Bettina why he needed her letters: "write soon, that I may again have something to translate."[33] The ground for groundless speaking was that women were excluded from the discourse. In 1800, that was true in a literal sense. Fichte's *Science of Rights* provided the shimmering proof that women, who had been destined by nature to love and marry, were "utterly annihilated by marriage as far as the state is concerned."[34] A power superior to the state—as the mere work of mortal men—commanded that women did not belong to themselves after they married, but to their husbands, and from this the conclusion followed that "women are ineligible for public offices."[35] Women could not become education officials, or any other kind of official, for that matter. The only discursive function that fell to women was that of an alphabetizing mother who existed so completely as voice and meaning that she no longer had anything to do with discourses or their textuality.

The grounding of all discourse transcended the discursive order, which was the state.

As soon as postal conditions underwent a change that put an end to the exclusion of women from discourse and included them instead, this transcendental signified, as the ground of a speaking that encircled nothing, vanished. At that historic moment, Romantic correspondence fell prey to madness. This madness was the insight that the writing of love letters was sustained only by the mail.[36] Kafka's "love letters" would become Romanticism's horizon.

CHAPTER NINE

The Logistics of the Poet's Dream: Kleist

The educational histories from which the text of the world was woven resulted from the specific form of being for the exchange of letters—and were thus the result of communications technology. But if it was essential that the threads of the postal net opened up the text of "the world," it was no less essential that they be forgotten. After all, the nature of education itself prevented insight into its *techné*. Education ultimately was defined so that it obeyed its own internal functionality (not as a technology per se), and not the postmasters' schedules and commands. Education's technology was delivered to it and invisible to it. The oblivion of the postal system was inherent in its formative concept—the story of an individual who extinguishes all contingencies to make everything that occurs a necessity. Literary theory, which is doubly obligated to the education of individuals, is therefore itself a substantial obstacle to any insights into technology. The inability to recognize the postal determination of its own possibility without going insane comprised the ontopathology of literary theory. And for the same ontopathological reasons, literary theory made Kleist's letters to Wilhelmine von Zenge into a scandal: on letters that made clearly apparent that literature is a postal delivery it can only impose the anathema of "unspeakable impertinence."[1] The condemnation of history, of the Kleist family tradition, that was implied by Heinrich von Kleist's reception into the canon of literature is fully consistent with that anathema.[2]

It became necessary, once again, to condemn a nonliterary origin of the literary: the fact that Kleist, the former second lieutenant in the Prussian Regiment of the Guards, constructed the communications technology that was to become Kleist the author. Rather than being ascribed to his texts from the start, the author Kleist established himself as a subject of the postal system. He remained within the sphere of family tradition, not only as the poet whose works combined the careers of writer and officer,[3] but also as the poet whose letters combined the careers of writer and postmaster. His younger brother, Major Leopold von Kleist, had the same career as Gellert's brother: he was a postmaster.[4] And even if it was not Heinrich von Kleist himself who applied for the position of post-office director in Lünen (Westphalia), which was under French administration in 1808, it was still a relative with the same rank, Friedrich Wilhelm Werner von Kleist—possibly on orders from the secret service.[5]

In the house of his father, who was descended from an ancient but impoverished family of Prussia's military nobility, Kleist had known so little about his childhood in Frankfurt an der Oder that he was unaware of his own birth date.[6] Thus, he had to generate his authorship as an effect of the media. Whoever was not granted authorship as the memory of a motherly voice[7] was forced to reconstruct (at least partially) the discourse network of 1800. Authorship became woman engineering.

The woman that Kleist's schematics set in operation *quoad matrem* and qua engagement was the daughter of Kleist's brother's superior, Major General August Wilhelm Hermann von Zenge,[8] and Kleist's student in German grammar.[9] The latter circumstance provided the opportunity to exchange letters, even though Kleist and Wilhelmine lived next door to each other, and the former—the sphere of military nobility—regulated every instance of face-to-face communication. Thus, the military created a love in letters that could be nothing but a love of letters. Before the postal processing of data and women could start, however, Zenge—precisely because she was the daughter of a nobleman and military officer—had to be programmed with the latest version of the discursive function that had been the norm for bourgeois women since 1796. To that end, Kleist had Wilhelmine write her now sufficiently well-known essays, which were supposed to reproduce nothing other than Fichte's definition of women as by their nature excluded from the state's discursive order in accordance with the *Science of Rights*.[10] Wilhelmine was quite simply calibrated for her function within language and the postal system. Standardized in this form, she acquired the skill to translate all kinds of natural and other types of phenomena, that is, to read them as similes and metaphors of the eternal sameness that was her calling: The Individual. "With every . . . thought, you must thus ask either 'what does this suggest in relation to *the individual?*' or 'how is this similar when compared to *the individual?*' Because the individual and the knowledge of his entire nature must be the supreme focus of your attention, since it will one day be your business to educate individuals."[11]

Enter the business of interpretation. To ensure that its intermediate results became verifiable and could produce the effect of an educational history of the individual, a database had to be created: "But if you arrive at an answer, record the entire thought immediately in one of the notebooks designated for that purpose. Because we must *hold fast* to what we have *acquired* for ourselves—afterward, I'll also tell you another reason why it's good for you to write it down."[12] The modern diary, whose emergence at the same time as the private letter and the epistolary novel was no accident,[13] was the medium for storing such data. The diary made it possible to record one's own thoughts (in contrast to mere words, which no one can own as private property), and that allowed the interpretation of an original opinion and an individual character. The self's acquisitions were the acquisition of a Self. The database of thoughts for feminine letter writers and readers at one end corresponded to a compatible database of ideas for masculine letter writers and authors at the other. All metaphors of the individual in a woman's diary were addressed to the latter. The will to knowledge was a will to record:

> But I wanted to tell you another reason why it would be good for you to record your own thoughts. It is this. You know that I am now training for the authorial profession. I have already set up a little repository of ideas for myself, which I may well wish to share with you and submit to your judgment. If you provided a small contribution to it, you could have the honor of contributing something to a future personal acquisition as well.— Do you understand me?[14]

Thus the question induced by Fichte—"*Do women completely lack any influence on the government of state?*"[15]—received an answer. If Wilhelmine understood correctly, women had influence in the state insofar as they provided poet-officials with metaphorical knowledge about The Individual and his production, thanks to the postal network (the quintessential embodiment of which would be Goethe's postage-free network). Such metaphorics immediately were fed back to them via the post by these very poet-officials (*in spe*). What followed was the output of the "repository of ideas":

> The Main flows away from the bridge in a straight line, swift as an arrow, as though its goal already were in view and it must in no way be detained, impatiently set on the shortest route—but a vine-planed hill curbs its onward flow, gently but firmly, as a wife bends the impetuous will of her husband, and the stalwart stand shows the way to the sea—and the demure admonition is respected, and the well-meant remonstrance obeyed, as the river alters its impetuous course, not breaking through the planted hill, but flowing round it, with quieter run, while kissing its flower-decked feet.[16]

Once more, it turns out to be true that the technology of the metaphor is nothing but the metaphor of technology. Kleist's fictionalized Main, after all, was indeed nothing more than a disguised repetition of information that already had been provided about how the "influence of women on the government of state" was to be conceived: that is, by translating readings into one's own thoughts and translating these thoughts from their database—women—to the database of ideas—the author. Thus, these translations or metaphors received the delivery of their own metaphor. Kleist's childlike birthday wish reappeared as German Poetry and thus translated Fichte's theory on the state of natural law and civil servants into word and deed. The metaphor, raised to the second power, needed merely to be read: mothers make sure that men become respectable officials. The Main tells us so.

What the river said was addressed to Wilhelmine von Zenge on October 11, 1800. But unlike letters, the productions of an author—or of a repository of ideas—did not have just one woman reader, but rather as many as possible. Consequently, "a poet's dream" became reality in a letter to Caroline von Schlieben of July 18, 1801. The secret to it was recording:

> That is a landscape like a poet's dream, and the most exuberant fantasy hardly could conceive greater beauty. . . . Swift as an arrow, the Rhine flows on from Mainz in a straight line, as though its goal already were in view and it must in no way be detained, impatiently set on its course. But a vine-planted hill steps into its path and curbs its onward flow, gently but

firmly, as a wife bends the impetuous will of her spouse, and with silent stand shows the way to the sea—and the noble admonition is respected, and the well-meant remonstrance obeyed, as the river alters its impetuous course, not breaking through the planted hill, but flowing round it, with quieter run, while kissing its flower-decked feet.[17]

Main or Rhine, it made no difference: the repository of ideas never recorded signifiers, but only signifieds. What it stored under the address "river" did not have any meaning or referents itself because it was the universal meaning of "river." It was what the names of all rivers signified. Kleist's repository really was one of *ideas*: it constituted poetry as the logic of the signified.

On July 28, 1801, the poet's dream was posted for a third time to a third woman. Adolphine von Werdeck also had the pleasure of reading that a region was transformed into a poet's dream when a randomly chosen river wound its way past a randomly chosen vineyard.[18] And there were still more details on the signified "river," which Kleist's letters reproduced and combined in different variations. For Caroline von Schlieben, the Rhine was entirely assembled from three different ready-made parts that were reproduced a total of seven more times. Adolphine von Werdeck received a shorter version, but one that still installed three different ready-made parts that already had been sent out on five previous occasions.

A reconstruction of this part of the repository of ideas might look something like this:[19]

River	Sent to	Date
1. The *** flows away from the bridge in a straight line, swift as an arrow, as though its goal already were in view [and so on as above to] while kissing its flower-decked feet.	W. v. Zenge C. v. Schlieben A. v. Werdeck	10/11/1800 7/18/1801 7/28/1801
2. The *** winds now to the right, now the left, kissing one vineyard, now another, and hesitates between its banks . . .	W. v. Zenge W. v. Zenge C. v. Schlieben	10/18/1800 5/21/1801 7/18/1801

(continued)

River	Sent to	Date
3. That is a landscape like a poet's dream, and the most exuberant fantasy hardly could conceive greater beauty than that of this valley, now widening, now narrowing, now blooming, now weak, now laughing, now frightening.	C. v. Schlieben W. v. Zenge A. v. Werdeck	7/18/1801 7/28/1801 7/28/1801
4. Suddenly the river leaves its right bank and turns quickly in the direction of *** to kiss its darling.	C. v. Schlieben W. v. Zenge W. v. Zenge	7/18/1801 5/4/1801 5/21/1801
5. But serene and quiet and majestic, it flows on to ***, as surely as a hero in victory, and slowly, as though it would make its course complete— and a mountain (the ***) casts itself onto its path like an affront to youthful virtue. But it breaks through and does not hesitate, and the cliffs recede before it, looking down in wonder—but scornfully it hurries past them, yet without frolicking, and the only revenge it allows itself is this: to show their blackened image in its pristine mirror.[20]	C. v. Schlieben A. v. Werdeck	7/18/1801 7/28/1801

Five different pieces were assembled in six dispatches, each time in a different combination and assortment. The true name for "the most exuberant fantasy" is "reproduction." But that was not all. The first transcription of the poet's dream of a spouse's influence on a state official, taken from the repository of ideas on October 11, 1800, was preceded by the reading of poets and transcriptions from their works. Just seven weeks earlier, Kleist had sent the recently published *Wallenstein* to Zenge as part of a parallel reading program. There, in Act I of *Piccolomini*, the river-vineyard allegory was to be found:

Octavio:
My son! The road that man in life must tread,
On which prosperity awaits, this road will run
Along the rivers, crooked like valleys,
Circling the cornfield and the vineyard's slopes,
Respecting what is one man's, what another's,
More slowly, but more surely, to its end.[21]

What Wilhelmine von Zenge read in the letter of October 11 merely served to monitor and interpret her reading of Schiller since August 25. The circuit of interpretation was thus complete. Kleist—like Gellert and Goethe previously and Brentano afterward—sent German Poetry to his fiancée, who translated it into her "own thoughts," which in tandem amounted to The Individual, and deciphered the command to exert influence on future state officials by transferring those thoughts into his database of ideas. Having himself become a poet in this manner, Kleist fed the entire system of translation back to itself in an act of sheer autoreferentiality by answering with "a poet's dream," which itself merely interpreted poetry as the *metapherein* of the postal system. What circulated were thus merely metaphors of circulation—sustained by the dream of Poetry: the phantasm of The Mother.[22]

The site of the relay was an author who translated a translation into poetry composed of metaphors of The Woman, which were metaphors of a river of language or letters that provided education. But something else had to take place at this site, the "nexus of power in the economies of transport and circulation":[23] interception. How else could an author named Friedrich Schlegel have come to publish a text addressed "To Dorothea" that—according to all the legal knowledge in dissertations on *The Law of Letters*—should have been in Dorothea's possession? The address of the letter alone already is enough to express "animus transferendi dominii"—the will of the sender to transfer possession of the letter to the recipient.[24] Thus, Schlegel had to intercept the letter either before he sent it, which meant transcribing it, or afterward, which meant demanding its return. Women who did not know their calling were not the only ones who had to write to themselves. Men who wanted to become authors had to do the same.

The act of interception or copying transformed the address into a dedication: it no longer was the materiality of the letter that it signed over and posted, but instead the immateriality of its thoughts, which were protected by copyright in their individual form.[25] What made a letter into a literary work was the formation of a distinct and new form of being for the address by way of its doubling. The semiotic requirement that an individual name had to meet in order to ensure that a letter could be sent by mail was that it be an address, and not a dedication. When such a name was recoded as a dedication, the sending of the letter became something that for all intents and purposes never occurred: the letter no longer could be delivered, no longer could be posted, and therefore it could be published.

Kleist's schematics had organized the bifurcation of the address from the very outset—how could it be otherwise? The letter to Wilhelmine von Zenge of September 15, 1800, not only insisted on being a mere repetition of what slumbered darkly in the souls of women, it also insisted that the clarity of repetition required a change in medium. The letter was interrupted and did not resume until three days later. On September 16, however, Kleist took out a new piece of paper and wrote an essay that started with a transcription of the letter's last paragraph and proceeded to discuss the philosophy women could not do without—and that therefore could be entitled simply "On Philosophy: To Wilhelmine." The supplement, however, was not addressed because Kleist himself was that address. While the addressed letter was transferred to Zenge's possession, the nonaddressed supplementary letter fell under the protection of the copyright law[26] and thus remained in Kleist's possession. Consequently, Zenge received the responsibility of carefully preserving these letters, since they contained passages that were intended for a public audience and that corresponded to so many gaps in Kleist's diary that he planned to fill with them later.[27]

The media status of poetry in the Age of Goethe corresponded to supplementary letters such as this: a printed text without an address, which was meant to be understood as a private letter addressed to each individual feminine reader. If Bettina at first mistook Goethe's works for love letters written to her,[28] and later mistook the letters' personal address for the authorial name of Goethe, she was merely taking the postal-literary system at the word of its princes and complying with its technical conditions. It was upon this ability to translate private mail into state mail (on the part of poets) and state mail into private mail (on the part of feminine readers) that poetry had been founded around 1800.

PART TWO

On the Way to New Empires 1840–1900

CHAPTER TEN

System Time (Registered Letter II)

Addresses, 130 years after Lichtenberg. Letters travel between a street number in Berlin and a street number in Prague. The postal genre that ensures the text's arrival at its feminine recipient is still the registered letter. But the moment of delivery is a different one:

> My home address is Niklasstrasse 36. But what, please, is yours? On the backs of your letters I have seen three different addresses. Is it in fact No. 29? Does it annoy you to get registered letters? I send them not only because I am anxious, though that is one of the reasons, but because I feel they are more likely to come straight to you, instead of aimlessly shuttling about, like those ordinary letters that sadly ply their way; and I always imagine the outstretched hand of a smart Berlin mailman, who, if necessary, would force the letter upon you, even if you were to resist. A dependent man cannot have too many allies.[1]

Superimposing a fantasy of letter delivery from about 1780 onto the postal system of 1912 reveals striking alterations. The postal system had become "one of the most perfect inventions the human mind has ever stumbled upon"[2] in the wake of Lichtenberg's proposals for its optimization in the very moment that the sender, who had taken over its role, abolished it as an institution. It became such an invention in Kafka's view when postal employees came to be nothing but the sender's nameless accomplices, who together took over in their turn the function Lichtenberg has taken on himself. A gang of minions who had no master *per definitionem* practiced the delivery of letters as an unreserved application of force, just as the letter writer had practiced it as an unreserved fantasy of authorship at the last epochal caesura.

This substitution can be assigned a historical date. Until 1827, the year the Prussian Post established municipal service for the city of Berlin,[3] there had been no such thing as postmen in German lands (with the exception of Vienna).[4] That is why Lichtenberg still had had to sacrifice himself in the service of the post—if only on paper. The year 1827, by contrast, does not merely mark the date when it became necessary to delegate the transfer of letters to postal agents in a systematic manner. The beginning of letter delivery's integration into the postal system also indicated the possibility of ascribing an accomplice's body or that of a proxy to the letter's subject or to the subject of the text (*sujet d'énoncé*). Precisely this systematization of proxy in the acts of delivery by the postal system provided the historical a priori for Kafka's famous delegation of body movement—the business trip on matters of an engagement or wedding—to the subject of the text, which was relegated to a position inside the letter. Modeled on *Wedding Preparations*,[5] Kafka's delegation allowed him to reserve the subject of the speech act (*sujet d'énonciation*) for communications technology alone.[6]

Integrated into the system, however, the postman himself heeded the historical condition for the possibility of his own existence: a condition that was provided by retired Artillery Staff Captain Gottlieb Carl Neander when he introduced standard street signs and house numbers in Berlin.[7] Up until then, addresses had been extremely complicated constructions, which included descriptions of entire routes or places, the large signs of shopkeepers being used whenever possible to indicate the building's location.[8] After 1806, however, Berlin addresses like Felice Bauer's essentially no longer needed the names of specific places or people, and because of this, ordinary letters always could also not make it directly into the hands of their recipients, something Kafka felt very acutely. Instead, they shuttled sadly between standardized addresses. Under conditions such as these, registered letters no longer had the function Lichtenberg assigned to them, that of measuring distance, but instead the function of physically submitting bodies to their addresses, of transforming them into subjects of the postal system. This is the index of a rupture in the form of being for posted texts, and it could not be more radically conceived.

Earlier, in 1780, the registered letter had been a technology for withdrawing the withdrawal of context, which itself belonged to the structure of written work, in order to bring about the Eucharistic moment when the context of the letter's text—this "set of presences which organize the moment of its inscription"[9]—coincided with the totality of presences that organized the moment of its reading. Such withdrawal meant the reader's presence at the writer's presence at what he had written: the obliteration of the symbol-constituting rupture in context for the sake of a perfect postal system. Now, by contrast, in 1912, the registered letter was a technology for expressly affirming that very rupture by grafting the letter's text onto another context in a moment of violence. The being of signs became simultaneously palpable and violent.

Kafka's fantasy of violence, in which the moment of delivery was a grafting, did not just remain on paper. It was realized almost exactly one year later, when the correspondence between Kafka and Bauer reached a definitive low point and Kafka took on Ernst Weiß, a fellow writer and an opponent of any marriage between Bauer and Kafka, as an employee who was literally supposed to force letters on people. "Well," Kafka wrote to Grete Bloch, who helped bring about the catastrophe,

> early in December [1913] I asked this Dr. Weiss to take a letter from me to F.'s office. In the letter I said little more than that I had to have news from or about her, which was why I had sent W. so that he could write to me about her. While she read the letter, W. was to sit beside her desk, look around, wait until she had finished reading, and then, since he had been given no further instructions and was most unlikely to get a reply (for why should *he* get one when *I* never did), he was to go away and let me know how she looked and how she seemed to be. And this was precisely what happened.[10]

Kafka's fantasy about the delivery of registered letters arrived at the reality of a controlling glance that was no less physically present than an "outstretched hand." And what Weiß did as postman and accomplice was nothing less than what Lichtenberg could only dream of doing: he "observed" the "face" the recipient "made upon delivery." The letter foisted upon her in this way doubles the violence of its delivery in sheer autoreferentiality. Felice Bauer reads her own reading of it so that Ernst Weiß can see and Kafka can find out what she reads and how she reads it. As though it happens in a precise and perverse recurrence of Lichtenberg's fantasy, the written work and the context of its reading are identical. The effect of reading such a letter, where what is written transpires in real time, is merely that the message merges with the self-presentation of the medium. Felice Bauer receives what is registered in registered writing: the registration of a body for its address. Immanuelkirchstrasse 29, Berlin NO. Receipt, signature:[11] Felice Bauer.

One could risk a thesis: the form of being for letters (the function of which is considered here to be their "meaning" or content) is the same as the form employed for assessing their value. Lichtenberg's model for the registered letter assigned values of meaning to words according to the distance between bodies, which was measured by the letter in successive stages, and that model coincided with the contemporaneous method for assessing the postage of letters, which assigned monetary values to words in the same way. In Kafka's case, the registration of a feminine addressee corresponded to a form of appraising registered letters in which the calculation of distance played no role whatsoever. As it was established by Heinrich von Stephan, the concept of the registered letter indeed had existed only as a paradox since its introduction in 1874. The concept of the registered letter had been around exactly as long as the elimination of the object it described. The reason for this: the appearance of Kafkaesque quantities of letters. "Over the course of decades, the treatment of registered dispatches had to be increasingly simplified because their numbers swelled to quantities that the operation could not handle. While registered dispatches initially had to be individually certified on cards by number and according to the location of mailing, summary registration was introduced in the exchange between railway post offices manned by officials as early as the year 1874."[12] What led to the elimination of registered letters worthy of the name, the swelling numbers of them in quantities that could be handled only statistically, quantities that therefore were the nightmare of every postal official before 1874, precisely fulfilled the wish of Kafka's dream:

> The night before last I dreamt about you for the second time. A mailman brought two registered letters from you, that is, he delivered them to me, one in each hand, his arms moving in perfect precision, like the jerking of piston rods in a steam engine. God, they were magic letters! I kept pulling out page after page, but the envelopes never emptied. I was standing halfway up a flight of stairs and (don't hold it against me) had to throw the pages I had read all over the stairs in order to take more letters out of the envelopes. The whole staircase was littered from top to bottom with the loosely heaped pages I had read, the resilient paper creating a great rustling sound. That was a real wish-dream![13]

Kafka's dream celebrated the demise of registered communication at the ground(lessness) of all discourse: white noise, into which the signals of all transmitting networks were discharged once their frequencies had been "heaped" or added up. But if the power of noise, whether it be Brownian molecular motion or crosstalk between networks, is to become audible and imaginable, then in the former case, the real must be able to move through technical channels such as a telephone line, for example, and in the latter case, communication must be treated as a closed system (not in the sense of thermodynamics, but of Shannon's model of communication).[14] What this means is that signals transmitted by the communications system at a given time t_n are not viewed as the function of a data source or receiver—not, let's say, as the expressions or intentions of people looking for the understanding of other people—but instead as a function of factors in the system of communication itself. Hence Kafka's comparison of the postman to a steam engine, which was anything but coincidental. The postal system had become a closed system, like the industrial system, which had been revolutionized by the steam engine, which in turn was functional thanks to Watt's invention of the centrifugal-force governor. According to the definition given in a treatise with the noteworthy title *On Governors* written by none other than Clerk Maxwell, a governor maintains the performance of machines at a constant ("uniform") level independent of all fluctuations in power or resistance.[15] Thus, machines could be brought up to standards that made it possible to predict the development of entire branches of the economy with the help of the emerging field of statistics. And as economic systems, those branches became accessible to the theories of people like Charles Babbage. Kafka's analysis, which was no less precise because it was dreamed, stated that the output of the postal system is uniform and dependent on postal standards in analogy to the output of machines. The link between people and the postal system might with good reason thus be called a man-machine interface. But it was someone else who dreamed. Kafka's wish-fulfillment dream of letters increasing to immeasurable quantities merely repeated another dream, which had been realized seventy-two years before. That event marked a rupture in the history of the letter's form of being, one that separated Lichtenberg and Kafka: the closure of the postal system to form a technical system.

CHAPTER ELEVEN

Postage One Penny: Rowland Hill's Post Office Reform

Advantages of the Penny Post, When is a pun not a pun?
—*James Joyce, 'Finnegans Wake'*

London, January 10, 1840. Rowland Hill, former school director and Utilitarian, noted something in his diary on account of which the English press, the Parliament, and broad segments of the population had been up in arms for months:

> January 10th.—Penny Postage extended to the whole kingdom this day! . . . I have abstained from going to the Post Office to-night lest I should embarrass their proceedings. I hear of large numbers of circulars being sent, and the *Globe* of to-night says the Post Office has been quite besieged by people preparing their letters. I guess that the number despatched to-night will not be less than 100,000, or more than three times what it was this day twelve-months. If less I shall be disappointed.[1]

He was not. The following entry reads: "January 11th.—The number of letters despatched last night exceeded all expectation. It was 112,00, of which all but 13,000 or 14,000 were prepaid. Great confusion in the hall of the Post Office, owing to the insufficiency of means for receiving the postage."[2]

The flooding of St. Martin-le-Grand's sorting hall with letters that night was not merely the primal scene of wish-fulfillment dreams like the ones authors would have in 1900, but also a rupture in the history of media technology. Rowland Hill's idea of the penny post and its realization took Justi's postage theory to its most extreme conclusion, but more than that, it produced a new way of thinking about the postal system and a new form of its being. After Hill's acclaimed treatise *Post Office Reform: Its Importance and Practicability* was published in 1837, the postal system was a closed system that obeyed its own economy and therefore required the knowledge of professionals. Hill set about researching the economy of the postal system in order to establish an organization of words appropriate to the media. From then on, signifiers led an independent life that intersected with the life of humans only in the area of politics: the politics of the unconscious, the Grand Other, or chance.

Once he had completed his investigation of the English postal system, Hill made up a list of its faults, at the very top of which he placed the fundamental characteristic of the traditional postal system itself (prior to the discovery that the nonpayment of postage increased the costs of delivery, since the postman also would have to collect the postage): the "taxing" of the letter's value, "that is, ascertaining and marking the postage to be charged on each [letter]."[3] The remarkable discovery that the very method of assessing value upon which Lichtenberg's wish-fulfillment dream had been based would prevent the postal system from becoming the "most perfect invention the human mind has ever stumbled upon" led Hill to three conclusions: (1) the postal rate had to be standardized, (2) postage had to be radically reduced, and (3) "means to induce prepayment" had to be adopted.[4] The most perfect invention would therefore not be the senders' delivery of their own letters, but the one-penny stamp. In making his plans for penny postage, Hill started with the theories developed in the discourse of police science during the eighteenth century: First of all, the number of "letters . . . passing annually through the [Post] Office" would be greatly increased by suppressing the illegal conveyance of mail. The extent to which the English postal monopoly was systematically violated must indeed have been considerable: "illicit correspondence was carried on throughout the country in systematic evasion of the law, if not in open violation of it, to an extent that could hardly have been imagined."[5] It was alleged that only one-sixth of the letter traffic between Manchester and London passed through the post office.[6] Then the number of dispatches would be increased by using the mail to distribute circulars and to issue new ones. Finally, the volume of mail would be increased "by an enormous enlargement of the class of letter-writers."[7] In Hill's reformulation of von Justi's theorem of postage, the postal administration's losses resulting from reduced postal rates, "even if large would be more than compensated by the powerful stimulus given by low postage to the productive power of the country."[8] Ultimately, Hill transformed Justi's theorem into the somewhat opaque law (reminiscent of Newton's) that the increase in consumption equals the reciprocal value of the square of the price, so that a reduction of postage from sixpence to one penny would result in a thirty-six-fold increase in traffic.[9]

The proposal to reduce postage, of course, was nothing new—not even the postal rate of one penny was new. In 1680, a customs officer, William Dockwra, introduced a penny post in the City of London, which had not had postal delivery up until then: between four and five hundred receiving offices were opened for letters from one end of the city to the other. Letters deposited for a penny were delivered at least fifteen times daily within the London city limits, and at least five times a day to the suburbs.[10] Although Dockwra had to relinquish his flourishing enterprise only two years later to the duke of York, who was in possession of the postal monopoly, and although the one-penny postal district was limited to a range of ten miles in 1711, with the scale of rates and their differentiation according to distance rising steadily beyond those limits, the London penny post did not cease to exist. On the contrary, after a relevant law was passed in 1765, it was imitated in all the larger cities of Great Britain. By the middle of the 1830's, penny posts operated locally throughout the entire United Kingdom, with the exception of London, where penny postage was doubled in 1801.[11]

In the light of this history, Hill's idea—as simple as it was profound—was thus to think of all Great Britain as a single city, that is, no longer to give a moment's thought to what had been dear to Western discourse on the nature of the letter from the beginning: the idea of distance. A city expanded its limits in postal terms to the borders of a country: the General Post Office was absorbed by the penny post. Mail—following Rowland Hill's insight—had nothing to do with distance. There is no relationship between the postal expense of letters and the distance of transmission. One could compensate for the differences in cost that emerged from varying geographical distances, Hill's investigation showed, merely by eliminating the expenses involved in calculating distances alone, not to mention by the savings derived from rapid, large-scale, and therefore inexpensive letter processing, which individual "taxing" prevented and only the standardization of spaces and signifiers allowed.[12] "The result," Hill later told the English Parliament in a speech, "was a thorough conviction in my own mind that the inland rate of postage ought to be the same for all distances, and that provided the postage of letters were prepaid, the rate might be reduced as low as 1 d. throughout the United Kingdom (Applause)."[13]

Henceforth, Mother Earth became a grave for bodies alone; the graphemes of letters—despite their etymology—ceased to find their ground, that is, to perish and be interred, by means of inscribing or engraving themselves. Instead, as "Mother Ground,"[14] Mother Earth crossed out graphemics itself—once Steinheil found her technical nature to be the best possible electrical conductor for closing telegraphic circuits in 1838 (a year after Hill published his proposal for the penny post).[15] The dates of the earth's disconnection from the postal system and its nearly simultaneous reconnection to telegraphy stand in unison: telegraphy, which made distances irrelevant on a global scale, became the basis of the British Empire; its beginning was marked by the fact that letters ceased to represent *territorium*. In order to do justice to the magnitude of the *tabula rasa* that Rowland Hill's reform ultimately made of Great Britain, a demonstration is in order to indicate how deeply postal rates actually had been engraved in the geography of the United Kingdom:

> In Great Britain . . . the postage on a single letter delivered within eight miles to the office where it was posted was . . . twopence, the lowest rate beyond that limit being fourpence. Beyond fifteen miles it became fivepence; after which it rose a penny at a time, but by irregular augmentation, to one shilling, the charge for three hundred miles, and thenceforward augmentation went on at the same rate, each additional penny serving for another hundred miles. . . . As if this complexity was not quite enough, there was as a general rule an additional charge of a half-penny on a letter crossing the Scotch border; while letters to or from Ireland had to bear, in addition, packet rates, and rates for crossing the bridges over the Conway and the Menai; or, if they took the southern route, a rate chargeable at Milford. Lastly, there was the rule . . . by which a letter with the slightest enclosure incurred double postage, and two enclosures triple; and the postage however, being regulated by weight whenever this reached an ounce, at which point the charge became quadrupel; rising afterwards by a single postage for every additional quarter of an ounce.[16]

The eradication of all the territorial markers and individual names that once had defined the exchange of letters, the removal of the world from the postal system (and the elimination of its distances) that ultimately found its conclusion in the World Postal Union: these were the conditions for Rowland Hill's second great idea: prepayment, or the delivery of postage payment from the actual posting—indeed, from the actual existence—of letters. After the introduction of prepayment, the post no longer was a matter of what was said, but rather of what *could* be said. Prepayment made the time dimension of letters handled by the postal system just as irrelevant as the spatial dimension had become after uniform postage. The form in which this negation of the bonds connecting words to time and space has come down to us is, of course, the postage stamp.

Rowland Hill certainly did not invent the postage stamp either; not even this was his achievement. That honor went to a Monsieur de Vélayer, to whom in 1653 Louis XIV had granted the privilege of installing several "boëttes" in every district of Paris, into which all men and women (the arrangement was said to be especially popular among the mistresses of noblemen) could deposit their letters.[17] Such letters merely needed to have a Parisian address, consisting of at least a name and a street designation,[18] and—as the court author Pellison reported—an adhesive ticket, which was stamped with a special mark and bore the inscription: "Port-payé le *jour* du *mois* de l'an 1653 ou 1654."[19] The very first stamps were thus canceled by their dates. In his *Instrvction povr cevx Qui voudront escrire d'vn quartier de Paris en vn autre, & avoir responce promptement deux & trois fois le iour sans y enuoyer personne*, Vélayer gave an argument in support of his invention that would reappear in Rowland Hill's work: "because the principal aim of this establishment is to insure a prompt response, which would not be possible if the Commissioners who carry the aforementioned Letters from house to house were obliged to wait for payment at every stop."[20] The separation of postal revenue at a given point in time from the dispatches actually circulating at a time increased the speed of delivery and thus allowed for an increase in its frequency.

It may have been no accident that de Vélayer originally had been a reporter of petitions in the Council of State and therefore was responsible for all the infamous lives that would have passed beneath the threshold of history and disappeared if the power of the absolutist state had not granted them the written petition, the denunciation, as a medium and a ritual of speech.[21] The *petite poste* of the *maître des requêtes* heralded a technological shift in the mode in which beings such as these appeared: the "easy possibility of letter writing" (in Kafka's words) appeared in place of the Leviathan's ear. Even in his day, Rowland Hill still would see the postage stamp as a means for intercepting and processing the people's unheard(-of) noise. The birth of the postage stamp from the disposition of the police: this endless murmuring, as the order's (i.e., the police's) Other, was dangerous only as long as it continued to be noise beneath the threshold of history; therefore it had to be controlled by a halt, a relay, an *epoché*, in consequence of which it was compelled to become a historical datum. The danger emanating from the noise of the people was dispelled as soon as it was intercepted by a network that controlled, redirected, sorted, and calculated it, thus ensuring that its waves were not emitted at unanticipated speeds or in unanticipated directions.

This was precisely the intention that had led to the foundation of a General Post Office in England in the first place. In order to make sure the letters of businessmen and other private persons passed through official channels—and especially through London—Thomas Witherings was appointed Master of the Posts for Foreign Parts in 1632. Three years later, a plan was put in action that established interconnections among all areas of Great Britain and linked them to overseas postal systems—that is, to the Taxis system—as well.[22] But the outspoken mistrust of the people confronted both the sudden request that they place letters into the hands of men employed by the state and the fact that all letters had to pass through London. Such fears were not unfounded, as it turned out by 1661 at the latest. With the lease of the General Post Office to Colonel Henry Bishop, its bureau "for the survey and inspection of letters" fell into the hands of the infamous conspirator Major John Wildman ("the soul of English politics")[23]—who was in secret the actual holder of the lease. This bureau "was nothing more nor less than an office for collecting intelligence by intercepting the mail, nearly all of which was made to pass at some stage through the London office." Wildman did indeed wind up in jail on charges of conspiracy against the crown, but "there is no doubt" that collecting intelligence by intercepting the mail "had been one of the activities of the Post Office ever since its earliest days."[24]

Once Rowland Hill had minimized the "vacuum of leadership" in the state's postal monopoly by extending Dockwra's penny postage to Withering's (or Wildman's) channels and hence vacuuming up the people's subversive W.A.S.T.E., every exchange of letters was subject to standardized speeds and frequencies. So too was propaganda, which formerly had been conducted mouth to mouth and which in all ages for various reasons herded together the gang that was then called "the people." Tristero's Empire, this Counterempire of History, the Post-Histoire, receded still further into the distance. In discourse, the postage stamp achieved what the centrifugal-force governor had done for the steam engine: it prevented explosions. This connection exists in more than mere metaphors: in a memorandum on his own inventions dated December 1832, Hill included a "Pendulus Mechanism applied to Steam Engines."[25] Kafka's dream comparison of the postman to a steam engine hardly could have turned out to be more precise.

In light of all this, it seems only sensible that Rowland Hill reinvented de Vélayer's postage stamp in order to guarantee that even the illiterate could use the postal system. Hill's first proposal for making prepayment accessible to the people—as stated in a letter to the chancellor of the exchequer—merely had envisioned the issue of "stamped covers and sheets of papers . . . sold at such a rate as to include postage."[26] But those who intend to suck up lives that previously had passed below the threshold of all discourse and to absorb them into the class of letter writers cannot make that discourse a prerequisite for those lives. "Persons unaccustomed to write letters would perhaps be at a loss how to proceed." They might want to bring a letter written on unstamped paper to the post office, for example. Then the official behind the counter obviously would sell them a stamped envelope in which they could enclose the letter and to which they would have to add only the address. But what, Hill worried, if the person bringing the letter could not write? To ensure that even the illiterate could not slip through the gaps in the postal net, Hill resorted to the means of issuing "a little bit of paper" that was "just large enough to bear the stamp and covered at the back with a glutinous wash, which the bringer might, by applying a little moisture, attach to the back of the letter so as to avoid the necessity for redirecting it."[27] Now that we have postage stamps, those of us who take letters to the post office can be illiterates, one and all.

By the time the third reading of the Penny Post Bill passed on July 29, 1839, two thousand petitions with a quarter of a million signatures already had been received by the House of Commons calling for the introduction of this unprecedented measure of discursive regulation. Thus, the *Times* could proclaim the bill a "cause of the whole people of the United Kingdom."[28] After an endorsement was extracted from the king himself, penny postage became law on August 17, 1839. The first one-penny postage stamps were issued only months after the official launch date for the penny post, that is, on May 6, 1840. By this time, however, the half-million stamps that the printing presses were able to dump into the market every day were insufficient to satisfy the demands of the British to bring their letters to the post office like an army of illiterates.

CHAPTER TWELVE

The Standards of Writing

Once upon a time, sending had meant finding a home in the police. Once upon a different time, sending had meant finding a home in the civil-service state and in motherhood. After May 6, 1840, sending meant finding a home in the postal system itself. Thus, the postal system closed itself as a system, and so came to an end an epoch of written communication based upon the "idea," which Kafka doubted and Luhmann refuted, "that people can communicate with one another by letter."[1] As the penny post closed the system of the postal system, it also enabled the insight of systems theory that this idea was merely a convention produced by the communications system "post" in order to enable further communication.[2]

The closing of the postal system as a system: this meant that the grounds for the postal system no longer transcended the postal—neither in the direction of the well-being of the state nor in the direction of the transcendental signified of a Mother who was both Nature itself and the absolute origin of The Individual. No longer was The Individual the grounds for posting, which now were provided by the laws of a postal economy. The theory of the postal system therefore had to stop celebrating anthropological truths and start computing the technical standards of the system using the single criterion of their suitability to the media. This criterion was dictated by the economy of the medium itself. Media rationality, *Medienräson*, emerged at the site where political rationality, the *raison d'état*, once had held sway. The individualization of letters produced by the process of registration—in which every letter was assigned an individual number, route, and "biography"—corresponded to a rationality that was completely foreign to the postal system after Hill. *Medi-*

enräson demanded the elimination of "taxing" procedures and the taxonomy of fees that had been projected onto geography, as well as the introduction of a standardized price for signifiers that made it possible to pay the debt for their transmission on a massive scale independently of their existence (prepayment). Signifiers no longer followed the rationality of meaning and its comprehension, but instead the rationality of a medium that subjected them to a standard that always preceded the possibility of meaning (as the standard value of meaning).

The postal system now could process signifiers (quasi-)mechanically: penny postage achieved the standardization and mechanization of all interfaces between the postal system and the people. Small machines organizing the routine bumps and grinds of writing stamped the distinction that made the postal system not only a closed system, but a technical system as well. At the site of postal input and output operations, such machines distinguished between a data source and a sender and between a data destination and a recipient. These differences were integrated into a general model of communication by Claude Shannon so that he might disregard both data sources and destinations—such as humans who transmit messages and other humans who understand them—as factors in the mathematical theory of communication. Once communication was subjected to standards that preceded the category of meaning, standards like the penny postage or the binary digit, processes such as expressing opinions or understanding them lost significance for the theory of communication.[3] And once the standardization of senders and receivers had made the operation of the postal system independent from data sources and destinations, it was possible to formulate a communications theory that did not depend on the question of intention or understanding. Shannon's theory specifically applies only to systems that are subjected to the historical a priori of prepayment. "The system must be designed to operate for each possible selection, not just the one which will actually be chosen since this is unknown at the time of design."[4] The prototype of such a system was the penny post, which, with the introduction of prepayment, became the first postal system ever to function "for every possible selection" and not just for letters that actually had been written (or chosen). In fact, the letters themselves might not even have been conceived at the time the stamps were purchased. After prepayment—that is, after the emergence of media rationality in our culture—people have become obsolete with regard to communications theory.

At present, all sending finds a home (or is epoch-making) in communications systems that were designed in accordance with the standard of prepayment—or in ones that function with regard to every possible message, thanks to a "presemantic" standard for signifiers. Because of this, mechanical interfaces determine our everyday postal existence. Everyday life and all of the machines that go into making it up thus date back to Rowland Hill and 1840. The postage stamp made the sender's presence at the postal counter just as superfluous as the recipient's presence at delivery. If the sheer quantities of standardized data were not to overload the system's capacity for processing them, consignment and delivery had to become the well-known standard inputs and outputs that mailboxes and mail slots routinely process every day. As a matter of principle, the postal system functions only in the absence of data sources and destinations.

MAILBOXES: "ALWAYS ONE IN THE NEIGHBORHOOD"

The mailbox is a historical function of the postage stamp; its inventor therefore was de Vélayer, and not Hill. Mailboxes had existed independently of postage stamps, of course, like the ones the French had introduced to German territories west of the Rhine in 1794,[5] or the ones mounted in front of Prussian post offices after 1824[6] (not to mention the dismal history of the delivery box as medium for anonymous denunciations).[7] But these mailboxes had allowed only the input of letters for which the postage had not been paid, and therefore were at odds with the purpose of Hill's reform, since they depended on a "postpayment" that systematically obstructed standard delivery. By contrast, the "pillar letterboxes" Hill proposed for construction after he read an article in the *Times* in November 1840[8] had the function of managing the massive quantities of discourse produced by the penny post by automating their consignment. It was thus only in their media union with postage stamps that mailboxes assumed the omnipresence[9] that transformed them into training equipment necessary for getting used to permanent connectedness in a psychotechnical manner.

Mailboxes generated a condition of maximal productivity and optimal possibilities for controlling written discourses. Only four years after Hill's mailbox initiative, the production of this condition was celebrated in Vienna by none other than Adalbert Stifter, following the reintroduction of the Viennese municipal postal service—fresh evidence that power not only is watching and listening, but compels action and speech as well.[10] Since "all of the terrain belonging to the main post office in Vienna . . . [is] divided into districts, and in each of these districts [there is] a letter collection box,"[11] one not only can send letters "twice daily to all parts of the city" and receive answers in return, "but also send letters to the entire world with the greatest of ease, since the above-mentioned collection boxes are set up in both the city and the suburbs at such intervals that there is always one in the neighborhood."[12] The postal system, as a system of beginning and end points separated by great geographical distances, had been transformed into a topology of neighborhoods. Thus, the act of sending could slip under the threshold of consciousness that separated time-wasting holiday indulgences from the normal, motorized mechanism of everyday life.

The effect of this evasion of consciousness was that Freud, working in the same Vienna sixty-seven years after Stifter's jubilant response, would be able to found a psychopathology of this everyday life produced by mailboxes.[13] The distinction between normal and abnormal individuals depends precisely on the question of whether or not neighborhood mailboxes had made the leap over the threshold of consciousness.[14] In discussing Freud's text, it generally is forgotten that the condition necessary for the possibility of malfunctions is an unconscious mechanism that people must have acquired at one time or another through training. A mistake at the mailbox, which is an unconscious malfunction, is thus preceded historically by another mistake, a failure as a result of a new standard of everyday life. In 1877, a report of the English postmaster general assessing the population's level of training in the medium noted:

> that in Aberdeen a man was noticed who gave himself much trouble trying to put a letter into the opening of a street hydrant that was being repaired. The similarity of this device to the pillar letter-boxes common in England had, as closer inspection of the hydrant revealed, already misled three different correspondents into depositing letters in this container, unsuitable as it was

to further conveyance. This is by no means an isolated incident. There is hardly any opening onto the street that is not occasionally mistaken for the slot of a mailbox by some uninformed person.[15]

The advent of permanent connectedness transformed random openings at random locations into connections. In the perceptual world organized by the senses' telematic hookup, things no longer appeared as things, but rather as disguises. Hydrants or cellar windows were disguised interfaces (Windows, indeed) of a ubiquitous informational network. Things became ears.

The flip side of being blessed with an omnipresent neighborhood of miniature transmitters that transformed the world into a design of postal instruments was paranoia—as Kafka's story "The Neighbor" reveals. In the case of the mailboxes Stifter had greeted with such euphoria, this paranoia was completely justifiable. As early as 1786, after all, Emperor Joseph II had indicated in secret instructions to the viceroys of the hereditary Austrian lands that it was "appropriate" to place the operation of the so-called "minor posts" and their mailboxes "into the hands of such persons whose integrity and loyalty would be guaranteed by the police. It is unnecessary to point out on the one hand how well such an institution could be used for certain reconnaissances, and what exceedingly great caution is demanded on the other, in order not to go too far in the matter and thus infringe too much on the credit of the institution and on civil liberty."[16]

So much for the concept of civil liberty as an absolutist listening device designed or disguised as a blessing to humanity with the veneer of convenience. So much, too, for a phenomenology that thinks it is possible to explain what the media are via experiences of their design (what since then is referred to as their "user interfaces"). It is in any case someone else who is jubilant. In the case of Stifter, it might well have been his namesake, Adalbert Zaremba, the head of the Viennese chancery of secret codes.[17]

MAIL SLOTS: " . . . TO SAVE US FROM VIOLENT REVOLUTION"

Unlike penny postage, the postage stamp, and the mailbox, the counterpart at the output end—the ominous slot everyone has in their door—appears for once to have been the actual invention of Rowland Hill. Once prepayment had eliminated the post office's task of collecting revenues, and "distribution" had become "its only function,"[18] the delivery of letters could be mechanized as well—a step that was necessary in order to increase its frequency. A topic of major importance for *Medienräson*, after all, was the economy of time: "One means of economising the time of letter-carriers, which I had contemplated from the first, was to induce the public to provide themselves with letter boxes to the doors of their houses; and I now suggested to the Postmaster-General the expediency of addressing a circular on the subject, in his name, to the inhabitants of London."[19]

While people were converting their doors to the slot design, which was intended to make them into purely standardized addresses, Harriet Martineau, a successful writer and author of the popular *Illustrations of Political Economy*, wrote in plaintext to an American friend about the meaning and purpose of the project:

> Our greatest achievement, of late, has been the obtaining of the penny postage. I question whether there be now time left for the working of beneficent measures to save us from violent revolution; but if there be, none will work better than this. It will do more for the circulation of ideas, for the fostering of domestic affections, for the humanizing of the mass generally, than any other single measure that our national wit can devise. . . . We are all putting our letter-boxes on our hall-doors with great glee, anticipating the hearing from brothers and sisters,—a line or two almost every day. The slips in the doors are to save the postmen's time,—the great point being how many letters may be delivered within a given time, the postage being paid in the price of the envelopes or paper. So all who wish well to the plan are having slips in their doors. It is proved that poor people *do* write, or get letters written, *wherever* a franking privilege exists. When January comes round, do give your sympathy to all the poor pastors' and tradesmen's and artisans' families, who can at last write to one another as if they were all M.P.'s.[20]

These were words that sealed the fate of postal empires where only aristocrats, members of Parliament, and poets had the privilege of circulating masterly discourses, using their names as prepayment.[21] Postage stamps (which Martineau had in mind only in the preliminary form of stamped envelopes) and mail slots transformed every letter writer into an

FIGURE 4. Penny stamp, nineteenth-century England.

M.P., an aristocrat, or a Goethe. It no longer was the timbre of a calling that put discourse in circulation, bringing writers to confessions of individuality, but a standard whose stamp inaugurated at a stroke a discursive sovereignty, doing so in the name of an anonymous media economy. The image of the young Queen Victoria that adorned the first postage stamps by the millions did not make her the queen of all discourses circulating beneath her portrait, but had the opposite effect—since it demanded it be continually canceled and struck out. Thus, the London press harbored the suspicion that "this untoward disfiguration of the royal person has been the studied work of ministerial malevolence and jealousy, desirous of rendering the royal benefactress, if possible, as odious as themselves."[22] Uniform postage granted the "franking privilege" or discursive sovereignty to all—and to no one alike—so that the nation, which was poor and numerous, would not make a revolution, but instead write letters and have letters written to it. Harriet Martineau said so with unsurpassable clarity.

Postage stamps and mailboxes, which in the hands of the secret police had been instruments for luring criminals and enemies of the state into the trap of communication during the seventeenth and eighteenth centuries, became industrialized England's supreme counterrevolutionary instrument in the nineteenth century, an instrument that submitted the uncontrollable murmuring of the people to the state's standards of writing. The queen carried her head to market for the price of a penny in order to ensure that it would not roll [see Figure 4]. The postage stamp prevented revolution because it was the revolution. No wonder the slots in doors celebrated by Miss Martineau were spurned in other places: in answer to the survey that the postmaster general assigned Hill to prepare, the postmaster general received an indignant query from the marquis of Londonderry asking if the postmaster general seriously thought that he, the marquis, would saw a slot into his mahogany door.[23] The noble privilege of postage shifted from the renowned to the nameless in order to give power the ability to control the "chaotic night" that, according to Klüber, presided where no mail—read no postage stamp—existed.[24]

With the standardization of delivery via the mail slot—as democratic as it was counterrevolutionary—the nondiscursive conditions were provided for discursive events such as Kafka's *Letters to Felice*. Martineau's expectation to receive a line or two from one of her brothers or sisters almost every day not only anticipated Kafka's demands on Felice Bauer nearly word for word,[25] it also called for the invention of the postcard. And such an expectation was itself evoked by nothing other than the conversion of the postal system to a media-rational economy. The economy of maximal time utilization, the discourse of which from now on began to write itself (with regard to the dispatching of letters) after Rowland Hill's post-office reform, was the historical a priori for love letters that desire nothing but "a line or two every day."

Once postage stamps, mailboxes, mail slots, and systems-integral postmen had come into existence, what enabled the calculation of further communication no longer was an individual, a soul, a person, or a subject. Since all such terms are according to Luhmann "nothing more than what they effect in communication,"[26] we are cognitive operators, now that we remain systematically absent in order to effect media-rational communication, only to the extent that we are addresses. This means that our culture switched over to a new logic of identity at the middle of the nineteenth century. Once the name was replaced by an anonymous street number—the dissemination of which, according to Benjamin, is a measure of progressive normalization[27]—and once the body was replaced by the counterrevolutionary, democratizing mail slot, identity no longer was a question of biographical depth, but of potential addressability. In the final quarter of the nineteenth century, with the lapse of "the addressee's acknowledgment of receipt" in the delivery of court mandates,[28] such addressability ultimately became synonymous with the legal definition of the person. We exist in the eyes of the law as long as only one mail slot is to be found at the address recorded by power. To withdraw addressability or to make access to the slot in the door impossible therefore is a violation of the fundamental laws of human existence. Revealing our existence in the form of an address is consequently a matter for the police. So it was stated, only ten years after the introduction of the penny post, in an article "On the History of the English Postal System":

> Some letters have an address no ordinary mortal could decipher: mysterious handwriting, orthography and indication of the residence still more mysterious, apparently destined to conceal the addressee from police investigations for a century. Such letters go to the "Blind Letter Office . . . and in no time at all the skillful clerk solves the riddle of the Sphinx. Sometimes it costs a few drops of noble perspiration, but like a bloodhound with the highest pedigree, the letter usually gets its man.[29]

The meaning is plain to see. Letters are bloodhounds, and bloodhounds, of course, are used by the police to track down criminals. Letters sniff out the addresses we owe to power, which has taken up residence in the technology of communication, in order to confine us to an identity. The solution to the riddle of the Sphinx, "Man," is thus the result of police investigations. Formerly a product of letter exchange in the form of education for the civil service or for motherhood, in the eyes of Kleist or Brentano, a person now became the product of letter exchange in the form of an arrest. We post bail for our existence with the payment of addressability: we are, insofar as letters can take us into custody. Thus, there is indeed "no destination before the arrival."[30] Only at the moment of the letter's delivery is there a destination, an address, our existence. The letter therefore is not delivered to the address, but the address is delivered by the letter; there is no place before its arrival, no identity before the address.

In Goethe's postal empire, where a transcendental norm—the gender-specific "highest calling of the soul"—had governed the writing of letters, proof of identity as the interpretation of individuality had been the grounds for all written communication. Once *Medienräson* and its standards began to govern all letter writing, identity became a function of delivery. This explains why, according to its own rationale, a text was submitted around 1900 in the form and under the media-rational title of *The Notebooks* and not *The Letters of Malte Laurids Brigge*: "And I mean to write no more letters. What's the use of telling anyone that I am changing? If I am changing, then surely I am no longer the person I was, and if I am something else than heretofore, then it is clear that I have no acquaintances. And to strange people, to people who do not know me, I cannot possibly write."[31] The reasons why Brigge writes a diary could not be more clearly drawn from communications technology. In the postal realm, identity exists as a cognitive operator only in relation to the letter's sampling velocity. Because Rilke defines identity as a function of frequency with regard to statements about change, identity exists only under the constraints of Shannon's sampling theorem, which states that identity is completely definable as the function of time $f(t)$, provided that the number of samples is equal to twice the highest frequency in their bandwidth: $2TW$ letters are required, where T is the interval that delineates the function in Brigge's case (i.e., Rilke's Paris interval, 1902–1903).[32] In Shannon's technical language: "If a function $f(t)$ contains no frequencies higher than W cps, it is completely determined by giving its ordinates at a series of points spaced $1/2W$ seconds apart."[33]

Provided that one takes Brigge (alias Rilke) at his word when he says that 3 weeks in Paris correspond to the same number of years elsewhere, the sampling rate that Shannon required is calculable in his case. If the frequency of change in Brigge's identity was once equal to $1/3$ per week, here it equals 52, since the same change that previously was spread out over 156 weeks now occurs in 3. Thus, according to Shannon's theory, Brigge would have to write a full 104 letters every week in order to be still recognizable as Malte Laurids Brigge. In a case such as this, one might well prefer to write nothing at all. That Brigge's letters, had they been written, merely would have produced a series of Others and turned acquaintances into pure strangers, that the cognitive operators indispensable for calculating and imputing correspondence were canceled out, resulted from a violation of the sampling theorem. Identity, runs the fundamental prerequisite for Brigge's repudiation of the mail, is a function of time produced by the medium—discrete time, in the case of letters, which is the master clock frequency for the medium of the postal system.

Letters ceased to be the classical medium for the production and recording of subjectivity and its development because the interpretation of obscure meanings no longer was decisive proof of identity (as identity in change). Such proof was provided instead by the postal materiality of identity: its character as an interval. The "time of that other interpretation"[34] is a digitized time, an age that has in the meantime dawned inside computer circuits and electronic data networks. Below the threshold of a certain master clock frequency, the Self becomes Other—or noise. Once the mail slot and the time economy it enabled vouched for the identity of addresses, a self that was responsible for its own sentences was something the communications networks needed to invent so that people would not stop writing letters, because people no longer were themselves:

> In a network such as the one . . . modern, twentieth-century technology is creating via electronic interconnections (telephones, televisions, computers, the postal service, etc.), it is necessary to invent or to establish something that belongs to the statement that is produced and heard, something to which it can be attributed. . . . On principle, someone must be addressable as the producer of statements, and on principle someone must serve as the statement's recipient.[35]

Since nothing circulates in postal channels unless a self remains identical to itself for at least $1/2W$ seconds (minimal correspondence) and thereby guarantees the coherence of its statements, in an act of preventive justice, the postal system rules out the insanity defense. Anyone who dissociates at a frequency more than half that at which he or she writes and receives letters—as Malte Laurids Brigge did, in communications-theoretical terms—no longer is a self, but insane. Letters from nonselves such as children or the mentally ill, however, amount to nothing more than waste in postal channels, and therefore cannot be posted. Every man and every woman who deposits a letter in a mailbox concludes a contract with the postal system,[36] after all, and people who have not completed their seventh year of life or are otherwise in a "condition of diseased disruption of mental activity"[37] are incapable of concluding contracts. Children and other lunatics thus are "not capable of transferring possession of letters written by

[them] or of taking [possession] of extrinsic letters."[38] The postal system consequently assumed no liability for such dispatches. Everyone who mails letters also makes a sworn deposition to power that he or she does not suffer from childhood or any other mental illness.

And therefore W.A.S.T.E. exists, pure and simple. That, of course, is the acronym for a postal system in Thomas Pynchon's *Crying of Lot 49*, which sends only the messages of children and the insane, and therefore posts the absolutely unpostable. Those who are excluded from the postal "there is" await an empire where the world is made up of everything that is waste, and they do so *per definitionem* in silence.[39] Because anything that cannot be posted does not exist, Tristero's Empire is history's precise Other. Since the dawning of the media age, people's ability to preserve the memory of themselves for the duration of a sampling interval is techno-genic. The anthropological conditions for the exchange of letters changed into historical ones. If in Justi's day the unity of self-consciousness had been transcendental and the possibility of writing letters therefore given a priori to man, since Rowland Hill, the knowledge that "man himself must first have become *calculable, regular, necessary*" in order to achieve such ends was long overdue.[40]

ENVELOPES

Standardizations bring about chain reactions. In the same way the penny standard resulted in the standardization of postal interfaces, mailboxes and mail slots in turn induced proposals for the standardization of letters themselves in order to bring letter writing up to a standard that corresponded to the writers' permanent connectedness and the increased frequency of deliveries. "Every one now uses envelopes," Captain Basil Hall wrote in a letter to Rowland Hill, "which save a world of time; and if you were to furnish the means of closing the letter by an adhesive corner a still further saving of time would take place."[41] The result, of course, was the invention of the adhesive envelope. And once again, mechanized mass production followed on the heels of standardization. On December 15, 1840, Rowland Hill's brother Edwin invented the legendary envelope-folding machine, which later became a sensation at the London World Exhibition in 1851.[42] The standard envelopes it produced enabled still further mechanization of postal channels in the next generation of the Hill family: in the 1850's, Rowland Hill's son Pearson invented the stamping machine.[43]

But that was not all. Even before he set out to increase and accelerate the circulation of textual communication by bringing it up to standard, Rowland Hill made sure in the first place that there was a material basis for the discursive proliferation expected from penny postage. In 1835, he received His Majesty's Patent No. 6762 for inventing a rotary printing press. Louis Robert already had launched the production of continuous paper in 1799 using what came to be known in English as a Fourdrinier, a machine in which the web of paper is formed on an endless traveling wire screen, which Bryan Donkin steadily improved after 1803[44] and which the English papermakers Henry and Sealy Fourdrinier perfected in 1847. And in 1811, Friedrich König had invented the high-speed press, which combined all the stages of work involved in the printing process within a single rotary motion.[45] What was lacking was a synthesis of the two technologies—but only until the day Rowland Hill combined the Fourdrinier's new machine for the production of endless paper rolls with a printing technique that involved mounting the typeface on a cylinder and so enabled the application of ink without any interruption in the press's rotary movement.[46] Hill's machine simultaneously printed eight thousand double-sided and sixteen thousand single-sided sheets of newspaper per hour, thus surpassing the production levels of traditional high-speed presses ten times over. And newspapers, after all, were not the last ones to benefit from Hill's radical postage reduction five years later (which they promoted with appropriate propaganda, for example in the *Times*). The increase in transmission capacity via the penny post might have been complemented by an increase in the production capacity of the medium for storage. But Hill's efforts were frustrated by lack of access to a government stamp, which every page of printed newspaper had to bear, according to the wishes of the Inland Revenue Department at the time. Every single sheet of English newspaper thus had to pass through the government Stamp Office, a production route that was completely inconsistent with the rotary printing press, which processed endless rolls of paper. Hill's requests for permission to attach the government stamp to his machines were left unanswered, and as a result,

England had to wait another thirty-five years for the introduction of rotary printing.[47]

Had Hill succeeded with his printing press, the only thing missing would have been some kind of reading machine, and all of England's written communication would have been completely standardized and mechanized, from production right through distribution to reception.

CHAPTER THIRTEEN

Hill/Babbage/Bentham: The Mechanical Alliance of 1827

The model for machines that economize time and discourse as remorselessly as the penny post is to be found in disciplinary systems—as we have known since *Discipline and Punish*. Nowhere was this more unconditionally true than in precisely the case of the penny post. Rowland Hill, after all—as the member of a family that represented something of a task force for radical Utilitarianism in England—had worked at reforming the English educational system literally from his childhood on, striving to transform schools into disciplinary machines that were constructed on the principle of maximal time management.[1] In the beginning, characteristically enough, there was the reform of the school bell at Hill's school, where his father was principal. The bell was sounded at such irregular intervals that the tormented twelve-year-old Rowland did not rest until this deficiency in time management was remedied by a clear delegation of responsibility and a reform of the system of punishments.[2] Hill eventually became principal of the boarding school, and in 1822, he and his brother Matthew published their *Plans for the Government and Liberal Instruction of Boys in Large Numbers*: blueprints for the construction of surveillance machinery that produced exhaustive time management as the function of a system of power-action feedback.

"Soon after Midsummer," Hill reported in his diary in 1816, "I established a Court of Justice in the School. The judge is chosen monthly by the boys. The sheriff and the keeper of the records are chosen in the same manner, the attorney and solicitor-general are appointed by me. The judge appoints the inferior officers, as the clerk and crier of the Court, the constables, etc. The jury consists of six boys, chosen by ballot."[3] Two years later, the system of self-surveillance was completed with the introduction of an elected magistrate: "This officer shall have the appointment of the constables, who shall be under his direction. These officers shall constitute the police, and their duty shall be the detection, and, in some cases, the punishment of crime. . . . It shall be considered the duty of the magistrate to examine into every offence, and punish the aggressor as early as possible after the offence is committed."[4]

"Quis custodiet ipsos custodes?"—one of the "most puzzling of political questions" according to the testimony of probably the greatest surveillance expert of the time[5]—found its answer in a system where power, although nominally given to the leader, actually was produced by an entire apparatus in which the watchmen were themselves the watched.[6] There had been similar institutions of microjustice in schools long before the Hill brothers, of course. But in their efforts to increase control within pedagogical institutions, both Batencourt in the seventeenth century and Demia at the beginning of the eighteenth had simply had their students replicate the pedagogical macrosystem in its entirety as a microsystem.[7] At Hazelwood and Bruce Castle, by contrast, the Hills mapped a state model rather than a pedagogical model onto their schools, thus suggesting that the state was itself a gigantic pedagogical machine. But above all, the Hills replaced previous systems of punishment with a microeconomy in which the general equivalent was time. Every student had a number of coupons, of which a certain quantity represented the value of a day off from school. Every transgression resulted in the judge sentencing the students to hand over a certain number of time units, and the sheriff kept precise records regarding the status of each student's individual account.[8] All actions thus could be expressed in time, exchanged with time, and transferred into an economy of time capitalization. If not the origin of the postage stamp as a historical fact, this was at least the origin of its standardizing and economizing function. The introduction of a standard for signifiers was anticipated by the introduction of a standard for time, the one-penny postage stamp by the one-minute time stamp. The penny post was the result of applying the principle of a disciplinary system to a system of communication. It was founded—in the not-unbroken tradition of Justi—on a time economy developed and tested in the schools and police institutions of the Hills. After Rowland Hill's time stamp, the time economy was based on debt itself, just as the economy of the postal system was based on the debt emerging from the circulation of signifiers after the postage stamp. This meant that the general equivalent made possible by the circulation of signifiers no longer was the interpretation of the signified, the concept,[9] but the postage stamp itself.

The exchange value of symbols, the signified, no longer found expression in the timbre of a calling or a transcendental signified, but instead in the characteristic stamp of the postal medium: denominations of postal value rather than denominations of value in meaning, standards rather than norms. The result was that the process of circulation no longer produced individuals and their education, but media systems and their empires.

The prototype of the modern English communications system was a school, Bruce Castle, which became a "machine" in one of Rowland Hill's metaphors, a machine in which power differentiated time and occupied it completely in order to channel every individual moment to its predetermined use: "Indeed the whole machine of school (for such is the regularity of our proceedings that the appellation is not misapplied) is now become so perfect that we are able to appropriate every minute of the day to its respective use; and the bells ring, the classes assemble, break up, take their meals &c. with such clock-like regularity that it has the appearance almost of magic."[10]

A phenomenon as magical as this, of course, did not remain a secret to the other machine fanatics in England. It was thus no accident that Charles Babbage, constructor of the Difference and Analytical Engines, sent both of his sons to Bruce Castle. Rowland Hill became acquainted with Babbage on the occasion of his son's first day at school, and Babbage's biography even surmises that during a parental visit to Bruce Castle he might have given Hill the idea of applying rational principles to the postal system—the same principles that led the former to construct a disciplinary machine and the latter a calculating engine.[11] The abstruse structure of transport costs had led Babbage to believe that "the costs for determining the price of an article must form a portion of its costs in every case." [12] It was no different for the postal system, where the cost of assessing the letter's value contributed to the expense of its conveyance— and for that reason, Babbage spoke out in favor of uniform postal rates. Moreover, in order to eliminate the letter's physical as well as its representational relationship to the earth, Babbage came up with a "means for transmitting letters enclosed in small cylinders, along wires fixed to poles on towers, or on church steeples."[13] Babbage's main concern in this—as in the construction of his machines—was standardization: from the development of a technical writing necessary for its construction, which Babbage wanted to make standard for all patent writing, to the standardization of English production of screws and nuts, to the standard logarithmic tables that were to be calculated and printed by the Difference Engine. Discipline, according to Foucault, functions "as machinery for adding up and capitalizing time,"[14] and therefore is itself an adding machine. If so, Babbage's Difference Engine had given concrete form to the metaphor of the school to which he sent his children and was also the medium that transferred the principle of time capitalization from the disciplinary machine to the postal machine. As a metaphor of discipline, the calculating engine could become the *tertium comparationis* of the school and the postal system.

But Babbage, the constructor of the first Universal Calculating Engine, was not the only one to hardwire his plans to those of Rowland Hill in 1827. Jeremy Bentham, the constructor of the first Universal Disciplinary Engine, also paid a personal visit to Hill's school at Bruce Castle that year. In 1822, Rowland Hill had sent a copy of his *Plans for Government* to Bentham, who read it with such enthusiasm that he tossed all of his own plans for school reform out the window.[15] Such enthusiasm is hardly a cause for surprise: after all, Hill's school machine realized all the basic principles of the panoptic machine, which sought to establish an uninterrupted state of surveillance produced by those who were being watched themselves. Both machines manufactured time that was completely occupied by power—that "marvellous machine,"[16] the Panopticon, created a permanent state of visibility, just as the magic of Bruce Castle created a time continuum, neither of which allowed a single minute to escape the clockwork of power.

If Bentham had not died in 1832, undoubtedly he would have greeted the penny post with a new level of enthusiasm. The solidarity between the Panopticon and the penny post existed not so much at the level of power production, after all, but was more a matter of the rationality of power that underlay both. This rationality, this fundamental characteristic, per-

haps the most decisive thing about panopticism in general, consisted of
the ability to separate the machine's "political technology" from its specific use.[17] A groundbreaking transformation in the technology of power
had occurred: functionalization. The penny post and the Panopticon were
technologies consisting entirely of relationships between factors that were
utterly interchangeable. The Panopticon was a diagram, a universal and
"abstract machine."[18]

> To say all in one word, it will be found applicable, I think, without excep-
> tion, to all establishments whatsoever. . . . No matter how different, or even
> opposite the purpose: whether it be that of *punishing the incorrigible, guard-
> ing the insane, reforming the vicious, confining the suspected, employing the
> idle, maintaining the helpless, curing the sick, instructing the willing* in any
> branch of industry, or *training the rising race* in the path of *education.*[19]

The active intentions of power, and therefore the social classes of bodies
entered into the panoptic machine, were randomly interchangeable, that
is, variables in a functional calculus. The penny post functionalized its recipients the same way the Panopticon did: it made no difference who was
entered at the other side of the mailbox or mail slot. The network ex-
trapolated from its nodes; the system was closed with regard to the data
or content it processed. And as if the penny post actually was a Panopticon that integrated the most diverse bio-political functions, each member
of the Hill family who had once held a post in systems specializing in discipline switched over to a job within the postal system. Thus, for example, Rowland Hill's brother Frederic, who became an inspector of prisons
in 1835, moved on to the Post Office in 1851.[20]

The radically democratic character of both the Panopticon and the
penny post lay in abstraction or universality. In the fabric of power,
everyone was interchangeable, and with regard to the functioning of
power, all were equal. For that reason and that reason alone, nobles such
as the marquis of Londonderry resisted slots in their mahogany doors—
not to mention the power of penny postage to mobilize the masses. People sent letters by penny post, Harriet Martineau wrote, as if they were
one of the ones in power—and for the simple reason that even the latter
were still in power only "as if" they were. The Panopticon was applica-
ble to every kind of bio-politics, Bentham wrote, whether it be education,

healing, production, or punishment. Contents and applications were programs that ran (or would run) on machines like the Panopticon, the penny post, or the Analytical Engine (the computer's precursor) only because such machines were blind to them. Programs for the Analytical Engine, Ada Lovelace wrote, could compute every type of process involving relative change between two or more random elements.[21] That the machine or power became abstract, Deleuze has said, merely meant that it became programmable. But power itself became machinelike in the process. The rationality of power—functionality or universality—requires the prior standardization of the data it processes—via postage stamps or punch cards, it makes no difference. And it formed a mechanical alliance among the machines of Bentham, Hill, and Babbage, which processed numbers, discourse, and bodies in accordance with the same economic principles. Disciplinary machine, postal machine, adding machine: after their interconnection was established, bodies, discourses, and numbers were one and the same with regard to the technology of power: data, and as such, contingent.

CHAPTER FOURTEEN

Mail in 1855: A Misuse of Love Letters

The invention of the postage stamp already implied its export across the borders of the land and the empire of Great Britain. What eliminated borders as far as the postal system was concerned, or at least made them anachronistic, could not very well be confined within such boundaries itself. In places where the democratization of discourse via postage stamps had not "protected" the so-called "good people" from "violent revolution," as it had in Harriet Martineau's England, a revolution was at times precisely what was needed in order to introduce that democratization (or postage stamp). So it was in France, where the July Monarchy's aversion to all forms of tax reduction (and postage was seen as a tax) thus far had succeeded in preventing a *réforme postale*. Owing to such resistance, postal reform likewise was set in motion with equal success after the February Revolution: Etienne Arago, the head of postal administration, and Saint-Priest, the French Rowland Hill, both pushed for state discursive regulation in the form of tax reduction and the *timbre* post. Given the political function Harriet Martineau ascribed to the penny post, it hardly is surprising that the Cavaignac government considered the "humanization of the masses"[1] by mail such an urgent matter after the July Insurrection that it was prepared to carry out postal reform even at the expense of the elimination of the salt tax—a sacred cow in all French revolutions.[2] Only the envelope, the mass production of which had resulted from postal reform in England, would remain unknown to the French. When several liberals attempted to set the maximum weight for the minimum postage at 10 instead of only 7.5 grams, Goudchaux advanced the paradoxical argument that a higher maximum would benefit only the wealthy. Heavier letters, that is, were merely the result of using envelopes, "a new and thoroughly aristocratic fashion."[3] On August 24, 1848, the National Assembly passed a resolution in favor of introducing a penny post along the lines of the British model: a uniform rate of twenty centimes and obligatory prepayment, that is, postage stamps.

In the German lands, where the state was more prone to making revolutions than the people, the postage stamp became a condition for realizing the German-Austrian Postal Union.

But a tiny postal district beat all European and non-European states to the punch in importing Hill's innovation: the Canton of Zurich, the home of Gottfried Keller. It was here that a misuse of love letters[4] commenced in 1843, which was to reach Berlin seven years later, at the same time as Keller. The malaise that Keller was forced to witness as it spread to Berlin between 1850 and 1855 and that produced a certain Viktor Störteler might have borne the name of Rowland Hill on two counts, were it not for the fact that the media, unlike literature, are fundamentally anonymous. What scandalized Keller was a literary machine that ran the same way as Hill's postal machine, that is, for no reason. Or at least not for a transcendental reason, which is what turned writers into renowned authors—like Keller—who were the true sons of their symbolic fathers, "Goethe and Tieck."[5] Viggi, by contrast, wished to join the ranks of the hack writers' army engaged in a different sort of literature, the style and content of which were not translations from the mouth of Mother Nature, at whose altars Goethe and Tieck once had made their sacrifices, but instead were dictated by the output velocity of the new rotary presses, which it had once been Rowland Hill's job to maximize.

Such presses, Benjamin wrote, changed the structure of literary production near the end of the first third of the century. "Through the feuilleton, belles lettres gained access to a market in the daily newspapers."[6] On these "thousands of gray pages,"[7] as Keller described the products of the rotary press, a literature emerged that was written not by unmistakable, individual authors, but by hack writers who were as randomly interchangeable as their pseudonyms. Hack writers produced standard literature for a medium so large in capacity, due to its speed of reproduction, that it ruled out the author's irreplaceability, which had made a Goethe out of Goethe, from the start. Not for nothing had Goethe's publisher, Georg Joachim Göschen, been of the opinion as early as 1804 that "one could perhaps print much, but never anything good" on Friedrich König's high-speed press.[8] The secret of production for the writer-subjects of the rotary press was not individuality and personality, but simply the technologies that showed how even more words could be made from words and nothing but words: nothing good, that is, in the sense of Classicism.

"Kunibert vom Meere" copies his lectures out of a book stolen from the library; "George d'Esan" translates the feuilletons of French newspapers into German. Keller certainly left no doubt about what constituted authorship: possession of copyrights to the speeches or texts one circulated.[9] But standard texts have no originator; they spring from the sourceless drift of words and never leave it. And because what words already had said was long since forgotten in this continuously branching mail, hack writers simply made only words about the making of words itself. In other words: they made modern literature. "I had nothing to write about except writing itself, so to speak. When I dipped the pen in the ink I wrote about this ink."[10] Keller denounced the very autoreferentiality that literary theory now sees as the characteristic feature of modern literature; he incriminated the folly of a doubling that allowed writing to make itself its own subject matter—a folly Flaubert wanted to see subsume literature itself at the end of *Bouvard et Pécuchet*: the copying of books, all books, including the book *Bouvard et Pécuchet*. The catalogue of all the catalogues that do not contain themselves. . . . It was with this paradox, Foucault wrote, that modern literature began.[11]

Once Viggi sets about making his wife, Gritli, the muse of his literary production, everything proceeds like a caricature of the correspondence between Kleist and Wilhelmine von Zenge, which indeed itself was only a caricature of Romantic correspondence distorted to the point that it became recognizable. Here, no differently than for Kleist or Brentano, a reading program stands at the outset of letter writing. But instead of including *Wallenstein* (for the former) or Goethe's poems (for the latter), Viggi's program contains nothing but titles like *Spring Letters from a Lonely Woman*[12]—books that at best might induce pleasure in a woman reader, the same sort of pleasure that had spread like an epidemic called "feminine reading addiction" in the eighteenth century, but that certainly could not establish an acquaintance with her inner person. Books that affect the body rather than effecting education are works of the devil: "For the devil had got into her husband and he presented her with every bit of boring and heartless affectation and pseudo-aesthetic rubbish he could lay hands on."[13] As though he were quoting from Kleist's letters to Zenge, Viggi gives lectures on the usefulness of observing Nature and advises his wife, again no differently than Kleist had advised his fiancée, to "note down similar observations and then show him what she had written."[14]

Yet the function for which Viktor Störteler tries to train his wife is not that of a reader, but of a discursive clerk. The purpose of the postal madness Viggi unleashes is not to enlighten Gritli as to her "highest duty," as the transcendental source of language and consequently of individuals, but instead to entice her into a simple lust for making words, as befits her foil in the text, Kätter Ambach, who "liked [nothing] better than writing letters."[15] If Gritli's duty nevertheless catches up with her at the end of the novel, when she gives true love (and for Keller, too, especially for him, this meant motherly love), then Keller was responsible, and not Viggi. The latter's postal machine skips over the very condition that made it possible for Romantic correspondence to function as the logistics of the poet's dream and the education of mothers: the condition that women could not make literature, but only intimate confessions. Viggi treats a woman's words not as translations of Nature, but as what they are: words. He takes for granted what Fichte had disproved in his *Science of Rights*: that clear and publishable texts could be produced on both sides of the gender divide. Instead of translating the meaning of her (or Wilhelm's) words for his wife and feeding them back to her (and then publishing the translation, as Schlegel did), Viggi wants to make a facsimile of Gritli's letters on the spot.[16] This amounted to nothing less than equating the intimate handwriting of letters with the typeset characters of a book. The difference that had allowed knowledge of women's letters and diaries to qualify its owners as psychologists and poets in 1800 thus might have been erased. Unlike Gritli, who translates Wilhelm's belletristic art into authentic love, Viggi treats all letters like postcards: they are addressed to a public audience from the start, always already are underway, are public, and are not in need of interpretation.

Once women no longer were excluded from writing that enjoyed the status of printed text, the discursive order that once had been the order of gender began to wobble; once love letters were misused as postcards, gender differences melted away. In her function as relay between the two men, Gritli writes "like a court clerk";[17] that is, she writes as only men had written up until then. The position she accepts or invents in the communications system is a job that one day would be reserved as a career for women. Copying manuscripts, opening and connecting discursive channels, would be the role of countless women typists and operators in 1900. This future had gotten underway even before the first publication of the *Misused Love Letters*: in 1863, the first woman telegraph operator had been appointed in Baden on personal orders from Grand Duchess Luise.[18] The technical media of transmission opened up jobs for women at the nodes and switchboards of discourse, rather than relegating them to its source (like letters) or to the site of its reception (like books). When Gritli "twists the sex,"[19] she assumes a role in the discourse that previously had been reserved for the secretaries of the spirit. As the first operator in the history of literature, Gritli transfers the text of letters into a mode that already heralded the power of this discursive function under the conditions of future reproduction technologies. After all, it is only by processing their original handwriting into waste that the two men receive delivery of their ephemeral existence from circulation (the one as author, the other as lover). The original, the authentic handwritten text, already is wastepaper by the time the stamp is purchased—its disappearance was the condition under which literary production could operate.

But Gritli was not the only one to effect the suspension of gender difference in literature: this is equally true of her author-husband, who plans to publish their correspondence under a title that dissolves the names of a man and a women into a single, genderless being: "Kurtalwino."[20] And the same was true of Keller himself, who, in admitting the possibility of hommo-sexual correspondents and the misuse of love letters, also had to admit the fact that "in the psyche, there is nothing by which the subject may situate himself as a male or female being."[21] Except for the handwriting and signature, there is nothing about the letters or their content that could identify the gender of their authors. Discriminations of bodies and gender were the discriminations of a discursive order that created literature by means of postal feedback between the handwriting of women readers and the poet's printed text. The suspension of such discrimination thus produced hermaphrodites. The author and women's rights advocate

Fanny Lewald and the author Adolf Wilhelm Stahr, who provided the models for Kätchen Ambach and Viktor Störteler and who had inspired Keller to write the novella in the first place, were a single "bisexual ink animal" in Keller's eyes.[22] The Age of Goethe came to an end with the distribution of all discursive functions of the postal system to both sexes, which could be explained only with the help of theories on infantile sexuality.[23] The novella, however, went one step further. In the relation of sexuality to truth, it broached the subject of the postal margins of the hermaphroditic turn, albeit belatedly.

These margins inscribed the wayward drift of words, which was literature and pleasure to Viggi and Kätter, with an economy that admittedly did not produce any works of literature, but did produce a market for literature in the daily press. "He [Viggi] was already having difficulty paying the postage on all the meaningless letters, the printed or lithographed circulars, manifestoes, and prospectuses that daily flew hither and thither and were worth less than nothing. He sighed as he cut off the postage stamps from the ever shorter strip, while the solid, profitable, and stamped business letters grew fewer and fewer."[24]

By penny post and in no other way was the feuilleton-novel finally able to arrive in villages like Seldwyla. That dispatches could flit back and forth on a daily basis was not merely an effect of the postage stamp—to be more precise: it was an effect of prepayment. It also was the condition necessary for the dissemination of daily newspapers and their feuilletons beyond the city limits of the metropolis. Letters that circulated through the channels of the postal system and at its frequency thus were devoid of content—at least as far as individuality and intimacy were concerned. Such letters were subjected to a standard that was not established with regard to them at all, but rather with an eye to modern technologies of reproduction. At bottom, the postage stamp and rotary press were utterly in unison, not only in a historical sense—take Hill's biography for example, which proceeds from the invention of the rotary press to the invention of the postage stamp—but also in a direct sense. The use of prestamped envelopes, which initially was earmarked by Rowland Hill as a means of prepayment and which later found its unlettered version in the postage stamp, was first proposed for the dispatch of newspapers by Charles Knight.[25] Knight was the publisher and editor of *Penny Maga-*

zine, the journal of the Society for the Diffusion of Useful Knowledge, to which both Rowland Hill and Charles Babbage belonged. Keller's mention of lithography therefore was anything but coincidental: it marked the achievement of an "essentially new stage"[26] in the technology of reproduction. Invented by the Munich actor and author Alois Senefelder in 1798,[27] lithography allowed graphics "to illustrate everyday life"[28]—because it was the first medium that could keep up not only with the presses, but also (as Benjamin forgot) with the frequency of penny post delivery.

Postage stamps treat all letters as potential printed matter. In the system of a postal system that would not and could not exist without stamps, letters circulate only under the historical a priori of technical replicability. The standard to which all handwriting and intimacies are subjected is the distribution of printed matter. Viggi's idea of making facsimiles of his and Gritli's letters simply obeys the postal system's command: it merely recognizes letters as what they always were capable of being after Rowland Hill. And love letters that could be addressed to everyone are indeed "worth less than nothing." But once there are stamps, the very existence of which implies media of reproduction, it seems that sending love letters by mail is possible only at the price of their misuse.

Because letters still could be posted only on the a priori historical condition of their misuse, they did not serve for the construction of subject matter in either psychology or pedagogy. They ceased to exist as media technologies of the soul or the individual. As a result, however, it no longer was possible to ignore the implications for literature, which had made itself the mouthpiece for psychiatry and pedagogy. One possible response was to stop talking about love, as Kafka did, in order to talk about the postal system. Another was to issue a repudiation of the postal system and letters, as Keller did, and to prescribe a program of rehabilitation in the bosom of Nature for pedagogues like Wilhelm, who had become entangled in the simulacra of the post. Such a program cleansed and refined them for true love, the authenticity of which was proven not by the text of letters, but by the symbols of a genealogy revealed and concealed by the earth itself (the Celtic grave). But literature could not speak of such love. After all: "Love is a postal system. If it were not for the distances and accesses, the routes and relays, the disruptions and connections, the divisions and channels—we would know nothing of love."[29] The postal system's entry into the age of media rationality, its formation into a closed system of communication that processes information using standards prescribed by the technical media of reproduction, puts an end to an epoch of literature in which the postal system was not yet a misuse of love letters and literature was still a *scientia sexualis*. Keller himself put an end to this end in his novella, even if it was an improbable one: in 1874, when the *Misused Love Letters* were published in part 2 of the *People of Seldwyla*, everything spoke against the eventuality that the love letters Viktor Störteler and Kätter Ambach "had rewritten" should "long since [have] vanished into oblivion,"[30] according to the end of the novella. After all, the World Postal Union had only just been founded in Bern.

CHAPTER FIFTEEN

The World Postal System, or The End of the World

The good fortune of an omnipresent neighborhood, which Viennese mail-boxes presented to Stifter in 1844, owed its existence to a *Medienräson* that—as Keller's novella illustrates—emphasized precisely the closed nature of information systems with regard to a discursive function such as authorship, which is at odds with standardization *per definitionem*. Thus, developing the logic of neighborhood was not left up to poets like Stifter, but was assigned instead to mathematicians—and paranoiacs. In 1852, nine years after the postage stamp had begun to infiltrate the European states and to establish an international communications system, two London mathematics students presented Augustus DeMorgan with a problem: was it possible to demonstrate as either true or false the proposition that the countries on every political map could be shaded in only four colors such that all neighboring countries had a different color.[1] Once the letter had become universally addressable by "attaching a stamp," the size, shape, location, economy, and climate of any given country were completely irrelevant in cartographic terms, and the *couleur* of any given state was merely a mathematical property. "No longer does any political, physical, cultural, economic, or linguistic boundary obstruct the route of such a letter in the channels of the World Postal Service."[2]

There was as yet no World Postal Union when DeMorgan confronted the Four Color Problem in 1852, but there was a German-Austrian Postal Union, which had been founded on April 6, 1850, as the first international postal district to eliminate all the territorial definitions and boundaries of individual postal administrations within its jurisdiction. "All state territories . . . belonging to the German-Austrian Postal Union shall . . . represent an undivided postal district in matters pertaining to the mail."[3] Arti-

cle 10 of the treaty mandated the erection of a homogeneous space for the
flow of information, and Article 18 named the means for accomplishing
it: "For exchange correspondence inside Union states, prepayment shall
take place on principle, and collection shall occur via postage stamps as
soon as feasible."[4] "As soon as feasible" meant seven months later in the
case of Prussia—that is, when the first Prussian postage stamps were issued on November 15, 1850, after the postal administration already had
been directed to manufacture and sell stamps "by means of which the
prepayment of letters may be effected as provided under the terms of the
tariff by affixing them to the letter" on December 21, 1849.[5] After the
prepaid stamp utterly had banished differences in distance from the face
of the earth (and thus the earth itself from union territory), the postal systems for each of the seventeen member states could select the shortest
route inside union territory. And above all: "The collection of special
transit postage from correspondents shall cease for all correspondence . . .
transported within union territory."[6]

It was not the Taxis and their Goethe who established the empire as
Klüber had dreamed of it, a region without transit postage, but Rowland
Hill and his postage stamp. That empire would not be known as the Holy
Roman Empire or German Poetry, but as the German-Austrian Postal
Union, or the World Postal Union. And because its neighborhoods eliminated the world as a space of distances in terms of both communications
technology and cartography, the condition for the empire's possibility was
situated beyond The Individual. The demonstration that every single one
of its neighborhoods could be produced with the aid of a four-color standard was not provided by DeMorgan and his successors, after all, but by
a computer in 1976.[7] Showing remarkable historical clairvoyance, the
American postal system in turn celebrated this demonstration with a special stamp that conjoined the medium of the message ("Four Colors Suf-
fice") with the message of the medium in a moment of sheer autoreferentiality [see Figure 5].

The homogenization of space in terms of media economy and semiotic
technology obeyed the commands of another spatial revolution in transport technology—at least in the case of the German-Austrian Postal
Union. Such was explicitly the matter at hand in the "written proposition" with which Austrian Court Chamber President von Klübeck and

FOUR COLORS
SUFFICE

FIGURE 5. U.S. postal system as an example of autoreferentiality.

Prussian Postmaster General von Schraper made the first drive toward a mutual postal union. "The establishment of extensive railway connections cutting across state frontiers," Klübeck and Schraper wrote to the several German postal administrations, "will give a completely different structure to international transportation in the immediate future. There will ensue the urgent necessity to select the shortest route for the transport of correspondence."[8] Because railways—and telegraphy, one would need to add—must have produced uniform space from the very beginning, the postal system had no choice but to bring the legal regulations and norms of symbol processing up to the standards of these technologies. At a conference in Dresden to which Klübeck and Schraper had invited representatives of the German postal administrations in 1848, such plans were frustrated in a remarkable manner by the fact that intelligence regarding "the postal norms and institutions existing in the German states"—that is, the endless differentiations of rates, laws, and units—quite simply was unavailable.[9] Consequently, in a second attempt at postal union in 1849, Prussian Minister of Commerce von der Heydt had to connect in series the homogenization of space and the standardization of weights and measures. Articles 6 and 7 prescribed the geographical mile (7420.438 meters = $1/15$ of an equatorial degree) as the exclusive standard for measuring distance and the customs pound (500 French grams) for measuring weight.[10]

With the founding of the German-Austrian Postal Union, the realization of Klüber's dream appeared fleetingly on the horizon of history: a postal empire that was to have the former states of the Rhenish League as its nucleus and a communications technology answering to the name of Thurn and Taxis. As early as 1842, after all, Austria had introduced a postal rate that was so uniform one might almost have called it "English." And on the basis of that uniform postage, postal treaties were concluded the same year with Bavaria, Baden, and Saxony, and the following year with Thurn and Taxis, thus bringing Austria together with southern and central Germany in a uniform system.[11] And yet: neither Austria as a European power worthy of the name nor Thurn and Taxis survived the end of the postal union that emerged from the confluence of these efforts. No history leads from the German-Austrian Postal Union to the World Postal Union—as historical scholarship would like to have it—but instead there is a rupture, or a war. Before a postal privy councilor by the name of Stephan could make history with the inauguration of the World Postal Union, which was founded at the Assembly House of the Estates in Bern on October 9, 1874, another history had to be put to an end.

Immediately following the outbreak of war in 1866, Heinrich Stephan presented a memorandum to the Prussian General Post Office calling for the elimination of the Thurn and Taxis Post. Such proposals, of course, had found a welcome ear in that office for centuries. On July 17, 1866, Stephan therefore already had authorization to march into Frankfurt am Main with the Prussian troops, where he summarily confiscated the Taxis postal administration on behalf of the Prussian government.[12] A declaration was extorted from the members of the General Postal Administration stating that they were prepared, "without impinging on the oath of service we have sworn to H[is] H[ighness] the Prince of Thurn and Taxis, to comply unhesitatingly with the regulations of the R[oyal] Pr[ussian] Administration under the prevailing conditions, and to refrain from anything that could be detrimental to the interests of the [R]oyal Pr[ussian] Government."[13] In protest, the princely General Post Director Baron von Schele suspended the performance of his official duties, and Stephan severed the connection between the princely General Post Administration and His Serene Highness in Regensburg.[14] "It is the postal Königgrätz that is being fought here, and I am at once both commander in chief and a fighting soldier!" Stephan wrote to his wife on September 20, 1866.[15] Prince Maximilian Karl von Thurn und Taxis signed a formal capitulation in Berlin on January 28, 1867: in return for a settlement of merely three million talers (Taxis had demanded ten million), all of his postal rights were transferred to the Prussian state on July 1, 1867, along with all accessories in mobile and stationary property, inventory, and so on. Thus, the former postal empire had been wiped off the map once and for all,[16] and thus, too, its own dream of a world postal empire had gone up in smoke. Yet in 1841—more or less directly in response to English postal reform—Taxis Postal Secretary Johann von Herrfeldt already had attempted to lay the "Foundations for a World Postal Union"—as his memorandum was entitled.[17]

Finally, when the war of 1870–71 broke the resistance even of France, which had feared for its revenues from transit commerce, nothing more stood in the way of realizing the plans for a world postal system that Stephan already had formulated in a "Memorandum on the General Postal Congress" of 1868.[18] On July 1, 1875, the Treaty for the Foundation of a General Postal Union went into effect, thus transforming the European states, Russia, Egypt, Turkey, and the United States into a "single postal district"—according to Article 1[19]—within which all political boundaries completely vanished with regard to the postal exchange of letters. Nietzsche was thus off by only a week when he wrote to his sister on July 8, 1875: "Today is the day the postal treaty of all nations goes into effect. With the same stamp I devote to you today, I could reach America, Spain, Asiatic Russia, etc."[20] With the same stamp, but *only* with a stamp. The fungibility of all conceivable nations, after all, was an effect of Article 6 of the treaty: "The postage of dispatches can be effected only by means of the postage stamps valid in the country of origin."[21]

In the years that followed, the elimination of the world (and removal of its distances) continued at a frantic pace, as the hegemony of the World Postal Union grew in size. During the first two years, such expansion was carried out under the banner of network hookups for the colonial empires. The admission of British India and the French colonies occurred in 1876. In 1877, the British and Spanish colonies, the Dutch East and West Indies, Dutch Guyana, and the Portuguese and Danish colonies joined, as did Japan, Brazil, and Persia.[22] A topology of the margin, in which the center of the empires was at once the point where all its margins intersected, a topology in which all points could be reached by the same postage stamp, transformed the conception of the exotic, which, due to the time-consuming travel and inaddressable remoteness involved, usually had been defined as a Utopia. Geographical spaces became jumbled subsets of postal space. "Natives of Southwest Africa adorned with orange-colored robes and riding on oxen and dromedaries," one lecturer told an audience at the Society for Geographical Studies and Colonies (of all places):

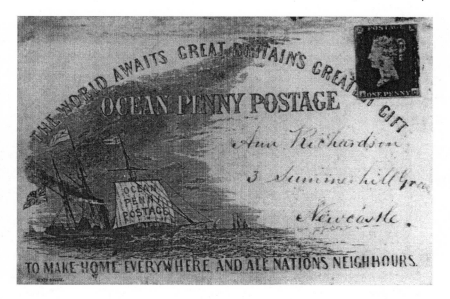

FIGURE 6. Ocean penny postage.

are the representatives of the German transport and express mail; khaki-clad Ascaris and half-Arabs are the swift foot messengers in East Africa, who pass through swamps and lagoons to cover fifty miles a day. Thus, even when he has become estranged from all other manifestations of culture, and even when all the other elements of connection fail, the German colonist finds a piece of world mail, and in it a courier of the homeland greeted with joy.[23]

In the World Postal Union, the homeland was sublated. "To make home everywhere and all nations neighbors" had been the goal promoted on the envelopes of an Anglo-American society as early as 1850.[24] Founded by the Connecticut philanthropist Elihu Burritt in 1847, the League of Universal Brotherhood had given itself the mission of providing America and the entire world with ocean penny postage, which was to be a gift to every homesick European emigrant [see Figure 6]. Transatlantic and transpacific penny postage would create a homeland of global dimensions, thus making homesickness impossible once and for all.[25] As the plan was realized, however, its pure-hearted benevolence increasingly revealed the distinctive features of imperialism. The Colonial Penny Postage

Association was brought to life as early as 1853, and in addition to Burritt, its members included Sir John Lubbock and Baron de Rothschild. Yet the empire's emergence from the one-penny stamp did not become an actual event until 1898. After decades of effort on the part of Henniker Heaton, an Australian emigrant who had returned to England to become the "Marconi of hearts,"[26] the first Imperial Postal Conference passed a resolution in 1898 calling for the introduction of imperial penny postage.[27] Burritt's dream of a ubiquitous homeland thus found a home in the British Empire. Lord Salisbury got to the point of the matter when he described Heaton as a "supporter of mine, who is engaged in sticking the Empire together with a penny stamp."[28]

Nor did Burritt's "Ocean Penny Postage Campaign" remain entirely without consequences elsewhere. In 1862, the American postmaster general, Montgomery Blair, appointed himself the spokesman of Universal Brotherhood and initiated the first international postal congress, which took place the following year in Paris and was remarkable for two reasons. The first is its recommendation for the introduction of the metric system in the calculation of distances and the gram as the unit for measuring weight. The second is the name of one of the two British delegates: Frederic Hill.[29] In 1878, at the second World Postal Congress (again in Paris), Elihu Burritt and his league finally were cured of their homesickness, only a year before Burritt's death: the member states of the World Postal Union resolved to introduce worldwide uniform postage at a rate of twenty-five centimes for letters. "Distance thus had ceased to be considered a factor in the collection of postage for letter conveyance the world over."[30]

In the symbolic world—as the discourse of Universal Brotherhood illustrates—global uniform postage anticipated an effect that would be produced in the world of bodies, according to Virilio, only with the supersonic vectors of airplanes and long-range ballistic weapons: the development of an "artificial topological universe: *the direct encounter of every surface of the globe.*"[31] Once the mailbox had created a ubiquitous neighborhood of contact, the World Postal Union made "all nations neighbors," or, in Virilio's words, effected *"the juxtaposition of every locality, all matter."*[32] Since the inception of the World Postal Union, the end of the world is everywhere. Not merely in the sense that the distances separating one place from another had become anachronistic,[33] but also in that the world's margins had moved into the immediate vicinity of a neighborhood everywhere: "The offing was barred by a black bank of clouds, and the tranquil waterway leading to the utmost ends of the earth flowed somber under an overcast sky—seemed to lead into the heart of an immense darkness."[34] The *limes* that drew the line between the ecumenical and its barbaric exterior ran through the hearts of both empires and people. The Thames flowed into the Congo (the Belgian colony with that name joined the World Postal Union in 1866). And because books are letters in time, history itself fell within the territory of the World Postal Union. Conrad's novel thus could begin with a nineteen-hundred-year flashback that addressed the British Empire itself at—and as—"the very end of the world, a sea the colour of lead, a sky the colour of smoke."[35]

Yet the literary techniques of mail and flashbacks corresponded to empirical media of transmission. Thanks to the International Telegraph Union or the World Postal Union, the evil present in distant colonies like India or Australia could strike terror into people's hearts in the metropolis. And these media thus made detective stories possible, stories in which the murderers (who always already have gotten away) exist only postally and the detective solves the case by comparing postmarks and the times required for the arrival of letters, or by studying the Lloyd's registers and the routes of ocean liners. The detective's name is Sherlock Holmes and one such story, which has practically nothing but absentee characters, is called "The Five Orange Pips."

"One day," the only other person present in the story besides Holmes and Watson reports, before fate closes his mouth, too, for all time and the story goes on to thematize discursive margins, "—it was March 1883—a letter with a foreign stamp lay upon the table in front of the colonel's plate. It was not a common thing for him to receive letters, for his bills were all paid in ready money, and he had no friends of any sort. 'From India!' said he as he took it up, 'Pondicherry postmark. What can this be?'"[36] The contents of the letter consist of the colonial wares of the story's title, which—counted and weighed—become the writing on the wall for an Englishman who once followed the Thames into the heart of a darkness that in this case bears the name "Florida." It is as though Burritt's Universal Brotherhood were giving lie to its own name. A universal brotherhood known as the Ku Klux Klan is sending threatening letters to Merry Old England, letters in which the threat of murder emanates from their standard format. The orange pips take on a deadly sense only with the delivery of postal margins—envelope, stamp, address, return address. Such marginalia itself presupposes the discursive system of the World Postal Union (or rather, India's admission to it seven years before the narrated incident). The effect is that the time for action—or for living—available to recipients of the pips is determined entirely by the difference between the speed of the letter and that of the murderers following behind. The conveyance time of the renowned "Indian Overland Post" from Calcutta via Ceylon, Bombay, Brindisi, Bologna, Turin, Mont Cenis, Macon, Paris, and Calais to London[37] is the measure of narrated time. The senders' identity thus is ascertained by correlating the marginal dates that the discursive system of the world postal service had stamped onto the letters with the dates that the murderers' personal transportation had left behind in the registers of Lloyd's (the availability of which in turn depended on Lloyd's telegraphic network).[38] And because identity is nothing but the quality of being the destination of dispatches, in Holmes' case, the media of research and the media of prosecution coincide: post and telegraph. Once the international transport media had become the content of the international communications media (in order to confirm once more McLuhan's axiom that the content of a medium always is another medium),[39] the police knew the whereabouts even of nomads and—due to the time advantage that the post and telegraph have over travel—could arrest them, as well (and the nomads could escape such arrest only by means—the quite terminal means—of a shipwreck).

The World Postal Union transformed the concept of post itself: once global, uniform postage had obliterated the difference between homeland and foreign lands in the letter's form of being, the word "post" was essentially an abstraction from the various material carriers by which information was sent on the earth. All means of transportation, no matter what kind—whether dromedaries, khaki-clad Ascanis, Trans-Siberian or Central Pacific Railways, carrier pigeons, or steamships—always would fall within the concept of "post." As the technical media themselves finally were integrated slowly but surely into the postal system—in Germany, completely, less so in other states—"post" became synonymous with the concept of a General Medium of Transmission. On January 1, 1876, only half a year after the world postal system was launched into operation, telegraphy was placed under postal jurisdiction in the German Empire.[40] The concept "post" was further expanded to include the telephone in 1892 and finally even radio in 1908.[41]

It was thus only a matter of consequence when, in the year that the World Postal Union was founded, Heinrich Stephan informed the Berlin Scientific Association that the maneuverable airship would become the vehicle of postal transportation in the future—once political boundaries and geographical distances had ceased to exist as far as the calculation of communication was concerned. The space homogenized by the standardization of global communications traffic found its mirror image in the "desolate and empty" expanses of an "ocean of air"[42]—the terrain of the world postal system would be the *tohu wabohu* prior to the beginning of Creation. Departure for the prehistoric end of the world: it would, Virilio wrote, "indisputably come with the generation of vehicles that eliminate the space of the human race."[43] Stephan himself called the propulsion principle of these "vehicles" by its rightful name: "the generation of forward motion from the repulsion of rockets."[44] Stephan's description of the airship merely brought Kleist's *Project for a Cannonball Postal System* up to date with the latest standards in the technology of artillery weapons. And there it finally would be realized in the opening pages of Thomas Pynchon's magnificent novel, *Gravity's Rainbow*, when Captain Geoffrey ("Pirate") Prentice catches sight of a German V2's condensation stream over London one world-war morning, and a voice on the telephone informs him shortly afterward that "there's a message addressed to him, waiting at Greenwich. 'It came over in a rather delightful way,' the voice high-pitched and sullen, 'none of *my* friends are that clever. All *my* mail arrives by post. Do come and collect it, won't you Prentice.' Receiver hits cradle a violent whack, connection breaks, and now Pirate knows where this morning's rocket landed, and why there was no explosion. Incoming mail, indeed."[45]

CHAPTER SIXTEEN

The Postcard

In the relatively short span of time between the introduction of the penny post in England by Rowland Hill in 1840 and the founding of the World Postal Union in Bern in 1874, during which the modern postal system came into being, nothing less than an entire discursive space was, if not destroyed, then at least deconstructed. Within this space, written discourses had circulated insofar as they were translations from the Mother's mouth, metaphors of The Individual, which continually received Truth at the other end of the postal channel and thus were confined within the orbit of an endless task of interpretation: a space in which discourse could be posted because it existed in the mode of recourse to a transcendental origin. Interpretability, the mode of being for translation, paid the postage for the communicability of such metaphors. The World Postal Union, by contrast, founded discursivity not on the ineluctable precondition of transcendental meaning, but on standards that always preceded the possibility of meaning (prepayment). It closed the circuit of the postal system, producing a communications system of planetary dimensions, the establishment of which coincided with the end of the world—insofar as the "world" is the concept underlying a psychologically teleologicized universe. The World Postal Union thus deprived the private letter, which was the medium of a discourse rooted in the ineluctability of The Individual, Nature, Meaning, and so on, of its "metaphysical foundations" (foundations that turn out to be anything but metaphysical, however, as soon as they are traced back to the real, historically specific rules and practices that constituted the apparatus for their formation and transformation).

The form in which the World Postal Union deconstructed the letter was the postcard, which thematized the letter by making it dysfunctional.

The postcard spread the news everywhere that subjectivity, as a product of the letter's confidentiality, had been addressed to a public audience, and it did so precisely for the reason that it lacked the confidentiality of the letter. The symbols conveyed by the postcard recall an origin not in the voice of intimacy, but in printed matter. The postcard is "a letter to the extent that nothing of it remains that is, or that holds,"[1] or that could gain entry to the archives of the "will to truth"—a letter that is litter.[2] And, as Derrida noted, the postcard "destines the letter to its ruin"[3]—an observation that describes with utmost precision the role planned for it at its inception. Heinrich Stephan's memorandum on a "post page"—the founding document of the postcard, in a manner of speaking—was distributed to the participants of the fifth conference of the German-Austrian Postal Union in Karlsruhe on November 30, 1865. In it, Stephan conjured up the postcard as a means for overcoming the two-thousand-year history of a medium whose final manifestation was the enclosed letter:

> The letter's form has, like many other human institutions, undergone many a transformation over the course of time. In antiquity, wax tablets containing its text were bound by rings. The letter was thus, so to speak, a book. Then came the form of the scroll, which lasted into the Middle Ages. This in turn made way for the more convenient form of folding, or the envelope. . . . The material was influential in this: the tablet, parchment, paper. . . . The present form of the letter does not provide sufficient simplicity and brevity for a substantial number of communiqués. Not simplicity, because selecting and folding sheets of stationery, using envelopes and adhesives, attaching stamps, etc. result in inconvenience; and not brevity, because once a regular letter is written, custom demands that one not limit himself to the bare facts.[4]

The *Brief,* German for "letter," in terms of etymology no longer legitimately can be called "brief." The classical ideal of epistolary style, *brevitas,*[5] spelled the doom of the letter itself. This was so because style no longer was a matter of the individual for Stephan, as it had been in Buffon's time, but instead a matter of a media economy. The postal privy councilor's media theory implied a rhetoric of materiality. Consequently, a strategy aimed at reforming style—in which the ideal was frankly the telegram[6]—had to undertake the task of transforming the materiality of the letter itself. After all, it seems that the traditional epistolary *dispositio* and its five parts had been inscribed so ineradicably into the Western soul that no amount of pedagogy could relieve the affliction. A cure could be effected only by means of a surgical operation that sliced the "digressions [that] afflict both sender and recipient" from the letter and so from the soul as well.[7] Stationery's reduction to an exposed, one-sided card in nine by fourteen centimeter format (which was introduced in Germany in 1873 and would become the worldwide standard in 1878)[8] delivered the people from the history of epistolography because it left nothing of the epistolary *dispositio* intact except for the *petitio* and the minimized *salutatio* and *conclusio* in the form of the address and return address.

The operation Stephan performed with the postal objectification of the soul was not a painless one. The most agonizing part undoubtedly was the incision that sacrificed the confidentiality of the letter by removing the envelope. In fact, the elimination of the legal-postal construct of individuality initially led to Stephan's failure: the exhibitionism that the postcard was to practice did not in any way escape Stephan's superior, General Postal Director Philipsborn. In 1865, Philipsborn thus rejected its introduction due to the "indecent form of communication on exposed post pages."[9] The nudity of communication, as Philipsborn recognized, would be nothing but the communication of nudity. And indeed: why else had stationery been folded and sealed or concealed in an envelope in the first place, if not to tease the discourse of sexuality from the soul, thus giving rise to its confessions of intimacy—the procedure by which the Western individual had to achieve legitimation in the modern period? Because the material conditions for the confidentiality of the letter had been sites for the production of sexuality, the postcard was synonymous with the exhibition of that sexuality. The postcard was scandalous because on behalf of the economy of information exchange it rejected an intimate mode of speech that had been capable of teasing true confessions from the soul. Among other things, after all, truth was also the result of the limitations on access to the discourse.[10]

The power of the institutions that had governed knowledge of the human soul and its sexual secrets in the nineteenth century was based on a monopoly on advance information. And because of this, the discourse of the postcard, which in principle was addressed to everyone, appeared to be immoral (even if no one actually read it, it was still a "communication legible for everyone").[11] Philipsborn's condemnation therefore was a belated effect of the postal system of 1800. Because the sexualization of souls had been a logic of address (see Kleist, see Brentano), the postcard, legible for everyone, brought about the desexualization of these souls. And this was precisely what constituted its immorality. The postcard, which is a publication, in Joyce's perceptive eyes,[12] dismantled the difference between an obscure, feminine discourse—that is, Nature itself—that was addressed exclusively to the civil servants of the spirit and a clear, masculine discourse that spoke the truth, insofar as it was a translation of the first discourse, and was addressed to the world as literature or philosophy. The texts of postcards thus were inaccessible to a hermeneutics of the soul: they were "open and radically unintelligible."[13]

Stephan's proposal of 1865 could be summarized as follows: as a postal technique, the soul no longer was up to the standards of a modern (which is not to say "postmodern") postal system. The reservations about the postcard thus hardly come as a surprise: people were very fond of the spiritual welfare that folded stationery and envelopes assured them. In his memorandum, Stephan himself had counted on an "initial shyness [of the public] with regard to public communication," which would have to be overcome.[14] And in fact, after the introduction of "correspondence cards" in the territory of the North German League, the Imperial Post Office indeed received requests that postcards be provided with adhesive flaps.[15]

While the days of modesty were numbered, but not yet over in Bismarck's League, the telegrammatic reform of epistolary style—which Stephan had conjured up only *per analogiam*—was taken quite literally in Vienna. "Because the flowery language, inscriptions, assurances of the most undivided esteem, etc. that are at once unavoidable in a letter are repulsive," Emanuel Herrmann (it probably was no accident that he was a professor at the Military Academy in Vienna-Neustadt) made an appeal in the *Neuen Freien Presse* for the acceptance of "cards in the format of a normal envelope" as mail, provided that "they contain no more than twenty words, including the address and the signature of the sender."[16] "With this postcard," Herrmann wrote, "we would create a kind of postal telegram, which, with the exception of the speed of its dispatch, would share nearly all the advantages of telegrams. . . . one could limit oneself to unavoidably necessary expressions, as has long been the custom in telegrams. We would soon possess a special language of telegram letters, which could compete boldly with that of Tacitus."[17] In contrast to the situation in Germany, the demand for discursive abbreviation, or the renaissance of the classical Latin *brevitas*, thus found a receptive audience in Austria. On October 1, 1869, the "correspondence card" was introduced there (although without the limitation to twenty words Herrmann requested) by Department Councilor Baron von Kolbensteiner, who later became director of the General Post and Telegraph in the Austrian postal administration and, incidentally, also had participated in the Karlsruhe conference of 1865.[18]

In Germany, by contrast, the postcard did not see the light of day in the world of media until Bismarck had performed his services as midwife. Philipsborn, who had tried unsuccessfully beforehand to prevent a meeting between Stephan and Bismarck, retired in May 1870—Bismarck already had proposed Stephan to the king as the new director of the General Post.[19] Now nothing stood in the way of introducing the "indecent form of communication on exposed post pages." Correspondence cards were officially accepted as mail by a general decree of the chancellor on July 1, 1870. (In practice, they had been allowed since June 18.) Once the denuding of the discursive sphere of intimacy not only had been achieved but actually was enjoying tremendous success[20]—after the "initial shyness of the public" had been surmounted—the only hope remaining for the salvation of humanity's spiritual welfare was to transfer the action of folding (after its material disappearance) to the symbolic realm. Where the area protected by the confidentiality of letters left off, the domain of intelligence agencies began.

For discourse, postcards represented enemy territory. Thus, the "art of secret writing" prescribed for the military and diplomats in such situations found its "application on imperial postcards" in 1875. Avé-Lallemant, a police officer and author of the renowned *History of German Knavery*, wrote that the number of postcards used would "still increase tremendously if postcards, by their nature and properties, did not lack the confidentiality of the letter, upon which the use and usefulness of the mail is principally founded."[21] The readers of the illustrated family magazine *Der Hausfreund* (and it was probably not entirely an accident that it was precisely these readers) then learned that this "drawback" easily could be remedied "by the use of a simple cipher script."[22] A demonstration was

furnished with, of all texts, the "Traveler's Night Song," in which friends
of *Der Hausfreund* were supposed to practice deciphering subjectivity:

> lvsvh rbbvd xzfwvbd
> zik hly
> zd rbbvd nzfwvbd
> ifflvhvik ul
> arlc vzdvd yrlty
> uzv mevxvbvzd itynvzxvd zc nrbuv
> nrhkv dlh srbuv
> hlyvik ul rlty.[23]

This is cipher as plaintext. After all, it hardly could be made more clear
that Goethe's empire was not of Stephan's world. What was meant as the
salvation of humanity's spiritual welfare merely confirmed its irretrievable
loss once more. And it did so for the simple reason that statement operations performed within a formation of statements established by the historical a priori of the media cannot in turn renege on that formation; re-
vision itself was subject to that a priori and perpetuated its effects. The
echo of an original voice, its tone and breath—unregulated by any me-
ter—disappeared beneath a simple exchange of written characters, marking the point of no return for the salvation of souls after the fashion of
nature poetry in the year 1780. Thus, the events that were postcards and
the World Postal Union within the realm of discourse crossed out and surpassed the intentions of the soul-guarding policeman. And it hardly seems
accidental that Avé-Lallemant stumbled onto this particular poem, which
celebrated the invention of the motherly voice as the secret of subjectivity
like no other.[24] Avé-Lallemant's "cipher script" was supposed to "preserve the confidentiality and peace of family life,"[25] and thus, in its application to the "Traveler's Night Song," did not preserve just any secret, but
the secret of family life itself. By citing the psychogenic lullaby of the
Mother, the proposal for saving the soul by means of cryptography cited
the origin of the soul itself—and in the same stroke placed that origin beyond reach in the past perfect of history. The intimacy of linguistic com-
panionship prior to all articulation that the Mother's voice had endowed
melted away in the heat of an intimacy endowed by the code manipulations of intelligence services. The secret of the latter did not lie beyond the
text, but on this side.

The task of salvaging meaning on imperial postcards thus was assigned not to the discipline of hermeneutics, but to a cryptoanalysis born
in war. According to Avé-Lallemant's account, the "enciphered letters of
spies" that fell into his hands during the German-Danish War had delivered the model for intimacy on postcards.[26] As a means for making the
postcard's message the consoling promise that the silencing of speech
would be a peaceful rest, the application of military cryptography thus
was among the spiritual duties of a ministry that meanwhile had seen the
strategic military value of lullabies. In its application on postcards, the
"Traveler's Night Song" was psychological warfare and nothing else.

On July 1, 1870, Stephan introduced the postcard in Germany. The
French declaration of war ensued on July 15, and by July 24, Stephan had
mobilized a field postal system and turned it into an instrument for realizing his plans for a new mass medium: "Since almost everyone remaining
behind had a friend or relative with whom he or she corresponded among
the troops going off to war, the field-service postcard made its way into
every segment of the population and thus made propaganda for ordinary
correspondence cards as well."[27] So that the war might initiate a modern-
ization drive in the discursive practices of the masses, Stephan had his
"field-post correspondence card" distributed to the troops free of charge
[see Figure 7].[28] Henceforth, the postcard proved to be a "invaluable
means" for achieving the homeland's omnipresence and for bearing the
consolation of the motherly voice—as the ultimate definition of the homeland—to the farthest front. By December 1870 alone, ten million field-service postcards had been mailed,[29] defending the souls of the German
armies' soldiers, souls whose military value was beyond question—as far
as its influence on fighting morale was concerned. Consequently, the true
calling of the field post assigned by Stephan referred to the same "breath"
that sustained the "Traveler's Night Song": "It [the field post] is the voice
with which the individual soldier speaks to his loved ones at home."[30] Beginning in 1870–71, it was on the battlefields of war that Elihu Burritt's
programmatic demand achieved fulfillment: "to make home everywhere."

And once the Franco-Prussian War had helped to bring about the postcard's mass-media breakthrough, not only in Germany, but [Figure 7] in
occupied France as well (the first French postcards were put in circulation
by Rosshirt, the "Administrator of Posts in the occupied French territo-

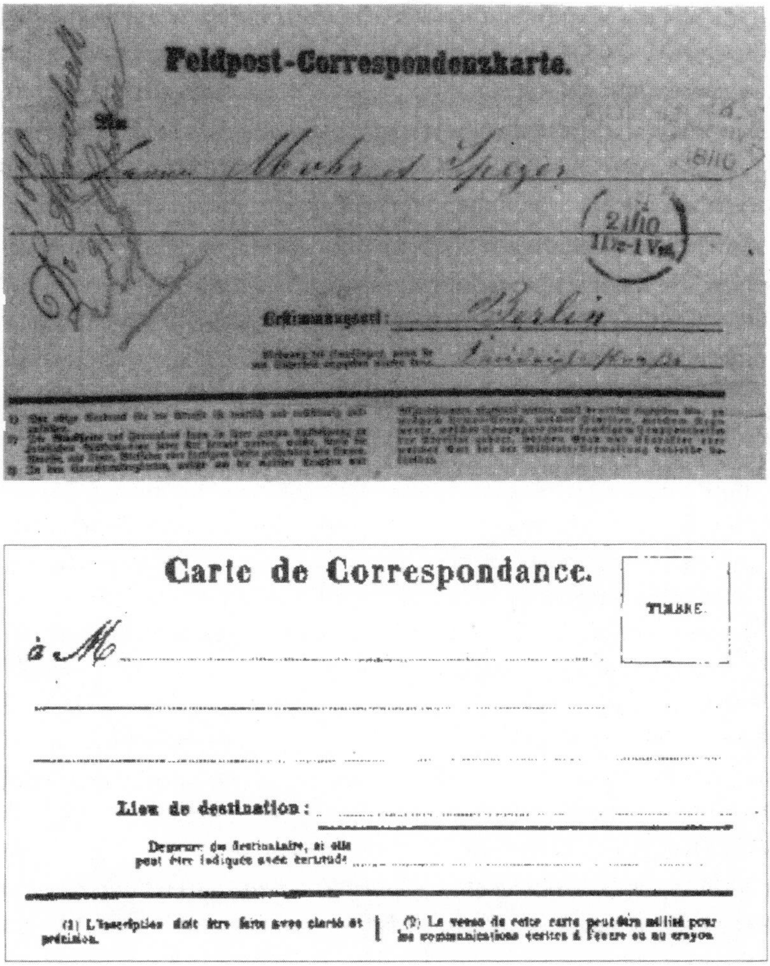

FIGURE 7. German and French versions of Stephan's "field-post correspondence card."

ries"),[31] the founding of the World Postal Union was practically unavoidable. Because it constituted the quintessence of the modern postal standard, the postcard implied the elimination of the world. It was the virus of the world postal system: it forced old postal districts to adopt the norms of the world post and thus to succumb themselves.

The postcard was the first information carrier of the postal system to be conceived on the basis of a standard format from the outset. Stephan's memorandum of 1865 already had foreseen postage that was valid "regardless of distance";[32] the stamp was to be printed on the card, and a standard format and address ensued with its introduction. "Such a post page," Stephan wrote, "will now be conveyed by the postal system free of charge, since the postage was paid with the form's purchase . . . Nothing is paid for the form itself."[33] In principle, the postcard was therefore nothing but a stamp that could be written on; it reduced the materiality of communication to its bare economy. It was a stamp that paid postage for nothing but itself—the stamp's self-postage. The message of a medium with a materiality consisting of self-reference to its own standards thus was the discursive system of that medium itself. Boundless testimony for this fact was given by postcards that bore an address identical to the return address and thus annulled the distance they factually crossed. Such a postcard, for example, was mailed in Chemnitz on May 24, 1878; the first of its six addresses sent it to Alexandria, and from there it went on to Singapore, then to Yokohama, then farther on to San Francisco and New York, and from there to its sixth address, which was at once its return address: a certain Ludwig Ploss in Chemnitz [see Figure 8].[34]

The "round-the-world postcard," which anticipated the "empty orbiting of the world" that according to Virilio travelers were to experience in the age of jet airplanes,[35] celebrated the elimination of the world because the distance it effectively had covered in circling the globe added up to exactly zero. But it was precisely this and nothing else that made the round-the-world postcard a "witness to the performance capacity of the world postal service."[36] The postcard's message was the World Postal Union.[37] In accordance with a resolution passed at the World Postal Congress in 1878, all postcards on earth continued for decades afterward to bear the impression UNION POSTALE UNIVERSELLE.[38]

Every conceivable caption on a postcard thus could be only a postscript

FIGURE 8. Message as discursive system of the medium: postcard bearing an address identical to its return address.

to this message. According to Derrida, Joyce's *Ulysses* transformed the universe of the ancient *Odyssey* into the very same union: "a whole game of postcards perhaps suggests the hypothesis that the geography of trajectories around the Mediterranean Sea in *Ulysses* might well have the structure of a postcard or the design of a map that traces postal messages."[39]

When a medium with a message of self-reference to its own discursive system emerged, the letter was sent to its ruin. The postcard is the final misuse of love letters. And this is above all due to the fact that its origin was not the psychogenic voice preceding all letters as a transcendental requirement, but printed matter. In 1865, Stephan's plan to unleash the postcard on the world of media had fallen through, but the dispatch of exposed printed cards—the so-called "advisements"—in fact already had been permitted in the Prussian postal district since June.[40] Two years later, the General Post Office issued a regulation on the subject, ruling that the dispatch of exposed cards at the reduced rates for printed matter was inadmissible in those cases "when the cards contain any additions or alterations of content after printed completion, with the exception of place, date, signature, etc. *Check marks at the margin* for the purpose of directing the reader's attention to a particular place, however, *shall be permitted*."[41]

This minimal exception to the general ban on handwritten postcards gave two Leipzig book dealers, Friedlein and Pardubitz, a brilliant idea: they drafted a "Universal Correspondence Card," the reverse side of which was printed with twenty-eight sequentially numbered questions and statements [see Figure 9].[42] Every single one of these cards, which were indeed truly "universal," thus represented a consummate occasion register. The purpose of this register, however, was not to give guidance in writing, as had been the case for the Baroque *artes dictaminis*, but to make writing unnecessary. Opposites such as the receipt of a document and its absence, arrival and departure, birth and death came together on the card as it is possible to do only in language. The universal postcard referred to a given fact of life only on the condition of its contingency: things might just as well have been different. In a discursive order such as this one, where things were expressed by placing legally permissible "check marks" by the appropriate number, congratulating someone on a wedding meant no more than not sending "condolences on a sorrowful occasion."

1 Melde(n), dass {mein / unser} Reisender Herr _____
  binnen Kurzem bei Ihnen eintreffen wird.

2. Zeige an, dass ich binnen Kurzem bei Ihnen zur Empfangnahme
   Ihrer Ordres eintreffen werde.

3. Danke(n) für gütigst ertheilten Auftrag, Ihnen dessen beste
   Ausführung versichernd.

4. Melde(n). dass Ihre gef. Bestellung ausgeführt, heute auf ge-
   wünschten Wege abgesandt wurde.

5. Ersuche(n) um gef. Einsendung des entfallenden Betrages mittelst
   Postanweisung.

6. Haben Sie meine (unsere) Sendung vom vorgestrigen Tage erhalten?

7. Melde(n), dass ich (wir) bis heute ohne Nachricht von Ihnen
   geblieben bin (sind).

8. Bitte(n) wiederholt um Antwort in der bewussten Angelegenheit.

9. Melde(n), dass das Gewünschte nicht mehr zu haben oder ver-
   kauft ist.

10. Melde, dass ich morgen von hier abzureisen gedenke.

11. Melde, dass ich bis nach Eintreffen weiterer Nachricht von
    Ihnen hier bleiben werde.

12. Bitte(n) um Uebersendung des angezeigten Prospectus, Probe,
    Muster oder dergl.

13. Bitte(n) um nähere Auskunft in der betr. Angelegenheit.

14. Bedauere(n) nicht auf gemachte Offerte oder Vorschlag eingehen
    zu können.

15. Bestätige(n) den Empfang d. letzten Schreibens oder Sendung.

16. Melde(n), dass ausführliche Antwort baldmöglichst erfolgen soll.

17. Bedaure(n) Ihnen melden zu müssen, dass die betr. Stelle besetzt ist.

18. Zeige an, dass die gewünschte Sache besorgt ist.

19. Theile, mit dass sich Alles hier wohl befindet.

20. Zeige an, dass ich jetzt wohne wie untenstehend angegeben.

21. Melde, dass ich heute glücklich hier angekommen bin.

22. Melde, dass ich von meiner Reise wieder zurückgekehrt bin.

23. Bringe mich ihnen in empfehlende Erinnerung.

24. Gratulire zu dem stattgefundenen frohen Ereigniss.

25. Gratulire zum Jahreswechsel, (Geburtstag).

26. Condolire zu dem betrübenden Ereigniss, und versichere herzliche
    Theilnahme.

27. Wegen Bezug und Benutzung. der U. C. K. wollen Sie die betr.
    Stellen der Vorderseite gef. beachten und sich behufs Bestellung
    an Unterzeichneten wenden.

28. Bitte(n) um Zusendung von 100 Stück U. C. K. gegen Nach-
    nahme des Betrags von 15 Sgr. durch Postvorschuss.

(Bei Frankoeinsendung des Betrages in Postmarken folgt Franko-Expedition.)

Name u. Adresse } _____
des Absenders. }

FIGURE 9. Friedlein-Pardubitz "Universal Correspondence Card."

Total entropy governed the speech acts possible in the technology of postcards, that is, the possibilities for transforming the "printed postcard into a genuine correspondence card."[43] The only information a "check mark" provided was that every other number had been equally probable. When what you say means only that you are not saying something else, then you are not saying very much. Which says nothing against the fact that no human speech meant anything more. In a story by Borges, a provincial governor, poet, astronomer, and chess player sets out to write a novel: instead of deciding on one of the various possibilities for the plot's development, he simply plays out all of them at the same time.[44] Every chapter of this *Garden of the Forking Paths* is a Universal Correspondence Card with check marks by all the numbers.

Yet the General Post Office initially refused to allow anything to be said on postcards at all. On the grounds that check marks would "endow printed matter with the character of a letter,"[45] it simply prohibited literature all together. After all, literature had not functioned in any other way in 1800: as a printed text that every single feminine reader was allowed and supposed to hallucinate as a letter personally addressed to her.

Yet despite such obstacles, the Friedlein-Pardubitz Universal Correspondence Card came to be the prototype for the "Whizz Bang" or "Quick Firer," the British Field Service Post Cards that were sent off by the millions during the First World War.[46] Form A.2042 reduced the entropy of war as a source of information almost to zero [see Figure 10]. The field-service postcard established a prestabilized order of salvation for the world in which sickness was possible only as a prelude to recovery, wounds only on condition of their treatment, and there was only one place you could go: home. "Where are we going?" a Romanticism homesick for its Mother had asked, only to answer, as if the destinies of people were determined by a transcendental Field Service Post Card: "Home, all the time."[47] In 1914, Romantic optimism certainly no longer was transcendental, but rather was an effect of the first communication to be mechanized by preprinted forms. The standardization of the utterable via postcards was simply the only economic form possible for discourse under the conditions of a battle of matériel. Even the normal field-post letters contained nothing but an endless litany of optimistic stereotypes. And how could it have been otherwise: when asked why he had not wanted to

NOTHING is to be written on this side except the date and signature of the sender. Sentences not required may be erased. If anything else is added the post card will be destroyed.

I am quite well.

I have been admitted into hospital
{ sick } and am going on well.
{ wounded } and hope to be discharged soon.

I am being sent down to the base.

I have received your
{ letter dated _____
{ telegram " _____
{ parcel " _____

Letters follows at first opportunity.

I have received no letter from you
{ lately
{ for a long time.

Signature }
  only. }
Date _____

FIGURE 10. British Field Service Post Card ("Whizz Bang" or "Quick Firer").

tell the people at home what the war was really like, Robert Graves responded: "You couldn't: you can't communicate noise."[48] Once the world became noise, the absolute grounds (or groundlessness) of information, everything that was utterable, became a postcard text: referenceless.

The flood of field-service postcards during the war of 1870–71 and the flood of their civilian successors in the founding years of the German Empire did not make the Friedlein-Pardubitz Universal Correspondence

Card obsolete, but instead brought to full fruition the possibilities inherent in the principle of printed matter's conversion into private matters. Paper manufacturers produced printed cards for every situation that might conceivably require a private letter, cards that could be transformed into personal greetings by filling in the blanks. For example:

> Have _____ most heartfelt congratulations on the celebration of _____ birthday tomorrow! Birthdays are milestones on the road of life! May it be granted to _____ that _____ be able to look back on many, many more of the same in a spirit of gladness. Where would _____ rather linger in spirit than with _____? _____ wish for _____ with heart and soul that the kind heavens grant all _____ wishes the fulfillment that _____ noble heart so fully deserves. Spend the day in untroubled joy and think of _____ loyally devoted _____.[49]

The occasion register no longer was represented by a single card—as it had been with Friedlein-Pardubitz and its military adaptations—but instead by an entire postcard repository containing appropriate cards for every occasion, which once had been only a number to be checkmarked. With the advent of this postcard repository, the age of technological replicability had dawned for the repository of ideas of 1800.

In the form of preprinted postcards, Kleist's poet's dream finally came to fruition. The postcard repository, after all, contained not only greeting cards, but also "idyllic descriptions of the natural beauty that the traveler enjoys ' . . . meters above sea level.'"[50] For ten pfennigs, anyone could become a Kleist in 1880. Postcards put descriptions of nature in circulation that gained pseudoreference only by the insertion of geographical names and specifications, exactly as Kleist had inserted the signifiers "Rhine," "Main," or "Elbe" into one and the same description of a river valley as the occasion required. These handwritten reproductions, which had simulated the productions of "the most exuberant fantasy" in the years 1800 and 1801, merely were substitutes for the World Postal Union and its media yet to come. "Swift as an arrow, the _____ flows on from _____ in a straight line, as though its goal already were in view and it must in no way be detained, impatiently set on its course. But a vine-planted hill, the _____, steps into its path and curbs its onward flow," and so on.[51] Such was the straightforward text of a postcard that had had the status of printed matter from the outset. The printed postcard "deconstructed" Kleist's postal "training for the authorial profession" by inverting the discursive strategy of Romantic correspondence. While Kleist's letters to Wilhelmine von Zenge had attained the status of printed matter ten years before it became a separate category of postal material (and then only in Bavaria)[52] by passing through a postal chain of translations from the Mother's mouth, the postcard took the opposite historical route: starting out as printed matter, it gradually conquered the domain of the handwritten text in order finally to become a phenomenon of the voice as the medium of the homeland. The printed postcard turned Kleist's letter inside out like a glove: the latter's objectivity—the handwritten text's global status as printed matter—was the former's subjectivity. Its "idyllic descriptions of natural beauty" were standard texts, just like Kleist's descriptions of the Rhine valley. Kleist's letters to Zenge defined Romantic authorship as the absence of a World Postal Union. And therefore they reappeared as postcards after 1874.

That today standard descriptions of nature are rare to say the least is, of course, due to something everyone knows: they were replaced by the mass-produced commodities of a particular media technology that the nineteenth century brought forth and that brought about the end of the Gutenberg Galaxy in the channels of the postal system: photography. In 1879, the royal Bavarian court photographer Alphons Adolph invented a photographic picture postcard that was reproducible in print.[53] In addition to standard postage, standard format, and standard text, there now was a standard picture, as well. With the advent of the picture postcard, visual memories departed from the human soul, only to await people thereafter on the routes of the World Postal Union. The picture postcard opened up the territory of the World Postal Union as an immense space of forgetting, the object of which was the world itself. As early as 1859, photography's merciless triumph over the world had been celebrated by the Boston author and doctor Oliver Wendell Holmes, who radically proclaimed its authority in matters of stereophotography by equating the mental eradication of the world with the physical. Once the usefulness of things had passed on to photographic images, things themselves could disappear:

> Form will be separate from substance in the future. In fact, the substance
> in visible objects is no longer of much use, unless it serves as a pattern
> for creating form. Just give us a few negatives of a noteworthy object
> photographed from various perspectives—we need nothing more. Then tear

the object down or light it on fire, if you want to. We might have to forego some luxury perhaps, since the color is lacking, but form and light and shadows are the most important thing, and even color can be added and will possibly be fetched from nature by and by.[54]

The annihilation of things was the photographer's living and his service. That the mass medium of the picture postcard had taken the place of memory and experience was clearly recognized in 1898 by a German photographer who praised it as a new source of revenue for his colleagues in an article in the professional journal *Das Atelier des Photographen*: "We have struggled to offer the public photographs that are truly beautiful, and indeed we have come so far that there are presently a large number of people who prefer, in place of several large folios rendering a few of the town's main features, to buy an entire series of these postcards, which they do not plan to send, but to include in their album as their own, desirable memories."[55]

If personal memories turned into picture postcards, they did so because the postal epoch of human communication, which had allowed literature to function as a letter and letters to function as literature, had been followed by a postal epoch of phantom communication via the industrial mass production of printed matter. This epochal caesura was something a telegraph battalion lieutenant had to learn about from personal experience in 1901. In May and in civilian clothes, he had set out with a young lady for a bicycle ride to Werder, where he had his picture taken, lady and bicycle included. His bad luck started when the photographer added his keepsake photo to a collection of pictures he sold to a dealer. The latter was so taken by the lieutenant, lady, and bicycle that he delivered ten thousand copies of the picture to the Wertheim department store in Berlin. Thereafter, not a day went by when the pitiable lieutenant was not haunted by the visitations of his keepsake picture in dozens of copies.[56] Since Henry Fox Talbot invented the negative, original and private visual memories always have been reproductions and thus might potentially flood the boulevards in massive quantities. At the same time, Kleist's case reveals that the originality of memory, as it was vouched for and glorified by literature in the cult of authorship, already had been a reproduction, even in the original. The originality of difference or repetition thus became an event in media history long before Derrida. That history left behind traces in which the destinies of media can be read and in which the end of history always was on the way: Heinrich von Stephan's postcard addressed to Heinrich von Kleist.

Once memories circulated as picture postcards that could be sent anyplace on the globe for ten pfennigs, traveling itself became unnecessary. Agencies such as the International Picture Postcard Bureau in Weimar (where Wilhelm Meister's educational travels apparently had been entirely forgotten) could assume that burden. Around 1900, that office hired a world traveler "who is beginning a trip around the world planned to last 4–6 months, on which he will send artistically made postcards with views of the mailing location from 40 of the most interesting points in the world to submitted addresses. The price is set at 10 marks for the entire series."[57]

At the moment that travel became obsolete in the age of the World Postal Union, writing lost its monopoly on the exchange of information. Text had been degraded to the form of a universal inscription of the world that continued to exist only in the form of free-floating visual memory in the channels of the postal system. The text on picture postcards took over the precise function that supplementary handwriting had performed in Kleist's letters or on printed postcards it provided the photo with a pseudoreference. Only the caption that no postcard lacked (initially it appeared only on the front, later on the back as well) gave the photo its meaning.[58]

The claim to possession of memories made with the help of picture postcards was correspondingly uncertain. Because possession had to be demonstrated with the inscription of an address or return address, and since picture postcards were anything but legitimate legal identification, identity itself was fundamentally threatened by the bona fides of those who wished to link it to a personal history. The sailor W. B. Murphy—whose profession traditionally had a bad reputation with respect to credibility—provides evidence of this with the shipwreck he suffers in the opinion of Leopold Bloom. Murphy tries to prove his story about cannibals in Peru with an eyewitness account using, of all things, a picture postcard showing—according to the caption—Indians in Bolivia: "Mr. Bloom, without evincing surprise, unostentatiously turned over the card to peruse the partially obliterated address and postmark. It ran as follows:

Tarjeta Postal. Señor A. Boudin, Galeria Becche, Santiago, Chile. There
was no message evidently, as he took particular notice."[59] Consequently,
it is not only the discrepancy between the story's Peru and the picture's
Bolivia, but also that between the sailor's name and the "fictitious addressee of the missive which made [Bloom] nourish some suspicions of
our friend's *bona fides.*"[60] Bloom's method of securing evidence disen-
gages the place pictured on the card from the story and identity of its
owner and thus appears to be the photographic negative of Sherlock
Holmes's detective work in "The Five Orange Pips," which reconstructed
a history from the relationships between place, sender, and recipient.
"One never knows who belongs to whom, what to whom, what to what,
who to what," Derrida wrote in the margin of Murphy's postcard. "There
is no subject of belonging, any more than an owner of the postcard: it remains without a designated addressee."[61]

Who is not familiar with Bloom's gesture, turning a postcard around
for a glance at the caption? As long as the caption remains unfound, the
visual memory in the picture remains silent: a dream image that remains
indecipherable. Once memories had photographic carriers, they no longer
were available to literature as signifiers. Thus, for example, Kafka's literary texts can reflect images only as uncaptioned picture postcards.[62] And
these transport images that cannot not be remembered, what they mean
is lost on the way from sender to addressee—the glance no longer can
come to rest upon them. Uncaptioned picture postcards glide past the
glance without leaving a trace in the memory of the observer. They are the
positive form of forgetting.

The Telegraph: Land and Sea

In 1800 and 1801, Kleist's repository of ideas had circulated nothing but postcards that defined authorship and imagination as historical supplements for the World Postal Union. Nine years later, postal discourse—and therefore literature—had the alternative, according to Kleist, of choosing between the dispatch of postcards and a new communications technology: telegraphy. The options Kleist presented for postal discourse in the *Berliner Abendblätter* in October 1810 contained the situation *in nuce* that would dominate all writing in the 1870's as the alternative between a World Postal Union and an International Telegraph Union. The *Project of a Cannonball Postal Service* and its (probably fictitious) reply unfurled nothing less than the future discursive order after Samuel Thomas Sömmerring had presented the first electric, or electrolytic, telegraph to the Munich Academy of Sciences in 1809: "It has been recently invented in order to expedite communications from the four corners of the globe, an electrical telegraph; a telegraph that by means of an electrophorus and a metal wire can transmit messages with the speed of thought, or, better said, in less time than chronometrical instruments could measure."[1]

Although his source was a report on Sömmerring's invention in the *Nuremberger Korrespondenten* on August 16, 1810, it seems as though Kleist had read Sömmerring himself. The latter's memorandum, after all, does indeed speak of the impossibility of determining the velocity of an electric impulse chronometrically: "In calculating the *velocity* at which the electrical agent moves, my limited experiments have indeed not been sufficient to observe even a single difference, whether the communications cables were one foot in length or several thousand."[2] Sömmerring's telegraph worked on the basis of contemporary neurological knowledge, that is, by means of water's decomposition into hydrogen and oxygen—and therefore the telegraph cable, in Sömmerring's words, was nothing other than "a rough physical analog of a nerve center, the individual fibers of which in the same way isolate both the received sensation impression in general and the smallest electrical spark in particular and transmit them to the brain."[3]

How did an author like Kleist, whose writings propagated the most advanced state of modern military strategy, respond to the telegraph? He attempted to bring literature up to the new standard of communications technology: if the telegraph was an analog to the nervous system, then literature had to find an analog to the telegraph, which was suitable "for dispatching only very short and laconic messages."[4] "Therefore . . . we propose a *projectile* or *cannonball* express: an institution that, with suitably situated artillery stations spaced within firing range of each other, would discharge, from mortars or howitzers, hollow shells, which have been stuffed full not of powder but letters and packages, and which could very easily be observed in flight, and wherever they might fall, short of some morass, be retrieved."[5] In order to make letters—the literary and pedagogical effects of which he had tested better than anyone else—competitive with the newest medium of communication, Kleist proposed that correspondence no longer be delegated to postal administrations, but to artillery detachments, instead. The proposal was historically precise and completely consistent with his literature. Kleist moved in the circles of the Prussian army reformers, most of whom belonged to artillery divisions,[6] and his practice of mobilizing literature as a means to unleash guerrilla warfare on Napoleon made it only appropriate that this "bourgeois" branch of weaponry should become the new logistics of the poet's dream. And nothing other than the effective mobilization of Napoleonic communications and leadership technology had led to the demand for Sömmerring's invention of the telegraph in the first place.

On July 5, 1809, the day of Wagram, Sömmerring had dined with the Bavarian minister, the future Baron von Montgelas, who requested him to have the academy work out proposals for introducing an optical telegraph, the extraordinary advantages of which he had learned to appreciate only a few months before. On April 8, Andreas Hofer had initiated the rebellion in Tyrol, and the Austrians crossed the river Inn the following day. The French envoy Otto reported the surprise invasion to Berthier in Strasbourg via courier, and Berthier sent it from there by telegraph to Napoleon in Paris. As a result, Napoleon—again using the telegraph—was able to bring his troops to bear so quickly that on April 16, he was able to promise King Max I his return within fourteen days to Munich from Dillingen, where the latter had fled together with Montgelas. And indeed, the promise was fulfilled only ten days later.[7]

Kleist's cannonball postal service thus represented a literary technology of mobilization in answer to the Napoleonic optotelegraphic technology of mobilization. There are sources to document this. Kleist's proposal was in fact not Kleist's proposal at all. It already was to be found in General–Brigade Inspector Carl Friedrich Lehmann's *Ideas on the Symbolic Language of Professor Bergsträßer and the Express Mail of Advocate Linguet*, which was published in 1795. Inspired by Johann Samuel Halle's 1786 study *Magic, or the Magical Powers of Nature*—in which Dom Gauthey's telegraphic proposals were discussed—Lehmann suggested that "an express postal system might be constructed using certain howitzers, set up at stations every half mile, and also grenades filled with letters, which are to be shot back and forth out of these howitzers."[8] According to Lehmann, such a postal system might "send a packet [*Partheygen*] of letters from Berlin to Königsberg in Prussia in approximately four to five hours' time."[9] The proposal of the Cistercian monk Dom Gauthey to which Lehmann referred consisted of the "transmission of written information with a weight of several ounces across one hundred miles in six hours on an arrow, from station to station, using a strong enough bow."[10] And precisely this historical prototype for Lehmann's cannonball post, seized upon by Kleist, was mobilized in the latter's *Battle of Hermann* as a means for inspiring the defection of Germanic princes allied with Varus and their national unification in a war against Varus (and Napoleon).[11] Kleist's arrow post in *The Battle of Hermann* thus was not only a concession to antiquity,[12] in which the play was supposed to be set, but at the same time the historical precursor of his cannonball postal service. Gauthey's arrow post from *The Battle of Hermann* finally was translated into Lehmann's/Kleist's medium of the cannonball post by the German *Wehrmacht* in the Second World War. In order to inspire the defection not of Rhenish League princes but of Red Army soldiers, propaganda companies on the Eastern Front fired texts at the Russian lines with cannons and mortars.[13] The ninth scene of Act 5 of *The Battle of Hermann*, which was read by the supreme command of the German Army, the *Oberkommando der Wehrmacht*, according to contemporary accounts,[14] could not have been staged with more precision.

The alternative to public telegraphy—or general mobilization—known as the cannonball post was a service that transported nothing but postcards: like the ones Kleist sent to feminine recipients in 1801 or the ones sent by British soldiers in the form of Field Service Post Cards during the First World War. According to Kleist's fictitious response to his own *Project*, the alternative was "a postal system that . . . in response to the question 'How are you' . . . always would arrive with answers like 'I am as well as can be expected,' or 'Not half bad,' or 'By gum, things are wonderful!' or 'I've put my house in order,' or 'My books are finally balanced again,' or 'I married off both my daughters recently,' or 'Tomorrow with cannons booming we shall celebrate a national holiday.'"[15] Kleist's repository of ideas of 1800 resembled the Universal Correspondence Card of Friedlein and Pardubitz or the Whizz Bang. Only two ways were open to discourse if it was to become something that actually could be posted: the standardization of codes or the standardization of information. The first option, telegraphy, did not transmit a material data carrier (the letter), but the information itself. By encoding the message so that it could be transmitted by light or electricity—as the positioning of regulators and indicators in optical telegraphy, as a series of impulses in its electric version—telegraphy made it possible to optimize the speed of transmission. The second option, the postcard, made it possible to optimize what was transmitted, the "world"—at the price of a high level of entropy. Once reality caught up with Kleist, everything either was rapid, highly entropic (i.e., informative), and therefore secret, or slow, not very entropic, and therefore public. The optical telegraph and letter mail in Kleist's time—the National Security Agency's SPINTCOM[16] network and the telegraphy of intelligence services in ours. Kleist's cannonballs posted the attempt to dissolve this boundary: to find the possibility of increased speed in addition to increased data flow so that the telegraph would be publicly available—or in other words, so that the public would be militarized. The

Project was anything but a joke. On the contrary, it was situated in the historical context of plans and efforts to introduce an optical, or indeed an electric, telegraph along the lines of the French model even in Prussia.[17] Once the first optical telegraph line had gone into operation between Paris and Lille in 1794, there was no lack of proposals on such matters in Prussia—especially after an anonymous eyewitness account concerning the *Newly Invented Long-Distance Writing Machine in Paris* was published the same year.[18]

On April 1, 1795, a transportable field telegraph was demonstrated between Spandau's Juliusturm and the Bellevue Palace in Berlin—the first telegraphic experiment to be performed before high-ranking state officials in Prussia. In attendance at the Spandau Fortress was Franz Carl Achard, the director of the Physical Class[19] at the Royal Prussian Academy, to whom Europe also owed its liberation from expensive West Indian sugar cane. In Bellevue, King Frederick William II, Prince August Ferdinand, and a commission from the academy were present.[20] But while the Convention and Napoleon (after 1801) were constructing telegraph lines in all directions throughout France,[21] Prussian proponents of the telegraph did not fare any better than Achard for a long time afterward. Despite, or perhaps even because of, his telegram—"The telegraph is the interpreter of the hearts of the faithful subjects of Frederick William, Father of his People, Protector of the oppressed, beloved by his subjects as he is feared by his enemies"—nothing came of Achard's efforts except for the supreme applause of his uncomprehending royal majesty and a gift of five hundred talers.[22]

Only a meeting between two literary figures, one of Weimar Classicism and the other of Berlin Romanticism, accomplished the introduction of optical telegraphy in Prussia. The captain in *Elective Affinities*,[23] Philipp Friedrich Carl Ferdinand Baron von Müffling, had been commissioned in 1816 to conduct topographical surveys of the Rhineland (the new Prussian territories), and in 1819, meanwhile promoted to lieutenant general, he filed a petition to the king requesting permission "to perform experiments with an optical apparatus that had become known to him."[24] But with the resignation of Minister of War von Boyen, which followed in the wake of the Reaction then predominant in Prussia, Müffling's proposal initially disappeared without a trace. Von Hake, Boyen's successor, knew whose spirit had fathered Müffling's proposed cannonball post only too well. Müffling's telegraph not only made it possible to conduct war with a strategy that ensued from the establishment and defense of a "Fatherland" instead of a dynasty, it also called for a telegraph company "that was part of the militia," and thus was associated with the notorious repute of Scharnhorst, Gneisenau, and Kleist.[25] Not until 1830—after renewed intervention on the part of Müffling (by now the commander of the General Staff)—was a telegraph commission formed under Hake's successor, Lieutenant General von Krauseneck. The latter soon discovered, however, that the shutter telegraph Müffling had recommended— apparently a version of the Edelcrantz system commonly used in Sweden[26]—did not work.

By this time, however, Kleist's *Project of a Cannonball Postal Service* already had borne its belated fruit. In 1830, Postal Privy Councilor Carl Philipp Heinrich Pistor had presented a *Memorandum on the Establishment of Telegraphic Lines Within the Royal States* to the minister for foreign affairs, von Bernstorff. Pistor had known Kleist personally as a member of the Christian-German Dinner Society to which Kleist, Gneisenau, Clausewitz, Adam Müller, Arnim, and Brentano had belonged,[27] where possibilities for the production of German patriotism had been debated. And as an enthusiastic player of the violin and an experimenter with non-electric telephones, Pistor provided the inspiration for E. T. A. Hoffmann's Councilor Krespel.[28] In 1810, as if in response to Kleist's cannonball proposal, Pistor founded a workshop where astronomical, mechanical, optical, and physics instruments were manufactured. It was there that Pistor's model telegraph originated, as did a large number of the telescopes used at the stations. Pistor's telegraph was an adaptation of a device that a lieutenant of the British Royal Navy, Barnard L. Watson, had set up on the routes from Wheatson to Liverpool and Holyhead (Pistor had traveled to England himself to study the apparatus)—which was in turn modeled after Sir William Pasley's Second Polygrammatic Telegraph.[29] The Pistor-Watson-Pasley telegraph turned out to be good, and an Immediate Commission for the Construction of Telegraph Lines was founded on October 16, 1831, under Krauseneck's chairmanship. One of the members of that commission was a major from the General Staff by the name of Franz August O'Etzel.

O'Etzel was the liaison connecting Müffling and Pistor, Goethe's captain and Hoffmann's Krespel. As a chemistry student, he initially had made friendly contacts with the upcoming scientific elite of France at Berthollet's Paris residence: Gay-Lussac, Arago, and Poisson. He attended Napoleon's self-coronation, became acquainted with Laplace, and finally with Alexander von Humboldt, who also was a guest at Berthollet's home. In the summer of 1805, O'Etzel accompanied Humboldt to Naples, where they observed an eruption of Mount Vesuvius while O'Etzel conducted barometric readings at the volcano.[30] In 1806, O'Etzel concluded his studies in Paris and took a state appointment as an assistant in the paint laboratory at the Royal Porcelain Factory in Berlin—a position he resigned only two years later when the French took control of the Prussian mining and smelting operations.[31] After leaving his post at the Royal Porcelain Factory, O'Etzel acquired an apothecary shop (on Post Street), and between 1808 and 1810 he moved in the circles of the Berlin Romantics—in the same circles, that is, as Pistor. Here, O'Etzel became acquainted with Chamisso, E. T. A. Hoffmann, and Fouqué—as well as Clemens Brentano and Achim von Arnim,[32] both of whom lived for many years at the home of Postal Councilor Pistor.[33] With the help of Friedrich Friesen and Friedrich Ludwig Jahn, O'Etzel founded a fencing club and a swimming school: institutions for training the Prussian Freedom Fighter.[34] With military training as their explicit objective, Scharnhorst, Gneisenau, and von Stein already had demanded the introduction of physical exercise in the schools in 1806, and Friesen founded the German Fencing Society in 1808.[35] Swimming, on the other hand, had been introduced as a military and sports exercise by Ernst von Pfuel, who had restored the Age of the Greeks in the heart of his friend Kleist by going swimming in Lake Thun.[36]

All of this brought results in rapid succession. O'Etzel became a recruit of Kleist, Gneisenau, Friesen, and Pfuel for the Battle of Hermann, which lay ahead: in 1810, he joined Brandenburg Ulan Regiment No. 3. Four years later, he received his first mission that required hands-on experience with the telegraph: he destroyed a French station. Shortly thereafter, during the Battle of Paris, Müffling noticed the ordinance officer Etzel at the headquarters of Field Marshal Blücher. As a result, Müffling sent O'Etzel to Koblenz to survey the new Rhine provinces in 1816.[37] Four years later, he returned to Berlin as an officer in the Senior General Staff. Pistor thus must have been an old acquaintance of O'Etzel's in 1831. His telegraph replaced Müffling's, which had proven to be too fragile. Then, in 1833, however, the Prussian field telegraph organization was adjourned indefinitely, while the decision had been made in 1832 to construct a state telegraph line from Berlin to Koblenz, and Major O'Etzel received orders to carry it out. In the spirit of Kleist, Hoffmann, and the Prussian army reformers of 1810, what was then the longest telegraph line in the world was completed in 1833. As was only proper, the line and its "telegraph corps" were placed under the authority of the General Staff, and therefore under O'Etzel, who was named the first Prussian telegraph director two years later.[38]

After his return to the General Staff in 1820, O'Etzel had given instruction on surveying theory and military geography at the General Prussian Military School.[39] Here he met a certain Georg Simon Ohm, who had formulated the law bearing his name in 1826:[40] the basic law of electricity, and therefore of electric telegraphy as well, which O'Etzel decided was more efficient than the optical type only a few years after the Berlin-Koblenz line had gone into operation. Measurements of telegraphic speeds had revealed something remarkable: raising the level of data in parallel transmission increased telegraphic speed much less effectively than raising the level of data transmitted in series. The grand treasury of symbols for the Prussian telegraph, which transmitted six indicator positions per cycle in parallel sequence, only doubled the speed of telegrams relative to the French telegraph, which transmitted only two indicator positions and one regulator position in parallel. The French telegraph could transmit a single symbol approximately twice as fast as the Prussian, so that both systems functioned at approximately the same speed, but with the Prussian telegraph requiring the use of twenty times as much code.[41] This discovery ultimately spoke in favor of introducing the serially transmitted dots and dashes of the Morse telegraph. O'Etzel was so convinced by the mathematical laws of communication (bad weather—nothing out of the ordinary in Prussia—and short days in winter also played a role) that he pushed for the introduction of electric telegraphs (with official support from Alexander von Humboldt) as early as October 13, 1837—once von Dönhoff, the Prussian envoy in Munich, had reported the success of Steinheil's experiment with electric telegraphy to the Prussian Ministry for Foreign Affairs on September 11.[42] At the Palace of Sanssouci, O'Etzel was allowed to give Frederick William IV a demonstration of an electromagnetic device he had invented himself in 1840—the following year, however, the construction of a conductor failed due to the same problem that had forced Claude Chappe to abandon his plans for an electric telegraph and to develop the optical version as early as 1791: insufficient insulation.[43]

In 1846, when General O'Etzel received an essay entitled *On the State of Telegraphy and Its Possible Improvement*, which promised to solve all insulation problems by laminating cables with a strange new substance known as gutta-percha,[44] he thus immediately requisitioned its author, a second lieutenant in the artillery division, to the Telegraph Commission of the General Staff. The lieutenant's name: Werner Siemens.[45] In 1848, the year of revolutions, Siemens and Halske, the mechanic who had helped him found the Telegraph Construction Institute in Berlin the year before, constructed the first telegraph lines from Berlin to Frankfurt—where the Paulskirche Parliament was meeting—and Koblenz. One year later—against the opposition of the military—the telegraph was made available to the general public[46] and placed under the administration of the Ministry of Commerce. Kleist's proposal for militarizing public discourse by means of the electric telegraph—alias the cannonball post—thus finally had been realized.

The military, however, had a hard time adjusting its chain of command to accommodate the telegraph. Only after the introduction of Morse instruments at railway offices, as a result of which large numbers of Siemens needle telegraphs taken out of service were to be had cheaply, did the Army begin to construct a telegraphic network for its fortresses. The acquisition of Morse instruments and the training of field telegraph units were finally approved in 1856. Nevertheless, it still took until April 20, 1859—the day general mobilization was declared—before the first step was taken to organize the system.[47] Kleist's proposal of transforming soldiers into postmasters met with the declared opposition of officers like Wilhelm Rüstow: never, Rüstow maintained, would "mindless wires" replace the officer on horseback; a battle could not be directed from the telegraphic bureau.[48]

Well, if not a battle, then at least a war. Precisely that was proven at the Battle of Königgrätz by Helmuth von Moltke, who had been named the commander of the General Staff in 1858 after presenting his much acclaimed concept of "deployment from widely separated areas, with assembly of the various armies at the theater of decision, the battlefield."[49] The "possibility [for this] was created especially by the telegraph, in connection with the construction of railroad networks in all countries. It [the telegraph] allowed the military leadership to be simultaneously present at all the positions of an army of operations."[50] In 1866, the effect of the telegraph was not to put limitations on the independent tactical decisions of commanding generals, as Rüstow had feared, but instead to limit the significance of such decisions: "a system of war was adopted that made strategy more, and tactics less, important."[51] Actual evidence against Rüstow's claim could not be reported until Count Alfred von Schlieffen did so in 1909, after the field telegraph had gained tactical importance with its division into four zones—state, base, army (or corps and reserve division), and finally cavalry.[52] Henceforth, Schlieffen wrote, "the general will be situated farther back, in a building with roomy offices, where *cable and wireless telegraphs, telephone and signal apparatus* are at hand. . . . There, in a comfortable chair behind a big desk, the modern Alexander has the entire battlefield before him, from there he telegraphs electrifying words."[53] What Rüstow had declared impossible had come true: "mindless wires" had replaced the general on his steed, or in other words: the First World War.

What was valid for a military leadership supported by a telegraph cable was no less valid for enterprises specializing in such cable: both were present simultaneously at all positions of an army of operations. After Nottebohm, the director of the Prussian state telegraph, imposed an embargo on the firm of Siemens & Halske, the Siemens brothers began setting up a new base of operations for world history itself—as a conflict between Leviathan and Behemoth, the sea power of England and the land power of Russia.[54] While one brother, Carl, laid the cable for the Russian Empire in Saint Petersburg, the other brother, William, produced technical know-how for the English monopoly on sea cables in London, where the Siemens brothers had a branch office. Just as members of the Taxis clan once had occupied all the control points in sixteenth-century Europe in order to connect the Habsburg Empire to the base of a relay postal system, the Siemens brothers occupied the nineteenth-century metropolises of the great European powers in order to construct international cable telegraphy.

At the same time, however, the Siemens brothers also proved how much the law of recurrence dominated their own history. To wit, there had been transfer of Russian-English technology even before the history of the Siemens firm began. Artillery Lieutenant Werner Siemens's interest in the telegraph first had started the day he saw and tested a Wheatstone needle telegraph at the home of a friend and brigade comrade named Soltmann.[55] But the invention Siemens subsequently improved was itself an improved model—and Wheatstone, the inventor of the relay, was himself a relay. In 1836, William Fotherhill Cooke, a retired officer of the East India Company's Army, was able to take a close look at the needle telegraph of a certain Pavel Lvovitch—better known as Baron Schilling von Cannstatt—during one of Professor Muncke's lectures in Heidelberg. Lvovitch alias Schilling was a Russian envoy to Germany, as well as a personal acquaintance of Sömmerring's. In 1832, he had given Czar Nicholas a demonstration of his five-needle telegraph in Berlin, exhibiting it as a medium of absolute control urgently needed for Russia's continental empire. Alexander von Humboldt, who was present at the demonstration, also attempted to convince the czar that Russia definitely needed the telegraph.[56] And just as Schilling von Cannstatt had his eye on the telegraph's use for Russia's continental empire, the India veteran Cook immediately saw its value for rapid military operations in geographical space—whether it was a matter of resisting demonstrations at home or uprisings in the colonies as soon as possible: "The memory of Peterloo was still green, so that Cooke saw the value of his invention to Government in its being enabled 'in case of disturbances to transmit their orders to the local authorities and, if necessary, send troops for their support; while all dangerous excitement of the public might be avoided.'"[57] But Cooke was a soldier, not an engineer. He therefore took his rather dilettantish instrument to Michael Faraday and then finally to Charles Wheatstone. To a certain extent, Carl and William Siemens thus were walking in the footsteps of Cannstatt and Wheatstone-Cooke under the banner of a single business name. The role the Siemens brothers were to play in the Crimean War therefore can be seen as that of telephone operator relaying the second *facteur*'s reply to the first, the product (or interception) of which had founded the Siemens firm's technological advantage.

In 1853, the Siemens brothers—as if they were Cannstatt and Wheatstone—laid cable for their joint partners Russia and England on both sides of the front. Confirming Pynchon's postulate "that the real business" of war "is buying and selling,"[58] Werner smuggled the cables for constructing the Russian telegraph through the English blockade so that the line to the Crimea could be finished just in time to report the expected fall of the Sevastopol Fortress back to Saint Petersburg.[59]

The rest of the telegraph's history is in principle nothing but the continuation and universalization of the Crimean War. From then on, the front ran between land and sea powers, or rather *the* sea power, England. In the former, telegraphy ordinarily became a state monopoly, and such states gradually hooked themselves up on the basis of international treaties: in 1850, the German-Austrian Telegraph Union was founded on the model of the postal system; in 1865, the International Telegraph Union (the only country not represented was England).[60] In the sea power, by contrast, telegraphy was left to the private sector. And because submarine telegraphy did not produce any state treaties (as land telegraphy had), but rather an international exchange of capital with entirely new dimensions, the future predominance of the submarine cable—or of England—already was preprogrammed. If the World Postal Union transformed the world into a collection of picture postcards on the basis of the postage stamp, the Eastern Telegraph Company transformed it into an empire on orders from the Colonial Defence Committee and on the basis of the telegraph.

In 1857, Werner Siemens addressed his *Theory for the Laying and Inspection of Submarine Telegraph Connections*—and therefore the theory of the British Empire itself—directly to the English cable industry as represented by the firm Newall & Company, which had laid the world's first submarine cable beneath the channel between Dover and Calais in 1851.[61] England was not quite so pleased, however, with the Siemens' Indo-European line from London via Prussia, Russia, and Persia to Calcutta, which went into operation in 1869[62]—nothing would be easier, after all, than tapping or cutting a cable. The Eastern Telegraph Company therefore was assured of the government's gratitude (and its money) when it laid a sea cable the very next year from London via Gibraltar, Malta, Alexandria, Suez, and Aden to Bombay, a cable that had practically no contact with non-British shores (the weak link of Egypt was eliminated in 1882). As the insight grew that "the maintenance of submarine cable communication in time of war is of the highest importance to the strategic and commercial interests of every portion of the British Empire,"[63] the Colonial Office increasingly pursued the goal of providing the British colonies with cable via "all red routes."[64] Such a project amounted to nothing less than spanning the globe with a network of telegraph cables that touched only on British soil. The "all red system," which—as Kennedy has written—became a true fetish for the navy and the Colonial Office,[65] revealed the world-historical importance of such obscure islands as Ascension, Norfolk, Rodriguez, Fanning, and the Cocos: once they had become on-land points for the "all red" cable, nothing less than Great Britain's "existence as a nation"[66] depended upon their possession. In the end, of course, this could not be kept a secret from the poet who brought imperial existence as a nation home to the British as no other would. For once, Rudyard Kipling sounded a topic all the way to the bottom and therefore to the literal ground of the Empire and his literature.

> Here in the womb of the world—here on the tie-ribs of earth
> Words, and the words of men, flicker and flutter and beat—
> Warning, sorrow, and gain, salutation and mirth—
> For a Power troubles the Still that has neither voice nor feet.
> They have wakened the timeless Things; they have killed their
>   father Time;
> joining hands in the gloom, a league from the last of the sun.
> Hush! Men talk to-day o'er the waste of the ultimate slime,
> And a new Word runs between: whispering, "Let us be one!"[67]

Only the last word of this was untrue. The command given by the "Deep Sea Cable" of the sonnet's title in the "deserts of the deep" was not to become one, but to become "British." In 1911, the "all red system" was complete.[68] Over 70 percent of the world's cable was in British hands,[69] and the British had a monopoly on gutta-percha, the only known insulating material.[70] The extent of this superiority would become visible on the morning after the English declaration of war on August 4, 1914. Although the German Empire had managed to connect every part of its network with the home country and with every other part of the network without relying on English cable,[71] German cable companies in foreign countries still depended almost entirely on the on-land points of foreign coasts. As a result, the German Empire easily could be dissociated as far as cable technology was concerned: on August 5, 1914, the cable steamer *Alert* cut the German cross-channel cable, and the cable between Monrovia and Pernambuco was tapped on September 13, 1915. The German companies' cable stations in foreign countries were closed and confiscated.[72] The destruction of the English cable stations, by contrast—on Fanning Island by the cruiser *Nuremberg* on September 7, 1914, and on the Cocos Islands by the *Emden* on November 9, 1914—remained almost entirely without effect.[73]

The logistics of Sherlock Holmes, that virtuous user of the telegraph, emerged simultaneously with the construction of the "all red system"—that is, the possibility that a brain like that of Poe's Dupin (who still had been confined to the distance he could cover on foot, and thus to the space of a European capital) could extend over the surface of the entire globe. With telegraphy, a new form of police knowledge based on photography and anthropometry became effective for the first time: from now on, the knowledge identifying an individual and conveying him to himself could be made available anywhere in the world. That such knowledge of things and people could be sent infinitely more quickly than things and people themselves not only enabled worldwide manipulations of the commodities exchange, but also a new conception of the individual that did not depend on location. "The telegraph has made the arm of the law long," the statistician Karl Knies wrote as early as 1857 (thus anticipating Sherlock Holmes's method of identification and pursuit in *A Study in Scarlet* or "The Five Orange Pips"),[74] "so long that it reaches to the furthest regions of the Continent and the ships in the harbors of coastal cities."[75] In telling fashion, a double-needle telegraph installed by Wheatstone and Cooke on the railway line between Slough-London and Paddington first demonstrated the usefulness of electric telegraphy by sending a criminal to the gallows in 1842. For the first time, it no longer was of any use for the murderer—a man named Towell, who had killed his lover, Sarah Hart, in Slough—to escape by train, since his "telegraphic signalment" had reached Paddington early enough for him to be arrested immediately upon his arrival.[76]

In no other age, Knies wrote, could the telegraph have had the importance it did in this one, "which has witnessed the almost immeasurable proliferation and acceleration of personal transportation precisely through the invention of the railway."[77] The transportation of people and information, which still had been one and the same twenty years earlier—that is, mail—now was divided into two competing camps: railway and telegraph. The former dispersed evil (bodies); the latter dispersed law (symbols). Once visual memories were standardized by picture postcards and the technology of individualization devolved into photographic police archives, which became ubiquitous after the facsimile telegraph,[78] the places where one could be forgotten by the media became rare: "the clear sketch of his likeness [rushed] ahead of the criminal" everywhere he went.[79]

When the telegraph was not busy transmitting the top-secret information of the military or police mug shots, the ticker tapes of stock-market rates were clacking away over its lines—as even a child knows. In 1815, on the day after the Battle of Waterloo, the second Rothschild of London, Nathan Mayer, succeeded in what was then the greatest stock-market speculation of all time simply because the state alone had access to Napoleon's optical telegraph—and the English Admiralty's[80]—and as yet no one had realized Kleist's proposal for a cannonball post:

> In response to pessimistic rumors circulating after Blücher's defeat at Ligny, government annuity rates had reached their lowest point. Rothschild bought up the entire supply, since he had been informed of the Allied victory earlier than the public. To wit, he had made sure that the news could reach him in London a few hours in advance, thanks to a carefully prepared system of relay horses over land and a fast sailboat across the North Sea.[81]

Once the Western Union Telegraph Company had laid a second transatlantic cable leading directly to the New York Stock Exchange Building, thus making instantaneous reactions to the international markets feasible as a rule,[82] this sort of thing became part of everyday life.

The postal monopoly on every type of data transmission was melting away, and in light of this fact, *The Diagnosis of Our Time* obviously read "cultural decline" for Hendrik de Man, the uncle of the literary theorist, while in 1874, the founding year of the World Postal Union, the same diagnosis had revealed the beginning of *post-histoire* to Gottfried Keller. As narratives that in a contemplative way recorded things as they happened, history and historical fiction did not testify to the nature of things, but only to a certain state of media technology and the conditions for its possibility: a relay postal system that subsumed the exchange of information and commodities and directed them in parallel transmission. In 1874, which was not only the founding year of the International Telegraph Union, but also the year the Anglo-American Telegraph Corporation laid the first durably functional telegraph cable between Ireland and Newfoundland, Keller's "Misused Love Letters" already had defined the history of literature as an epoch of the nondelivery of those very letters. Now, in the preface to their appearance as a book, this literary metadiscourse was itself published as the postscript to an epoch that was gone forever. Because the delivery of *res gestae* such as Waterloo had devolved to the telegraph, and consequently "the opening or sending of dispatches and a hundred similar things . . . fill up the day . . . nothing happens any more among [the people of Seldwyla] that would be worth noting in a contemplative way, and so it is time to reap yet a small, late harvest in their past."[83] For the poet without access to a telegraph, events became dead letters. Because text no longer was the common bearer of *res gestae* and *res narratae* now that there was a telegraph, even historical fiction like the Seldwyla novellas no longer had recourse to the actuality of narrated events. As a system for recording and processing occurrences, the novel could fall back upon past events, that is, on what already had been written. The novella became historicist, not historical. But while prose escaped with nothing more than the black eye known as historicism, poetry had to look forward to the much crueler fate the telegraph had in store for it.

A pot of boiling water awaited poetry. That was the situation in 1852, just three years after public use of the telegraph started in Prussia, at least according to a novel by Karl Gutzkow entitled *The Carrier Pigeons*. Leontine Simonis, a lonesome palm from Heinrich Heine's Orient and the daughter of a Jewish businessman, feels misunderstood and alone among the "railroad shares, exchange notes, bank transactions" of her brothers, cousins, and uncles. Her fanciful soul finds understanding only from a doctor of philosophy named Moritz Sancho, who writes poems and, of course, is penniless. "There could be no question of a correspondence" during summer vacation, however, since "Leontine hardly would have dared to accept a line from Sancho that came to her by postal route."[84] Consequently, the romantic young lady suddenly is married off to an extremely prosaic merchant, and the philosopher-poet plunges into spiritual distress. Finally, after a long separation, he dares another attempt at poetic rapprochement. For a long time now, "he had observed that Leontine climbed up inside a small, lovely tower attached to her villa every day, where she kept a number of pigeons and fed them regularly. To him, this care for the pigeons was symbol of the lasting and indestructible poetry that remained in Leontine's heart."[85] Thus, a key is quickly fashioned to fit the castle's lock, a poem, that is, that conjures up the pigeons as couriers of a future love correspondence:

> From mine eye 'twill ne'er disappear
> The image: Imprisoned troubadour,
> To whom oh! a pigeon's hope alone!
> She comes! A note! It flutters in the winds—
> What might I find written within?[86]

But the poet who interpreted a woman's occupation with media as potential service to masculine authorship in 1852 ran headlong into a trap. At the same dinner at the merchant's home that Sancho uses as an opportunity to slip his poetic offer of communication to the adored Leontine, his sacred symbol of poetry is served up to him as a side dish, with vegetables. All of Leontine's attempts to conceal it merely bring the terrible truth to light: the would-be "birds of Aphrodite"[87] turn out to be "our old carrier pigeons, which will have served their term of duty in three days, when the electric telegraph is opened." "Haven't you ever seen my wife," the husband continues in explanation to the poet who has fallen from the clouds, "when she climbed our little tower at twelve noon and waited for the transactions my pigeons brought me from Brussels? The telegraph signals them from Paris to Brussels; the electric cable from there has just been completed."[88] Thus, the lady who was to have been Sancho's partner in a carrier-pigeon correspondence—but who has long since been retrained as an ambitious housekeeper—slaughters the poet's postal system *in spe* and drops it into a pot of boiling water. It is hard to imagine a more crass illustration of the end of poetry as an epoch of the postal system.

Devouring the postal system showed poetry for what it had been all along and thus immediately put an end to it. Poetry that devoured girls' letters, as Goethe's had done, lost its footing once the letter-writing muses and women readers of earlier times had placed themselves in the service of the electric telegraph and its economy. After Werner Siemens's gutta-percha press, it was dangerous to interpret women's attendance to postal carriers as the cultivation of poetic symbols. Once women had defected from their postal duties to authorship and had taken up positions as telegraphic assistants in the international stock-market business, it was quite simply their job to sacrifice obsolete systems of postal communication (even if poetry fed upon them) when electrical ones surfaced.

After the Age of Goethe had been served up as dinner to the Age of the Telegraph, the alternative to Keller's choice—defining the narrated time of literature as the prehistory of the technical media—was a literature subjected to the historical a priori of Rowland Hill's economy of symbols or the International Telegraph Union, and thus itself became an event under highly technical conditions. The symbol economy that depended on the standards of worldwide postal formats and transmitting capacity is known in literary history as expressionist style, and in the history of the media as telegram style.

The unsurpassed laconicism of August Stramm's poems merely followed the economic laws the telegraphic medium had imposed on discourse, insofar as it passed through the strettos of signifiers or through the cable network of the world telegraph system.[89]

And that was no accident: in 1909, the senior postal assistant Stramm received his degree in Halle after submitting his *Historical, Critical, and Financial-Political Investigations on the World Postal Union's Postage Rates for Letters and Their Foundations*. These foundations were nothing but the laws of the symbol economy dictated by the technical standards of the telegraph. Even "a cursory glance at the former and current telegram rates of all countries shows that the length of the conveyance route . . . is completely disregarded in many cases."[90] This was so simply because it made no difference whatsoever—as Sömmerring already had discovered—whether electrical current traveled one foot or many thousand. Strict seriality in data transmission thus made rigorous price standardization necessary for messages. "The telegraph is a courier borne on the wings of lightning," Knies wrote, quoting Kleist, "but it never takes along more than *one* letter."[91] This circumstance had compelled the German Empire to switch its telegram rates from group to single-word charges on March 1, 1876—the previous lump-sum fee for twenty words merely had produced the effect "that wire correspondents thereby were forced into the habit of diligently adding unnecessary titles, verbose clichés of cordiality, and otherwise meaningless padding to telegrams."[92] An initiative for restructuring rates in this manner subsequently was passed at the London conference of the International Telegraph Union in 1879.[93] The result of such a technogenic symbol economy was that the average length of telegrams dropped from 18.32 words to 11.9 in 1881, and that August Stramm's poems sometimes contained as few as eight words, as is the case with "In the Fire" (and would therefore have cost only forty pfennigs in telegram fees, plus twenty for the base rate).

Even Prussia's optical telegraph, with its endless transmission intervals of up to thirteen hours per telegram, had produced this kind of abbreviated phrasing, which not even the style of royal sovereigns and the etiquette afforded them could escape. A telegram text such as "His Royal Highness the Duke of Cambridge held a grand hunt in the local forest and on this occasion caught sight of the R[oyal] Prussian telegraph, which is located not far from the Office in Liebenburg. The same Supreme Highness let His pleasure at the purposeful institution and the punctuality with which it performed its service be known to the attending telegraphist" became this laconicism after being pruned on principle of all forms of etiquette and passing through O'Etzel's code book: "Duke Cambridge held hunt here in forest at station 23 let telegraphist know pleasure at good institution and punctual service 18 Oct. three thirty stop."[94] Thirty-five years later, such monarchical ignorance of the appropriate forms of etiquette demanded by telegraphic technology provoked the Franco-Prussian War.[95]

That the price standardization of information via the postage stamp and the disregard for differences in distance even within the territory of the World Postal Union took place under the influence of the telegraphogenic time economy is possible in the case of letters and actually is documented in the case of postcards. In 1837, the year of Rowland's memorandum on post-office reform, Charles Wheatstone had discussed the telegraph's value for the "public good" with Hill at the Social Community, a kind of cooperative living arrangement for scientists.[96] And according to Hermann's 1869 proposal, the postcard was to be nothing but a "postal telegram" containing "no more than twenty words, including address and signature of the sender"—in accordance with the current group rate for telegrams. "Fire's" eight words thus would have found just enough room on Hermann's "postal telegram." Information exchange, Stramm wrote in his dissertation, was subject to the "principle of economic viability, of producing the highest possible values with the least possible expenditure"[97]—and expressionist lyric poetry was no less so. The expressionist "work of art does not become significant in that it can be interpreted" or "that one knows what it is supposed to mean," Stramm's friend and publisher Herwarth Walden wrote, but instead, via the most economical ratio possible between the expenditure of words and their effect. It had "nothing to do with . . . spirit"[98] simply because it had everything to do with telegraphy.

The characteristic style of Stramm's lyric poetry—contraction of nouns, verbs, and/or adjectives—was nothing but an effect of the word fees that the telegraphist encountered day in and day out and that the Imperial Post and Telegraph Administration [*Reichspost- und Telegraphenverwaltung*, or RPTV] regulated using veritable lexicons of expressionist lyric. "The more progress the public makes in using the most laconic telegraphic style possible, predetermined ciphers or abbreviated forms of address," in other words, the more they trained to become expressionist literary artists, "the more the telegraph's gross revenues decline."[99] Consequently, the so-called *Little Stephan*, a postal handbook to be found in every office during the expressionist epoch and assuredly on the desk of the senior postal assistant Stramm, contained exhaustive vocabulary lists, but lists that did not contain any signifieds on the right-hand side, merely definitions of the word count. The confrontation between these definitions and a selection of Stramm's neologisms conveys the principle of creating the highest possible values with the least possible expenditure as the originator of both [see Table 1].

TABLE I. Stramm's Lyric Poetry Versus the RPTV

Expressionism (Stramm)		RPTV	
to count as[100]		to count as[101]	
blauspielfroh	I word	abhier	2 words
hagelgelb	I ''	anglogerman	2 ''
tottoll	I ''	billigstmöglich	2 ''
hartscharfkantig	I ''	lebendfrisch	I word
Sonnsiegklänge	I ''	Zehnpfundgans	3 words
blaublaß	I ''	braunblond	I word
lichtgeblendet	I ''	eilreist	2 words
frechgespreizt	I ''	seeverpackt	2 ''
trügeneckend	I ''	morgenabend	2 ''
glühewehe	I ''	gutbonig	I word
gähnmund	I ''	ersttätig	I ''
goldhellrot	I ''	aprilalt	2 words
schreikroll	I ''	einsmodel	2 ''
schamzerpört	I ''	zweizink	2 ''
Allwege	I ''	Drangdraht	2 ''
flammzerissen	I ''	starkmusterig	I word
welttiefhohe	I ''	Russenfläue	2 words

Why did a postal inspector defect to lyric poetry? Because the readers of his poems let him count a word like "sunvictorysounds" [*Sonnsiegklänge*] as one word (and therefore as art), while the telegraph administration at the German Imperial Postal Service would treat it as mercilessly as it treated a "tenpoundgoose" [*Zehnpfundgans*], that is, as a three-word word. The *Little Stephan*'s lyric poetry therefore contained its own definition in contrast to Stramm's: cheapestpossible pressurecable [*billigstmöglicher Drangdraht*]—to count as four words.

CHAPTER EIGHTEEN

The Virgin Machine

The low efficiency of telegraphic transmission determined by its sequentiality did not merely produce aftereffects such as the word fee and the expressionist word art published in *Sturm*. It also led to the inventions of direct sound recording and transmission. The phonograph's principle was bestowed on Edison by a device that, by mechanizing the telegraph's key-entry functions, increased the speed at which telegrams could be entered beyond anything humanly possible. Edison recorded Morse code signals by hand on perforated strips of paper and then fed them through the machine at a rate that surpassed his own record speed as a telegraphist[1] and that also promised to rescue his colleagues from the professional disorder of "telegrapher neurosis" (loss of hand control at the key, followed by cramps, etc.).[2] During his experiment, Edison noted that the dots and dashes on the paper strips produced a "slightly musical, rhythmic tone resembling a faint human voice" as they passed beneath the steel needle.[3] The "replication" of a voice that no one and nothing ever had recorded before sent Edison on his way to invent the phonograph.

At about the same time (1873), a Scottish pedagogue who instructed deaf-mutes in Boston was experimenting with a different method for increasing the transmitting capacity of expensive copper telegraph cables: the multiple telegraph. While Baudot and Edison were busy developing phase multiplex procedures, Alexander Graham Bell spent his free time on something he called a "harmonic telegraph," later known as the frequency multiplex, by means of which he sought to transmit a harmonic chord and to resolve it into its component tones at the receiving end using resonators. Such tones then could be used as carrier frequencies for signals. Bell had been pursuing this idea since Alexander J. Ellis, the prominent phonetician, had personally referred him to Helmholtz's treatise *On the Sensations of Tone as a Physiological Basis for the Theory of Music*. At almost the same time, the young Bell had become acquainted with none other than the renowned Charles Wheatstone, who gave him a demonstration of an improved version of Kempelen's speech machine.[4] Perhaps the young Bell misunderstood Ellis, thinking that Helmholtz had succeeded in electrically transmitting vowel sounds using his resonator piano.[5]

In any case, Bell's imitation of Helmholtz at once helped and hindered him in inventing the telephone. Occasionally, of course (after his flight from tuberculosis-plagued London to the New World), he also experimented with Léon Scott's "phonautograph," which he improved by implementing the ear of a human cadaver and used to produce feedback between written and spoken oscillation curves for his students.[6] But in terms of communications technology, Bell, the reader of Helmholtz, returned again and again to the latter's principle of intermittent currents—even after the possibility of transmitting speech via "undulating" currents had been demonstrated by accident. And because of this, he remained (in the words of his biographer) "incapable of thinking in terms of a membrane transmitter and receiver."[7] Consequently, the telephone never has been patented. All of the patents Bell submitted concerned "improvements of telegraphy" and included his telephone inventions only in supplementary clauses. But Bell cannot rightfully be called the inventor of the telephone. Unable to think of the human ear phonautograph as anything but a storage medium for voice oscillations, Bell had to be hooked up to the telephone by an operator. That job went to a woman: Mabel Hubbard, the operator of all future operators.

Alexander Graham Bell met her at Sara Fuller's School for Deaf-Mutes in Boston, where she became his student in 1871.[8] She had lost her hearing from a case of scarlet fever at the age of five, and her father, Gardiner Green Hubbard—a lawyer who had made a fortune from patent-dispute cases—subsequently set out to reform the system for deaf-mute care in America. In order to prevent his daughter's complete loss of speech—a fate considered to be unavoidable at the time—Hubbard imported the so-called "oral method" from Europe and along with it the scandalous conviction that deaf persons spoke only when they had no language of their own—that is, no sign language. "A fair trial can only be made," Hubbard demanded, "where articulation and reading from lips are the only medium of communication taught and the only one allowed."[9] In other words: deaf persons speak as operators or not at all.

That was reason enough for Hubbard to make contact with Bell, whose oral methods of teaching were based on his father Melville Bell's "Visible Speech" system, which was just then enjoying sensational success. Hubbard quickly recognized that there was capital to be made from the telephone experiments of this bitterly poor teacher of deaf-mutes. But Bell wanted nothing other than to teach deaf-mutes to speak and to get his frequency multiplex to function. And he wanted Mabel Hubbard. Thus, the deal eventually was brokered that produced the largest media conglomerate of all times: as dictated by her father, Mabel wrote to Bell, whom she feared more than loved, that she would not marry him unless he already had developed a patentable telephone.[10] Hubbard sold his daughter to Bell for the price of the telephone. It was not just after, but even before, the telephone's invention that women were "especially good at making it work."[11] Hubbard subsequently financed Bell's telephone experiments, and in 1875, he founded the Bell Patent Association, in which he, Bell, and Thomas Sanders each held 30 percent of the shares, the remaining 10 percent going to Bell's technical assistant, Thomas A. Watson. Yet for all that, the telephone submitted for patenting (by Hubbard) in 1876 merely consisted of a harmonic telegraph tipped at a 90-degree angle and soldered to a membrane. In 1877, Bell married Mabel, a woman who was as deaf and mute as his mother (Eliza Grace Bell, who later would attain worldwide literary fame as the flower girl Eliza).[12] On the same day, his father-in-law founded the Bell Telephone Company. No wonder Bell wrote his fiancée: "The telephone is mixed up in a most curious way with my thoughts of you."[13] The rest is history: the National Bell Telephone Company (where, incidentally, Emile Berliner—the future inventor of the gramophone record—worked in the technical division)[14] was founded in 1879, and a year later the American Bell Telephone Company followed, which in turn gave birth to the American Telephone and Telegraph Company in 1885, a daughter organization responsible for constructing "long lines." (In 1899, the daughter swallowed up her parents.)[15]

The move away from the frequency multiplex, which led to the development of the mass-producible telephone—by replacing a deaf-mute woman "in a most curious way"—was in truth the decisive step in its direction. In 1915, the telephone caught up with its own origin, or rather its nonorigin, with the invention of the "wave filter," which made possible what Bell neither had wanted nor had been able to achieve with his Helmholtzian tuning-fork transmitters and receivers: the transmitting route's separation into different frequency bands.[16] For the telegraph, this achievement meant that its message could be sent over telephone lines in the future, either in the form of base telegraphy at frequencies from 0 to 150 Hz, which played no role in speech transmission, or as eighteen-channel tone-frequency telegraphy via a single unused telephone channel. Telegraphy became a subset of telephone frequencies. The optimization of its efficiency—the irony of fate—was precisely what spelled the doom of the telegraph as an autonomous medium. Its existence had depended on its weakness. In the years that followed, the kilometers of telegraph line dropped steadily in number. The fulfillment of Bell's dream of the frequency multiplex via his "improvement of telegraphy" had led to a result of which he never would have dreamed: "specialized telegraph networks were absorbed everywhere."[17]

In 1898, a year before Mabel became Ma Bell, she published the history of the speech training in which she herself had been the first subject: *The Story of the Rise of the Oral Method in America*. This text itself was subject to the law of the discourse it described—and as a result, someone else was speaking whenever the pronoun "I" appeared. As the first experimental subject of the Oral Method in America, Mabel had read her speech from the lips of her father; therefore, in the discourse she gave on that method, she could appear only in the third person: "My own interest in the education of the deaf and my earnest efforts to introduce what I believed to be a better method of instruction than the one then in use, sprang from my anxiety for my little deaf child."[18] Because the self was occupied by her father, all that was left for Mabel was to speak using lines that did not belong to her, no differently than operators in switchboard offices would do afterward by the tens of thousands. On principle, such operators were neither senders nor receivers of discourse, but instead the third persons in whom all first and second persons were founded and in whom they foundered. The operator's function practiced the truth that "only because in everyday speaking language does *not* bring itself to language but holds itself back, are we able simply to go ahead and speak a language."[19] In other words: "The operator was not allowed to use her own words."[20]

That holding back or epoch of the postal service opened up the opportunity for countless women to occupy roles in the discourse that previously had been reserved exclusively for men. For technical reasons alone, the telephone made it necessary to install the third person, who lacked the capacity to establish individual discourse, in what in Germany was a civic post. The renunciation of all claim to the discursive authority of "I" that "permits each speaker to *appropriate to himself an entire language*"[21] could not be expected from male subjects, whom the state continued to train for personal responsibility and the ability to appropriate language. Consequently, women became indispensable as third persons. Only women could commit the speech act dictated since 1881, which linked the third person with a deixis and, according to Benveniste,[22] is impossible: "Operator. Number please."[23]

In Germany, because civil servants frequently were transferred over the course of their education and were trained to be independent selves who hardly could be subjected to a prohibition on the use of their own words,[24] The Office overturned Fichte's verdict against women in governmental posts by creating a position for them that was as impossible as the sentences they pronounced: the position of a nontenured civil servant or salaried public employee—an operator. As telephone operators, women professionalized a discursive authority that, according to Kafka's analysis of the postal situation around 1900, defines the fundamental role of speaking: "They were given the choice of becoming kings or kings' messengers. As is the way with children, they all wanted to be messengers. That is why there are only messengers, racing through the world and, since there are no kings, calling out to each other the messages that have now become meaningless. They would gladly put an end to their miserable life, but they do not dare to do so because of their oath of loyalty."[25]

Civil servants, of course, swear oaths of loyalty, and were thus appointed as discursive authorities of the first person, who established an individual discourse for which the speaker assumed responsibility: in the name of the king. Kafka's postal officials, by contrast, are not the subjects, but the operators of speech. They are third persons, one and all, who can establish only a discourse that shares the status of postcards: without reference, owner, or designated recipient.[26] Already in Kafka's first fragmentary novel, Raban—yet another clerk in an anonymous office—reflects the status of discourses for which neither the speaker nor the operator assumes responsibility, since they are grounded in the third person:

> One works so feverishly at the office that afterwards one is too tired even to enjoy one's holidays properly. But even all that work does not give one a claim to be treated lovingly by everyone; on the contrary, one is alone, a total stranger and only an object of curiosity. And so long as you say "one" instead of "I," there's nothing in it and you can easily tell the story, but as soon as you admit to yourself that it is you yourself, you feel as though transfixed and are horrified.[27]

Raban is just another courier without a king. The stories he recites have the status of standard texts: without an author or an owner, they are nothing but precisely that—recitals, which (after Herder) means they were not internalized. Anyone who says "one" is not saying anything himself, but merely relaying information. At the same time, however, someone who says "I" is not saying anything, either. Because there is no king in whose name the official self can take responsibility for speech, the speaker assumes the entire language as his responsibility and is veritably beaten. Kafka's couriers are therefore like children or lunatics—which, indeed, amounted to the same thing, according to the letter of the civil law regarding the inability to conduct business: by law, they could not send letters or gain ownership of the ones addressed to them. There was a reason why children wanted to be couriers: that was precisely what they were by law.

The circumstances of Kafka's courier metaphor had quite non-metaphorical properties. After all, the insight that authors were couriers for the postcards known as literature was fully consistent with the situation of German postal officials after 1871. The Charter of the Constitution of the German Empire stated the following with regard to the courier's oath of loyalty in 1871: "It is the duty of all civil servants of the postal and telegraphic administration to comply with imperial ordinances. This duty is to be recorded in the oath of loyalty."[28] Yet a law of the same year stated that precisely these imperial ordinances no longer were to be issued. "In light of the rapid advances being made in transportation, commerce, and industry, and further in light of the development and improvements experienced by the entire system of transport," Moltke argued in justification of the bill, it seemed necessary "to issue rules on specific operations and the performance of postal service, not via legislation as before, but by a [departmental] regulation"[29] that the Imperial Post Office could pass on its own: "It would create . . . a substantial impediment . . . to the postal administration's flexibility and its quick detection and consideration of defects as they present themselves, if matters of postal operation were . . . determined via legislation."[30] In the name of the emperor: discourses in the name of the emperor—for example, laws—were an impediment to postal action. An imperial law decreed that the postal service no longer was governed by imperial laws. From then on, postal officials acted in the name of the emperor when they did not act in the name of the emperor; the only imperial ordinance with which they were required to comply by the oath of loyalty was no longer to comply with any imperial ordinances: voilà Kafka's courier, pledged to kinglessness.

The telephone ultimately procured an endless number of incarnations for this legal paradox. Switchboard technology made the end of auctorial discourse into a women's profession—simply because women, unlike male officials and poets used to discursive power, did not "want to put an end" to their "miserable life" as operators, but much rather preferred to begin professional careers. As the first woman telephone operator in history, Miss Emma Nutt had launched that career itself in 1878, when she was hired by the Boston Telephone Despatch Company, the first firm founded under the license of Hubbard and Bell. Soon, thousands followed her from the army of employment-seeking women left behind by the American Civil War. It was especially easy for them to do so, since men (in the lovely words of one of the first female telephone operators) were "complete and consistent failures" as switchboard operators.[31]

In Germany, State Secretary Heinrich von Stephan initially stood in the way of men's disconnection from the communications service. In 1872, even before the age of telephones was underway, he explained to the Reichstag "that no institution is less suitable for the employment of women than the Imperial Communications Offices."[32] (Stephan seemed here to be playing on the double entendre in the German word for communications—*Verkehr*, literally "intercourse"—which also inspired public discussion and countless cartoons for years to come.) Two hundred fifty women telephone operators were hired in 1874, but Stephan was able to close the breech in his woman blockade two years later. The preliminary decision to employ them finally was made in 1881. The same year that the Remington marketing department discovered that the armies of unemployed women also were practically destined to make a commercial hit out of the first mass-producable typewriter,[33] the first telephone switchboard was set up on Berlin's Französische Strasse.[34] Once the multiple switchboard (which allowed several thousand connections to be made from a single seat) was introduced in 1885, Stephan finally had to clear his ramparts under pressure from the crown princess and later empress. In 1887, the first "female assistant workers for telephone service" were hired as nonbudgeted civil servants.[35] Yet in spite of this, the massive entry of women into the rooms of the unyielding postal administration did not begin until after Stephan's death in 1897. His successor, Major General Victor von Podbielski, opened up all areas of postal administration to women by decree as early as February 1898: "As the first area of employment in the postal service, the operation of typewriters in the official chanceries (official rooms) of Post Offices 1, the railway post offices and especially the General Postal Administration were opened to women by the February Decree of 1898. . . . Here a number of chancery clerks are constantly occupied with written work, much of which is suitable for typewritten script."[36] On July 17, 1897—Stephan was not yet cold in his grave, so to speak—the Prussian Ministry of Commerce and Industry issued a regulation deeming typewritten script to be permissible in communications with the government.[37] From then on, women did not merely write like chancery clerks—as Gritli Störteler once had done for the postal administration of the *Misused Love Letters*—but also instead of chancery clerks.

With Lilian Sholes (the daughter of the Remington's inventor and the first female typist in history)[38] and Mabel Hubbard (the daughter of the future founder of AT&T), the beginning of the end had arrived for the asymmetrical distribution of gender in discourse. While the typewriter delivered "the resources of the printing press" not only into the hands of poets, but also those of stenotypists,[39] the switchboard began to erode gender boundaries in the law regarding civil service in Germany. These two developments augmented each other in the same way that all new media fundamentally are at one among themselves and mutually interchangeable: the telephone "sped the commercial adoption of the typewriter. . . . In no time at all, the telephone expanded the work to be done on the typewriter to huge dimensions. Pyramids of paperwork rose on the basis of a small telephone network inside a single business."[40] The acceleration of business and command routes by means of the telephone (which only women typists were capable of handling with their record number of strokes per minute) left the elitist pride of male chancery clerks (who wrote calligraphically, but slowly) intact, but it also left them without jobs. As early as 1907, women already held 10,489 positions as nontenured officials, which was equal to a share of 87 percent of all official positions in the telephone service, nontenured and otherwise.[41] Tenured— that is, male—civil servants survived only in the ecological niches they owed solely to the prudery of directors. "The service of telephone communication has today become an exclusively female profession," the women's corner of an illustrated magazine gleefully proclaimed as early as 1905, "our male colleagues, after all, are only employed in supervising or as low-level officials for night shifts."[42] In 1912, the "greater dexterity (of women) at the machines"[43] out-trumped the higher education of the men once again, when the adding machine procured their entry into the postal money order offices, which had been opened in 1909.[44]

The last bastions of women's exclusion from communications institutions, which as yet still had been neglected in a situation where the technical media demanded couriers and not kings, finally were swept away by the First World War. At its end, a full seventy-five thousand women civil servants and wartime auxiliaries stood in the service of the RPTV. Nor were they to be dismissed after the war—a regulation issued in view of the strategic situation on December 15, 1917, made sure of that.[45]

Like all other social safeguards for women, however, this regulation applied only on one condition: their single status. Until 1929, "wedlock dissolved the contract of employment on the day of the marriage ceremony."[46] Should their highest duty, providing the state with new civil servants and raising them, catch up to the undepletable numbers of women at the switches, they were "utterly annihilated" as operators of the public machinery as a result—as indeed they always had been according to Fichte's interpretation. In the war against the telephone and typewriter, Kleist's "highest duty" and Fichte's conclusion based on that duty flowed once more from the pen of the education officer and privy councilor Pierstorff in 1899:

> A man devotes himself to his profession for his entire life and is conscious of this from the very beginning. If he marries, then his professional occupation is not affected by this. It is different for women. The majority marries sooner or later. . . . For women who have a professional life, the wedding vows bring with them the abandonment of their former careers. After all, life's other task awaits them, in the fulfillment of which the wife's highest duty and satisfaction lies now and forever more, the profession of spouse, the mother of the home.[47]

The Truth of the bureaucratic state's transcendental proviso demanded that mothers be removed from circulation. Marriage became the sole gender characteristic upholding the state: "The distinction between man and woman in the civil service, which cannot be cleared away without shaking the foundations of disciplined civil service, lies in the exclusion of the married woman."[48]

Women were married either to their machines or to a man. At the same time, telephone technology long since had denied the sacrament upon which its church was founded to the priestly caste of a bureaucracy informed by the exclusion of women. The analog channels of communication had destroyed the monopoly that had existed from time immemorial on transmitting discrete signals. From then on, women were included in state institutions for the same reason that once had justified their exclusion as the transcendental origin of the mind's presence to itself (named the individual or the civil servant): the voice. Because the frequency range of a woman's voice was encompassed more completely by the frequency band that the telephone transmitted (originally 1000 to 1500 Hz, after the introduction of the first intermediate amplifier to 2000 Hz, since 1929 to 2400 Hz),[49] it simply was more suitable for telephone transmission than a male voice. Thus, Undersecretary Fischer had explained the connection between girls and the media to the clueless Bebel[50] as early as 1894—when Stephan was still alive and kicking. Turning first to physics and then to the erotic, Fischer explained: "His question is with regard to the young girls who have been employed in the telephone service for about three years, and, if I dare say so myself, with much success, for one thing because their sound waves are more easily understood due to the higher voice register of the feminine organ, and also because the caller becomes friendly when a woman's voice comes through to him on the telephone. The trial runs have thus been quite positive."[51] In 1898, after Stephan's death, the Reichstag was able to hear it from the mouth of the state secretary of the Imperial Postal Service himself: "With regard to the ladies' question, I must repeat that women in particular are especially well-suited for telephone service because their vocal range is three tones higher, and as a result they are more easily understood than men."[52]

The technical standards of the channel were at one with its eroticization in the form of the media's self-advertisement. And that was no accident: the voice became an erotic partial object in the same breath that made it recordable and transmittable as something real via the gramophone and telephone—and therefore an object for the research of physics. That the voice included women in the discourse instead of excluding them thus implied a fundamental shift in the linguistic *episteme*.

As long as the voice was a presence that vanished in what it was, the definition of its true nature was delegated to the fields of philosophy, Classical/Romantic poetry, psychology, and anthropology, whether it was defined as "the concrete shape born from the spirit";[53] or the pre-articulate grounding of the perception of sound itself, which became the origin of the world that endowed meaning (as it was in Pestalozzi's pedagogical theory of the mother's voice);[54] or the remembered and infantalizing origin of poetry (as in Tieck's *Sternbald*);[55] or the "sacred music" in which The Mother known as Nature had swaddled The Individual after its ontogenic and phylogenic birth (as in E. T. A. Hoffmann's theory of the mechanism, or natural metaphysics).[56]

All that changed abruptly after 1877. The media of sound recording and transmission did not merely show physicists and physiologists that the existence of the voice is grounded in the parameters of frequency, amplitude, and phase. Worse still, they allowed these parameters to be individually manipulated and thus made it possible to analyze what had been seen as the indivisible foundation of all syntheses in the Romantic era. There had been voice physiologists even before the invention of the telephone, of course, just as there had been acoustics in physics. But the sound transmitters of such scientists never really advanced beyond the technical state of Romantic machine magic or carnival sensations. In 1835, Johannes Müller had acquired the larynxes of corpses and blew in them "in order to study the production requirements for specific vocal sounds *in concreto*"[57]—the result sounded "like a carnival pipe with a rubber membrane."[58] Helmholtz had experimented with tuning forks, using resonators to regulate their sound energy; others like Toepler and Boltzmann in 1870 or Rayleigh in 1877 still were tinkering with the organ pipes Kempelen had used long before.[59] The voice itself was ruled out as an object of research or as standard output due to lack of the necessary equipment.

It is thus no wonder that after 1877 (four years before Stephan set out to spread news of the telephone to the rest of the people) a downright rush began, with physiologists, medical scientists, and physicists flocking to the new media of sound transmission and recording. As early as 1877, Du Bois-Reymond was able to use the telephone to confirm Helmholtz's hypothesis of timbre's independence from the phase delay occurring due to the induction between transmitter and receiver.[60] In 1878, Ludomar Hermann presented the bold hypothesis that either the general law of induction or Helmholtz's theory would have to be discarded because of the telephone. Even if induction itself did not produce a change in timbre, Hermann argued, the change still had to occur because of the increase in the amplitude of higher partial tones in relation to the amplitude of lower ones, which was caused by induction.[61] In response, Helmholtz reached for the telephone in order to defend his theory of vowels.[62] Next door, scholars also were making telephone calls with frogs: while Tarchanow in Saint Petersburg used the telephone as a receiver for the electrical currents of frog muscles (and thus as a galvanoscope)—and heard "a distinctly musical tone on the telephone"[63]—Hermann used it the other way around, as a transmitter: "Of the vowel sounds, 'a' affects the frog preparation most intensely, next come 'o', 'ou', 'e', and the weakest is 'i'."[64] Finally, in 1891, Hermann presented the theory of vowels he had worked out on the basis of telephonic transmissions. "The essence of vowels," according to Hermann's theory, was not to be found "in distinct ratios of intensity among the harmonic partial tones of a sound," but in "a definite tone, intermitting or oscillating with the period of the note."[65] This was a first step in the direction of formant theory. In 1892, Hermann Gutzmann, the first private instructor of phoniatry, began to use the restricted telephone frequency band of 1000 and 1500 Hz for his "Investigations on the Limits of Linguistic Perception"—after the consistent perceptive distortion of his name into "Butzmann" or "Dutzmann" on the telephone made him aware that "sounds with similar acoustic character [in this case *b*, *d*, *g*, phonetic stops] are consistently confused" in the process.[66]

Ultimately, Carl Stumpf reached for the telephone in 1921 to confirm his formant theory of consonants.[67] Karl Willy Wagner, the president of the Imperial Office of Telegraph Technology, then reached in turn for formant theory: the damper series connected to telephone lines made Stumpf's predicted formant regions unmistakably audible and allowed Wagner to use them as a basis for redefining the frequency range necessary for sufficient comprehension on the telephone.[68]

But feedback of this sort between standards and the objects they measure, between technology and physiology, was part of the agenda after Boston otologist Clarence John Blake had procured the cadaver ear for Alexander Graham Bell that showed him the possibility of membrane-directed currents, and after Blake in turn used that possibility, in the form of the telephone, to develop a supra-individual method for testing hearing.[69] Collaboration in Germany went just as well: on Helmholtz's personal advice, Werner Siemens constructed the membrane of his telephone in the form of an ear drum.[70] But such connections between engineers and physiologists merely marked the beginning of a symbiotic coalescence between two entire research disciplines. To the same extent, technical laboratories were set up at the physiological and anatomical institutes of universities, and departments for research on speaking and hearing were established at media firms and governmental institutions. In 1905, the British General Post Office began to administer articulation tests.

But a physiology of the voice and hearing that actually suited the specific needs of the media was not founded until 1913. Irving B. Crandall, a professor of physics and chemistry, joined the research staff of Western

Electric (an AT&T daughter company, of course) that year with the specific goal in mind of "arriving at an accurate physical description and a standard for measuring the mechanical operation of the human ear in terms that we can directly apply to our electrical and acoustical instruments."[71] The voice and ear became elements of a technical communication system *inter pares*: "it was apparent that great advantages would come from similarly analyzing speech and hearing; for an accurate knowledge of every part of a system, from the voice through the telephone instruments to and including the ear, would permit more intelligent design of the parts under control."[72] Harvey Fletcher, Crandall's successor, who joined the Department of Physical Research at Western Electric in 1916, initiated "the first major phase in the investigation of language, speech, and comprehension."[73] From then on at the latest, "the nature of speech" no longer was defined as the soul or "self-manifesting subjectivity," but instead as manifestations of frequency and amplitude. Consequently, "its interpretation" was not the business of philosophers and linguists, but of engineers and physicists, who viewed the voice as nothing more than an element in the telephone system. And as precisely that, the voice included women, rather than excluding them. Their vocal range not only was better situated in the band of telephone frequencies, it also was substantially more conducive to the articulation of language—as Fletcher determined: "A filter system which eliminates all frequencies below 500 cycles per second eliminates 60 per cent. of the energy in speech, but only reduces the articulation 2 per cent. A system which eliminates frequencies above 1500 cycles per second eliminates only 10 per cent. of the speech energy, but reduces the articulation 35 per cent."[74]

Conclusion: after the invention of amplifier tubes, nothing spoke in favor of men's voices on the telephone. Women's voices, by contrast, not only were not the obscure, pre-articulate origin of the clear and distinct articulation of men, but themselves were *claire et distincte par excellence*. In an epoch of the postal service where psychogenic voices did not count at all, but system-compatible ones counted all the more, women were predestined for the role of couriers operating without a king. The technical media, which produced their own conceptions of the body, and consequently of the soul as well—conceptions that suited them—thus created a career for women at precisely the site where they dismissed auctorial discourse. And for that reason alone, media conglomerates can use the prevention of literature as a means for self-advertisement.

It cannot be said more clearly: whoever leases telephone service from AT&T thereby undersigns a "terrible loss" for literature [see Figure 11]. The postal epoch of the sonnet is defined as the telephone's absence—and is therefore irrevocably past. However countless the ways that lyric poetry transmits meaning, it is helpless against the discount percentages guaranteed by AT&T's standard rates for signifiers per time unit. Precisely because the capacities of telephone lines are not countless, but limited, literature in the form of love letters was left by the wayside. Just as women typists turned poetry into a countable quantity of keystrokes—all of which had their price[75]—women telephone operators (or their automatic rate meters) turned declarations of love into a counted quantity of discourse minutes (or in the age of ISDN, bits per second). And these, too, all had their price: the theme of countless pop songs ("and the operator says 'forty cents more for the next three minutes'"),[76] money, "the most annihilating signifier possible of every signification,"[77] annihilated even romantic love, which indeed is poetry by definition alone and therefore "signification" at the highest level. But this does not obstruct good business for the telephone companies—as the above-mentioned pop songs go to show. Because the "ways" of telephone lines transmit voices not in the form of fantasized magical melodies, but instead as sundered objects, they are a way or a medium with which the "ways" of love letters cannot compete. "The right choice" is therefore not Elizabeth Barrett, but Ma Bell. Not for nothing are the postal service and the telephone industry competing communications services in the United States (and recently in Germany as well, as the era of Stephan gradually nears its end).

Thus, the competitive advertisement in Figure 11, which in any case uses the elimination of *the* epistolary romance in nineteenth-century English literature as promotional material, conducts a rather precise analysis of the Romantic scene of letter writing. The sonnet emerges in the field between two poles: between the quill on one side and the beloved's miniature in the medallion on the other. These poles organize two lines of vision that converge in the eye of the woman writer—who is at once also the observer. Such is the primal scene of Sentimental-Romantic letter writing: the woman writer's wandering glance weaves the unbroken or in-

If Elizabeth Barrett and Robert Browning had AT&T's 60% and 40% discounts, it would have been a terrible loss for English literature.

And of course, she wouldn't have had to restrict her feelings to a mere sonnet's length, either.

After all, you can always think of one more way to tell someone you love them when you're on the phone.

Let us count the ways you can save. Just call weekends till 5pm Sundays, or from 11pm to 8am, Sunday through Friday, and you'll save 60% off AT&T's Day Rate on your state-to-state calls.

Call between 5pm and 11pm, Sunday through Friday, and you'll save 40% on your state-to-state calls.

So when you're asked to choose a long distance company, choose AT&T. Because with AT&T's 60% and 40% discounts, you can satisfy your heart's desire without exhausting your means.

Reach out and touch someone.

AT&T
The right choice.

FIGURE 11. AT&T long-distance advertisement.

dividual threads of text into the imaginary. As it rolls up, the paper gains an interior space: it is the medium of subjectivity and not, let us say, a postcard. And Gellert's ink bottle—forming a right triangle with the quill and the portrait—stands ready to tip over should the letter threaten to be finished. Letters were glances that reflected the glance of the Other. Therefore, the letter Elizabeth Barrett wrote was not a letter at all, but the soul itself. Love's postal territory was not the penny post, but the imaginary: "I love thee to the depth and breadth and height / My soul can reach, when feeling out of sight / for the end of Being and ideal Grace."[78] By contrast, the "one more way" AT&T customers have over the poet is not a "way to tell" at all, but rather a way to "reach out and touch someone," as the company says itself. And this is not done with the soul, as it is in the sonnet, or metaphorically, but via the electromagnetic transmission of bare sensual stimuli. The scope of the imaginary voice, which had reached out to the boundaries of existence and eternity and had outlined The Individual at once in the form of the Mortal and—*qua* poetry—the Divine, was canceled out by the scope of the technogenic partial object, which coincided with the worldwide networks of cable and radio. Ever since, speaking means touching.

The genealogy of AT&T's slogan meanwhile dates back to the earliest phase of electronic communications technology. In 1795, the Spaniard Francisco Salvá made a proposal to Barcelona's Real-Academia calling for the use of Leyden jars in order to telegraph between Matar and Barcelona. By means of cables, twenty-two Leyden jars in Matar were to be hooked up to twenty-two people in Barcelona, each representing a letter of the alphabet:[79] a long-distance typewriter composed of human bodies that would have become signifiers under electrical shock treatment. More than a hundred years later, Ma Bell's "touch" was implemented by a worthy successor to Alexander Graham Bell, the deaf-mute instructor Rudolf Lindner from Saxony, who modified the telephone to construct the "tele-touch device" he used to convey a realistic impression of sounds to his students. A series of single-contact microphones, each of which was activated only by singing a specific tone (the membranes had been tuned to various specific frequencies), replaced the receiver. In each of the microphone's circuits, an induction coil was activated, and the specific electrical currents were then fed to the corresponding fingers of the deaf-mute to be alphabetized. When the instructor spoke on the telephone, "every tone was felt in a different finger."[80] Finally, in 1980, Dieter Wellershoff's novella *The Siren* transformed the historical reality that on electrical channels, speech is always touch, into literature as telephone sex:

> He pulled the telephone over and dialed her number.
>
> Her soft, whispered "hello" answered him. . . .
>
> The tone moved him, touched him, and the rest of his resistance and caution abandoned him. . . . Sighing, he said "I can't sleep. I have to think about you constantly. I'm crazy about you."
>
> "Me too," she said. "I've called out to you. Every minute, I'm calling you."
>
> "I feel it," he said, "how do you do it?"
>
> "I'm naked. I'm touching myself."
>
> "I feel it," he said.
>
> "Do it too," she said. "Please."
>
> "I will," he said.[81]

One could hardly obey AT&T's command to "Reach out and touch someone" more precisely.

Once women defected to media conglomerates, which would make the elimination of literary works via telephone sex into a means for self-promotion, media war, rather than love, ruled the relationship between authors and women readers. It is no accident that Wellershoff's professor of pedagogy can defeat the telephone siren only by mobilizing another medium, the gramophone. The phantasma of Romantic love, that on the field of literature women could participate in the phallic pleasures of the One Spirit, melted away once women ceased to obey the will to knowledge. Because they would rather dream of being desired as discursive clerks at media conglomerates like Remington and AT&T, or at state enterprises like the RPTV, the discourse of authorship ran headlong into the void.

The text had lost its power over women. The discovery by Raban, whose name was merely a cipher for Kafka's,[82] that "even all that work does not give" authors, who were only discursive clerks in anonymous offices, "a claim to be treated lovingly by everyone"[83] expressed precisely that insight, painful as it was for authors. Such a claim to love on the part of auctorial discourse was precisely what had made the hearts of women readers fly to the poets since Goethe's *Werther*. Indeed, that very claim had founded Classicism itself, with its cult of authorial names. Once women, due to their "skill with machines," became the indispensable agents of the media and of communications offices, the demigods of handwriting were pushed out in the cold.

In such a critical situation, nothing was left for writers to do but become media specialists themselves. The postal service had to take the place of love. The Romantic logistics of the poet's dream spilled over into the "madness"[84] of a postal war of nerves.

PART THREE

Mail Beyond Human Communication

CHAPTER NINETEEN

Typewriter and Carbon Paper

At the end of June 1912, Franz Kafka went on a so-called "Thalia journey" to Weimar and Halberstadt, a visit to the parlors of great German poets. The result of the journey was a weighty suspicion: "Do you suppose it is true that one can bind girls to oneself by writing?"[1] he wrote Max Brod from the Jungborn Sanitarium. He was referring to the custodian's daughter at the Goethe House in Weimar,[2] whose name furthermore was Margarethe, and to whom Kafka wrote as often as he liked (despite the fact that he was "of no more importance to her than a pot").[3] In the primal author's shadow, knowledge of what had been the secret of Classical/Romantic authorship was beginning to stir inside the budding author of books: an epistolary love between Spirit and Nature, or between the author and his feminine readers. Thus, the lines Kafka received from Goethe's posthumous clerk were "literature from beginning to end."[4]

But "text" is a rather coarse euphemism for what Kafka set in motion only two months later. In order to bind a girl to him, beginning on September 20, 1912, Kafka exhausted the entire potential of current transmissions technology. He mobilized not only every kind of letter and every technical medium, but beyond them and most importantly, the media standards of the postal system themselves: transmitting speeds and delivery frequencies. The author armed his desk as a command headquarters for the entire media system standing at his disposal. And not without good reason. Power, as its "greatest expert" among the poets[5] knew very well, no longer resided at the Goethe House in Weimar, but in buildings such as Carl Lindström Incorporated in Berlin. Its feminine allies now called themselves not Gretchen, but women stenotypists and operators. A devil, or the ancient logistics of the poet's dream, no longer was enough to bind one such ally, Miss Felice Bauer.

Instead of worshipping translations of their private affairs into the poet's auctorial handwriting, women now put the typescript on paper themselves. At the author's end, a historical transposition thus had to assume the place of translation. Piece by piece, Romantic literature's postal system had to be modified for the technical media and the conditions of information exchange in the age of the World Postal Union. A series of substitutions occurred in the process—as Politzer already recognized:[6] the claim to love was replaced by the claim to letters, the transcendental origin of the text by the standards of the postal system, phantasma by madness, the bio-politically disciplined individual by the dead body that rotted by day and rose to the text (not to life) only at night, the hallucination or childhood memories of a voice by the strategy of postal dispatching, and: The Woman/Mother/Nature by a secretary. Once writing had been desexualized, the loves of the author were at best media alliances, and at worst media wars.

Such altered conditions already had applied to Postal Assistant August Stramm around 1900. His beloved and later his wife, Else Krafft, the daughter of a Bremen newspaper publisher, had written articles and poems on her typewriter when she was only seventeen years old and was considered to be a talented journalist. "When there was nothing more important to do just then, her typewriter sang, and in no time at all a page was filled with verse or prose."[7] Once women no longer were excluded from discursive technologies, The Woman was lacking as the Other and the ground of all words and printed matter.[8] In view of such *écriture automatique* on the part of Else Krafft, nothing remained for Stramm but verse production, which was performed with just as much media expertise, but was dictated by the symbol economy that employed him as a postal clerk. It was said that Mrs. Else Stramm was not very taken with her husband's telegraphic style.[9]

Nor did Kafka become an author until after he had placed his writing on the basis of the text-processing technologies that informed his routine, bureaucratic intercourse with texts in his clerk's existence at the Worker Accident Insurance Agency. And even that required the intervention of a woman typist. Felice Bauer had made her career in a way that was open to women only after there were technical media for which men had proven "complete and consistent failures" and big companies that escalated such failure at an exponential rate via feedback between women, who administered the mass production of technical media, and the technical media itself, which in turn called for more women. After concluding her training at school, Bauer had started out as a stenotypist at the Odeon phonograph company in Berlin-Weissensee. In 1909, she moved to Carl Lindström Incorporated, where she rose to the rank of *Prokurist*, an officer of the firm entrusted with its power of attorney, within three years. Willy Haas even suspected she might make it as far as director.[10] By the end of 1912, Carl Lindström Incorporated was "the largest German manufacturer of phonographic equipment"[11]—the company produced large quantities of dictating machines (the "Parlograph," a sensational success) and phonographs (the "Parlophone" reached an annual production rate of 400,000 pieces in 1913), including coin-operated "fully automatic phonographs for salons, restaurants, etc." Acoustical jacks, phonograph needles, and other replacement parts were produced by Carl Lindström as well. Most of the correspondence between Kafka and Bauer falls within the year 1913, which was also the year of the company's extraordinary expansion: Lindström merged with the firm Grünbaum & Thomas, thus becoming the majority stockholder in Favorite Talking Machines, the Lyrophon Works, and the Dacapo Record Company.[12] The following year, the company also absorbed the Polyphon Company. Lindström equipment was to be found on five continents. The firm was especially proud of its exports to African and overseas colonies—in 1914, Kafka's traveler would promptly reencounter the phonograph as an instrument of torture in the "Penal Colony."[13]

Kafka's request for a "factory brochure"[14] from Bauer was not a futile one—along with it, he probably received an article from the *Phonographic Magazine* of December 12, 1912, which reported the distribution of gramophones in the French penal colony at New Caledonia.[15]

On August 13, 1912, while on a trip to Budapest, the *Prokurist* of the successful Parlograph Division of this multinational conglomerate came to Prague, where she visited the Brod family (she was a cousin of Max Friedmann's, the businessman who was married to Max Brod's sister). It was a momentous day for Germanic literature. At nine o'clock that evening, Kafka arrived, along with the manuscripts of the fragments to be included in the *Observation*, his first published book, the sequence of which he wanted to discuss with Brod.[16]

Yet for all that, communication between Kafka and Bauer was not initiated by words, either spoken or written, but by the photographs from Kafka's "Thalia journey" to Weimar, which he handed over to her "one after the other." Among them was a picture of Kafka and Margharete Kirchner:[17] it showed both of them (though out of focus) sitting on a bench; the custodian's daughter at the Goethe House was looking at Kafka, while Kafka looked in the direction of the camera. Thus began the game of enticements: when Felice Bauer looked at the photo, she was forced to repeat the glance of the woman it portrayed. A vanquishment such as this she would not leave unanswered. Shortly after Kafka had demonstrated his power to captivate the glances of women, she demonstrated her power to banish the very word of men. Later, when Kafka unfolded his manuscripts, Bauer mentioned something "which so amazed me that I banged the table. You actually said you enjoyed copying manuscripts, that you had also been copying manuscripts in Berlin for some Mister [*Herrn*] (curse the sound of that word when unaccompanied by name and explanation!) and you asked Max to send you some manuscripts."[18]

Banging on the table and callous swearing marked receipt of the sensational announcement that the typewriter gave women a pleasure readied for them by Misters whose namelessness referred to the very Master [*Herr*] or Adonai who was utterly nameless for all Jews because he replaced The Name itself. As the great Other governing the desires of women, he immediately garnered Kafka's damnation. Kafka's photographic power, after all, was nothing compared to the power of the typewriter. The jealousy regarding the control over her desires that Bauer offered to his friend—while scorning his manuscripts with neglect as they lay on the table—mobilized Kafka's fighting spirit. He too, they would see it yet, was a master of published discourse, a master over the lusts of women. The cover letter Kafka sent to Ernst Rowohlt the next day along with his manuscript demonstrates such a fighting spirit: "Dear Herr Rowohlt, I am herewith transmitting to you the short prose pieces you wished to see. They might well make a small book. While I was assembling them for this purpose I sometimes had the choice between appeasing my sense of responsibility and my eagerness to have a book of my own among your fine books."[19]

Answering a typewriter with a book implied a tragic confusion of reading and writing (or copying), as the future would tell. But the fight went on. On the very same day, Max Brod received a written announcement that the intertwining of books and women did not refer to Brod's manuscripts, but to Kafka's: "Good morning! Dear Max, while arranging the little pieces yesterday, I was under the young woman's influence, and it may well be that some silliness resulted, perhaps only a secretly comic sequence. Please look it over once more and let my thanks for that be included in the enormous thanks I owe you."[20] A major artery in the network of Romantic authorship thus had been constructed: a secret love relationship between the poet and the woman as muse. As the translator of intimate experiences into public charades—or works of literature—the author related that connection to his publisher and revealed it to his reader and interpreter: the classical construction of literature as a love letter designed for interception.

But the postal system was still only halfway reconstructed, and the fight not even half won, since it had been won only against the masculine reader. What was missing, obviously, was feedback between the author and the woman by means of which her pleasure would be declared his pleasure and thereby brought under his control. In the two-front war that the letter writer was fighting for the sake of his authorship, his fellow author obviously saw the typewriter merely as a means for putting office clerks out of work—or "driving the spirit out of humanity by mechanistic labor"[21]—and thus received the most old-fashioned kind of evidence for an authorial existence. The female *Prokurist*, by contrast, received the most modern form of evidence possible. But Kafka still had to wait a while to deliver it. In all probability, he wrote not only the first letter to his future beloved, but also his name under the publishing contract for his first book, on September 20, 1912.[22] Now, with that signature invested, he finally could inform Felice Bauer—by typewriter—that the typewriter, or the pleasure of women, was the condition that made writing possible for authors such as himself: "One thing I have to confess, bad as it sounds, and ill as it accords with what I have just said: I am an erratic letter writer. Yes, and it would be worse still if I didn't have a typewriter; for if my mood doesn't happen to feel equal to a letter, there are still my fingertips to do the writing."[23]

Writing on a machine was *écriture automatique*, and so was not under the influence of a creative subject's moods. The machine abrogated the rule, cherished in the Age of Goethe, that what wrote letters was the soul itself. In place of the connection between bodies and souls, fingers and moods, the machine established a difference.[24] Thus, the Manichean instrument solved a problem that consistently had spelled the doom of Kafka's earlier writing: the impossibility of distinguishing between the subject of the text and the subject of the speech act—or: the impossibility of putting copies in circulation. Precisely this dilemma had frozen Raban, alias Kafka: the writer of the text could not pass on the "I" to his copy in the text, as though its function as a shifter had been suspended. The impossibility of replicating "I" foiled the attempt at putting the doppelgänger Raban in circulation. And the *Description of a Struggle* reflected the same impossibility of setting the text free from the body: "It's the same as it was at the party last week. Someone is reading aloud from a manuscript. At his request I myself have copied one page. When I see my handwriting among the pages written by him, I take fright. It's without any stability. People are bending over it from three sides of the table. In tears, I swear it's not my handwriting."[25]

If transcriptions made for others always had been referred back to the person of the copyist, as happened to the fat man (one of the many metamorphoses of the narrator who speaks in the quote above), since he did not use a typewriter, Felice Bauer's career would have been impossible. That is, it would have been impossible for her as *Prokurist* to sign (typed) copies of phonograms "per pro. Carl Lindström," "per pro. Strauß," or "per pro. Heinemann."[26] That was precisely what the doppelgängers in the *Description of a Struggle* and Raban never could do: speak for Franz Kafka *per procurationem*. Georg Bendemann and Gregor Samsa are the first to be agents in this sense, both on the constituted level of texts—the former is a proxy for his father in business, the latter a traveler *per procurationem* for his firm—and also on the constituting level, as the doppelgängers and agents of their author. The typewriter separated what was written from the person of the undersigned; it allowed the possibility of signing for oneself "per pro."—as though the one speaking and taking responsibility for his speech by saying "I" was a different person from the one named by the signature. Kafka saw the typewriter as such a means to exonerate the signator by withholding his identity (or the characters that allow his identification):

> I could never work as independently as you seem to; I slither out of responsibility like a snake; I have to sign many things, but every evaded signature seems like a gain; I also sign everything (though I really shouldn't) with FK only, as though that could exonerate me; for this reason I also feel drawn toward the typewriter in anything concerning the office, because its work, especially when executed at the hands of a typist, is so impersonal. This otherwise praiseworthy caution, however, is complemented and canceled by the fact that I sign even the most important things with the said FK, without reading them, and that owing to my forgetfulness anything that has once left my desk has, so far as I am concerned, never existed. Would all this make me, who recently sought a position in your office, highly commendable?[27]

The answer is simple, but has to be given three times: as an office clerk, "yes," as author, even "to the highest degree," but as a lover, "no." Love letters—and what else could the "most important things" have been that Kafka was writing and underwriting in his office?—that are typewritten and separated from the sender by an act of forgetting so radical that, once sent, they never existed—such letters are not love letters at all.

But for the same reason that such texts were useless as love letters, they were useful for promoting literature. This was true in two respects. First, mechanical word processing, as Bauer herself had confessed on August 13, was the appropriate way to bind girls to oneself by writing in the year 1912. It allowed Kafka to execute a merger in the name of authorship between his desk at the Worker Accident Insurance Agency and Carl Lindström Incorporated—the power that bound girls in droves—so that he could make one of its clerks the clerk of his writing. (Not only did Kafka study the firm's brochures and propose wide-reaching systems of media alliances to Bauer, he also imagined himself as her director.)[28] That merger provided him with a strategic position outside the family's sphere of discursive power, and from there, such a sphere of power could be reflected, and indeed reflected as power over the media. The opening of a strategic position opened up the conception of strategies themselves for the first time. After all, the "Judgment," which was written down in a single night two days after the first letter to Bauer, deals with a fight between a father and son over access to the mail.

Whoever had access to the mail also had at his disposal the existence of its addresses, and therefore the life and death of its senders. Georg succumbs because he forgets "to take [his father's] writing things away from" him[29]—which enables the latter to occupy the communications channel to Russia and to declare Georg's letters incapable of delivery. If Georg had written his letter on a typewriter, a "writing thing" destined like no other to destroy the despotic power of fathers (as Bram Stoker's *Dracula* demonstrates most emphatically), the mail to Russia would have remained beyond the grasp of his father.

That was reason enough for Kafka to withdraw his handwritten texts from the reach of fatherly writing things by making copies of them on the typewriter or, in a case such as the "Metamorphosis," by having someone else make the copies for him.[30] While handwritten letters were "dead letters," the typewriter made it possible to mail both letters and literature. With this machine, the postal system had created the strategic condition for the possibility of Kafka's literature. After all, Christopher Latham Sholes, the inventor of the first mass-producible typewriter (the Remington No. 2), had been a postmaster by trade.[31]

And precisely what Georg forgot in the "Judgment"—to disempower his father's writing things by using the typewriter—had been put in practice by Kafka two days earlier. On the day he sent the first letter to Bauer, Kafka also typed a letter to his friend Max Brod, who was just underway to Italy with Felix Weltsch—the very typewritten letter that was lacking in the "Judgment." Its message was a copy of the message in the letter to the *Prokurist*—as if to prove that tearful swearing no longer was necessary to mail a copy: "Dear Lucky Ones, I am giving myself the pleasure— a very nervous one, to be sure—of writing to you in the middle of office hours. I would not do so if I were still able to write letters without a typewriter, but this pleasure is irresistible. If mood isn't quite sufficient, as is usual, the fingertips are always there. I must assume that greatly interests you, because I am writing this in such great haste."[32] The letter dealt with nothing other than the possibility that there was such a letter. It encoded the plan for a network of writing, the negative of which contained the

"Judgment." To that end, it not only quoted the glad tidings of *écriture automatique* as the hope for writing itself, which had just been written down and addressed to Berlin, but also quoted the pleasure of typewriting, which the message's first recipient had announced in Brod's home on August 13. And with salutations that turned his friends into Felices, the letter still was directed to her address. Instead of falling into the hands of his father, as happened in the "Judgment," all the letters went to the beloved stenotypist. Her pleasure no longer excluded, but included, an author armed with a typewriter. From then on, he was not only in league with a power the father could not reclaim, but also with one that—under the cipher of Odradek—was to become a pronounced "worry of the housefather." Initially, this alliance of powers was to have been openly named in the "Judgment": in the handwritten text, Frieda Brandenfeld first was described as a jeweler's daughter, then as a factory owner's, and finally as the daughter of a "cinematography owner" (before Kafka, for reasons of disguise, replaced the entire passage with the description "a girl from a well-to-do family").[33] Carl Lindström Incorporated had been founded as the Lindström Company through a merger between the Lindström Workshops and the Salon Cinematograph Company in 1904.[34]

But the letter to the two Felices, Brod and Weltsch, was not the only copy Kafka had made of the fateful lines. A third copy of the text was also in existence, a carbon of the first letter to Bauer, as Kafka informed her *en passant* five and a half months later: "But I really was a different person when I wrote that first letter, a carbon copy of which (it is the only letter I have a copy of) I found a few days ago during a perfunctory tidying up of my desk (which never gets tidied in any other way)."[35] When Kafka rediscovered copies or (as occurred more frequently) unsent letters in his desk during the course of this correspondence, it never was by accident. In the same letter, somewhat farther down, Kafka expressed concern that Bauer might fall victim to the delusion "that at some time I might yet turn into a useful human being with whom a steady, calm, lively relationship would be possible. If this is what you think, you are under a terrible misapprehension; as I have told you before, my present state (and today it is comparative paradise) is not an exceptional state. Don't succumb, Felice, to these misapprehensions!"[36]

Such a warning did not come out of the blue. By the beginning of

March 1913, after all, the correspondence had just reached its first low point—judging by the quantity of letters sent.[37] The impending setting aside of written communication due to wedding preparations and the springing of the familial trap had started to become apparent. In this critical phase, the "chance discovery" of the carbon copy of the first typewritten letter recalled the fact that the actual site of letter writing was the office, where anonymous processing of texts into carbons had become routine once the English chemist and physicist Sir Joseph Swan accidentally had invented carbon paper during his experiments with electric light.[38] (In 1878, Swan presented a mass-producible lightbulb in England, at nearly the same time Edison did in the United States.)[39] Such office technology, when applied to love letters in an alliance with the typewriter, did not make the letter writer seem very "commendable" for "a steady, calm, lively relationship," as Kafka had explained in reference to the anonymity of typewritten letters in the letter of December 20–21. After all, letters that existed simultaneously as a carbon copy were *per definitionem* "not of a personal nature . . . like private letters, but instead . . . of a bureaucratic nature."[40] They were open invoices, and the issuing authority could demand payment on the basis of his carbon copies.

The continued existence of the copy in Kafka's desk was the continued existence of the "original difference" between the fingertips that took care of the writing and the moods of an individual who signed responsibly. Kafka thus could go back to the handwritten text very quickly: indeed, he had a copy in his desk documenting the typewritten a priori of the correspondence.

The letter of September 20 did not initiate the correspondence, but it did establish its rules by fixing the bureaucratic a priori for all private matters. The foundation of the correspondence between Kafka and Bauer was not a contract, with a marriage contract on its horizon, but instead a pact[41] based on a promise: it was valid as long as what was promised actually came true, that is, the promise of a closeness conveyed by letters must never be carried out. The invoice was filled in that it remained open. The pact accordingly read as follows: writing shall mean recognizing the condition that a difference exists between the subject of the text and the subject of the speech act,[42] that the subject promising closeness, longing, and love in the letter is not identical with the subject of the letter writer, the subject of the speech act. This meant the letters were literature or forgeries on principle.

What the copy of a typewritten letter promised was nothing other than what was also the state of knowledge in expert criminology at the time: the possibility of fraud was becoming the condition for writing. "It cannot be denied that the typewriter is being used increasingly for the production of falsified documents."[43] While expert detectives and chief inspectors insisted on being able to document individuality for every typewriter, they also left no doubt as to what individuality in the age of standardized mass production was: a mechanical defect. Osborn resorted to every conceivable finesse of detective work in order to disprove Kafka's acknowledged opinion that the typewriter's "work" was "so anonymous," or that "typescript [guaranteed] the forger" an "impenetrable shield, behind which he could hide."[44] This possibly was the case for a brand new machine. But once it had been put in use, "a typewriter's individuality can ultimately be proven with absolute certainty" "by means of deviations and defective letters resulting from normal use or accidental damage."[45] Just as Freud had deciphered unconscious individuality in the defects of speech, criminologists deciphered individuality in the defects of machines.[46] In the scientific evidential paradigm produced by the technologizing of discourse around 1900, individuality exists at best in the form of a pathological symptom in the everyday life of people and machines. The individual is a sign of decline, of downfall, the creeping destruction that is normal use or normal life.

Insofar as the individuality of the writer of a typewritten letter could be proven not through confessional procedures, but only by the defects in pure signifiers, the promise the typewriter and its typist had given to Kafka abrogated the rules governing its own functions: it freed postal exchange from "the illusion . . . that the signifier has to answer for its existence in the name of any signification whatever."[47]

Because the individual was at best a sign of wear and tear or a series of typographical errors (as documented in the case of Kafka's letter of September 20),[48] the signifier answered for its existence solely in the name of the typewriter and of carbon paper. Consequently, proclamations of love were not confessions, but the machinations of bureaucratic technocracy. The *terminus ad quem* of such fraudulent machinations would be wedding preparations that were interminable because the text's doubling at the origin of the correspondence deconstructed both the assurance that the writer would vouch for the conditions of discursive sincerity and the guarantee that the meaning of words actually was the one the writer had intended.

Yet: since the annulment of the promise implied by the exchange of letters—as it was implied by any use of language—was itself the subject matter of a promise that the letter embodied, the promise that rescinded the promise's rules for speech acts continued to function only as long as no reference was made to that promise. Because one and the same medium (the postal system) processed both the pact and what it covered, Kafka revoked the content of the promise at the moment he referred to its existence, at the moment, that is, when he took the copy of the typewritten letter out of the drawer. A letter that promised difference had to be a slip of the tongue.

The original pact therefore did not establish a legal order for the correspondence that might have allowed the legitimation of discourses via a third party; it established an agonal order, instead. The stage of discourses became the stage of a drama in which subjects embodied nothing but strategies. The role of the typewritten letter was thus not so much to state a difference as it was to inscribe that difference onto all postal exchange. It set off a war in which Kafka would mobilize the entire dispatching power of the postal system.

CHAPTER TWENTY

The Poet's Printed Matter in Extremis

Kafka could leave the battlefield of his private postal war (he had been woefully unable to participate in the Great War) only when he bore away the wound of catarrhal apicitis of the lung in 1917. Thus, a five-year struggle to reconstruct the postal system of Classical authorship under the conditions mandated by the age of the World Postal Union came to an end. Felice Bauer married a Berlin businessman shortly afterward, and Kafka declared his "general bankruptcy."[1] The typewriter had promised the author the felicity of making girls attached to him by writing and remaining anonymous himself, but only at the price of the transitive character of literature, that is, at the price of author deification and the love of women readers. Bauer never gave a moment's thought to the idea of placing her typist's art in the service of poetry, either as a muse or a reader. Nothing and no one prevented her from seeing Kafka as a better factory owner than a writer.[2] Nothing and no one prevented her from telling the author Brod to his face that she had been unable to finish reading *Nornepygge Castle*—whereupon Kafka, the shocked young author faced with such an obstruction to the function of women readers, "really froze with horror—for myself, for you, for everyone."[3] The epistolary inspiration of earlier times became the mailing of newspaper articles and factory brochures. At the best, addressing poetic works to women readers might have become dictation into Bauer's Parlograph: neither the one nor the other had anything to do with love.

But poets could not dream of a desexualized exchange of information between women and men. The dictation of a Berlin professor that Bauer's typewriter recorded three times a week met with Kafka's jealous suspicion that—as if it were Romantic poetry—it occurred only for the purpose of ensnaring Bauer in the slings of the imaginary: "But I have just glanced at your last letter again and wonder whether you shouldn't give up your work with the professor. I still don't know what kind of work it is, but even if he were to dictate the most precious words night after night, it wouldn't be worth while, if it tired you."[4] "Nothing but jealousy"[5] at the "pleasant temptations at the professor's"[6] to which he submitted the stenotypist governed Kafka's relationship to Bauer's profession; therefore, preventive ignorance about the nature of such work seemed to him the best strategy for turning Bauer's eyes and ears to his own "precious words." No wonder the postal system, just in the nick of time, committed the blunder of losing the very letter in which Bauer gave an account of her work at the professor's.[7] No wonder, because Kafka already had declared in his third letter to Bauer that letters were lost—if at all—to consciousness alone;[8] in the unconscious, by contrast, letters apparently lost were either ones that never should have been written or ones that never had been written.

But suppression alone was not enough to break the power of nameless Misters over the mind of his beloved. The literary text had to face direct competition from the dictations that occupied her every other day. There was nothing else for the author to do but to construct in a postal manner at the margin of his poetic art the transitive properties that literature had lost to dictation on typewriters and Parlographs:

> This spring, at the latest, Rowohlt of Leipzig will publish a *Yearbook of Poetry*, edited by Max. It will include one of my short stories, "The Judgment," which will be dedicated "To Fräulein Felice B." Is this dealing too imperiously with your rights? The more so since this dedication was written a month ago, and the manuscript is no longer in my possession? Could it be looked upon as a valid excuse that I forced myself to omit the rest of the sentence: "(To Fräulein B.) so that she does not receive presents only from others"?[9]

The precious words of the poet were supposed to suppress the precious words of the professor that Bauer had declared it her pleasure to type. There could be even less doubt about this, insofar as "this dedication was written a month ago," that is, after the "Judgment" had been written down—as Bauer easily could have calculated from the date on the letter—or after the day she received Kafka's first typewritten letter, in which the reference to her remark on August 20 about typing out copies was evident. That the words a stenotypist heard and transcribed were seen as presents by Kafka is an example of a confusion about the professionalism of feminine dealings with writing that was typical of poets around 1900. Typists, for whom every syllable had a price, clearly did not think much in general of presents in the form of words. And hence Kafka's caution in not telling her about the dedication until after it had become a fait accompli and no longer could be rescinded.

The dedication turns printed matter into a matter of letters. It is assigned to the "margins of the title," yet does not itself belong to the text. Instead, it mediates between the title, whereby the text becomes the property of the state and the archives of law,[10] and the text itself, which it in turn sorts into a private archive of letters. But what precisely does a dedication give? After all, it does not transfer ownership of the physical body of the text, as the address of an actual letter does (even if "for F." is written at the top of every printed copy of the "Judgment" right up to the present day, those copies still do not belong to Bauer), anymore than the individual form of phrases and verbal contexts did (they are protected by copyright law and remain in the possession of the author or publisher). The dedication signs over the "material content," the "ideas" that are "transferred to the reader when he appropriates them by intellectual effort."[11] The dedication creates the very same postal properties that had been implicit in Goethe's poetry—as the feedback from Bettina as a feminine reader testifies—thanks to Thurn and Taxis. At the same time, it also declares that these "ideas" are mysteriously indebted to the person named in the dedication.[12] "To Dorothea" and "for F." are isomorphs. In the topology of the textual margin, the dedication restores—if necessary, by force—the power of the authorial name to address stories as private love letters to women readers.

> Yesterday I received the proofs of your short story. How beautifully our names unite below the title! When you eventually read the story, I hope you won't regret ever having consented to your name being mentioned (of course it is only Felice B.). For no one, no matter to whom you may show it, could like the story. You can take comfort, at least some kind of comfort, from the fact that I would have added your name even had you forbidden it, for the

dedication, although only a tiny and dubious one, is nevertheless an unquestionable sign of my love for you.[13]

A story no one would like needs a dedication to ensure that it reaches at least one feminine reader. In the face of the Parlographic dictators who were enticing women readers away from literature by addressing them in a professional manner, Kafka brandished the regimental colors of authorship: the "unquestionable sign" of love between the writer and the feminine reader.

Unlike the "Judgment," the *Observation*, Kafka's first book, had been a wartime operation in his struggle for the mind of a woman since his first encounter with Bauer. Over the pages of the *Observation* the battle had started, and there it would have to be decided. With and within those pages, Kafka therefore proved that printed matter and matters of letters were merely two sides of the same sheet of paper as far as he was concerned—quite literally. Using the excuse that he had no stationery at hand, Kafka wrote Bauer a letter on the back of a page from the proofs to the text "Children on a Country Road": "How do you like the type sample (needless to say, the paper will be different)? No doubt the typeface is a little too consciously beautiful, and would be more appropriate to the tablets of Moses than to my little prevarications. But now it's being printed that way."[14] The cat was out of the bag: a Nameless Master dictated not only to Felice Bauer, but to Franz Kafka as well. But the self-representation of an author as the typist of God, who used the printing press to transform the advocative "prevarications" of handwriting into the (truly) oversized typeset letters of the law, made little impression on a typist who transformed handwriting into typewritten text herself every day by the pile — especially since as a *Prokurist* she was fairly certain that power no longer resided in divine law, but instead in new technical media.

The poet's claim to kisses as a reward for his book[15] thus found no resonance whatsoever; nor did any of Kafka's other requests for Bauer's commentary on his work. Before submitting herself to the author–feminine reader feedback loop, she preferred to read every other book imaginable. She favored *Silhouettes* of an entire palette of authors over the one real author who wrote her palpable letters. Bauer never was as enamored by Kafka's "glimpses into endless perplexities"[16] as she was by Herbert Eulenberg's educational crash course for the "culturally deprived in Germany," which, in the form of "literary sketches," dealt with forty-five poets and writers at a pace suitable for typists. As she said herself, she valued Eulenberg's book because it was the exact opposite of "endless perplexities," that is, "pithy and clear,"[17] and therefore conformed to the stylistic demands of stenographic business letters or telegrams. In the preface to the first edition, Eulenberg himself wrote poetry about the situation of creative writing in an age of this kind of feminine reader's love:

> One likes not to buy just learned books,
> A dirge not new in Germany,
> No question of good ones ever at all.
> They don't sell well, old funeral shrouds.[18]

The shrouds or texts of grave robbers sold all the better, however: precisely because "everyone can read them,"[19] Eulenberg's sketches went through no less than nine editions between 1910 and 1912.

That was reason enough for Kafka, the weaver of funeral shrouds, to erupt in jealousy: of "men and girls," businessmen and secretaries, author-idols and their feminine readers:

> I am jealous of Werfel, Sophocles, Ricarda Huch, Lagerlöf, Jacobsen. My jealousy is childishly pleased because you call Eulenberg Hermann instead of Herbert, while Franz no doubt is deeply engraved on your brain. . . . *But you ought not to read the Silhouettes.* And now I see that you are even "very enthusiastic" about him. . . . But other people are to be found in your letters as well; I want to start a fight with them all, the whole lot, not because I mean to do them any harm, but to drive them away from you, to get you away from them, to read only letters that are concerned solely with you, your family, and the two little ones, and of course, of course, me![20]

Once media power and education no longer were one and the same, it was all over for the poets' and thinkers' mastery of all discourse, over for their self-appointed pedagogical power to decide the reading material of their subjects or serfs, especially the feminine ones. Thus, for example, Kafka's repeated demand for a list of Bauer's books remained futile.[21] Authors fell into an impotent rage against competitors who no longer sought to be successful with women readers by urging them to penetrate the author's spirit via hermeneutics, but who instead used texts that satisfied the minds of women readers, minds warped by typewriters, cinematographs, and gramophones.[22] To their horror and consternation, authors discovered that once women made careers of the typewriter and the talking machine, they could judge printed matter with competence they had gained not from the mouth of a pedagogue (and that means from other printed matter), but on the basis of an expertise in the media that was specific to women.

Kafka was not alone in this. On the typewriter that he used to type out the "chaos of smudges and scriggles" representing the handwritten form of his books, Vladimir Nabokov could manage a speed of "some three hundred words in one hour," according to his own admission, and therefore decided (while trying to earn a living as a Russian writer in Paris during the 1930's) "to hire an expert typist, to whom I would dictate my corrected manuscript in the course of approximately thirty carefully planned afternoons."[23] Thirty afternoons became four years—as his semi-autobiographical memoirs record, which weave together poetry and women instead of *Poetry and Truth*—and the typist Anna Ivanovna Blagovo became his second wife. The marriage was a product not of mutual love, but mutual abandon. Out of pure "lust," the poet became "reckless"[24] with regard to the typist's recklessness concerning his power of language. It was quite true, after all, that *rapport sexuel* did not write itself—the typewriter wrote it down:

> Our first session proved pretty awful. . . . She asked me not to go so fast. She put me off by fatuous remarks: "There is no such expression in Russian," or "Nobody knows that word (*vzvoden'*, a welter)—why don't you just say "big wave" if that's what you mean? . . . After three hours of work, I examined the result of her dainty and impudent rattle. It teemed with misspellings, typos, and ugly erasures. Very meekly I said that she seemed unaccustomed to deal with literary (i.e. non-humdrum) stuff. She answered I was mistaken, she loved literature. . . . Did she know Morozov's poetry? No, she did not much care for poetry in any form; it was inconsistent with the tempo of modern life. I chided her for not having read any of my stories or novels.[25]

Women such as Miss Blagovo or Miss Bauer, who were absolutely and entirely legitimized by their machines, were fully immune to the Eros of the masculine power of language when it was not "pithy and clear" or when it clashed with the "tempo of modern life" (which amounts to the same thing). Poets therefore had to guard jealously over the fate of their literature, distribution.

It was no accident that Kafka sent Ernst Weiß, a bitter adversary of the technical media in any form, into the Carl Lindström building in December 1913 in order to force Bauer into a written correspondence. Ten years later, Weiß finally would discover the true fate of literature in its being undeliverable to readers, which he called "essentiality." His polemic was directed against the cinema, telephones, phonographs, and the "wireless transmission of concerts, sermons, exchange rates, and stock market reports,"[26] and so against the tendency of the technical media to submit the output of Mozart, Luther, and the New York Stock Exchange to one and the same set of standards. But the technical media did not destroy themselves, as Weiß boldly had prophesied for such a "weak, lowly, common thing." Instead, they produced so much competition for the "striving toward essentiality" known as literature that Weiß—just as Kafka had done in the "Judgment"—burst out with the desperate question: "What poet is to work for a public he can't captivate for the simple reason that it doesn't exist?"[27]

The poet's printed matter was in extremis. When literary works ceased to capture the distorted minds of the public as love letters, a lonely writing took their place, writing that could not be delivered and that no longer pronounced any truth about life because it had replaced life itself. Without much grief, Eulenberg's dirge had declared that the fabric of literature was a funeral shroud; Kafka drew from this the obvious conclusion that poets were the deceased: "What I need for my writing is seclusion, not 'like a hermit,' that would not be enough, but like the dead. Writing, in this sense, is a sleep deeper than that of death, and just as one would not and cannot tear the dead from their graves, so I must not and cannot be torn from my desk at night."[28] The author's study was a Dead Letter Office, a bureau for letters that could not be delivered. Herman Melville's Bartleby, the hack writer who had been a clerk in a Dead Letter Office all his life[29]—before he occupied the same site in the discursive system that would be taken by stenotypists a generation later—was the prototype of the modern author.

But for that very reason, the postal system took the place of love (of poets). Only writers of dead letters or dead letter writers had to rearm their desks as command headquarters for complete postal systems. They were forced to establish and to calculate technically a textual circuit that replaced the circulation of blood. Literature could create a niche for itself within its own incapacity for delivery only when that incapacity became the postal principle of the interminability of a correspondence made up of love letters. Mail became the vehicle for a carefully planned obstruction of communication. The correspondence with a dead(-)letter writer never ceased to deal with such incapacity for delivery.

Kafka's letters thus were the exact opposite of a Romantic novel, and not, as Politzer claimed, his only "completed novel" in the sense that Romanticism meant by the term. As Jens Schreiber was able to demonstrate, Romantic novels always allowed the reader to forget that love—the imaginary failure to recognize the impossibility of describing sexual relations—was sustained by the text alone.[30] Kafka, on the other hand, never ceased to insist upon precisely that point. Love was a postal system. To say that, and to call the saying of it "love," was madness: "Love must be ignorant in order to forget speaking. . . . Love therefore tumbles into madness when it becomes clear-sighted. In madness it becomes clear that love is sustained only by speaking, and in the final consequence that means practically by nothing at all."[31] "Madness" therefore was Kafka's name for the "many letters" to Bauer, which circulated on the basis of incapacity for delivery, and for the desired goal of his nocturnal writing as well.[32] And for good reason: because ultimately, such madness was the postal principle itself, which guaranteed the inability to conceive of correspondence.

In 1922, Kafka would write to his last epistolary love that letter writing was impossible for humans. In 1912, ten years earlier, this impossibility was a positive possibility known as the mail.

CHAPTER TWENTY-ONE

Mail, or The Impossibility of Writing Letters

How do I love thee? The answer Michel Cournot gave in place of Kafka is today as unsurpassed in its clarity as it ever was: "This correspondence demonstrates exactly how one being may touch, enchain, torture, enslave, destroy another being by the systematic and total use of the postal and telegraph services."[1]

Without the feats performed in advance by the General Staff, however, a total and systematically waged war is unthinkable—including wars that are fought by mail and telegraphy. Thus, Kafka was not unprepared. Five years earlier, using an arsenal consisting of a railway line, a telegram, and two letters, he already had tested his plan for the mobilization of the media in the struggle for writing. The code name under which the maneuver was executed was *Wedding Preparations in the Country*. And the outcome provided Kafka with more or less the same lesson that the German General Staff learned at the Battle of the Marne seven years later. While in Kafka's novel / war game *literature* (blue) had been compelled to surrender to the superior force of the *family* (red) and its transport media due to insufficient communications networks, the disaster of the Marne was caused by a lack of telephone lines between the individual armies and especially between those armies and the Supreme Headquarters.[2] And just as Raban saw illness as the only way to escape his misery, Senior General von Moltke made his exit with a nervous breakdown.

"The Great War," Kafka wrote to Moltke as much as to his own address in a 1916 appeal for "A German society for the establishment and support of a military and civilian hospital in Prague for the treatment of nervous diseases in German Bohemia," is "a war on the nervous system, more a war on the nervous system than any previous war."[3] That it was, because during the First World War, "nerves" was just another word[4] for telegraph and telephone lines, which indeed played a much larger role in the age of million-man armies than they had in all previous wars. Consequently, "nervous breakdown" was just another word for the Marne disaster. Not unlike modern armies, literature was dependent on the organization of the means of communication, so that the Military and Civilian Hospital for Nervous Diseases was a matter of life and death for authors, as well as for the commanders of the General Staff. "The telephone," the *War Diary of a Telegraphist* reported in 1916, "has taken over the exchange [of information] and in most cases has replaced the horse rides and car trips of adjutants and ordinance officers. It [the telephone] and the many, many wires form the nerves of the --- Army."[5]

That, however, is precisely what is not achieved in the *Wedding Preparations*. Unlike Kafka in 1912, Raban is not in possession of the carbon copy of a typewritten letter, and thus of a promise suspending the functions of letters: giving promises. There is no carbon paper to provide insurance against the superiority of bodies. Like a child or someone with a nervous disorder, Raban therefore is excluded from all use of the postal system. He cancels the values of every letter he writes by catching up with them on foot or by train. Raban runs across his friend Lement before Lement can receive the letter he wrote him that afternoon in hopes of preventing such a meeting.[6] He is rescued from the presence of his friend, however, by a reference back to the letter he had written his fiancée early that morning.

> "Wait, you just said now you advised me to stay here over tonight. I've thought it over, it couldn't very well be managed. I've written to say I'm coming this evening, they'll be expecting me."
>
> "That's quite easy, send a telegram."
>
> "Yes, that could be done—but it wouldn't be very nice if I didn't go—and I'm tired, yes, I'll go alright. If a telegram came, they'd get a fright into the bargain."[7]

Only the mobilization of a highly technical medium could have suspended the promise the letter gave to his fiancée. But such mobilization only would have led him back into the arms of his friend and also would have established a terrifying connection with the letter. Or so it seemed, in any case. Only after he catches up with the letter to his fiancée does it occur to Raban that he still could have postponed the trip had he not confused the speed of letters with that of bodies: "Yes, after all I have already accomplished it is certain that tomorrow I shall get to Betty and to Mamma, nobody can prevent that. Yet it is true, and was indeed not to be foreseen, my letters will arrive only tomorrow, so that I might very well have remained in town and spent an agreeable night at Elvy's."[8] Because Raban does not calculate the times of arrival for his dispatches, he is able to play his letters off only against friends who are present, not against an absent fiancée, and certainly not against telegrams. Instead, he falls into a trap between the addressees of his dispatches. Because the subjects of the letters cannot call on each other as witnesses, what they say has to be the responsibility of the subject of the speech act, whose "moods" are by no means disconnected from his fingertips.

That Raban tragically mistook the letter's time of arrival for his own (thus leading the *Wedding Preparations* into the dead end of the title) reflected the same principle of written communication that had viewed the letter as doppelgänger and an archivist of the individual a hundred years earlier. And—just as in that earlier time—Raban's mistake was an effect of the organization of empirical communications institutions. While the postal system and Ministry of Commerce were divorced in Germany, personal transportation and the transmission of information still were combined in a single department in Austria.[9] And just as the postal system and railways were under the same ministry, the positions of fiancée and mother were combined in the *Wedding Preparations*: a short circuit that resulted in the nervous breakdown of writing and the hero. Such an advance of the red lines was completely realistic, as the course of Kafka's correspondence with Bauer would illustrate. In fact, Kafka's mother would try to bring about precisely that short circuit: after she intercepted one of Bauer's letters, she tried to turn its sender into a secret agent in the service of familial discipline. Writing was defined as a "pastime" and declared to be harmless only on the condition that it was subjected to the familial regimen of sleeping and eating (a restriction that in Kafka's case strangled his writing).[10]

However, Bauer did not live in Jungbunzlau or anyplace else between Prague and the Sudeten Mountains (where Raban was heading), but instead in the capital of the German Empire, where the postal system and railways did not play into each other's hands—a lucky thing for Kafka, who had been able to uncover his mother's act of sabotage. The difference between those two institutions was the organizational requirement that guaranteed the body would not have to take the place of the letter. Instead, the whole postal system was mobilized systematically. Unlike Raban, Kafka would calculate the arrival times for his letters very precisely, so that they could refer to each other as authorities, and not to an individual responsible for all the letters signed by Kafka (or FK). Kafka later would call this "communication with ghosts."

How, then, did Kafka love Bauer? Let us "count the ways."

> In the first place, Kafka established a precise timetable of all the mail collections in Prague, and of all the deliveries in Berlin. Second, he made a timetable of Felice's movements between her residence and her office in order to ascertain at which moment of the day she would receive a certain letter, depending on whether that letter was addressed to her home or business. Third, he made note of the exact itinerary of the letters, through whose hands they would pass, whether at her home (the concierge, mother, and sister of the unhappy Felice) or at the office (the internal mail service, assistants, secretaries). Fourth, he made a comparison of the routes and schedules of registered letters, on the one hand, and express letters on the other. Fifth, he noted the amount of time necessary to send telegrams. In passing, it should be mentioned that at this time telegrams and express letters could be delivered from Prague to Berlin on Sundays and that there was even a delivery of regular mail on Sunday mornings. If one adds to this the fact that Kafka not only placed the words he had written in these envelopes, but hinted darkly at the words he had written but not sent, and that he also inserted at propitious moments insults he had drafted several weeks earlier—and if one adds furthermore that he put ten or twelve pages of a single letter in separate envelopes and mailed them at different times in different letter boxes, it is quite evident that Kafka, playing the game of "dispatching" to its maximum, using every postal method and timetable, had at his disposal a formidable artillery with which to reduce Felice to a state of confusion.[11]

That Kafka had such a formidable cannonball postal system at his disposal, however, is a "given" that—rather than being taken for granted—deserves some attention in its own right. Kafka was not the only one prepared "to attach a girl" to himself "by writing"; the postal system had made its own preparations as well. The year 1912–13, in which most of the correspondence with Miss Bauer falls, was not just any year. It was—at least as far as letter traffic is concerned—a record year for mail: 6,822,000,000 letters were transported by the RPTV in 1913,[12] including 208 letters from Kafka to Bauer. That figure would not be surpassed until the year 1927. Never again would as many trains be mobilized to convey letters as in 1912–13: a total of 17,303 every day[13]—an absolute record in the history of the German postal system. These trains provided the precondition necessary for Kafka's postal war, not only by speedily transporting mail back and forth between Prague and Berlin, but above all by making it possible to calculate the arrival times of letters—something that became possible only after they began to be transported by railway. "Only now can the correspondent calculate—and he should be able to do so nowadays!—the hour in which his letter will reach the hands of its recipient."[14] The highest number of telegrams sent in Austria was reached in 1913,[15] while the German record set for that category the same year was only a passing one.

But statistical probability was not the only thing calling for poetology in the form of a postal war of nerves in 1912–13. What scholars of German literature have yet to waste a single moment considering is the simple fact that "one man's attempt to take possession of a women with words, nothing but words, and furthermore primarily words of negation," which was "probably unique in human and literary terms,"[16] would have been absolutely impossible if the postal organization of letter traffic had not made the necessary conditions available around 1912. These conditions took the form of standards that had no more to do with the postal situation of a Novalis or a Hölderlin—whose fantasies and madness Politzer tried to take as a literary-historical context for Kafka's "love letters"—than they do with the postal situation of 1998. Between 1910 and 1914, the mail was delivered a full eight times a day in Berlin, including Sundays[17]—no wonder "the postman" became the "legendary hero" in the "postal chronicles" that were narrated to Bauer day after day.[18] In Prague, by contrast, the postman came only twice a day, and only once on Sundays.[19]

For that reason alone, Felice Bauer did not have a chance from the start: the armies of postmen were unevenly divided. Eight daily deliveries were the condition necessary for Bauer's receiving mail from Kafka as many as three times a day. Confronted by such a frequency, she had to fall behind and in tow, simply because of the logistics of the Austrian postal system at her disposal.[20] Kafka really should have dedicated the "Judgment" not to Bauer, but to Rowland Hill. After all, the postage stamp and the increased frequency of delivery it made possible were the historical a priori for Kafka's strategic position, which made writing the "Judgment" possible and which it reflects.

The remaining parameters for the exchange of mail can be found in Kafka's letters. The "interpretaments" indispensable for their analysis are (1) that a letter mailed in Prague no later than four o'clock in the afternoon was delivered to its recipient in Berlin during the course of the following day (and vice versa);[21] (2) that letters mailed in the evening were not in Berlin (or Prague) until two days later;[22] (3) that the time it took to transmit telegrams from Prague to Berlin came to approximately four hours;[23] and (4) that express letters were delivered within one day.[24]

On the basis of these invariables, which defined the firepower of the medium available to him, starting in September 1912, Kafka exhausted all the variables of information exchange and ordered into battle all postal modalities. Present and accounted for here were: ordinary letters, registered letters, express letters, supplemental letters, late, lost, undeliverable, and intercepted letters, mutilated letters, unsent letters, ordinary postcards, picture postcards, photographs, printed matter, and telegrams. The technical media, and above all the analog media, had a special role to play in this. The telephone was a medium of communication that Kafka only dreamed of using; in real life, he preferred to delegate a representative. Telephones, along with gramophones and Parlographs, formed the horizon of the exchange of letters.

With the differentiation of postal standards, the modern subject—whether Cartesian or Kantian in nature—faded from the territory of the world postal system. Subordinated to the historical a priori of an absolute maximum velocity that applied equally to all information, persons, and objects, time once had been able to appear as a constituent of objectivity prior to all experience—simply because the trinity of the postal system covered the entire conception of objectivity. In 1913, by contrast, the differentiated modes of dispatching used by the postal system allowed for manipulations of the time axis, which until 1848 had been surrounded by a postal blockade fully equipped with the philosophical blessings of inaccessibility. That blockade and the subject to whom such inaccessibility had been attributed were shattered once the postal system no longer registered different types of information carriers on the same time axis (not to mention the different types of information, persons, and goods). Since then, the chronological order of postal events at the receiving end always could fail to correspond to the chronological order at the transmitting end.

Schematically speaking: in cryptological terms, a "die" was rolled between the collection at mailboxes and the delivery by postmen. That is, a process was activated that generated the "confused sequence" of a chain of signifiers by writing them line by line into a register that was determined by a key and reading them out column by column.[25] In relation to a series of letters as a chain of signifiers, the postal system was a die in time, and its register was constructed with the key of the various speeds of transmission. Once the series of posted statements had been acted upon by the die of the post, it no longer was a duplicate of the series of posting actions. If it nonetheless was read as such, a phantom emerged as the result. The alchemy to which it owed its appearance is known as hermeneutics, insofar as one of its principles is to impute to coherence (of statements) a subject on the other side of the mailbox. Phantoms are figures of the imagination when, as virtual images of the postal origin of meaning, they are projected onto a surface on the other side of the mailbox, only to be interpreted there as images of transcendental origin. Felice Bauer's "empty face" was such a projectional surface:[26] a screen for phantoms. By contrast, phantoms are modern figures of madness when, as producers of meaning, they are situated inside the postal channels on this side of the mailbox—as the origin of precisely those images of origin.

Madness is a clear-sightedness that discovers a function of the symbolic in the imaginary. The method of this postal madness, which sustained Kafka's writing between 1912 and 1914, meanwhile no longer can be paraphrased. It can be reconstructed only on the basis of a meticulous record of the dice-rolling process. In order to accomplish this, the analysis must assume the standpoint of strategy. That is, instead of being duped by the virtual image of the letter writer Kafka that his letters to Bauer produce when published in the order they purportedly were sent, the analysis must reconstruct the phantom at the other end of the channel. A critical-paranoiac edition of the *Letters to Felice* would need to order them by the sequence in which they afflicted the sight of their victim. The result would be a reconstruction of the letters' discourse as it actually was promulgated; the price of such a reconstruction would be the authorial name Franz Kafka. What follows is thus—with regard to the letters from November 16–28, 1912—a conjuring of phantoms.

NOVEMBER 16, SATURDAY. K. writes a letter (1) to B. in which he complains that he has not received a letter ("Dearest, please don't torment me! Please!"), informs her of his expectation to receive a letter most certainly the following day, and promises something in the event that this expectation should be fulfilled: "A letter will and must come tomorrow, or I won't know what to do; then all will be well and I'll stop plaguing you with endless requests for more letters."[27] The foreseeable crossing of the letters in the mail—the prophesied or conjured one and the one just being written—thwarts the purpose of the letter and its complaint. "But if there is a letter tomorrow, then it will have been superfluous to greet you in your office on Monday morning with these complaints."[28] Let's say, Kafka writes, I hadn't said anything. The mail already will have canceled out what I am writing. This is a perversion of postal matters: instead of functioning as a medium for communication, the postal system functions as a medium that prevents communication. It's unnecessary, this letter I'm writing. If I'm right, then I'm wrong.

But that is not all—K. includes with the same letter (1) an undated letter (i) from the early phase of the correspondence that elevates precisely this cancellation (or deconstruction) of communication to the principle of the correspondence itself: "Once more what I am writing is not an answer; let questions and answers entangle themselves to their hearts' content."[29] K.'s letters are not answers because the letters they might answer are the ones that are just now being expected and will cancel them out. It is not an answer, but rather proof that—with eight daily deliveries against two—the expectation of the next letter always will quash the answer to the previous one. And because of this, the additional letter had not wound up in the mailbox earlier, but rather in K.'s drawer next to a carbon copy of the very first letter: "Nor is this the first time I have had to wait for a letter from you (though I'm convinced as always that it isn't your fault), which this old letter, enclosed, will prove."[30] And indeed, one reads in that letter: "I had resigned myself to the fact that there would be no letter from you today."[31]

K.'s "old letter" refutes Hegel. The truth that no letter would come "today" became anything but shallow, after all, by being written down and stored in K.'s drawer (not to say "sublated")—as Hegel had wanted to demonstrate with the truth that "now" was the night.[32] Of course, writing serves as a test of truth for K., as it had for Hegel, but instead of refuting the night, it demonstrates its ineluctability. (No one knew this better than Kafka, for whom night was never enough night.) The repetition of reading does not demonstrate that letters that do not arrive "today" are things that disappear (as night disappeared at midday in the philosopher's text), but instead proves to the contrary that the text's absence is a curse cast upon "today": No letter ever will arrive "today"— that is the law. Therefore (because all days are designated by the stored "today"), the additional letter has no date.

But: that law itself already has been crossed and canceled by a letter, and its charter therefore is an exception to itself. On that "today", after all, K. discovered an unexpected letter from B. at his office, "on sheets of the magnificent size of your writing paper, and . . . of most gratifying weight," and in it he found permission to "write to you whenever I like."[33] In other words, K. received permission to write letters that are not answers. The reference of the one letter (1) to the other (i) consequently demonstrates that no letters ever arrive, unless B. was to demonstrate the exception to that law every day. And because letters thus arrive only in exceptional cases, it is permissible—on the basis of the canceled law to which all the letters are subject—to write letters that are not answers. Because letters always could also not arrive (as Derrida, the reader of Kafka, discovered),[34] K. is justified in writing letters that are not answers, but instead references to the revocation of the law that no letter ever arrives "today". That is the law, or the curse, of the correspondence. By giving the permission that revoked the law, B. has invoked this curse upon herself.

NOVEMBER 17, SUNDAY. And the curse is fulfilled "today" as well, on this day. Just as prophesied, the Sunday delivery indeed cancels letter (1) and its affirmation of the Law of Eternal Incapacity for Delivery of all let-

ters. B. once again has revoked the law, and K. writes (2) that it was unnecessary to write letter (1).

NOVEMBER 17–18, FROM SUNDAY NIGHT TO MONDAY. But the revocation of the law always applies only to "today." Every exemption of a letter
from the curse of nonarrival that the postman procures expires at midnight.
Thus, Kafka renews his demand for revocation this very night in a letter (3)
that is not an answer: "Tomorrow your letters, dearest, dearest!"[35]

NOVEMBER 18, MONDAY. In the morning hours at his office, K. begins
to write B. a letter (4), which, however, is not sent. Instead, he submits a
telegram (5) at 2:30 P.M.:

> urgent = rp 10 urgent
> felice bauer berlin immanuel kirchstrasze 29
> are you ill = kafka + +[36]

Because the morning delivery has confirmed the curse, a telegram is the
only way to effect the cancellation of the cancellation (2) of the letter (1).
That is, it overtakes the letter (2) that was not mailed until Sunday afternoon and, of course, the nocturnal letter (3). Thus, B. must believe K. had
not received a letter from her either on Sunday or on Monday morning.
The law is thus fulfilled for her: no letter ever arrives; all letters are lost.
That, at least, is the message of the telegram, which asks a question (or in
fact is nothing other than a question about the missing revocation) confirming the unholy effect of the law that no letter will come today, a law
chartered by the letter alliance (1, i). In falling into B's hands after letters
(1, i), the telegram (5) functions as the cancellation of the cancellation of
the cancellation (which is the law itself). Unlike Raban's (potential)
telegram, it does not cancel a letter promising the writer would come, but
instead cancels letters that promised the cancellation of the law that letters never arrive. The result is that B. immediately sends a reply telegram
and an express letter to replace the letters that apparently have been lost.

NOVEMBER 18, MONDAY NIGHT (11:15 P.M. AND LATER). K. complains
(6)—probably referring to his letter (3) written Sunday night—that
"these unfortunate Sundays are beginning to be a regular misfortune in
our relationship."[37] Yet the agent of this misfortune is K. himself, since
between September 12 and August 13 (the heyday of the correspondence)
he wrote most of his letters on Sundays.[38] K. offers no explicit apology for

the traffic accident in the form of the telegram produced by this particular Sunday ("not one word of apology for all the worries and troubles I caused you with that telegram") due to the absence of the stipulated letters. In any case, he definitely should have received a letter Monday morning, since B. claims to have written one already Saturday evening. K., however, will claim that the letter—as the law demands—was lost,[39] just like Sunday's letter, which the telegram (5) had carried off into the night of unavoidable letter losses.

NOVEMBER 19, TUESDAY. A letter (7) reproduces the letter alliance (1, i). As he had in the letter of November 16, K. promises a restriction on the correspondence and calls an "old letter" to the stand as his witness, that is, letter (4), begun on Monday: "It is quite right that we should stop this madness of so many letters; yesterday I even started a letter on this subject which I will send to you tomorrow."[40] The fulfillment of the sincerity rule governing speech acts and thus the validity of the statement is postponed, put off until "tomorrow." Until then, the restriction on the restriction is valid that states "one would go crazy" if the madness were ended, and that madness is therefore unavoidable. Between the speech act and the intended content, a difference prevails: "the intention which animates utterance will never be completely present in itself and its content."[41] This difference is precisely what governs the strategic fate of the stipulated letter (4): in addition to the transcript of Monday morning, when the Curse of Eternal Incapacity for Delivery was fulfilled, it also contains the concession (given before the second mail delivery, and thus before the last possible absence of the postman's absence) that writing twice a day is "a sweet madness, nothing else,"[42] and therefore would testify to the intention animating the utterance of the letter of November 19 (7). The decisive factor, however, is that K. does not keep his promise and does not do just what letter (7) stipulated: that is, to send B. letter (4) the next day. Instead, K. will keep the letter in the by now well-known desk drawer for nine days. The sentence that it "is quite right that we should stop this madness of so many letters" thus remains canceled by the affirmation that stopping the madness merely means permitting madness.

NOVEMBER 20, WEDNESDAY. Instead of sending the stipulated letter (4) that was to animate with intention the utterance in yesterday's letter (7), K. sends a letter (8) further postponing the animation of the utterance "it is quite right" by anticipating the madness that would come once the flow of the "madness of so many letters" was dammed.

> Dearest, what have I done that makes you torment me so? No letter again today, neither by the first mail nor the second. You do make me suffer! . . . You've had enough of me; . . . it's not surprising at all; what is incomprehensible, though, is that you don't write and tell me so. If I am to go on living at all, I cannot go on vainly waiting for news of you, as I have done these last interminable days. But I no longer have any hope of hearing from you. I shall have to repeat specifically the farewell you bid me in silence. . . . I shall expect no further letters.[43]

The animation of yesterday's renunciation would have resulted in the death of the writer. The reason of letters spells death for their writer, just as madness spells life. Yet what is valid for the declaration that the madness would stop also is valid for the declaration of wanting to affirm the curse of letters from now on by expecting no further letters: the suspension of intention.

NOVEMBER 20–21, NIGHT FROM WEDNESDAY TO THURSDAY. At 1:30 a.m. the sincerity rule for speech acts is rescinded once more, by means of a letter (9) apologizing for the morning letter (8), and thus the writer is absolved from what he said: say I hadn't said anything: "Have I offended you with this morning's letter? . . . Please, dearest, forgive me! . . . All I can say is: Stay with me, don't leave me. And should one of my enemies from within write to you as he did this morning, don't believe him."[44] "There's someone in my head but it's not me":[45] I'm not writing you letters, it's someone else, whom you can't believe. But it cannot even be believed that he cannot be believed; after all, how is one to know if it is K. or his enemy who is saying it?

NOVEMBER 21, THURSDAY. Two letters reach K. The revelation that Kafka is not the writer of the *Letters to Felice* is followed at 3:00 P.M. by an express letter (10) that overtakes the letter of apology (9), or at least catches up with it. Both letters will be delivered to B. on Friday morning. The express letter recapitulates the letters' course of action since Saturday and offers an excuse for Wednesday's madness, claiming that (after Monday's catastrophe) there could be only one explanation for the postman's renewed absence: "owing to some curse that is upon me, you wanted to end it all."[46] Irrevocably, the Curse of Eternal Incapacity for Delivery had struck. Standing behind the magical shield of the two letters he received, K. actually is able to admit that the curse for once merely had consisted of K. (supposedly) forgetting Wednesday was a holiday (the Day of Prayer and Repentance). Since no mail was sent on Wednesday, he could receive the letters B. had written on Tuesday only on Thursday. But while K. is explaining all this, the farewell letter (8)—meanwhile no longer written by K.—arrives in Berlin, and B. responds immediately with a telegram. In it, she insists that despite Kafka's accusations, she most certainly did write a letter on Monday. Since, however, K. does not count her "express letter I had extorted by force,"[47] yet another letter is added to his list of lost letters. K. immediately informs B. of this by registered letter (11)—fearing that the express letter (10), which he had forgotten to post by registered mail, might meet the same fate that befell B.'s letter of Monday. The registered letter is followed, finally, by an ordinary letter (12), in which K. reports his discovery that meanwhile another person (another woman) had been talking in B's letters: that is, his own mother.

And so on, and so on. It is plain to see: the letters going back and forth between Prague and Berlin amounted to a single, self-registering, mad postal machine. They were a registry of lost, canceled, unnecessary, and forged letters—or letters that were written by someone else entirely. They exhausted the repertoire of defective postal speech acts. Austin or Searle would find nothing here they would not have to exclude from the theory of speech acts.[48] Mail, or the impossibility of writing letters.

What became of letter (4) in K.'s drawer still has to be reported. It surfaced again—as always, not without reason—fourteen letters later: in the form of an inclusion in the letter of November 28. Emerging from the depths of time, it gave the lie to "correspondence" as the name for an exchange of letters that were anything but co-responding (if "correspondence" means that letters make reference to each other in a shared context). It came in answer to a letter from Berlin that brought the news that B. had broken down in tears, apparently for no reason: "Perhaps really the only reason is that we write to each other too often. I am enclosing a letter I began on that telegram-Sunday [November 18 was in fact a Monday], but didn't dare finish at the time because of my misery when the second mail brought nothing. Read it like an ancient document. I no longer agree with every word I wrote then, but your tears reminded me of it."[49]

Kafka, or how to cross out what you say. Mail was not a means for correspondence, but precisely the opposite: a means to give answers that did not correspond, to fire off speech acts that blew themselves to pieces. The inserted letter was an "old document," just as the inserted letter (i) had been an "old letter." That is, it had an owner and a sender, but no author; it was remembered, quoted, but not meant; it was a dead letter in the catacombs of Kafka's writing shrine.[50] In the actuality that summoned it from the grave of the drawer, its intention was suspended: "I no longer agree with every word I wrote then." No wonder, given what that letter contained: the very conclusion that the writer of the letter, subject to the duty of correspondence, should have reached from the insight that the reason for the unreasonable tears was "that we write to each other too often" and that he now refused to reach in this way: "And that is why I beg you, let us put an end to this flood of letters that produces nothing but delusion, which makes one dizzy. To me they are indispensable, yet I beg you nevertheless. If you agree, I shall get used to writing less often, but certainly not otherwise, for it's a poison that lodges in the pit of one's stomach. Suggest how we should do it; I will listen to you, not to myself."[51]

An old, archival self corresponded with B. in place of the "frame self." The madness revealed in letter (9)—that "one of my enemies from within writes to you"—was a solid discourse network. It was someone else who was speaking; an implanted Other assumed the guilt that in the present context of the correspondence went to the letter writer. The subject of the *Letters to Felice* was nothing more than a sensual certainty: his truth was limited to the duration of a single night, and only during that night did he animate his letters with the soul of intention, only then did he take responsibility for what was said. His past, his memories, were a pile of dead letters in a drawer. The other K.s speaking in those letters corresponded with each other, bore witness, and gave promises, while the subject who had to keep them had dissolved under the first rays of the morning sun, once upon a dawn long past.

But there was more. It was no accident that the text of the inserted letter broke off in midsentence precisely at the word "restraint," only to be continued—as is known—in a telegram, the text of which ("are you ill") was fully incompatible with the offer of "restraint" in letter writing and had been stipulated in parentheses even before the break in the inserted

	Sa	Su	Mo	Tu	We	Th	Fr	Sa	Fr
K	1 + i[52]	2,3	4,5,6	7	8,9	10,11,12			
B		1+i	5	2,3	6,7	8	10,9	11,12	26+4i

FIGURE 12. Delivery series of Kafka's letters.

letter: "(The first mail has just arrived, and no letter from you. For heaven's sake, could you still be ill?)."[53] Reading this letter on November 29 invoked perforce the telegram, (5), in the context of which it belonged on its constituted level. In the context of letter (26) of November 28, by contrast, in which it belonged on its postally constitutive level, it voiced a request that was incompatible with the first context (but corresponded to the situation on that day): "to stop the many letters." The letter's two contexts canceled each other out: in principle, the letter was incapable of delivery. Only the context of the contexts was delivered, which the telegram (5) and letter (26) produced between themselves, a context that was not authenticated by any signature. And this merely stated that neither tears nor illness would find mercy in the eyes of someone who sucked the life out of letters.[54]

There still remains the question regarding the originator of these things, which exist only in the context of the confused sequence of letters [see Figure 12]. Who took responsibility for the sense made by the delivery series of K.'s letters?

Think of a "correspondence" sustained by lost letters at one end and dead letters at the other: by a woman's letters, which were under the spell of nonentity, insofar as they never were anything but coincidental exceptions to the law of their ineluctable absence, and a man's letters, which always already were canceled out by the text of another, enemy self. In order to recognize the originator of sense in the letter series, one merely needs to identify this enemy other self, to which Kafka referred in letter (9) as the medium of "a-respondence" and its clerks. Especially since that indeed is precisely what Kafka did: "Dearest Felice, we are being made fools of by the mail. . . . Somewhere within this rigid organization of postal services, there seems to be some diabolical official who is playing around with our letters, letting them go according to his whim—if only he really would let them all go!"[55] The coherence of the letter series no longer was guaranteed by a transcendental principle of order—an unevadable subject as the unity that dialectically underlies multiplicity (and even in recent theories of the letter still constitutes "correspondence" as an object of literary scholarship)[56]—and therefore a diabolical post official appeared behind the pack of letters as a figure of madness in the technical age of reason. His punctuation of letter delivery sustained the discourse of the subject who spoke in the letters, a discourse to which no subject beyond the mail can be imputed.

Once symbol processing functioned without a king, its institutions became the stronghold of parasitic powers. The interpretation of symbols thus no longer was the business of hermeneutics, but of paranoia. The spirit of the primal author was not what haunted the users of mail, but instead a conspiracy of subaltern discursive clerks. Just a year after Kafka's suspicion that the phantom of a postal official lurked behind every defeated postal speech act, Anton Wenzel Grosz presented an extremely precise and detailed criminological case study on the same problem at the mental hospital in Troppau, not far from Prague (the case under study was, of course, his own). According to it, Kafka's diabolical official was a member of an international gang of conspirators who, like Kafka's phantoms, were bent on sucking the life from lordly subjects of the Occident (identified by their coats of armor and noble titles). "They hire criminals as policemen + constables, as postmen, court ushers; even postal officials are in the service of the gang."[57] This parasitic organization, which later would answer to the name of Tristero in Pynchon's novel, forged the entire exchange of letters conducted among living people and was responsible for the curse to which all of Kafka's letters were subjected: never to arrive, forever. "All correspondence reaching me is either forged or not sent, or confiscated, as the case might be."[58]

Here, as in the case of Kafka, who gave up all of his letters as lost,[59] paranoia was merely a catastrophic form of the insight into the order of knowledge: whether it referred to the migration of criminological knowledge into the laboratories of experts in forensic evidence (for Grosz), or to the desire to study dispatching in brain pathways *in vivo* on the part of physiological knowledge (for Daniel Paul Schreber),[60] or the dream of taking possession of the material equivalent of telepathy—the telephone network[61]—on the part of psychoanalytic knowledge (for Ernst B.-F., the Basel hairdresser whose thoughts were stolen out of his head by a gang of doctors using "brain telegraphy").[62]

It was no accident, but in fact merely a matter of consequence, when in the last year of his life Kafka revealed the debt his insights regarding the hermeneutic production of phantoms owed to the censorship of the First World War. While in March 1922 Kafka still had substantiated the impossibility of communicating by letter on the rather vague basis of a "ghost which develops between the lines of the letter one is writing and even more so in a series of letters where one letter corroborates the other and can refer to it as a witness,"[63] the reasons he stated to the postal official Brod in October 1923 were, in his own words, "strategic":

> So if I do not write, that is due chiefly to "strategic" reasons such as have become dominant for me in recent years. I do not trust words and letters, my words and letters; I want to share my heart with people but not with phantoms that play with the words and read the letters with slavering tongue. Especially I do not trust letters, and it is a strange belief that all one has to do is seal the envelope in order to have the letter reach the addressee safely. In this respect, by the way, the censorship of mail during the war years, years of particular boldness and ironic frankness on the part of the phantoms, has proved instructive.[64]

The lesson of wartime censorship, which in any case pervaded a substantial portion of the *Letters to Felice*, was that the hermeneutic method of producing phantoms—by imputing a subject to a chain of contextual links as its originator—was a historical effect of the confidentiality of letters. It was not for nothing that Kafka was particularly mistrustful of letters and their envelopes, the postal requirements for subjectivity. It was not for nothing that during the war, he resorted to the new standardized forms of the world postal system that had undermined subjectivity and the phantom known as the individual from the start: postcards and the typewriter. "Dear Felice," he announced on April 14, 1916, "I'm going to send more postcards from now on, letters are too slow."[65] The reason for this was that postcards, which "by their nature and properties . . . lack the confidentiality of the letter, upon which the use and usefulness of the mail"—

and ergo the nourishment of phantoms—"is principally founded,"[66] passed more quickly through the censor's office than letters did. No sooner said than done. From the outbreak of war until the definitive end of the correspondence in 1917, Kafka sent 140 postcards to Bauer and only 29 letters to the phantoms. And when such postcards were written on a typewriter, like the one of August 22, 1916, the chances were even multiplied that they might escape the hands of phantoms who lived off the secrets in human letters: "A sudden thought: do use the typewriter one day, too. In which case it could well be longer than say last Sunday's note (nothing so far dated either Friday or Saturday), and typescript may pass through the censorship at greater speed."[67]

Wartime censorship of letters revealed that the confidentiality of the letter had been invented by phantoms in order to make love letters and their heartfelt texts things that could be posted. "Written kisses don't reach their destination, rather they are drunk on the way by the ghosts"[68] precisely because the possibility of writing and mailing kisses had been an invention of the ghostly "opposing side." That, however, was a lesson only wars and the media of postcards and typewriters that emerged from them could teach.[69] These media were the materialities that transformed the conditions of epistolary discourse in a way that made it possible for the first time to state the law defining what writing had been under the rule of the letter's confidentiality.[70]

The subsequently obvious impossibility of postal communication conducted by a means other than postcards, the theory of which Kafka devised in 1922–23 and the practice of which quite manifestly was the "a-respondence" of his correspondence with Bauer, does not at all suggest caving in to the choir of Kafka interpreters who confuse this impossibility with the meaning of Kafka's "work" (whether it be defined as unintelligibility or enigma or absurdity). To that end, one would first have to ignore the pile of 581 letters, postcards, and telegrams. It seems equally fruitless, however, to include this pile in the files of evidence in support of deconstruction and its theorems. Indeed, the game of endless cancellations, graftings, and decontextualizations demonstrates beyond a shadow of a doubt that the text of Kafka's letters between 1912 and 1914 is preserved in the traces of the very *différance* Derrida ultimately incorporated into his general theory of the postal system. It is equally beyond doubt that Kafka systematically suspended all the rules that the theory of speech acts prescribes for communication accessible to theory, and that this suspension was not accidental or "negligible" due to its "theoretical irrelevance."[71] On the contrary, it opened up the "general space of possibility"[72] for the correspondence in the first place. Finally, Kafka's law that letters reached him only as exceptional spells lifting the curse that letters never arrive seems to find a clear echo in Derrida's law that letters always also cannot arrive. Yet: Kafka's impossibility of communicating by letters did not have philosophical or linguistic foundations, but instead—as he explained to Max Brod in 1923—"strategic" ones. It did not lead to the rules of a "petty pedagogy"[73] that seeks to prescribe the interminability of reading, but instead to a war of nerves that produced the interminability of writing. Instead of producing interpretation that is fundamentally endless, the movement of *différance* produced an interminable stream of letters.

Dracula was not a linguist or a philosopher, but a warlord. Insofar as the deconstruction of correspondence had strategic reasons, it was the product of a historical situation determined by the media. The indisputably accurate claim that Kafka's letters to Bauer document the attempt to "use riddles . . . to secure a permanent stage of transition"[74]—permanent postponement of their arrival and thus a permanent state of being on the way—therefore includes, rather than excludes, power. The historical a priori of postal materialities (postage stamps, postcards, the World Postal Union, etc.) itself deconstructed the humanistic "idea that people can communicate with one another by letter" and made such deconstruction an overt game of power. Consequently, the securing of a permanent stage of transition was the effect of the power of the modern postal system—typewriters, stenotypists, and Parlograph departments included. The postal system's record year, 1913, not only deconstructed the humanistic sub-epoch of the postal system, but also was the historical site at which a deconstructionist general theory of the postal system became possible. The permanent stage of transition was a warrior's position (and therefore the position of the will to power) in a postal situation where truth was not proclaimed by kings, but was instead the result of polemics among couriers.

Only such discourse-analytical reflection on deconstruction (which itself will not elude deconstructionist reflection) prevents the autoreferentiality of Kafka's letters, in which the correspondence deconstructs itself, from imploding and leaving nothing behind but the inconclusive construction of an unending text or the letter's celebration of itself upon which deconstructionist studies of Kafka's *Letters to Felice* insist.[75]

The endless stream of letters, the naked factuality of writing as the autoreferentiality of letters, instead points to a realm beyond letters: to their Other, the reality of the technical media.

CHAPTER TWENTY-TWO

In the Presence of Noise

Irretrievably, Kafka's letters are under the spell of their Other, the noise of the analog media, their raison d'être and their end, their destiny. The horizon toward which the letters incessantly were striving—at once erasing and multiplying themselves in self-referentiality—was the end of literacy itself. But it was not an end in magical melodies like the ones that once had lulled to sleep the heroes of Romantic novels as the ideal readers of their epoch. It was not the lullaby of the Mother, whispering and murmuring endlessly in the sounds of nature and trickling through the pages of Romantic novels, into which the text sank as night was falling upon consciousness. Around 1912, letters were on the way to new and final shores, beyond The Individual.

On sleepless nights, in the dozy state when things sometimes take on a different appearance, the cellar's inhabitant became aware of what was driving them and where they were going. And when sleep, the most supreme and mollified of Kafka's gods, could be enticed to come by day, it brought dreams telling of the boundaries of language and the postal system. They spoke of something that could not be communicated, according to Robert Graves, because it was the ground and groundlessness of communication itself: the "mighty roar" into which the endless heaps of letters merged as the pages poured out from two dreamed registered letters, the "roar of the sea" in the two dreamed telephone receivers of the so-called "Pontus letter," or the endless tape of a peculiar teletype machine:

> Dearest, today I must have dreamt about you the whole time I was
> asleep. . . . The first [dream] was in some way connected with your remark
> about being able to send a telegram straight from the office. Well, I could

somehow send a telegram straight from my room, the apparatus actually stood beside my bed, possibly in much the same position as the table you pull up to your bed. It was a particularly spiky apparatus and, just as I am afraid of making a telephone call, I was afraid of sending this telegram. But I had to send you a telegram on account of some immense worry about you, and a wild desire for immediate news of you that was about to drive me out of bed. Luckily my worries about you make me resourceful, alas, only in my dreams. The apparatus was built in such a way that one had only to press a button, and at once the reply from Berlin appeared on the paper tape. I remember how, rigid in suspense, I watched the tape unwind, at first completely blank, as was to be expected, since no reply could come through until you had been called to the apparatus in Berlin. What joy, when the first signs of writing appeared on the tape; I remember my joy was so tremendous I really should have fallen out of bed. Then came a proper letter that I could read perfectly, the greater part of which I might even be able to remember if I wanted to. All I will say is that the letter scolded me in the kindest, pleasantest way for my anxieties. I was called a "glutton" and there followed a list of the letters and postcards I have recently received or that are on their way.[1]

The "most perfect invention the human mind has ever stumbled upon"—after Lichtenberg's self-delivered letter—was the telephone, as the telegraph's limiting value. The "apparatus" is either a telegraph—and apparently a Hughes telegraph (which printed out written symbols that could be read "perfectly," and not Morse code, for example)[2]—in which case the room in Kafka's dream is an office, from which he, like Bauer, could send telegrams directly; or the room is in fact his room, in which case the device is a telephone. Telegraphs, of course, are not to be found in private apartments, but the method of operating the apparatus in the dream does in fact precisely conform to that of a telephone—Kafka's personal way of using the telephone, that is. Indeed, the telephone's classical location next to the bed had been celebrated by Kafka's friend Max Brod just two years earlier in a poem entitled "Telephone"—one of Brod's rare references to his occupation.[3] But unlike the one in Brod's poem, the apparatus in Kafka's dream does not produce the vision of a white night shirt and the beloved who is dressed in it, but instead, that of a white ticker tape. As though the white noise of the telephone line became a "completely blank" ticker tape as the telephone became a teletype.

Literature's dream was a medium for instantaneous and continuous transmission that would postpone indefinitely the cut in communications traffic that letters quite simply require in order to become things that can be mailed in the first place. In the indefinite postponement of a cut on the part of the Other, who asks the question the subject can answer only by calling itself into being through an act of interpretation,[4] the letter clacking out over the Hughes device could deal with nothing other than the past and future letters from Bauer to Kafka—the mail of Babel. The endless letter, a self-registering postal system, deals with the noise of letters, with the white ticker tape itself, and thus with nothing at all. Indeed, the only letters with meaning are the ones not written, the interruptions, the cuts. Kafka went through the exercise a hundred times: "Nothing? You had letters from me on both Friday and Saturday, yet you don't write a single word? . . . This must have some significance, I tell myself, and it isn't difficult to work it out."[5] The cut that the dream telegraph promised to postpone was a call for the subject to surrender itself to the police installed in the construction of the mail: "Could not answer last letter. Had to say to myself your sole desire is to humiliate me. What else could your last letter mean, what else was the meaning of the otherwise pointless, never explained intervals between your letters."[6]

Intervals thus placed the subject in question. Endless letters, by contrast, or letters "invest[ed] . . . with a sense of infinity," had to mean nothing, ask nothing, and say "nothing essential," as Kafka already had established in one of his first letters to Bauer.[7] A continuum[8] produced by the delay or multiplication of cuts (as in film technology) would forget all about the call to which a soul—a self as the absent text's meaning—would have to respond. The continuum in Kafka's postal fantasy dream therefore was the effect of a double postponement: while the delay of the cut eliminated the letter, it simultaneously allowed the voice's presence to remain outstanding for an ever longer period of time. Such communication was no longer a letter and not yet a voice. Without an end and prior to all beginnings, it no longer experienced any farewells, but had yet never known a meeting.

This "permanent stage of transition" promised a text without end. Instead of being brought back to life by the touch of a voice, like the lyrical self in its grave—the telephone booth and its lifeless technology in Brod's poem[9]—Kafka sucked up a ticker tape like an insatiable vampire: the elixir of life for the Undead, securing his rest in his grave, which was his desk, his writing shrine. Unletters make the Undead.

The dream delivered the ground and groundlessness of the correspondence. That was not just a dream. After all, the telephone was the reason love letters flowed between Prague and Berlin at all rather than nothing. Without the telephone, the correspondence probably would have been at an end as early as November 9, 1912—with a letter that restrained both Bauer and Kafka from all further letter writing and tolerated continued communication only in the form of a blank postcard as a signal demanding the return of the letters.[10] The farewell letter already was written before the actual love correspondence began. The love letters were registered in the delay of posting that "last" letter, which ended up in Kafka's drawer next to the typewritten carbon copy of the first letter.

Instead, a telephone call arrived at Bauer's home. It was Kafka's declaration of love and ushered in the informal form of address ("Du") as well as the use of "dearest" as a salutation in Kafka's letters. The telephone conversation did not take place between Bauer and Kafka, however, but between Bauer and Max Brod. Brod had established his professional abilities with the telephone not only in poetry, but also in a career as personal consultant at the Prague Postal Administration.[11] He represented Kafka, just as his sister Ottla did in the dream. Kafka himself, on the other hand, developed an operating system governing the use of second-person singular pronouns in a letter that followed the telephone call: "The *Sie* glides as though on skates, it may have disappeared in the crack between the two letters . . . but the *Du* stands firm. . . . But what a word that is! Nothing unites two people so completely, especially if, like you and me, all they have is words."[12] Nothing but words, and therefore no bodies. And nothing but paper words at that, since the telephone showed up only as "Du" after the call had taken place and disappeared in the gap between two letters. The telephone gave the correspondence the quality of an unbroken electrical current, which indeed was nothing but the technical reality of a telephone line. However, the telephone expert Brod's telephonic speech act assumed responsibility for the use of "Du." Kafka could write love letters, and the postal system was liable for the results.

The analog was the *limes* of the mail. In the noise on the channels or in the crosstalk of the networks, communication is founded and founders.

This and the fate of literature under the conditions of analog communications technology was the subject of what is probably Kafka's most famous dream:

> Well, I won't sleep anyway, only dream. As I did yesterday, for example, when in my dream I ran toward a bridge or some balustrading, seized two telephone receivers that happened to be lying on the parapet, put them to my ears, and kept asking for nothing but news from "Pontus" but nothing whatever came out of the telephone except a sad, mighty, wordless song and the roar of the sea. Although well aware that it was impossible for human voices to penetrate these sounds, I didn't give in, and didn't go away.[13]

As the boundary of the senses, the daydream—a dream without sleep, being awake without being awake—was the dream of the boundary of meaning. The dream's path led the dreamer down to the sea, which divided the people from their Other, the realm of the analog media; it led to the place where the letters of people who had nothing but words became one with the pounding of the surf.

"Communication in the Presence of Noise": the title of an essay by Claude Shannon would read in 1940, which in itself is remarkable enough. Communication no longer took place in the presence of the Lord, who divided the waters so the chosen message or the chosen people might pass through without noise. Communication no longer took place in the presence of The Woman, whose wishes were heard and answered, as when Kleist wrote a love letter.[14] Communication is the presence of a Third, the presence of a parasite, as the French translation of "noise" signifies,[15] which could be an enemy or death (loss of information, thermodynamic disintegration). Just as a roll of the dice never eliminates chance, a signal never can eliminate noise (and the human voice never can pass through noise as the people of Israel crossed the Red Sea). This already gained expression in the fact that the ratio of signal to noise— $\sqrt{P/N}$ — did not itself provide any information about the number of amplitudes to be fairly well distinguished on a telephone receiver; the ratio of signal plus noise to noise was necessary: $\sqrt{(P + N)/N}$.[16] The muse's mouth of antiquity no longer stood at the origin of language, and no mouth of The Mother made the poet speak as in the days of Romanticism. Instead, a telephone transmitted the ground of all discourse, which was delivered to the human senses only by the media of acoustical recording and transmission: white noise.

Here, at the origin of language, where poets had felt at home since the eighteenth century, here the dreamer expected news about the situation of literature as a discourse of love. After all, the fate of the "consummate 'love poet' of European literature," of Ovid, the author of the *Amores* and the *Ars amatoria*, was to be announced in the "News from 'Pontus.'"[17] But in Austria, direct dialing still was unknown in 1913, even to Austrian daydreamers. Therefore, a second Ovid of the Habsburg Empire acted as agent or operator: Franz Grillparzer, the author of a cycle of poems entitled *Tristia ex Ponto*, operated the switchboard between Vienna and Rome.[18] It was through Grillparzer, who had written his poem "To Ovid" exactly a hundred years earlier, through Grillparzer, who had felt excluded from history like the man

> who was pushed to wild and desolate wastes,
> where a fortunate man ne'er was seen,
> on Pontus' far shores, whipped by the sea,
> by the rage of Rome's treacherous sovereign,[19]

through Grillparzer, one of his favorite poets, that Kafka hoped to be connected with Ovid.

But no one worked at the switchboards anymore; even complaints about a cut-off postal connection now seemed impossible. Instead, the daydreamer got to hear tones that were the acoustical *limes* of humanity. He heard what fenced in and cleared writing when it was defined as exile from love and as the total transmission potential of the postal system. In the background noise, at once the abyss of meaning in general and the condition for its possibility, a song could be perceived from a place remote from humans. After women as agents for the seizure of power and the expansion of the technical analog media had (like the dream's addressee) taken the place of the transcendental signifier, the ear no longer perceived the most familiar of all familiar voices at the boundary river of language, but instead the most remote and strangest—the voice of an inhuman, man-killing enticement to which antiquity had given the name "Sirens."

Kafka was not the only one to hear this voice. In 1907, in Maurice Renard's story "The Man and the Sea Shell," it also claims as victims a composer named Nerval, the Western system of musical writing, and—as the reader may suspect—in the end, the narrator himself, who all succumb to the noise from a "stehoscope"[20] only superficially disguised as a sea shell. The noise gives birth to a "sexual cry of goddesses" that—as the return of the real for existences grounded in writing (such as the fictional Nerval and the empirical Kafka)—is fatal: "At first I was only able to make out a gurgling of foam, then the hardly audible turmoil of the open sea. I sensed—how I can not say—that the sea was very blue and very ancient. And then, suddenly, women were singing and passing by . . . inhuman women whose hymn was wild and lustful like the scream of an insane goddess."[21] In the end, all that remained was a space "littered with blackened and torn sheets of music."[22] Such was the horizon and the vanishing line of literature around 1900: not *dissémination*, not the endless distribution of signifiers, but instead, hearing's plunge into the real. In 1907, Rilke also dealt with the topos of literature's origin in a poem entitled "The Island of the Sirens": narrating, the narrator Odysseus searches for the site that is the origin of narration, a silence that is nothing but the holding back of a song "no mortal ear withstands."[23] This is a silence, or a noise,[24] for which the eloquent Odysseus has no words because it is the origin of all words.

In Kafka's case, however, the "mighty" and obviously "wordless song" can be assigned a name and a date. Only five days before the "Pontus dream," Kafka had "thumbed through an old volume of the *Gartenlaube* from the year 1863," as he wrote to Bauer.[25] In doing so, he might well have run across an article entitled "The Music Telegraph," which described the telephone Philipp Reis had presented to the Physical Society in Frankfurt am Main on July 4, 1863. The apparatus Reis demonstrated represented such an improvement over the 1861 model that it was now able to transmit "*clearly and audibly* melodies sung at moderate volume with the doors and windows closed at a distance of circa 300 feet."[26] Like the frequency multiplex experiments of his successor Bell, Reis's experiments with the telephone were influenced by the way Helmholtz had configured his technical apparatus, which used tuning forks and resonators to prove experimentally that timbre originates from the ratio of amplitudes in harmonics. Consequently, the intermittent currents produced by Reis's apparatus could transmit periodic oscillations alone, and hence nothing but "wordless song."[27] In his dream, Kafka thus heard precisely what Bell had denied himself the privilege of hearing in exchange for Mabel Hubbard (who certainly was no Siren), only to have it resurface via Ma Bell as the frequency multiplex in every telephone line.

In the form of Helmholtz's jukebox, the "resonator" or quasi-"digital" stage of the telephone's development reappeared in *The Castle* as the human side of telephone networks:

> In inns and such places it [the telephone] may be of real use—as much use, say, as a penny in the music-box slot—but it's nothing more than that. Have you ever telephoned here? Yes? Well, then perhaps you'll understand what I say. In the Castle the telephone works beautifully of course; I've been told it's being used there all the time; that naturally speeds up the work a great deal. We can hear this continual telephoning in our telephones down here as a humming and singing, you must have heard it too. Now, this humming and singing transmitted by our telephones is the only real and reliable thing you'll hear, everything else is deceptive.[28]

What comes slamming through the telephone "as if it were trying to penetrate beyond mere hearing"[29] is the naked and raw being of discourse, its unadorned That. If the theme of the Pontus dream is the disappearance of "communication into noise," the speech of the village leader deals with communication that *is* the presence of noise. Language is not a medium for understanding, but instead an enticement for hearing to plunge from the treacherous heights of meaning into the reality of the media. Information and meaning have parted ways; the former refers to technical, the latter to semantic aspects of communication, and the semantic aspects, at least, are irrelevant to the technical ones.[30] The only thing that is authentic is the Real of speaking as it is delivered and revealed to humans by the medium of the telephone. Speaking in the telephonic medium as a form of communication, by contrast, is "merely a practical joke," as the village leader declared.[31] Either the truth is known, and nothing is understood, or the meaning is known, and one is deceived.

If the criterion "deceptive/trustworthy" is translated into the criterion "uncertain/certain," the village leader's discourse coincides with the discourse of information theory, which was just beginning to emerge in Kafka's time. A transmitting system whose output is governed by the greatest possible certainty would be a system that encodes messages in such a way that they are no more redundant than white noise. An ideal system would transmit a signal that approximates white noise in its statistical properties. This follows directly from Shannon's fundamental theorem, which specifically states that "it is possible to send information at the rate C [i.e., channel capacity] through the channel *with as small a frequency of errors or equivocation as desired* by proper encoding."[32] If one possessed a transducer that allowed the redundancy of a signal to approach zero, on the one hand, the rate of transmission would approximate the channel's capacity, but on the other hand, the message would consist of a sequence of symbols that all were equally probable.[33] There would be only one disadvantage to using such an optimal code: "The required delays at transmitter and receiver increase indefinitely."[34] The optimal code requires an indefinite delay in transmitting the message.

Shannon referred to this assertion on the part of his fundamental theorem as "astonishing" or "rather surprising." And that it is. We humans, who live inside our everyday languages like pet animals, are accustomed to think redundancy must be as great as possible at the time of encoding so as to minimize the probability of errors, and that the rate of transmission must approach absolute zero for the same reason.[35] The absolutely intelligible is at the same time the absolutely empty. What provokes astonishment is therefore the codes' departure from everyday language. Unlike the animal in possession of language, codes are not concerned with understanding in minimizing the probability of error, but with a transmission rate exactly equal to C. So misanthropic are the strategies of codes in contrast to those of languages. While the latter increase redundancy because they have to do with human communication, the former dismantle it (and therefore intelligibility as well, as anyone can see in a compressed text) in order to achieve a rate of transmission approximating channel capacity as closely as possible ($W \log (P + N)/N$).[36] Encoding no longer stands in the service of The Individual, but in that of communications systems. This is why humans are so in love with user-friendly interfaces, which bind codes to everyday language and its philanthropic redundancies. So much at least appears certain: the end of what is possible for the human voice, the speaking of a language that would completely lack redundancy (i.e., would consist of symbols that all were equally prob-

able and could be expressed in random order), the end of human communication, is the end of the postal system as well.

Kafka certainly tried to do his part in achieving that end. In the second
section of the Pontus letter, he proposed a sort of takeover of the postal
system on the part of Carl Lindström Incorporated that amounted to the
replacement of written communication with the circuitry of the analog
media. In point 2 on his list of proposals, Kafka still envisioned the transmission of dictation in typewritten form, which then would be transferred
to the postal system for further delivery.[37] But even that, the text's last remaining relay, was eliminated in point 5:

> Invent a combination of telephone and Parlograph. This really can't be too
> difficult. The day after tomorrow, of course, you will tell me that this has al-
> ready been accomplished successfully. . . . More difficult, but surely quite
> possible, would be a combination of gramophone and telephone. More diffi-
> cult, simply because one can't understand a word the gramophone says, and
> a Parlograph can't very well ask for clearer pronunciation. A combination of
> gramophone and telephone would not be of such great universal importance;
> it would only be a relief to people who, like me, are afraid of the telephone.
> People like me, however, are equally afraid of the gramophone, so for them
> there is no help whatever. Here, by the way, is a rather nice idea: a Parlo-
> graph goes to the telephone in Berlin, while a gramophone does likewise in
> Prague, and these two carry on a little conversation with each other.[38]

The end of communication for human beings—the beginning of communication for machines. The writing hand and the Western Individual attached to it ceased to be the interface of postal exchange, ceased to be relays or halts that posting had to take into account. In Kafka's plans, the
Imperial Postal Service did continue to exist as an "overlapping public institution,"[39] but de facto it grew dependent upon private industry, which
provided both the technology and the network.

As the oldest history of the modern postal system, the history of the
Taxis, shows, postal power ultimately resides with those who own and
maintain the hardware, and not with the institutions in the name of
which they operate. In Kafka's view, the postal system did not cease to exist with the emergence of analog technologies for recording and transmitting, it was simply transferred to media firms like Lindström. As an institution, however, the postal system appears to stand and fall with the

power of writing. Was this the end of the postal epoch? No, but it was the end of the modern sub-epoch of the postal system that had been based on writing and thus had seen the individual and its *cognitio* as the ultimate address of the reason for anything that exists. With the *clôture* of this sub-epoch, the epoch of the human individual in the history of communications technology was at an end. If Ovid's laments about lost postal connections could legitimate laments about the end of human communication in the noise of circuits, all writing from then on would have been the writing of *Tristia*. Rather than continuing on to the hundredth colloquium on "art in the age of the technical media" the lamentations over the end of the individual (as if such lamentations were the ultimate vocation of art), Kafka did not "wish to complain, but to make a generally instructive remark."

Such a standard has yet to be established. As everyone knows, the postal system as an institution was not demolished by gramophones, telephones, and the Parlograph, as Kafka had planned and perhaps even desired. He was mistaken insofar as he saw the media conglomerates' takeover of the postal system occurring at the level of signal transmission instead of signal processing. The end of The Individual as the universal interface for every type of data and the emergence of machine-to-machine interfaces—that is, communication without people—is not what informed the postal system of its end in the 1980's. The postal monopoly on the transmission of data will not collapse due to the differentiation of transmission (both the thing and the concept) into telegraphy, telephony (wireless or hard-wired), and television, a differentiation that has made available separate channels for text, sound, and image. Instead, its collapse will come as a result of digitalized transmissions, with which transmission itself will cease to exist for the history of the media after it becomes a subsystem of universal signal processing. Once transmission is irrelevant, text, sound, and image will be combined in one and the same digital signal-processing code, and the postal system in the form of institutionalized transmission will disappear.

The shift in the problematic of power from the level of transmission to the superordinated level of processing was achieved by wars. During the First World War, R.V.L. Hartley, who coined the term "information theory" and was one of the first pioneers in the field, already was working on the urgent problem of developing cryptography, not only for telegraphic, but also for telephonic, signals. The development of secret telephone systems led "perforce to the attempt to digitalize vocal transmissions,"[40] that is, to scan verbal language discretely such that it could be scrambled afterward. (Hartley registered a corresponding patent in 1921.) After all, when Shannon and others resumed Harvey's experiments at Bell Laboratories one war later, they discovered language's phonetic supply of signals to be so redundant that even the most sophisticated attempts to scramble the frequency ranges of vocal transmissions in order to make them indecipherable without a key resulted in nothing more than today's pop music at best. No matter how much the technicians tried to destroy language completely, the human ear was all that was needed in order to decode the resulting mess.[41] Consequently, the world inhabited by ears had to be abandoned by developing a procedure for translating the amplitude values of analog transmitting systems into digital form, or—in other words— transmitting anything that is analog, such as spoken language, telegraphically. The result was known as Pulse Code Modulation, or PCM. Its development had been pursued in the Bell Laboratories since 1943,[42] where technicians had learned about the Pulse Count Modulation patented in Paris by Alec H. Reeves of the International Telephone & Telegraph Company in 1938.[43]

In principle, PCM is a simple matter.[44] Under precise observation of Shannon's well-known sampling theorem, the analog entry signal first is sampled at a rate that is "at least twice the highest frequency in the input wave."[45] The result is a Pulse Amplitude Modulation (PAM), that is, a signal that is analog in one of its parameters (amplitude) and discrete in the other (time variable). The next step is the quantification of the PAM signal—its expression in thirty-two discrete incremental values, a number that was hardly chosen at random. "By quantizing we limit our 'alphabet,'" Oliver, Pierce, and Shannon wrote with an enthusiasm for methods of analphabetization peculiar to technicians.[46] Developing a circuit capable of distinguishing these thirty-two values turned out to be as difficult as ever. It was easy, by contrast, to construct a circuit that simply needed to determine whether an impulse had been transmitted or not. The third and decisive step in PCM is thus known as binary coding. Several impulses, each of which can be either "on" or "off," one or zero, are used

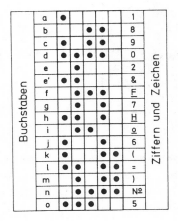

FIGURE 13. The Baudot system of telegraphic encoding.

as a "code group" in order to describe the amplitude of a single sampled value. Five impulses are necessary and sufficient to express thirty-two different values, since $2^5 = 32$. In other words: each of the thirty-two values is expressed by a symbol with five bits of information.[47] This in turn corresponds precisely to the five-bit code of Émile Baudot (today known as the Gray Code), which—due to its capacity to avoid errors—had become the standard code of automatic typewriting telegraphs after it was patented in 1874 [see Figure 13].[48] Baudot was the first to introduce machine-readable ON/OFF coding.

PCM is thus nothing but the reduction of language to telegraphy. And once analog voice oscillations had been reduced to Gray Code in sequences of thirty-two binarily coded digits, which were then transmitted at a rate of 8000 scans and 40,000 bits per second,[49] it was of course a simple matter to apply the classical methods of telegraphic encoding (such as the Vernam system) to the voice. Yet for all that, PCM did not achieve practical importance until the 1960's, when the transistor stood ready as an element capable of implementing the high telegraphic speeds required for rapid switching processes. From then on, PCM came to be decisive for the "revolution which is digitalizing almost every step in the telecommunications pathway."[50]

Revolutions tend to begin in secret. PCM initially found its application in cryptography, for which it indeed had been invented in the first place. In the 1980's (and perhaps even today), systems for encoding messages with the highest security clearance—such as the Pentagon's Key 9 System—continued to be based on PCM.[51] If German Telekom plans to bless the Germans with the construction of an ISDN (Integrated Services Digital Network) in the 1990's, it would mean that, once again in the history of communications technology, formerly top-secret military technology (PCM) would become the standard of everyday life. A development that began with Kleist's proposal for turning the artillery into a routine technology of postal transmission thereby would reach its momentary conclusion with the introduction of PCM at a standardized transmission rate of 64 kilobits per second, which would serve as the basic technology for a universal network of fiber-optic cables transmitting acoustical, optical, and symbolic data. The most highly classified information of the NSA (National Security Agency) thus would be transmitted over the same network as the afternoon mystery series or the everyday blahblah of people on the telephone. The difference between military and civilian communications technology would pass away, since radar signals and e-mail are all the same to PCM circuits.

While PCM's practical use was first established in the late 1960's, it already had produced immediate consequences for the development of information theories as early as the 1940's. After all, it was the technical condition for the possibility of reducing all information technologies to telegraphy: "Pulse Code Modulation represents the technical background for information theory's development from a systems theory of telegraphy into the transmission theory for all of telecommunications technology."[52] PCM was the prerequisite that allowed Shannon to transform his information theory—which emerged from his work for the Signal Intelligence Service at Bell Laboratories—into a general "mathematical theory of communication" (MTC). Not for nothing did the very first sentence of Shannon's communication theory refer to PCM, since like PCM it obtained "continuous information" "through a limiting process from the discrete case" and thus from the statistical structure of information in general.[53] Mathematics could make a profit from human physiology in the process: "Fortunately," analog messages could not be transmitted precisely—that would be completely impossible on a finite channel.[54] Only

God transmits exact reproductions—a fact that resulted in mysteries such as the Trinity. The ones transmitted by humans always are merely "high-fidelity." A certain discrepancy between original and reproduction always would be tolerable, provided it was not a matter of the Christian God's quality of reproduction (in telephone transmissions, a bandwidth of up to 4,000 Hz and a scanning rate of 8,000 Hz was completely sufficient), and therefore all analog information could be expressed digitally.

But that was not all. PCM also was the prerequisite for a *mathematical* theory of communication, that is, for a theory that could dispense with geographic parameters. This was so because after PCM, space no longer played any role in the design of communications systems. In all conventional electrical systems of transmission, the distance of transmission still had played an extremely important part, since the noise produced by relays was cumulative. The length of the system, that is, dictated the standard of quality required for each individual relay. Such was not the case with PCM: amplitude and phase were not transmitted, but merely columns of numbers in the form of impulses; the relay therefore simply had to register whether or not anything arrived.[55] While the technology of carrier frequencies made it seem to the ear that a "channel was useless" at an interference level of 10 µW and an interference gap of 20 dB, digital technology gave the impression of "very good reception" at the same levels.[56] "Practically, then, the transmission requirements for a PCM link are almost independent of the total length of the system. The importance of this fact hardly can be overstated."[57]

Indeed. "This fact," after all, quite simply meant that distance confidently could be neglected as a factor in theories of communication. What uniform postage had meant for the letter, digitalization meant for the medium of transmission: the negation of space.[58] If the postage stamp had canceled the spatial constant in the calculation of financial expenditure for a letter, the bit canceled the spatial constant in the calculation of the expenditure of redundancy for the channel. Distance, that is, no longer played any role in the relationship between capacity and rate of transmission. This in turn meant that communications theory no longer had anything to do with (letter) mail, and that is indeed becoming obvious as our letters are absorbed and transformed into bit sequences by fax machines and e-mail. Space was swallowed up by the theoretical properties of a single relay. The effect of this was that the properties of the "overall transmission system can be made to depend upon the terminal equipment alone."[59] The terminals and their industries alone will decide. The element that had been indispensable (in the form of the telephone) to Kafka's plans for media networks and that had guaranteed an existential basis for the Imperial Postal Service in a situation otherwise completely dominated by Carl Lindström or Edison thus itself had become a dependent variable.

Transmission shows up in the mathematical theory of communication as the loss of entropy. Equivocation is its measure, that is, uncertainty over the value of a transmitted symbol. What once promised employment and respect to hermeneutics until the end of time or until thermal death, the fundamental ambiguity and interpretability of every communicated symbol, now makes a living primarily for cryptanalysts in the form of equivocation. After all, the uncertainty about the value of individual bits that is called forth by interference on the channel is more or less indistinguishable from the uncertainty produced by enemy codes. "From the point of view of the cryptanalyst, a secrecy system is almost identical with a noisy communication system."[60] If there once had been uncertainty about whether one was inspired or seduced in the ages of religious symbols, and if there was uncertainty about what all this was supposed to mean in the age of literary symbols, there now is uncertainty about whether something is a coded message or merely interference in the age of digital coding.[61] Universal cryptanalysis has taken the place of universal interpretation. Literary scholars can draw their own conclusions from this.

Output with equivocation greater than zero can be a coding system as well as a noisy communication system (and what communication system would not be noisy, except perhaps that of angels?). As a result, Shannon's fundamental theorem provides proof that with optimal coding, information can be transmitted over channels with equivocation > 0 at an arbitrarily low rate of error (provided that $H(x) \leq C$, that is, that the entropy of the source is less than or at most equal to channel capacity).[62] At the same time, it also demonstrates that, again with optimal coding, it is possible to keep uncertainty about a symbol (that is, equivocation) constant at its initial value, regardless of how much material an enemy agent intercepts.[63] Once the transducer has eliminated all redundancies in the text to be transmitted $(D \rightarrow o)$, all letters are equally probable. In order to produce a message with the same properties as white noise, it thus is sufficient to apply any simple code to this compression result (substitution, transposition, Vigenère, etc.). The procedure for approximating an optimal rate of transmission is identical to the procedure for approximating optimal secrecy; in its basic design, an ideal system of transmission is identical to an ideal "secrecy system."

One should be careful, however, not to confuse Shannon's ideal communication system with the ideal of Enlightenment police science in 1800. The secrets of cryptology have nothing to do with the confidentiality of the letter. The optimal secrecy handled by MTC does not stand in solidarity with human communication or human hearts, but only with the reduction of entropic loss. An ideal system of transmission would experience no loss from entropy, be completely indecipherable, and—since $D \rightarrow o$—would be as unfavorably disposed toward people as white noise. The language of angels is a din human voices could not possibly hope to penetrate unless they spoke a language consisting of a sequence of symbols each of which was independent of its predecessor and all of which had equal probability. Such is the situation. Now that communication is the presence of noise and the absence of noise is therefore the absence of communication (a transmission with no entropic loss would be identical to the presence of God), transmission and thus the lines of communication in general are dominated by the rule of the code. With the dawn of the age of optimal codes, the epoch of the postal system known as human communication and the literature that lived off that communication were at an end. Lichtenberg's dream of a perfect postal system, which would have been continuous deciphering, reappeared in Shannon's designs for an optimal system of transmission. But in rigorous distinction from Lichtenberg's postal system, the message conveyed by Shannon's perfect post could not be delivered at all. The more optimal that codes, connections, and transmissions become, the more they distance themselves from humans and their redundant languages. If computer systems were not surrounded by an environment of everyday languages, there thus would be no software.[64] User interfaces alone provide humans with the narcissistic belief that everything that goes on is being delivered to them. Yet the expenditure in deeply layered surfaces already gauges the distance between humans and codes.[65]

In 1928, the very year that the age of information dawned with the publication of Hartley's essay "Transmission and Information" in the *Bell System Technical Journal*, the final sentence of Robert Musil's "Blackbird" already described the situation for human beings and their senses, once ideal systems of transmission had forsaken them. Faced with messages, "it's as if you hear whispering or just plain noise without being able to tell the difference!"[66]

Reference Matter

Introduction

1. Locke, 2: 149.
2. Ibid., 2: 3, 2: 131.
3. Ibid., 2: 150.
4. *Verstopfung*, also meaning "constipation." Translator's note.
5. Derrida, *The Post Card*, p. 65.
6. Ibid., p. 64.
7. Schottelius.
8. Pynchon, *The Crying of Lot 49*, p. 123.
9. Locke, 2: 9.
10. Pynchon, *The Crying of Lot 49*, p. 52.

Chapter One

1. Kafka, letter, end of March 1922, in *Letters to Milena*, p. 229.
2. *Zustellen* (along with the noun *Zustellung*) has a double meaning in German, and this pun is basic to the book, but untranslatable in a single term. It means "to deliver," but also "to block," "to render invisible," or "to make inaccessible." Translator's note.
3. Kafka, letter, end of March 1922, in *Letters to Milena*, p. 229.
4. *Das Unwägbare oder Unwëgbare*: "*wëgen*. . . . This verb, used transitively, means: to form a way and, forming it, to keep it ready. Way making [*Be-wëgen* (*Be-wëgung*)] understood in this sense . . . means to bring the way . . . forth first of all, and thus to *be* the way." Heidegger, *On the Way to Language*, pp. 129–30.
5. Heidegger, *The Principle of Reason*, pp. 23–24. *Zugestellt* is translated as "rendered" in the standard translation. Translator's note.
6. Ott, p. 83.
7. Kafka, letter, end of March 1922, in *Letters to Milena*, p. 229.
8. Ekschmitt, pp. 71–80.

9. Ibid., p. 122.

10. Innis, p. 48.

11. Hudemann, pp. 2–4.

12. Holmberg, p. 53–58; Rothschild, p. 29.

13. Hirschfeld, pp. 421–41. See also Wolfgang Riepl, pp. 459–62; Holmberg, pp. 104–30.

14. Vaillé, p. 98; Voigt, *Die Entwicklung des Verkehrssystems*, p. 816.

15. Ohmann, p. 40.

16. Cited in Herzog, p. 298.

17. Rübsam, p. 219.

18. Voigt, *Die Entwicklung des Verkehrssystems*, p. 836.

19. Popp, p. 6.

20. Dallmeier, p. 65.

21. This is highly evident, for example, in the case of England: in order to assert control over an increasing exchange of private letters, the queen issued a proclamation in 1591 urging that all letters be sent through state channels. In 1635, this ultimately led to the institutionalization of the General Postal Service in the United Kingdom. "It was the beginning of our postal services" (Staff, pp. 22–24).

22. Beyrer, p. 86.

23. Since Manfred Frank presumably does not believe in phantoms, he thinks it absurd to view the subject as a historical and therefore transitory figure—because thinking the end of the subject requires a subject (Frank, pp. 10–11).

24. Heidegger, *On Time and Being*, p. 9.

25. Derrida, *The Post Card*, p. 65. The technical sense of "counting" as the computability of information in a digitalized postal system will be discussed in the last chapter of this study.

26. Ibid.

27. Ibid., p. 63.

28. Vaillé, pp. 67–68.

29. Thus Beyrer states in a study completely unburdened by the issue under discussion here. Beyrer, p. 86.

30. Lacan, "Seminaire," p. 41.

31. Letter of d'Alembert, November 14, 1776, in Frederick II.

32. *Der Mensch*; there is no precise equivalent to this term in current English. *Mensch* refers to the concept of general humanity, in both biological and moral/ethical terms, as embodied within the confines of a single individual in a sense that is not gender-specific. (Like "man" in former English usage, however, it is assigned a masculine grammatical gender.) I have translated it as "human" or "human being" when the context primarily emphasizes humanity in the sense of a biological species. In its moral/ethical connotations, *Mensch* describes all of the potentialities of humanity, fully realized within the context of an individual. Such potentialities obviously are perceived differently in different time periods: in the Classical/

Romantic period, *Mensch* might thus perhaps best be understood as the morally autonomous, rational, self-actualizing individual and has been translated in this context as "individual" or "person." The moral/ethical aspect of the Classical/Romantic *Mensch* is in turn associated with the concept of *Bildung*, for which there is again no precise English equivalent. Literally "formation," the latter term refers to the educative process of forming the individual (as in the *Bildungsroman*) and has been rendered as "education," "formative education," "instruction," or even "training" as required by the context. The biological connotation of *Mensch* should be kept in mind in all instances, however; *Menschenbildung*, for example, can denote the "creation of human beings" and "education" at the same time. Translator's note.

33. Koselleck, pp. 70–71.

34. Cited in Friedlaender, p. 766.

35. Pedantically demonstrated in Siebenkees.

36. According to the testimony of Madame de Housset—the chambermaid of the Marquise Pompadour—Louis XV had "the duke of Choiseul pass on the secrets of the mail, i.e., excerpts from opened letters, a privilege the Duke of Argenson, his predecessor at the ministry, never had enjoyed. Choiseul abused the privilege, however, and amused his friends by reading from the whimsical stories and love intrigues he had discovered in this manner. Half a dozen *commis* at the Hôtel de la Poste made . . . a copy of the seals from letters they had been ordered to open, using a drop of quicksilver and holding the seal over a basin of warm water until the wax melted, then opened the letter, took the excerpt, and sealed it again. The intendant brought along the excerpts for direct recital every Sunday, just like a real minister." Cited in König, pp. 14–15.) Precisely this practice of interception provided the empirical background for Diderot's unspeakable methods of publishing the most intimate knowledge in *Bijoux indiscrets*. The shift from the speaking *bijou* as a euphemistic secondary metaphor to the speaking soul as a metaphor for the letter—which became perennial after Herder—precisely marks the transition from courtly to bourgeois dispositives of sexuality. (Whether the soul was a metaphor for the letter or for what the *bijou* stood for remains an interesting question in this context.)

37. Kafka, letter, end of March 1922, in *Letters to Milena*, p. 229.

38. Sautter, p. 101.

39. Voigt, *Theorie der Verkehrswirtschaft*, p. 865; Sautter, p. 102.

40. The speech was given during the Reichstag debate over the law regarding the Telegraph System of the German Empire on April 6, 1892. Cited in Wessel, p. 479.

41. Kafka, letter, end of March 1922, in *Letters to Milena*, p. 229.

42. So Kafka argued in his appeal for "the establishment and support of a military and civilian hospital in Prague for the treatment of nervous diseases in German Bohemia." Kafka, *Letters to Felice*, p. 580.

43. On the Foucault-Derrida debate referred to here, see Derrida, "Cogito and the History of Madness," in *Writing and Difference*, especially pp. 32–39, and Foucault, "Mon corps, ce papier, ce feu," in *Histoire de la folie*, p. 602. On the latter, see Wordsworth, pp. 116–25. Wordsworth accuses Foucault of having miraculously forgotten in 1972 what Derrida would insist on considering the technopolitics of the media in *The Post Card* in 1980. See also Eribon, pp. 144–47.

44. Foucault, *Archeology of Knowledge*, pp. 74, 186–87.

45. Heidegger, "Origin of the Work of Art," p. 190.

46. Turing, p. 15.

Chapter Two

1. Georg Christoph Lichtenberg, Enlightenment physicist, has left behind a body of work consisting mainly of aphorisms and fragments that make up his voluminous *Waste Books*. Translator's note.

2. Lichtenberg, first published in Joost, "'Briefe an Jedermann,'" p. 64; Joost places the date of the letter in the late 1770's.

3. Smolak, pp. x, xii.

4. Lacan, *Encore*, p. 87.

5. F. Kittler, "Die heilige Schrift," p. 155.

6. Derrida, *The Post Card*, p. 29.

7. Lichtenberg derived the term that he coined to describe his own writings, *Sudelbuch*, from the English "waste book," a ledger used in a system of accounting that is no longer employed today: "The merchants have their Waste book (*Sudelbuch, Klitterbuch*, it is, I think, in German), wherein they register from day to day everything they sell and buy, indiscriminately and without any order." Georg Christoph Lichtenberg, *Sudelbücher*, vol. 1, in *Schriften und Briefe*, ed. Wolfgang Promies (Frankfurt am Main, 1994), 1: 352.

8. Haller, *Tagebuch*, pp. 123–25.

9. "Die Gemschen sehn erstaunt im Himmel Ströme fliessen / Die aus den Wolken fliehn, und sich in Wolken giessen." Haller, *Die Alpen*, p. 22.

10. Ibid.

11. Ibid., pp. 57–58.

12. Ibid., p. 5. Daniel Casper von Lohenstein, a jurist and poet of the seventeenth century, was famous for the extensive apparatus of notes that he added to his historical dramas. In these notes, Lohenstein cross-referenced the details of his verses with history books, which he cited carefully by chapter, paragraph, and page number.

13. Zimmermann, cited by Heinzmann, in Haller, *Tagebuch*, p. 205.

14. Haller, *Tagebuch*, p. 205.

15. Joost, "'Briefe an Jedermann,'" p. 65.
16. Joost, *Lichtenberg*, pp. 288–89.   17. Raabe, pp. 60–61.
18. Bartholdy, p. 142.   19. Goethe, "Winckelmann," p. 5.

Chapter Three

1. Innis, p. 118.
2. Steinhausen, vol. 1, p. 5.
3. Vaillé, pp. 366, 370.
4. Quoted in Steinhausen, part 1, p. 102.
5. Erasmus, pp. 22–23.
6. Ibid., p. 74.
7. Pynchon, *Gravity's Rainbow*, p. 509.
8. Foucault, "Für eine Kritik der Politischen Vernunft," p. 65.
9. Harsdörffer, p. 76.
10. Campe, p. 87.
11. Derrida, *The Post Card*, p. 29.
12. "Alphabetization" is a term from social history that designates the spread of literacy among a population. See Friedrich A. Kittler, *Discourse Networks, 1800/1900* (Stanford, Ca., 1990), part 1, chapter 1. Also Rudolf Schenda, "Alphabetisierung und Literarisierungsprozesse in Westeuropa im 18. und 19. Jarhundert," in *"Das Pädagogische Jarhundert": Volksaufklärung und Erziehung zur Armut im 18. Jahrhundert in Deutschland*, ed. Ulrich Hermann (Weinheim and Basel, 1981), pp. 158–68, and François Furet and Jacques Ozouf, *Lire et écrire: L'alphabétisation des français de Calvin à Jules Ferry* (Paris, 1977).
13. Harsdörffer, pp. 29–30.
14. Gellert, "Briefe," pp. 97–98.
15. Ibid., pp. 162–63.
16. Gellert, *Briefwechsel*, letter 14.
17. "Hommo-sexual" is a Lacanian pun indicating the identification of "human" with "male" in Western culture, on the one hand, and the underlying homosexuality of all relations, on the other. Translator's note.
18. Tieck, *William Lovell*, pp. 307–8.
19. It is unnecessary to point out the obvious logocentrism of this ideal of the letter in detail. See Derrida, *Grammatology*. On Thot, see ibid., pp. 312–13.
20. Tieck, *William Lovell*, p. 60.
21. Haslam, pp. 38–39. On Matthews and some of his successors, see Siegert, "Gehörgänge ins Jenseits," pp. 51–69.
22. Campe, p. 28.
23. Gellert, "Briefe," preface (unpaginated).
24. Ibid.

25. Koselleck, p. 78. The same system was in operation at Schiller's *Carls-schule*, a preparatory school for education officials and for German Classicism. See F. Kittler, "Carlos als Carlsschüler," pp. 241–73.

Chapter Four

1. Klüber, *Wünsche*, pp. 6–7.   2. Obermeit, p. 68.

3. Steinhausen, part 2, pp. 334–35.   4. Goethe, *Werther*, p. 31.

5. Goethe, letter of September 14–19, 1775, in *Goethes Briefe: Hamburger Ausgabe*, 1: 192.

6. Ibid.

7. Ibid., 1: 194.

8. Goethe, *Werther*, p. 47.

9. It is possible to demonstrate Goethe's attention to the historical accuracy of the days of the week with regard to the dates on letters in *Werther*: a date is named in connection with a day of the week on a single occasion; Christmas Eve 1772, the day after Werther shot himself, was a Thursday according to Lotte. Goethe, *Werther*, p. 72. This was indeed the case in 1772, as anyone can prove to his or her satisfaction.

10. Goethe, *Werther*, p. 14.

11. Ibid., pp. 12, 53.

12. Ibid., p. 5.

13. "In the quiet of evening, the shade of my mother always hovers round me, when I sit in the midst of her children, my children, when they are assembled about me as they used to be with her. Then I raise my anxious eyes to Heaven and wish she could look down upon us and see how I keep the promise I made to her on her deathbed to be a mother to her children." Ibid., p. 40.

14. "Is, qui aperuerit vivi testamentum, legis Corneliae poena tenetur." *Corpus iuris civilis*, 46.10.1. "Qui testamentum amoverit celaverit eripuerit deleverit interleverit subiecerit resignaverit quive testamentum falsum scripserit signaverit recitaverit dolo malo cuiusve dolo malo id factum erit, legis Corneliae poena damnatur." Ibid., 48.10.2. See also *Cor. iur. civ.*, vol. sec.: *Codex Iustinianus*, 9.22, "Ad legem Corneliam de falsis."

15. Quoted in Friedlaender, p. 766.

16. Ibid., p. 769.

Chapter Five

1. Steinhausen, part 1, p. 104.

2. Ibid.

3. Gellert, "Gedanken," p. 184.

4. See the classical study by Bosse, "Dichter kann man nicht bilden."
5. Alewyn, pp. 102–3.
6. Gellert, "Briefe," p. 3.
7. Richter, p. 17 ff.
8. F. Kittler, *Discourse Networks*, p. 11.
9. Quoted in Gellert, "Briefe," p. 18.
10. Ibid., pp. 27–28.
11. Think of Kuhlmann's poetic combinations, for example.
12. Kant, p. 132.
13. Alewyn, p. 116.
14. Gellert, letter of March 14, 1759, in *Briefwechsel*, 2: 231.
15. Gellert, letter of January 22, 1759, in ibid., 2: 207.
16. Gellert, letter of February 26, 1759, in ibid., 2: 222–27.
17. "No, I want to teach you something better. We'll do it like this, sister. Write your letters on a folded page, and I will write the answer and critique next to it for you. But don't let Father help you. That's no use. I will see how you write. Now I'll make a start. Note this: write just as you would speak, and then you'll write a good letter." Goethe, letter of December 6, 1765, in *Goethes Briefe: Hamburger Ausgabe* 1: 19. See also Gellert, "Briefe," pp. 9, 46–47; Gellert had gleaned the catchphrase, which Goethe repeated to his sister, from one of the fourteen-year-old Lessing's letters to his sister Salome: "Write as you speak, and you will write beautifully." On this point and Goethe's relationship with Gellert in general, see Schöne, p. 193, and especially pp. 205–208.
18. Goethe, letter of December 6, 1765, in *Goethes Briefe: Hamburger Ausgabe* 1: 18. It was no accident that Richardson's epistolary novels—which Gellert likewise praised above all others (Gellert, "Briefe," p. 117)—were exempted from the novel-reading ban imposed on girls' minds (and not only by Goethe) in the second half of the eighteenth century. After all, the first of these novels, *Pamela, Or Virtue Rewarded*, emerged from Richardson's work on a letter-writing guide intended especially for women in the countryside—a commissioned work, moreover, that the printer Richardson had undertaken for two London book dealers (who saw such a guidebook as the prerequisite for the book market's access to rural areas); see Eaves and Kimpel, pp. 89–90. The "Briefe der Fr. von Montier," the "Lett[res] de Md. Montague," and especially the "Epistole di Cicerone," which were also among the texts Goethe prescribed for his sister's reading, were direct assignments from Gellert that Goethe passed on to his sister, who, as a matter of principle, never could have taken part in Gellert's classes (see for example Gellert, "Gedanken," p. 184). The ladies' college Gellert planned as a joke in one of his model letters (Gellert, "Briefe," pp. 163–64) thus had become a de facto reality by way of postal relays and in the person of his male student—a women's correspondence course.
19. Arnim, "Clemens Brentanos Frühlingskranz," p. 62.

20. Ibid., p. 24.
21. Klüber, *Das Postwesen in Teutschland*, p. 129.
22. Ibid., p. 5.
23. Alewyn, pp. 107–9.
24. Gellert, "Gedanken," p. 185.
25. Rabener, letter of May 7, 1749, cited in Alewyn, p. 114.
26. Gellert, "Briefe," p. 146.
27. Gellert, letter of December 11, 1759, in *Briefwechsel*, 2: 283.
28. Reiners, pp. 181–83.
29. Stephan, *Geschichte der Preußischen Post*, pp. 204–6.
30. Ibid., pp. 204–48.
31. Gellert, letter of March 27, 1959, in *Briefwechsel*, 2: 236.
32. Raabe, p. 4.
33. Ibid., p. 44.
34. Schlegel, "Vom Wesen der Kritik," p. 259.
35. Ibid., p. 251.
36. Ibid., p. 252.
37. Novalis, "Dialogen und Monolog," p. 429.
38. Ibid.
39. F. Kittler, "Über die Sozialisation," p. 104.
40. Goethe, *Apprenticeship*, p. 186.
41. Schlegel, "Goethes Meister," p. 266.
42. Ibid., p. 267.
43. Ibid., p. 259.
44. Schneider, *Die erkaltete Herzensschrift*, pp. 9, 16–20.

Chapter Six

1. As, for example, in the anonymous *Rationes dictandi*, mistakenly attributed to Alberich of Monte Cassino by Rockinger. See Adalbertus, p. 2 (editor's introduction): "Est igitur epistola congrua sermonum ordinato"; "Rationes dictandi," in Rockinger, p. 10, or the *Ars dictandi aurelianesis*: "epistola est oracio congrua suis e partibus conuenienter composita affectum mentis plene significans," Rockinger, p. 103.
2. On this conception of the "literary" as something necessarily prior to a history of literature, see Campe, p. xvi: "The 'literary' . . . indicates the site of a *point of intersection in a discourse network* at which literature is defined by non-literature."
3. Bäuml, p. 13.
4. Dambach, p. 9.
5. Foucault, *The History of Sexuality*, pp. 140–41.

6. Frey-Schlesinger, p. 433.

7. Justi, *Grundsätze*, p. 4. This was a key concept for Foucault in understanding the bio-politics of the eighteenth century: "Et cette 'biopolitique' elle-même doit être comprise à partir d'un thème développé dès le XVIIe siècle: la gestion des forces étatiques." Foucault, "Résumé," p. 106.

8. Siegert, "Netzwerke," pp. 540–41.

9. Foucault, "La gouvernementalité," p. 100.

10. Justi, *Die Grundfeste*, p. 382.   11. Ibid., p. 392.

12. Fontius, pp. 271–72.   13. Tieck, *William Lovell*, p. 9.

14. Justi, *System des Finanzwesens*, p. 186.

15. Stephan, p. 250.

16. Ibid., p. 239.

17. Ibid., p. 250.

18. With this a history began that would end in the English post office reform. To the extent that Rowland Hill was a more radical bio-politician than Justi, his mathematical theory of postage also was more radical.

19. Justi, *System des Finanzwesens*, p. 187.

20. Foucault, *The Order of Things*, p. 254.

21. Foucault, "The Life of Infamous Men," p. 89.

22. For a complete list, see Klüber, *Patriotische Wünsche*, pp. 32–35.

23. Klüber's favorite sample calculation involved a letter that, before the dissolution of the empire, could have traveled exclusively by Taxis Post from Hamburg to Lindau on Lake Constance and therefore would have cost only sixteen to eighteen kreuzers. In 1810, by contrast—since it had now to pass through six territorial postal services—the same letter cost between 70 and 80 kreuzers: "nothing makes correspondence more expensive than frequent, at times high, transit postage." Klüber, *Patriotische Wünsche*, p. 30.

24. Ibid., p. 131.

25. His *Staatsrecht des Rheinbundes* (Tübingen, 1808) earned him a reprimand from patriotic circles. See the *Allgemeine Deutsche Biographie*, s.v. "Klüber, Johann Ludwig."

26. This sympathy, which can probably be attributed to his loyalty for the Grand Duchy of Baden, allowed the region's postal service to continue under the administration of the otherwise unpopular princely house until the summer of 1811.

27. Klüber, *Patriotische Wünsche*, p. 65.

28. The princes of Thurn and Taxis. "Taxis" ("Tassis") means "badger" in Italian, and the heraldic animal of the house of Taxis is a badger. Translator's note.

29. Klüber, *Patriotische Wünsche*, p. 129.

30. The very same Johann Ludwig Bergius, whose *Policey- und Cameral-Magazin* were cited by Klüber as an authority in matters of "reasonable postal rate," gave absolute priority to the territorial principle over the much-hailed "con-

venience of the *publici*" in cases regarding the regulation of postal traffic with other states, whether it concerned the "treaties" that fixed procedure for calculating interstate postage or the argument that "a sovereign prince [can]not be blamed . . . if he sends letters and goods going to foreign lands along his own postal routes as long as at all possible." Bergius, p. 165. For Klüber, on the other hand, it would have been "Olympia" to remove the postal system from "police surveillance" altogether. Klüber, *Das Postwesen in Teutschland*, p. 130. Bergius' *Magazin*, incidentally, was completely dependent upon Justi; Klüber cited—without knowing or indicating it—a passage Bergius had lifted verbatim from Justi's *System des Finanzwesens*.

31. Letter of the Prussian Cultural Ministry to Hegel, June 17, 1820, *Briefe*, vol. 2, pp. 232–33.

32. F. Kittler, "Das Subjekt," pp. 408–9.

33. Klüber, *Patriotische Wünsche*, p. 12.

34. Ibid., p. 11.

35. Ibid.

36. Niethammer, quoted in Kittler, "Das Subjekt," p. 409.

37. Klüber, *Das Postwesen in Teutschland*, p. 129.

38. Ibid., p. 92.

39. Stephan, pp. 302–3.

40. Virilio, *L'horizon négatif*, p. 35.

41. Not even the love letter had fulfilled any kind of confessional function in the age of *ars dictaminis*. Quite to the contrary, it belonged—whether as an honorable *conciliatoria* or a dishonorable *amatoria*—to the demonstrative (or persuasive) class. Erasmus, pp. 203–5.

42. Steinhausen, part 2, pp. 303–4.

43. Klüber, *Das Postwesen in Teutschland*, p. 55.

Chapter Seven

1. It was in all probability the historian Christian Eduard Pabst (1815–1882), from Reval, who was appointed archivist of the Estonian Literary Society in 1874. See *Deutschbaltisches Biographisches Lexikon* (1970), s.v. "Pabst, Christian Eduard." Thanks for this should go to Heinrich Bosse in Freiburg.

2. Bartholdy, p. 148.

3. Visible traces of Goethe's privilege of postage appear in a private letter sent to the Frankfurt book dealer Carl Jügel on May 2, 1829, for example: the letter not only exhibits the black seal with the initials "JWvG" above it, but also bears the notation "fr[anco]" beneath the address without the postal official's usual notation of the fee, which would not have been lacking if Goethe had cleared the letter with something other than his name. See also Goethe, letter of April 30, 1829;

Autograph Collection of the Federal Postal Museum in Frankfurt am Main, E 1501. According to a response graciously provided by the Central Archives of Prince Thurn and Taxis in Regensburg, the *factum brutum* of Goethe's exemption from postage is indeed beyond question, but the files on postal exemption—from which conclusions about the details could be attained—have not yet been systematically evaluated because the materials are very widely dispersed.

4. Koch, p. 4; see also Piendl, p. 80; and Stephan, p. 282. When, after the founding of the German League, a postal monopoly again was granted to princes in Saxony-Weimar, which in the meantime had been promoted to the status of grand duchy, "the whole body of us servants appeared in becoming attire according to our respective ranks, and on our side recognized the supreme authority of the prince." Goethe, *Annals*, p. 443.

5. Goethe, letter of May 17–23, 1820, in *Werke*, part IV, 33: 36. Only a year before his death, the prince sent a "fossil" and postage-free "mussel" to Goethe. Goethe, letter of September 26, 1826, ibid., 41: 171.

6. Behringer, p. 116.

7. Goethe, *Poetry and Truth*, p. 411. Taxis postage was indeed the most bearable of the forty-three different rates in the former empire. See Stephan, *Geschichte der Preußischen Post*, pp. 204–48, and Klüber, *Das Postwesen in Teutschland*, pp. 28–29.

8. Arnim, *Goethe's Correspondence with a Child*, p. 188.

9. Ibid., p. 297.   10. Ibid., p. 34.

11. Ibid., p. 101.   12. Ibid., p. 121.

13. Ibid., p. 233.   14. Ibid., p. 246.

15. Ibid., p. 297.   16. Ibid., p. 76.

17. Ibid., p. 187.   18. Piendl, p. 87.

19. Dallmeier, no. 173.   20. Biedermann, p. 298.

21. Freiesleben, pp. 19–21.

22. Behringer, pp. 360–61. Also among the members of the Thurn and Taxis lodge was the director of the royal theater, Emmanuel Schikaneder, who is known for writing the text to the *Magic Flute*. Mozart belonged to the Viennese daughter lodge "At the Crowned Hope," and his composition fascinated Goethe, a fellow brother of the order in Weimar, so much that between 1796 and 1807 the latter made repeated attempts at writing *The Magic Flute, Part Two*.

23. In a (negative) recommendation on the constitution of a lodge in Jena, Goethe wrote in 1807: "Freemasonry definitely amounts to a *statum in statu*. Where it is once introduced, the government will seek to dominate it and make it harmless. Introducing it where it has not previously existed is never advisable." Cited in Wernekke, p. 31. For the specific purpose of co-opting Masonic activities in Jena and bringing them under state "supervision" (as Goethe expressed it), the Weimar lodge was reopened by Duke Karl August on Goethe's recommendation in 1808. Wilson, pp. 152–53. Infiltration of the infiltrators—as Daniel Wilson has

shown—was also the motive for Goethe's and Karl August's entry into the Order of Illuminaries. Wilson, p. 66.

24. Not to mention the Tower Society, which of course took Adam Weishaupt's Order of Illuminaries as its model; Freiesleben, pp. 63–64; see also Kittler, "Sozialisation," p. 84ff. Scholars like Rosemarie Haas and Wilson, who claim that "the goal of the Tower Society" was "not a system for the 'secret art of governing and of the world,' as in Weishaupt's model, but instead for the development of individuals," and who derive from this a "fundamental difference" between the Tower Society and Weishaupt's ideas, fail to see that the development of individuals was itself precisely the essential ingredient in the new art of governing—and of the world—for both Goethe and Weishaupt. See Wilson, p. 161.

25. Freiesleben, pp. 42, 43.

26. Wagenknecht, pp. 495–96.

27. Abbot, pp. 281–86.

28. The analogy between the Freemason's ritual passage and the "passage through life" was made by Goethe himself in "A Symbol," which begins with the verse: "The mason's trade / Resembles life, / With all its strife,— / Is like the stir made / By man on earth's face." "A Symbol," p. 296. See also Abbott, pp. 272–73.

29. Arnim, "Clemens Brentanos Frühlingskranz," p. 19.

30. Novalis, *Henry von Ofterdingen*, p. 159.

31. This escaped Foucault's glance, which was directed at French conditions to some degree. See Foucault, "What is an Author?" p. 124.

32. Arnim, "Clemens Brentanos Frühlingskranz," p. 540.

33. Goethe, *Journeyman Years*, p. 252.

34. Ibid., p. 253.

35. Lacan, "The Agency of the Letter," p. 15.

36. Goethe, *Journeyman Years*, p. 251.

37. Foucault, "What is an Author?" p. 118.

38. Adalbert Stifter, *Indian Summer*, p. 145.

39. Ibid.

40. In this passage, the German original plays on the double meaning of *Band* in German as both "volume" and "bond." Translator's note.

41. Kleist, letter of August 16, 1800, in *Werke und Briefe*, 2: 517–18.

42. Risch, p. 79.

43. Foucault, *The Order of Things*, p. 262.

Chapter Eight

1. The Hegelian Bruno Liebrucks briefly toyed with the idea, otherwise apparently unbearable for philosophy, that Hegel's absolute method did not so

much amount to cognition as to "projectiles that are guiding themselves to their goal." Liebrucks, p. 405. In other words, feedback loops in perhaps their most radical form of realization—missiles or missives of a postal service that has abandoned the sphere of humans.

2. This already was the case—with a single exception, Wieland's *Agathon*—for the founder of the genre's concept, Karl Morgenstern (see Martini, p. 63), and still was true of an inaugural dissertation in 1972 that documented the paradoxical existence of the *Bildungsroman* by using the concept of the "unfulfilled genre." Jacobs, p. 271.

3. The first among these was the "subject as civil servant." See Kittler, "Das Subjekt."

4. Arnim, "Clemens Brentanos Frühlingskranz," p. 19.

5. Foucault, *The History of Sexuality: Volume 1*, p. 59.

6. Ibid., p. 58.

7. Arnim, "Clemens Brentanos Frühlingskranz," p. 539. For the plain text, see F. Kittler, "Writing into the Wind," p. 20. See also Steig, pp. 264f.

8. Klaus and Liebscher, p. 651.

9. Goethe, *Gespräche*, 2: 474.

10. This passage, and with it the chapter as a whole, turns on meanings of "timbre" available in French, but not in English. It means not only "the quality of a sound," but also "stamp" and "postmark." Translator's note.

11. Schreiber, *Das Symptom des Schreibens*, p. 27.

12. Kleist, letter of May 1799, in *An Abyss Deep Enough*, p. 29.

13. Ibid.

14. "The," capitalized and crossed out, is a Lacanian notation that designates that woman does not exist as One, but in a plurality.

15. Kittler, *Discourse Networks*, p. 28. On the following paragraph in general, see ibid., pp. 25–69.

16. Kleist, letter of October 10/11, 1800, in *An Abyss Deep Enough*, p. 66.

17. Lacan, *Encore*, p. 36.

18. Kleist wrote in the same letter: "Your next goal would be to educate *yourself to be a mother*, and mine to educate *myself to be a citizen of state*." Letter of October 10/11, 1800, in *Werke*, 2: 578. This passage is omitted in the English translation. Translator's note.

19. Novalis, "Glauben und Liebe," p. 294.

20. Kittler, *Discourse Networks*, p. 51.

21. See "Gellert's Coup," above.

22. Kleist, letter of October 10/11, 1800, in *An Abyss Deep Enough*, pp. 67–68.

23. "I could stand before this letter as before the Inquisition, which could never take hold of the mind of an enlightened person, except to his destruction!" Bettina Brentano wrote in answer to her brother's hermeneutics of the soul. Arnim, "Clemens Brentanos Frühlingskranz," p. 145.

24. Kleist, letter of July 18, 1801, in *An Abyss Deep Enough*, p. 111.

25. Kleist, letter of September 13–18, 1800, in *Geschichte meiner Seele*, pp. 103–4. This supplementary letter was not included by Sembdner in the complete edition of Kleist's works.

26. Schlegel, "Über die Philosophie," p. 54.

27. Ibid., p. 42.

28. Foucault, "The Discourse on Language," p. 221.

29. Schlegel, "Über die Philosophie," p. 61.

30. Arnim, "Clemens Brentanos Frühlingskranz," p. 64.

31. Kleist, letter of September 15, 1800, in *An Abyss Deep Enough*, p. 62.

32. Fichte, pp. 448–49.

33. Arnim, *Goethe's Correspondence with a Child*, p. 97.

34. Fichte, p. 418. Translation modified.

35. Ibid., p. 446.

36. Schreiber, *Das Symptom des Schreibens*, p. 214.

Chapter Nine

1. Schrader, pp. 89–96. To explain what he feels is the "unspeakable impertinence" of Kleist's letter to Zenge, Schrader accused Kleist of impotence and, failing to recognize their strategic character, interpreted his letters as "love letters that cried out for the devotion, solace, and support of his beloved partner" (p. 95). Thus the phantasm of The Mother returns as a verdict exactly at the moment when a writer simulates it by technical—in this case, postal—means.

2. See W. Kittler, p. 34, with regard to Thomas Mann.

3. Ibid., p. 33.

4. Ibid., p. 37.

5. Breithaupt, pp. 49–50.

6. Haase, *Kleists Nachrichtentechnik*, pp. 41–43. Kleist's birthday, according to the parish register of the garrison in Frankfurt am Oder, was October 18. Sembdner, p. 13.

7. Together with one of his cousins, Kleist learned to read from Christian Ernst Martini, a private tutor who instructed them in accordance with his colleague Jung-Stilling's "usual school method," which meant that he "made them pray, sing, read, and learn the catechism." Jung-Stilling, quoted in Birkenhauer, p. 23.

8. Wilhelmine von Zenge, letter of June 16, 1803, in Sembdner, p. 33. On August Wilhelm Hermann von Zenge, see Priesdorff, part 5, pp. 63–64.

9. Birkenhauer, pp. 87–88.

10. Kleist, letter of May 30, 1800, in *An Abyss Deep Enough*, pp. 35–37. See also W. Kittler, *Die Geburt des Partisanen aus dem Geist der Poesie*, pp. 52–55.

11. Kleist, letter of November 18, 1800, in *Werke*, 2: 596.

12. Ibid., p. 595.

13. Schreiber, *Das Symptom des Schreibens*, p. 29.

14. Kleist, letter of November 18, 1800, in *Werke*, 2: 597.

15. Kleist, letter of May 30, 1800; ibid., 2: 508.

16. Kleist, letter of October 11, 1800, in *An Abyss Deep Enough*, p. 69.

17. Kleist, letter of July 18, 1801; in Kleist, *Werke*, 2: 663. The second instance of the passage is omitted in the English translation. The opening lines can be found in Kleist's letter to Wilhelmine von Zenge of July 21, 1801, in *An Abyss Deep Enough*, p. 115. Translator's note.

18. Kleist, letter of July 28, 1801, in *An Abyss Deep Enough*, pp. 118–19. Much of the passage has been omitted here as well. For the complete text in German, see *Werke*, 2: 674–75.

19. In each specific instance of reproduction, a geographical referent is to be introduced at ***. For rivers, Kleist's poet's dream utilized the postal variables Rhine, Main, and Elbe; for mountains: Rheingau, Hundsrück, and the Elbhöhen; for cities: Mainz, Koblenz, Dresden, and Bingen. Kleist reflected the status of the variable names by the occasional use of parentheses.

20. For English translations of passages 1–3, see *An Abyss Deep Enough*, pp. 69, 70, 115. For instances of repetition and passages 4–5, refer to the original German in Kleist, *Werke*, 2: 549, 2: 663, and 2: 674–75; 2: 580–81, 2: 651, and 2: 662; 2: 647, 2: 651, and 2: 662; and 2: 662–64 and 2: 675.

21. Schiller, p. 235 ("Piccolomini" 1, 4).

22. In light of such postal logistics, it is almost disheartening to be informed by Karl Heinz Bohrer that Kleist's description of the Rhine Valley (which, according to Bohrer, "belongs alongside Hölderlin's hymns to the most significant representations of the Rhine Valley in this epoch") was a "heroic idyll" mirroring the discovery of the contingency of existence (Bohrer, pp. 96, 101). Bohrer failed to notice not only the quotation of Schiller, but also his other reproductions, and thus the lack of all referentiality outside of that to Kleist himself. This is how literary scholarship functions as an obstacle to insights about technology.

23. Beyrer, p. 86.

24. Reichardt, p. 13.

25. Bosse, *Autorschaft*, pp. 60–61.

26. Burckas, p. 51.

27. "I am keeping a journal, in which I daily improve and perfect my plan. In my record of the day's events, therefore, I must occasionally repeat what I have written to you. I shall give myself free play in this, and one day piece out the missing parts from my letters to you. The story as a whole, I hope, will one day be of great interest to you. But you must be conscientious in calling for these letters; will you?" Kleist, letter of August 21, 1800, in *An Abyss Deep Enough*, p. 45. She would.

28. Arnim, *Goethe's Correspondence with a Child*, pp. 434–35.

Chapter Ten

1. Kafka, letter of November 6, 1912, in *Letters to Felice*, p. 29.
2. Lichtenberg, first published in Joost, "'Brief an Jedermann,'" p. 64.
3. Leclerc, "Post- und Personenbeförderung," p. 184.
4. At least none who belonged to the postal service: in the cases where there were in fact postmen, they were employed by the municipality and worked at their own risk.
5. Kafka, "Wedding Preparations in the Country," p. 11.
6. See Deleuze and Guattari, p. 31.
7. Drogge, p. 12.
8. For example, a typical letter address of 1862 (not for Berlin, but for London) read like this: "This / To Mr. Peter Le Neve att his house / in east Hardon Street att the / end of Gunpowder Alley from / Shoe Lane over against the Door / In the middle of Dead Wall / London." Quoted in Staff, p. 35. See also ibid., plate 2b.
9. Derrida, "Signature Event Context," p. 317.
10. Kafka, letter of January 28, 1914, in *Letters to Felice*, pp. 340–41.
11. Kafka, letter of October 10, 1912, ibid., p. 12.
12. Sautter, p. 121. When even this no longer was viable, the registered letter was completely eliminated in commerce between post offices.
13. Kafka, letter of November 17, 1912, in *Letters to Felice*, p. 47.
14. Shannon, *The Mathematical Theory of Communication*, p. 4.
15. Maxwell, pp. 270–71.

Chapter Eleven

1. Hill, 1: 390–91.
2. Ibid., 1: 391.
3. Ibid., 1: 247.
4. Ibid.
5. Ibid., 1: 300.
6. Ibid.
7. Ibid., 1: 256.
8. Ibid., 1: 257.
9. Daunton, p. 10.
10. Staff, pp. 37–46.
11. Ibid., pp. 55, 58, 71.
12. Stössel, p. 55.
13. "Testimonial to Robert Wallace, Esq.," cited in Hill, 1: 531 (appendix G).
14. Pynchon, *Gravity's Rainbow*, p. 604.
15. Hennig, p. 106.
16. Hill, 1: 296.
17. Rothschild, p. 110.
18. Velayér, p. 3.
19. Rothschild, p. 98.
20. Velayér, p. 2.
21. Foucault, "The Life of Infamous Men."
22. Staff, pp. 22–24.
23. As Disraeli described Wildman. Staff, p. 32.

24. Ibid., p. 32.

25. Hill, 1: 205.

26. Ibid., 1: 270.

27. Ibid., 1: 271. Hill thus drew upon a proposal James Chalmers, a book dealer from Dundee, had published in the postal reformers' propaganda organ, the *Post Circular*, which was edited by Hill's closest colleague, Henry Cole. Chalmers had proposed printing paper stamps that would be coated with an adhesive solution. Correspondents were to be able to buy these stamps at paper dealers and paste them to their letters by moistening their backs with a brush or a sponge. For the entire article, see Chalmers, p. 8f.

28. Quoted in Hill, 1: 341.

Chapter Twelve

1. Kafka, letter, end of March 1922, in *Letters to Milena*, p. 229.

2. Luhmann, p. 371.

3. Shannon, *The Mathematical Theory of Communication*, p. 7.

4. Ibid.

5. Leclerc, "Kleine Zeittafel zur Geschichte des Briefkastens," p. 58.

6. North, p. 13.

7. Siegert, "Denunziationen."

8. Hill, 1: 417.

9. Dopf, p. 64.

10. Foucault, "The Life of Infamous Men," p. 89.

11. Stifter, "Wiener Stadtpost," p. 126.

12. Ibid., p. 127.

13. Freud, *The Psychopathology of Everyday Life*, pp. 157, 235.

14. Ibid., pp. 152–53.

15. Fischer, p. 152. An undocumented copy of this and the following passage is found in Geistbeck, pp. 445–46.

16. Cited in Hartmann, p. 70.

17. Stix, p. 150.

18. Hill, 1: 271.

19. Ibid., 2: 90. In his famous pamphlet of 1837, Hill had written the following: "There would not only be no stopping to collect the postage, but probably it would soon be unnecessary even to await the opening of the door, as every house might be provided with a letter box into which the Letter Carrier would drop the letters, and, having knocked, he would pass on as fast as he could walk." Cited in Staff, p. 77.

20. Martineau, pp. 249–50.

21. In 1656, the privilege of exemption from postage was confirmed for members of Parliament and the nobility in England. Staff, p. 73.

22. Quoted in Hill, 1: 394.

23. Ibid., 2: 91.

24. Klüber, *Das Postwesen in Teutschland*, p. 129.

25. Kafka, letter of November 16, 1912, in *Letters to Felice*, p. 44: "But who insisted on a whole letter? Just two lines."

26. Luhmann, p. 387.

27. Benjamin, "Charles Baudelaire," p. 549.

28. Anonymous, "Entstehung und Entwickelung des Post-Zustellungswesens," p. 114.

29. Anonymous, "Zur Geschichte des englischen Postwesens," p. 284.

30. Derrida, *The Post Card*, p. 245.

31. Rilke, *The Notebooks of Malte Laurids Brigge*, p. 5.

32. Shannon, "Communication in the Presence of Noise," p. 161.

33. Ibid.

34. Rilke, *The Notebooks of Malte Laurids Brigge*, p. 32.

35. Schreiber, *Das Symptom des Schreibens*, p. 152.

36. Aschenborn, p. 73 (§6).

37. *Bürgerliches Gesetzbuch*, p. 60 (§104).

38. Reichardt, pp. 13–14.

39. Pynchon, *The Crying of Lot 49*, pp. 126–27. W.A.S.T.E. stands for "We Await Silent Tristero's Empire."

40. Nietzsche, *On the Genealogy of Morals*, p. 58.

41. Quoted in Hill, 1: 418.

42. Ibid., 1: 419.

43. Staff, p. 124.

44. Bosse, *Autorschaft ist Werkherrschaft*, pp. 135–41.

45. Bolza, p. 9.

46. Hill, 1: 225.

47. Ibid., pp. 226–27.

Chapter Thirteen

1. Foucault, *Discipline and Punish*, p. 154.

2. Hill, 1: 80.

3. Ibid., 1: 107.

4. Ibid., 1: 110–11.

5. Bentham, p. 45.

6. Foucault, *Discipline and Punish*, pp. 176–77.

7. Ibid., pp. 175–76.

8. Hill, 1: 107.

9. Goux, pp. 94–95. On the relation between money and language in general, see ibid., pp. 2, 42, 96–111.

10. Hill, 1: 113.

11. Hyman, pp. 64–65.

12. Babbage, quoted in Hyman, p. 115.

13. Ibid.

14. Foucault, *Discipline and Punish*, p. 157.

15. Hill, 1: 172.

16. Foucault, *Discipline and Punish*, p. 202.

17. Ibid., p. 205.

18. Deleuze, *Foucault*, p. 36.

19. Bentham, p. 40. Emphasis in the original.

20. Daunton, p. 14.

21. Hyman, p. 242.

Chapter Fourteen

1. Martineau, p. 249.   2. De Luna, pp. 312–13.

3. Ibid., p. 312.   4. Rothschild, pp. 348, 366.

5. Keller, "The Misused Love Letters," p. 15.

6. Benjamin, "Charles Baudelaire," p. 528.

7. Keller, "The Misused Love Letters," p. 16.

8. Bolza, p. 7.

9. Bosse, *Autorschaft ist Werkherrschaft*, especially pp. 50–64.

10. Keller, "The Misused Love Letters," p. 20.

11. Foucault, "Language to Infinity," p. 68.

12. Keller, "The Misused Love Letters," p. 23.

13. Ibid., p. 27.   14. Ibid., p. 25.

15. Ibid., p. 52.   16. Ibid., p. 40.

17. Ibid.

18. Korella, p. 27.

19. Keller, "The Misused Love Letters," p. 44.

20. Ibid., p. 41.

21. Lacan, *The Four Fundamental Concepts of Psycho-Analysis*, p. 204.

22. Keller, letter to Lina Duncker, March 6, 1856, in *Gesammelte Briefe*, 2: 154.

23. Freud, "On the Sexual Theories of Children," pp. 211–12.

24. Keller, "The Misused Love Letters," p. 61.

25. Muir, p. 474.

26. Benjamin, "The Work of Art in the Age of Mechanical Reproduction," p. 221.

27. Weber, pp. 16–17, 21–24.

28. Benjamin, "The Work of Art in the Age of Mechanical Reproduction," p. 221.

29. Schneider, "Nachrichten aus dem Unbewußten," p. 69.
30. Keller, "The Misused Love Letters," p. 94.

Chapter Fifteen

1. Appel and Haken, p. 153.
2. Risch, p. 79.
3. Treaty of the German-Austrian Postal Union, Article 10. Quoted from the complete transcription in Anonymous, "Der deutsche Postverein," p. 151.
4. Ibid., p. 153.
5. Stephan, p. 648.
6. Anonymous, "Der deutsche Postverein," p. 151. See also Stephan, pp. 419–20.
7. Appel and Haken, p. 155.
8. Quoted in Weithase, p. 15.
9. Ibid., pp. 16–17. Conditions had remained practically unchanged since Klüber's day: in 1846, sixteen (or thirty-two) postal institutions existed in the territory of the former empire. Thirty-two, since while Thurn and Taxis no longer held the post in fief, they still continued to administer the postal services in the sixteen states, but only in accordance with the varying principles of their princes—the badger had become a chameleon. The standard weight for a normal letter in these thirty-two institutions was $^1/_2$ lot Cologne weight, $^1/_2$ lot Viennese weight, $^3/_4$ lot, $2^1/_2$ hectograms, and 1 lot (p. 14).
10. Anonymous, "Der deutsche Postverein," p. 150.
11. Paikert, Gasser, and Oldenburg, p. 13.
12. Bartholdy, pp. 63–64.
13. Memorandum of the royal assessor of the General Postal Administration, Wilhelm Rippenberger. Cited in Piendl, p. 91.
14. Rippenberger, cited in Piendl, p. 91.
15. Cited in Bartholdy, pp. 67–68.
16. Vogt, p. 204. See also Rippenberger, quoted in Piendl, pp. 91–92.
17. Kämmerer.
18. Reprinted in Paikert, Gasser, and Oldenburg, pp. 32–34.
19. Ibid., p. 38.
20. Nietzsche, letter of July 8, 1875, in *Briefwechsel*, 2: 71.
21. Quoted in Paikert, Gasser, and Oldenburg, p. 41.
22. Ibid., p. 66.
23. Jung, pp. 25–26.
24. Paikert, Gasser, and Oldenburg, p. 12.
25. Staff, pp. 105–25, especially p. 108.
26. So he was described in the London *Times*. Ibid., p. 140.

27. Ibid., p. 137.

28. Ibid., pp. 142–43.

29. Paikert, Gasser, and Oldenburg, pp. 19, 22.

30. Veredarius, p. 375.

31. Virilio, *Speed and Politics*, p. 136.

32. Ibid.   33. Ibid.

34. Conrad, p. 30.   35. Ibid., p. 30.

36. Conan Doyle, "The Five Orange Pips," p. 220.

37. Veredarius, pp. 361–65. See also Weithase, p. 47.

38. The telegraph enabled momentary recordings of the global space of commerce. Just as photography initially had been unable to record objects in motion due to lengthy exposure times, the postal system had been unable to provide knowledge or registry for the positions of all ships on the globe at one and the same moment due to lengthy intervals of transmission.

39. McLuhan, p. 8.

40. Schöttle, p. 170.

41. Lerg, pp. 30–31.

42. Stephan, *Weltpost und Luftschifffahrt*, p. 39.

43. Virilio, "Fahrzeug," p. 30.

44. Stephan, *Weltpost und Luftschifffahrt*, p. 67.

45. Pynchon, *Gravity's Rainbow*, p. 11.

Chapter Sixteen

1. Derrida, *The Post Card*, p. 249.

2. Joyce, *Finnegans Wake*, p. 93.

3. Derrida, *The Post Card*, p. 249.

4. Stephan, quoted from the complete document reprinted in Anonymous, "Die Postkarte," p. 344.

5. Curtius, p. 487. See also Smolak, p. xiv. The argument here alludes in part to the etymological relationship between *brevitas* and the German word for "letter," *Brief*.

6. Stephan, cited in Anonymous, "Die Postkarte," p. 344.

7. Ibid.

8. Grosse, pp. 688–89.

9. Quoted in Meier, p. 262. See also Risch, p. 43.

10. Foucault, "The Discourse on Language," pp. 216–25.

11. Thus it was described in 1777 in an article in the French *L'almanach de la petite post*, which originally appeared in the Brussels *Soir* and reported the surfacing of mysterious "engravings on cards transported by the post." Ledât, p. 675.

12. Joyce, *Ulysses*, p. 417.

13. Derrida, *The Post Card*, p. 79.

14. Stephan, quoted in Anonymous, "Die Postkarte," p. 345.

15. Veredarius, p. 32.

16. Emanuel Hermann, "Über eine neue Art der Korrespondenz mittels der Post," cited in Kalckhoff, p. 8. On Hermann, see also Meier, p. 92.

17. Hermann, quoted in Kalckhoff, pp. 8, 10.

18. Meier, p. 262. See also Grosse, pp. 678–80.

19. Vogt, pp. 205–6, 210.

20. In Austria, 2,930,000 postcards were sold during the first three months after their introduction (between October 1, 1869 and January 1, 1870); in 1895, 2,000,000,000 were sent annually in the World Postal Union (Grosse, p. 674); in 1905, 77.8 percent of all dispatches with contents consisting of words were postcards (Sautter, p. 78), a proliferation that deserves to be called epidemic.

21. Avé-Lallemant, p. 8.

22. Ibid.

23. Goethe, cited in Avé-Lallemant, p. 15.

24. F. Kittler, "Lullaby of Birdland." See also F. Kittler, *Dichter Mutter Kind*.

25. Avé-Lallemant, p. 8.

26. Ibid., p. 7.

27. Kalckhoff, p. 25.

28. Ibid., p. 22. See also Bartholdy, pp. 90–91.

29. Veredarius, p. 30.

30. Stephan, cited in Risch, p. 49.

31. Kalckhoff, pp. 29–31. It is thus no wonder that France, as the only country in Europe to do so, would continue to reject the "carte postale" for years afterward.

32. Stephan, quoted in Anonymous, "Die Postkarte," p. 344.

33. Ibid. See also the general decree of July 6, 1870: "Only the amount on the stamps affixed is to be paid when the forms are used as correspondence cards; the forms themselves are supplied free of charge." Quoted in Kalckhoff, p. 12.

34. Veredarius, p. 366.

35. Virilio, *Speed and Politics*, p. 31.

36. Veredarius, p. 366.

37. The founding treaty mentioned postcards in Article 3: "Postcards must be prepaid. Postage amounts to half the postage rate for prepaid letters." Quoted in Paikert, Gasser, and Oldenburg, pp. 38–39.

38. Meier, p. 263.

39. Derrida, *Ulysse gramophone*, p. 62.

40. Meier, p. 262.

41. Quoted in Grosse, p. 682.

42. Kalckhoff, reproduction between pp. 10 and 11.

43. Grosse, p. 683.

44. Borges, pp. 27–28.

45. Grosse, p. 683.

46. Fussell, p. 170.

47. Novalis, *Henry von Ofterdingen*, p. 159.
48. Quoted in Fussell, p. 170.
49. Quoted in Veredarius, p. 32.
50. Ibid., p. 33.
51. Kleist, letter of July 18, 1801, in *Werke*, 2: 663.
52. Weigert, p. 27.
53. Hoerner, p. 27. Postcards with wood-block prints appeared on the market for the first time in 1875; there had been hand drawings on postcards since 1870–71 (Schultze).
54. Holmes, p. 119.
55. Frank Stolze, quoted in Hoerner, p. 38.
56. Hoerner, p. 36.
57. Ibid., p. 40.
58. Benjamin, "The Work of Art in the Age of Mechanical Reproduction," p. 228. See also Bolz, p. 30.
59. Joyce, *Ulysses*, p. 512.
60. Ibid.
61. Derrida, *Ulysse gramophone*, p. 65.
62. This has been shown by Gerhard Neumann: precisely because picture postcards make sense only on the basis of their captions, they resist all efforts at hermeneutic interpretation as soon as their labels are removed. "Yet, although Kafka on the one hand tries to suggest [the] triviality [of pictures] by any means possible, the identifying characteristic of triviality still is missing on the other: the simple and comprehensible intelligibility, the immediate, primitive symbolism, the posterlike character of a photo from an illustrated magazine or a picture post card. The symbol of triviality has been changed into its opposite, the absolute riddle, though indeed without depth or secrets. The picture, deprived of its triviality by its removal from all conventional contexts, resists interpretation in nothing less than an exemplary fashion, since it no longer offers any points of reference other than the broad label—which has been taken from it." Neumann, "Umkehrung und Ablenkung," p. 504.

Chapter Seventeen

1. Kleist, "Project for a Cannonball Postal Service," p. 245.
2. Sömmering, p. 408.
3. Ibid., p. 411.
4. Kleist, "Project for a Cannonball Postal Service," p. 245.
5. Ibid.
6. Görlitz, pp. 16–17.
7. Hennig, pp. 86–87. See also Pieper, p. 44.
8. Aschoff, "Von Abel Burja bis zum Fächer 'à la Telegraph,'" p. 113.

9. Ibid.

10. Aschoff, "Drei Vorschläge für nichtelektrisches Fernsprechen," p. 5.

11. Kleist, *Die Hermannschlacht*, p. 607.

12. W. Kittler, *Die Geburt des Partisanen aus dem Geist der Poesie*, p. 396.

13. Buchbender, p. 60ff. This reference is thanks to Bojan Budisavljevic in Oberhausen.

14. Schramm, vol. 4, part 2, p. 1811.

15. Kleist, "Letter from a Berliner," in *An Abyss Deep Enough*, p. 247.

16. The acronym stands for "Special Intelligence Communications." See James Bamford, *The Puzzle Palace* (Boston, 1982). Translator's note.

17. Experimentation with electric telegraphy preceded the invention and development of the optical telegraph in France as well. Difficulties in isolating the conductors and the loss of current over long distances made such a project seem unrealizable to Claude Chappe. On March 22, 1792, Chappe presented his definitive model of an optical telegraph to the National Convention. After Romme predicted that Chappe's telegraph would prove its worth in land and sea wars, an experiment was conducted on July 12, 1793 (over a 35-km line), which was evaluated by Lakanal, Danou, and Arbogast, who were members of the Convention. Lakanal (who was also responsible for the enactment of the first copyright law) made a report to the Convention that was decisive for the construction of the first line between Paris and Lille. The line went into operation under the direction of Abraham Chappe in August 1794. Herbarth, p. 19; see also Hennig, pp. 28–30.

18. Anonymous, "Abbildung und Beschreibung des Telegraphen," pp. 25–45.

19. The academies of science in Germany, Italy, and France were divided into "classes," usually a mathematical-scientific class and a historical-linguistic class. These were institutions comparable to faculties, not classes in the pedagogical sense. Translator's note.

20. Herbarth, p. 184.

21. Giehrl, pp. 71–75.

22. Drogge, pp. 6–8.

23. After the defeat of 1806, Müffling received his discharge with the rank of major and entered the service of the Duke of Saxony-Weimar as the vice president of the Provincial Diet. Ibid., p. 13. On his identity as Goethe's captain and his activities in Weimar, see F. Kittler, "Ottilie Hoffmann," in *Dichter Mutter Kind*, pp. 139–47.

24. Frobenius, p. 378.

25. Ibid., p. 379. The creation of a Prussian militia in 1812–13 during the "liberation wars" against Napoleon was a patriotic act, but one that aimed not at the defense of the king and the monarchy, but at the defense of the "Fatherland." During the Reaction that followed the restoration, Scharnhorst, Blücher, Gneisenau, and Kleist, who had participated in the militia's creation, became notorious

for this political attitude, as did the military officers named here. Their position was deemed "liberal" in contrast to that of the conservative monarchists. Translator's note.

26. Herbarth, pp. 22–24, 26, 41.

27. Haase, *Kleists Nachrichtentechnik*, p. 165.

28. Haase, "Nachrichtentechnik vs. Romantische Autorschaft," p. 55.

29. Herbarth, p. 49.

30. *Allgemeine Deutsche Biographie,* s.v. "O'Etzel, Franz August," vol. 6, p. 402.

31. Feyerabend, "August von Etzel," p. 80.

32. Pieper, p. 51.

33. Haase, "Nachrichtentechnik vs. Romantische Autorschaft," p. 56.

34. Feyerabend, "August von Etzel," p. 80.

35. Kittler, "Die heilige Schrift," pp. 332, 334.

36. Kleist, letter of January 7, 1805, in *An Abyss Deep Enough*, p. 159f.

37. Herbarth, p. 48.

38. Ibid., pp. 42–43. See also Feyerabend, "August von Etzel," p. 82.

39. *Allgemeine Deutsche Biographie,* s.v. "O'Etzel, Franz August," vol. 6, p. 402.

40. Hagen, p. 245.

41. Herbarth, p. 61.

42. Kunert, *Telegraphen-Landkabel einschließlich der Flußkabel*, p. 6. See also Hennig, p. 105.

43. Feyerabend, "An der Wiege des elektrischen Telegraphen," p. 165.

44. The dehydrated milky sap of the isonandra gutta, a tree native to the Malaysian archipelago. This material was thus quite exotic, and came to the lieutenant's attention only because he had a brother living in Britannia, which of course still "ruled the waves" at the time. Kunert, *Telegraphen-Landkabel einschließlich der Flußkabel*, p. 10.

45. Siemens, *Lebenserinnerungen*, p. 51.

46. "Availability," however, was a mild euphemism for difficult access to the new discursive technology, which was subject to tight restrictions: the sender of a private telegram had to present police clearance and bring two personal acquaintances as witnesses. Oberliesen, p. 111.

47. Frobenius, pp. 380–81.   48. Showalter, p. 49.

49. Görlitz, p. 76.   50. Groß, p. 203.

51. Van Creveld, p. 145.   52. Schmiedecke, pp. 136–39.

53. Alfred von Schlieffen, cited in F. Kittler, "Im Telegrammstil," p. 359.

54. Schmitt, p. 16.

55. Siemens, *Lebenserinnerungen*, p. 41. Afterward, Siemens developed Wheatstone's device further by combining it with a self-alternating system. The Siemens needle telegraph thus became the most dependable system available and was used for the Berlin-Koblenz line in 1848.

56. Hubbard, pp. 13, 28.

57. Ibid., p. 31.

58. Pynchon, *Gravity's Rainbow*, p. 105.

59. Siemens, *Lebenserinnerungen*, pp. 109, 111.

60. Fischer, p. 114.

61. Siemens, *Lebenserinnerungen*, pp. 119, 124–28. The treatise did not appear in print until 1874.

62. Ibid., pp. 185–88.

63. Colonial Defence Committee memorandum 417M, secret, July 7, 1910. Cited in Kennedy, p. 76.

64. Ibid., p. 77.

65. Ibid., p. 79.

66. Report of the Inter-Departmental Committee on Cable Communications, March 26, 1902, quoted in Kennedy, p. 76.

67. Kipling, p. 174.

68. London was connected to the Cape of Good Hope via Madeira, the islands of Cape Verde, Ascension, and St. Helena; the Cape of Good Hope itself was connected to Australia via Mauritius, Rodriquez, and the Cocos Islands, and to India via Mauritius, the Seychelles, and Ceylon; Halifax to St. Lucia via the Bermudas; and London finally even to India "in the opposite direction," via Canada and Australia (to name only a few of the "all red routes").

69. See Oberliesen, p. 22, regarding the situation in 1898.

70. As early as 1880, the India Rubber, Gutta Percha & Telegraph Works Co. (a daughter company of the Telegraph Construction & Maintenance Co.) had achieved a practical monopoly on the production of gutta-percha. Kieve, p. 117.

71. Kunert, *Telegraphen-Seekabel*, p. 351.

72. Ibid., pp. 349–58.

73. Ibid., pp. 709–10.

74. Conan Doyle, *A Study in Scarlet*, p. 85; "The Five Orange Pips," p. 229.

75. Knies, p. 222.

76. Hennig, pp. 125–26.

77. Knies, p. 222.

78. Frederick C. Bakewell had developed a procedure for transmitting images as early as 1847. "In this system, a metal folio was inscribed with 'insulating ink,' which was then wrapped around a rotational cylinder. Immediately afterward, the cylinder was turned by means of a drive assembly and the folio scanned thereby with a metal needle. At the receiving device, a similar metal needle traced on chemically prepared paper." Abramson, p. 147.

79. Knies, p. 222.

80. Aschoff, *Aus der Geschichte der Nachrichtentechnik*, pp. 24–25.

81. De Man, p. 93.

82. Voigt, *Die Entwicklung des Verkehrssystems*, p. 866.

83. Keller, *Die Leute von Seldwyla*, preface to part 2, pp. 252–53.

84. Gutzkow, p. 156.

85. Ibid., p. 170.

86. Ibid., p. 176: "Von meinem Auge will es nimmer schwinden / Das Bild: Gefangener Troubadour, / Dem ach! die Hoffnung einer Taube nur! / Sie kommt! Ein Blatt! Es flattert in den Winden— / Was würd' ich wohl auf ihm geschrieben finden?"

87. Ibid., p. 170.

88. Ibid., p. 173.

89. Lacan, "The Direction of the Treatment and the Principles of Its Power," p. 225. See also F. Kittler, "Im Telegrammstil," p. 361.

90. Schöttle, p. 286. 91. Knies, pp. 206–7.

92. Schöttle, p. 299. 93. Ibid., p. 300.

94. Exercise example from the "Instructions" of Prussian telegraphers (1835). Cited in Oberliesen, pp. 71–73.

95. F. Kittler, "Im Telegrammstil," pp. 362–63.

96. Hill, 1: 210.

97. Stramm, "Untersuchungen," p. 26.

98. Walden, p. 124.

99. Schöttle, p. 303.

100. Stramm, *Das Werk*, pp. 7–117. Stramm's word play is easily lost in literal translation: blueplayhappy, hailyellow, deadcrazy, hardsharpedged, sunvictorysounds, bluepale, lightblinded, freshspread, deceitsteasing, glowingwoe, yawntired, goldbrightred, shriekrisp, shameragetorn, allways, flametorn, worlddepthhigh.

101. *Der kleine Stephan*, pp. 217–21: fromhere, Anglogerman, cheapestpossible, livelyfresh, tenpoundgoose, brownishblond, expresstravels, seapacked, tomorrownight, wellboned, firstoccupied, Aprilold, firstmodel, twopronged, pressurecable, strongexemplary, Russianslackness.

Chapter Eighteen

1. Clark, p. 23.

2. Cronbach, p. 271.

3. Quoted in Vögtle, p. 42.

4. Bruce, p. 35.

5. Helmholtz had succeeded in using resonators that were tuned to the specific tone of an electric tuning fork and then opened and closed over a piano in order to synthesize the vowel sounds "u," "o," "ö," and "a"; Helmholtz, *On the Sensations of Tone*, pp. 119–23.

6. Snyder, p. 12.

7. Bruce, p. 123.

8. Snyder, p. 12.

9. Bell, p. 20.

10. Ibid., p. 186.

11. Maddox, p. 262.

12. On the manifold connections between George Bernard Shaw and the Bell family, especially regarding Shaw's *Pygmalion*, see my article "Switchboards and Sex: The Nut(t) Case," pp. 83–84.

13. Bruce, p. 209.

14. Fagen, p. 30.

15. Ibid., p. 34.

16. Hagemeyer, p. 112.

17. Küpfmüller, Ebeling, and Cramer, *Internationale Lehrkurse für den elektrischen Nachrichtenverkehr*; cited in Hagemeyer, p. 114.

18. Bell, p. 15.

19. Heidegger, *On the Way to Language*, p. 59.

20. Maddox, p. 369.

21. Benveniste, p. 226; emphasis in original.

22. Ibid., p. 228.

23. Leclerc, "Das 'Frollein,'" p. 147.

24. Sautter, p. 348.

25. Kafka, "The Eight Octovo Note-Books," p. 43.

26. W. Kittler, *Der Turmbau zu Babel und das Schweigen der Sirenen*, pp. 7–9.

27. Kafka, "Wedding Preparations in the Country," p. 8.

28. Cited in Aschenborn, p. 15.

29. Ibid., p. 303.

30. Ibid.

31. Cited in Maddox, p. 266.

32. Cited in Leclerc, p. 139.

33. F. Kittler, *Gramophone, Film, Typewriter*, pp. 193–94.

34. Genth and Hoppe, p. 135.

35. Leclerc, p. 141.

36. Wagner, p. 18.

37. Kittler, *Gramophone, Film, Typewriter*, p. 218.

38. Ibid., p. 286.

39. McLuhan, p. 260.

40. Ibid., p. 263.

41. Leclerc, "Das 'Frollein," p. 141.

42. Julien, p. 7.

43. Sautter, p. 350.

44. Wagner, pp. 18–19.

45. Wagner, p. 237; Sautter, p. 351.

46. Sautter, p. 349.

47. Cited in Kleemann, pp. 3–4.

48. Braun, p. 35.

49. Küpfmüller and Storch, p. 7. The range between the circuit frequencies of 3000 to 13,000 Ω, approximately 500 to 2000 Hz ($\Omega = 2\pi f$), appeared "necessary and sufficient" to telegraph director Ulfilas Meyer in 1921. See Meyer, p. 70.

50. On Bebel's blindness to the media and women, see his *Woman and Socialism*. Even after fifty editions, its socialism still continued to sleep through the new technologies of the media in their entirety—in this regard (and only in this regard) a prophetic book. In love with production in general, and with the classical branches of the eighteenth and nineteenth centuries (agriculture and the tex-

tile industry) in particular, Bebel viewed employees in service areas such as "communication" as "more or less parasites" long before Michael Serres. Bebel, p. 450. While Bebel praised traditional occupations for women in agriculture, laundry service, house cleaning, and "domestic services" in spite of relatively stagnant employment figures, he passed over the boom—caused by the typewriter—that women were experiencing in the area of "commerce and transport" (p. 252) in silence. At 76.7 percent, the women's share of "stenographer" positions in America was barely mentioned in the context of a statistic (p. 254). There is not a single word about women in the context of "telegraph, telephone, railways, and postal service" (p. 450), to say nothing of the fact that "because of the typewriter as well as the telephone, the percentage of American women working in jobs other than agriculture or domestic service rose from 20 percent (when it was first surveyed by the United States Census) to 42 percent." Maddox, p. 269.

51. Cited in Wagner, p. 76.   52. Ibid., p. 76.
53. Hegel, *Encyclopedia*, §459.   54. Pestalozzi, p. 247.
55. Tieck, *Franz Sternbalds Wanderungen*, pp. 169–70.
56. Hoffmann, p. 349.   57. Scherer, p. 49.
58. Ibid.   59. Fagen, p. 936.
60. Du Bois-Reymond, pp. 573, 582.
61. Hermann, "Über physiologische Beziehungen des Telephons," p. 98.
62. Helmholtz, "Telephon und Klangfarbe," pp. 488–89.
63. Tarchanow, p. 94.
64. Hermann, "Über physiologische Beziehungen des Telephons," p. 98.
65. Ibid., p. 544.   66. Gutzmann, pp. 250, 247.
67. Stumpf, p. 639.   68. K. Wagner, pp. 451–54.
69. Blake, "Verwerthung," pp. 434–39, 5–12; "Auswahl," pp. 29–31.
70. Siemens, "Über Telephonie," p. 47.
71. Quoted in Fagen, p. 929.   72. Ibid., p. 928.
73. Hagemeyer, p. 141.   74. Fletcher, p. 744.
75. F. Kittler, *Gramophone, Film, Typewriter*, p. 180.
76. As Dr. Hook and the Medicine Show lamented many years ago.
77. Lacan, "Le séminaire sur 'La Lettre volée,'" p. 37.
78. Browning, p. 248.   79. Salvá, pp. 3–4.
80. Lindner, p. 100.   81. Wellershoff, pp. 79–80.
82. Binder, *Kafka-Kommentar zu sämtliche Erzählungen*, p. 64.
83. Kafka, "Wedding Preparations in the Country," p. 8.
84. Kafka, letter of November 12, 1912, in *Letters to Felice*, p. 50.

Chapter Nineteen

1. Kafka, letter of July 13, 1912, in *Letters to Friends, Family, and Editors*, p. 80. Translation modified.

2. See Kafka's diary from June 29 to July 6, 1912, in *Diaries, 1910–1913*, pp. 288–300.

3. Kafka, letter of July 13, 1912, in *Letters to Friends, Family, and Editors*, p. 80.

4. Ibid.

5. Canetti, p. 111.

6. Politzer, p. 198.

7. Inge Stramm, quoted in Stramm, *Das Werk*, p. 407 (appendix).

8. Kittler, *Gramophone, Film, Typewriter*, p. 214.

9. Stramm, *Das Werk*, p. 408 (appendix).

10. Politzer, p. 197.

11. *Phonographische Zeitschrift* 14, no. 9 (1913): 215.

12. In addition, Carl Lindström already held majority shares of the stocks in Beka Record, the International Talking Machines Co., and Odeon (Bauer's earlier employer), and later he acquired the Homophon Co. and Fonotipia as well. It is plain to see: in spite of all the German propaganda, media conglomerates on the model of Siemens long since had become multinationals. All statistics regarding Lindström are taken from anonymous and untitled notices in *Phonographische Zeitschrift* between 1913 and 1919 (volumes 14–20).

13. W. Kittler, "Schreibmaschinen, Sprechmaschinen," pp. 117–40.

14. Kafka, letter of November 24, 1912, in *Letters to Felice*, p. 62.

15. W. Kittler, "Schreibmaschinen, Sprechmaschinen," p. 138.

16. Eight of the fragments were published in *Hyperion*, a newspaper edited by Franz Blei and Carl Sternheim, under the title "Observation" in 1908. In 1910, five of them appeared as "Observations" in the Prague magazine *Bohemia*. See Rolleston in Binder, 2: 2, 2: 9.

17. Reproduced in Wagenbach, p. 122.

18. Kafka, letter of October 27, 1912, in *Letters to Felice*, p. 16. Translation modified.

19. Kafka, letter of August 14, 1912, in *Letters to Friends, Family, and Editors*, p. 85.

20. Ibid. p. 84.

21. Brod, "Zwei Welten," p. 49. See also Brod and Borst, p. 494.

22. W. Kittler, "Schreibmaschinen, Sprechmaschinen," p. 88.

23. Kafka, letter of September 20, 1912, in *Letters to Felice*, p. 5.

24. W. Kittler, "Schreibmaschinen, Sprechmaschinen," p. 94.

25. Kafka, "Description of a Struggle," p. 44.

26. Directors of Carl Lindström Inc. See Kafka's letters of December 10–11 and December 22, 1912, in *Letters to Felice*, pp. 99–100, 117–18.

27. Kafka, letter of December 20–21, 1912, in *Letters to Felice*, pp. 115–16.

28. Kafka, letter of December 22, 1912, ibid., p. 199.

29. Kafka, "The Judgment," p. 87.

30. W. Kittler, "Brief oder Blick," pp. 57–58.

31. Martin, 1: 51. Sholes became postmaster in Madison in 1844 at the age of 25 and, four years later, postmaster in Milwaukee.

32. Kafka, letter of September 20, 1912, in *Letters to Friends, Family, and Editors*, p. 86.

33. Neumann, *Franz Kafka: "Das Urteil,"* p. 34.

34. W. Kittler, "Schreibmaschinen, Sprechmaschinen," p. 111. This origin became evident once more in 1917, when Lindström came to be one of the major financial backers in the founding of Ufa.

35. Kafka, letter of March 6–7, 1912, in *Letters to Felice*, p. 215.

36. Ibid.

37. After the frequency of Kafka's writing reached its absolute maximum in December 1912 with fifty-one letters, it dropped to thirty-four in January and then to thirty in February. In March, it rose once again to thirty-five, before falling to sixteen in May, when the second meeting between Kafka and Bauer took place in Berlin.

38. Faulstich-Wieland and Horstkemper, p. 27. Carbon paper is simply a different application of the material Swan ordinarily used to produce incandescent filaments for his vacuum bulbs.

39. Clark, pp. 102–3.

40. Ibid., pp. 22, 27.

41. Deleuze and Guattari, p. 29.

42. According to Todorov, this very difference is what constitutes narrative literature; Todorov, p. 147.

43. Osborn, p. 390.

44. Ibid., p. 389.

45. Ibid., p. 401.

46. On the relationship between psychoanalytic and criminological detection, see the now classical study by Ginzburg.

47. Lacan, "The Agency of the Letter in the Unconscious or Reason since Freud," p. 150.

48. Facsimile in Kittler, *Gramophone, Film, Typewriter*, pp. 224–25.

Chapter Twenty

1. Kafka, letter of September 30 or October 1, 1917, in *Letters to Felice*, p. 545.

2. Kafka, letter of January 25, 1915, in *Letters to Felice*, pp. 443–44.

3. Kafka, letter of October 27, 1912, ibid., p. 16.

4. Kafka, letter of November 3, 1912, ibid., p. 26.

5. Kafka, letter of November 7, 1912, ibid., p. 31.

6. Kafka, letter of November 6, 1912, ibid., p. 29.

7. Kafka, letter of October 29, 1912, ibid., p. 19.

8. Kafka, letter of October 13, 1912, ibid., p. 8.

9. Kafka, letter of October 24, 1912, ibid., p. 12. With a dedication in the form specified by Kafka, "The Judgment" appeared in Brod's yearbook, *Arkadia*, in June 1913. Kafka changed the dedication to "for F." in the story's separate publication for Kurt Wolf's book series *Judgment Day*. Kafka, postcard of September 22, 1916, ibid., p. 505.

10. Derrida, "Titel (noch zu bestimmen)," pp. 24–25.

11. Bosse, *Autorschaft ist Werkherrschaft*, p. 60. The decisive three-fold division upon which modern copyright law is based, the physical body of the book (the printed paper); "the matter, the content of the book, the ideas it presents; and the form of these ideas, the manner, the context in which, the phrases, and words with which it presents them," first was established by Johann Gottlieb Fichte in his *Demonstration of the Illegality of Reprinting Books* (1793).

12. Kafka, diary entry of August 14, 1913, in *Diaries, 1910–1913*, p. 296: "Conclusion for my case from The Judgment. I am indirectly in her debt for the story."

13. Kafka, letter of February 13–14, 1913, in *Letters to Felice*, pp. 192–93.

14. Kafka, letter of November 8, 1912, ibid., p. 33.

15. Kafka, letter of December 6–7, 1912, ibid., p. 92.

16. Kafka, letter of December 29–30, 1912, ibid., p. 132.

17. Kafka, letter of December 28–29, 1912, ibid., p. 129.

18. Man kauft, nicht neu ist diese Totenklage, / in Deutschland ungern nur gelehrte Bücher, / nach guten vollends ist fast nie die Frage, / Die gehen schlecht, sind alte Leichentücher." Eulenberg, p. vii.

19. Ibid., p. xxiii.

20. Kafka, letter of December 28–29, 1912, in *Letters to Felice*, p. 129.

21. Kafka, letters of February 10–11, February 14–15, and March 13–14, 1913, ibid., pp. 188, 194, 221.

22. On the writers' fury regarding cinemas, see Kaes, *Kino-Debatte*, p. 77ff. (Moritz Heimann, "Der Kinematographen-Unfug") or pp. 160–63 (Adolf Behne, "Die Stellung des Publikums zur deutschen Literatur"). On the overall relationship between literature and the technical media during the Weimar Republic, see Kaes, *Weimarer Republik*, pp. 159–314 (part 2: "Institution Literatur im Zeitalter der Massenkommunikation"). On stenotypists' professionally determined love of the movies, see ibid., pp. 352–54 (Rudolf Braune, "Was sie lesen: Drei Stenotypistinnen").

23. Nabokov, pp. 80–81.

24. Ibid., p. 104.

25. Ibid., pp. 98–99.

26. Weiß, p. 98.

27. Ibid., pp. 99, 100.

28. Kafka, letter of June 26, 1913, in *Letters to Felice*, p. 279.

29. Melville, p. 45.

30. Schreiber, *Das Symptom des Schreibens*, pp. 77–78.

31. Ibid., p. 214.

32. Kafka, letter of July 13, 1913, in *Letters to Felice*, p. 289: "*Simply to race through the nights with my pen that's what I want. And to perish by it, or lose my reason, that's what I want too, since it is the inevitable and long-anticipated consequence.*"

Chapter Twenty-One

1. Cournot, p. 60.

2. Genth and Hoppe, pp. 77–80.

3. Kafka, "[Appeal for] A German society for the establishment and support of a military and civilian hospital in Prague for the treatment of nervous diseases in German Bohemia," in *Letters to Felice*, p. 580.

4. In agreement with Schöttle, I have intentionally avoided using the term "metaphor." Once Du Bois-Reymond had recognized nerve fibers as actually being telegraphic cables, rather than merely being comparable to them, the use of the term "nerves" to refer to cables and wires did not reflect a current and merely metaphorical use of language, but instead was indicative of the state of knowledge at the end of the nineteenth century. "A popular and in fact very accurate comparison refers to the worldwide telegraphic network as a 'nervous system of the Earth, of the body of humankind, which at almost the same moment transforms every stimulus in each individual cell into a collective sensation of the entire body,' just as, conversely, the nerve fibers of humans and animals are in fact—and not just metaphorically—nothing other than telegraph lines" (Schöttle, pp. 4–5).

5. Anonymous, *Nerven der Armee*, p. 18. Thanks to Peter Berz in Berlin.

6. Kafka, "Wedding Preparations in the Country," p. 15.

7. Ibid., p. 18.

8. Ibid., p. 28.

9. W. Kittler, "Schreibmaschinen, Sprechmaschinen," p. 83.

10. Julie Kafka, letter of November 16, 1912, in *Letters to Felice*, pp. 45–46.

11. Cournot, pp. 60–61.

12. Sautter, p. 596. By contrast, the figure for Austria was only 2,049,922,720 for the same year. Anonymous, "Das österreichische Post- und Telegraphenwesen," p. 296.

13. Anonymous, "Post, Telegraphie und Fernsprechwesen," p. 554.

14. Knies, p. 94.

15. Anonymous, "Das österreichische Post- und Telegraphenwesen," p. 296. The record was set at precisely 23,342,840.

16. Politzer, p. 197.

17. Sautter, p. 160.

18. Rogozinski, p. 70.

19. Kafka, letter of November 3, 1912, in *Letters to Felice*, p. 24.

20. Kafka emphatically refused to ease this distress: once, when Bauer wanted to know when her letters were delivered so she would be able to calculate her letters as well (one learns from the enemy), Kafka answered with the demoralizing remark that her army was still at a preindustrial (quasi-mail-coach) level: "My poor dear one, you want to know when your letters arrive, so as to plan accordingly? But the mail is quite unpredictable; in Austria in particular it functions in a completely haphazard fashion, just like the Telegraph game at summer parties." Kafka, letter of December 5–6, 1912, in *Letters to Felice*, p. 89.

21. Kafka, letter of November 5, 1912, ibid., p. 27.

22. Kafka, letter of May 28, 1913, ibid., p. 263.

23. Kafka, letter of November 18, 1912, ibid., p. 49.

24. Kafka, letter of November 19, 1912, ibid., p. 50.

25. Figl, pp. 16–25, and supplement 4.

26. Kafka, diary entry of August 20, 1912, in *Diaries 1910–1913*, p. 178: "Miss F. B. When I arrived at Brod's on August thirteenth, she was sitting at the table. I was not at all curious about who she was, but rather took her for granted at once. Bony, empty face that wore its emptiness openly."

27. Kafka, letter of November 16, 1912, in *Letters to Felice*, p. 44.

28. Ibid.

29. Kafka, undated letter, ibid., p. 45.

30. Kafka, letter of November 16, 1912, ibid., p. 44.

31. Kafka, undated letter, ibid.

32. Hegel, *Phenomenology of Spirit*, p. 60.

33. Kafka, undated letter, in *Letters to Felice*, p. 45.

34. Derrida, *The Post Card*, p. 181.

35. Kafka, letter of November 17–18, 1912, in *Letters to Felice*, p. 48.

36. Kafka, telegram of November 18, 1912, ibid., p. 48.

37. Kafka, letter of November 18, 1912, ibid., p. 49.

38. Of the 308 letters written at this time, Kafka wrote 60 on Sundays, 49 on Thursdays, 48 on Fridays, 44 on Tuesdays, 42 on Mondays, 37 on Wednesdays, and 28 on Saturdays.

39. Kafka, letter of November 21, 1912, in *Letters to Felice*, p. 52.

40. Kafka, letter of November 19, 1912, ibid., p. 50.

41. Derrida, "Signature Event Context," p. 326.

42. Kafka, letter of November 18, 1912, in *Letters to Felice*, p. 73.

43. Kafka, letter of November 20, 1912, ibid., pp. 50–51.

44. Kafka, letter of November 20–21, 1912, ibid., p. 51.

45. Pink Floyd, "Brain Damage," on the album *Dark Side of the Moon*, EMI LP C 064–05249.

46. Kafka, letter of November 21, 1912, in *Letters to Felice*, p. 52.
47. Ibid.
48. Searle, pp. 54–71.
49. Kafka, letter of November 28, 1912, in *Letters to Felice*, p. 72.
50. *Schreibschrein*, a term used by Adalbert Stifter in *Indian Summer* (1857) to describe the scene of writing surrounding an ornate writing desk. Translator's note.
51. Kafka, letter of November 18, 1912, ibid., p. 73.
52. "i" designates an inserted letter.
53. Ibid.
54. Kafka, letter of June 22, 1913, ibid., p. 274: "Dearest, you cannot imagine the way I suck [*saugen*, "squeeze" in original translation] life out of your letters."
55. Kafka, letter of November 28, 1912, in *Letters to Felice*, p. 72.
56. Bürgel, p. 285.
57. Grosz, p. 39.
58. Ibid., p. 47.
59. "I am sure all my letters also get lost—the one from Kratzau, from Reichenberg, this morning's letter, the ordinary, the registered, the express letters, all of them" (Kafka, letter of November 27, 1912, in *Letters to Felice*, p. 69).
60. Kittler, "Flechsig/Schreber/Freud," pp. 56–68.
61. Freud, *New Introductory Lectures on Psycho-Analysis*, pp. 54–55.
62. Stingelin, pp. 58–59.
63. Kafka, letter of March 1922, in *Letters to Milena*, p. 229.
64. Kafka, letter of October 25, 1923, in *Letters to Friends, Family, and Editors*, p. 387.
65. Kafka, letter of April 14, 1916, in *Letters to Felice*, p. 464.
66. Avé-Lallemant, p. 8.
67. Kafka, postcard of August 22, 1916, in *Letters to Felice*, p. 492.
68. Kafka, letter of March 1922, in *Letters to Milena*, p. 229.
69. The Remington firm originally produced machine guns. See Kittler, *Gramophone, Film, Typewriter*, pp. 190–91. On the genesis of the postcard from war, see "The Standards of Writing" above.
70. Foucault, *The Archeology of Knowledge*, pp. 187–89.
71. Searle, pp. 54–71.
72. Derrida, "Signature Event Context," p. 327.
73. Foucault, "Mon corps, ce papier, ce feu," p. 602.
74. Schneider, "Kafkas Lockung," p. 115.
75. Rogozinski, p. 143. "Anyway, the correspondence with Felice would have tried the impossible. Fascinated by itself from the start, the letter celebrates its own cult, bewitches itself by its postal litany, by its amplitude, by the periodic frequency of its deliveries, by the syncopated enjoyment of its own repetition."

Chapter Twenty-Two

1. Kafka, letter of December 7–8, 1912, in *Letters to Felice*, p. 93.
2. Karras, pp. 252–309.
3. Brod, *Tagebuch in Versen*, p. 19.
4. See Freud's "fort-da game" (Freud, "Beyond," p. 15). See also Norbert Haas's commentary, especially regarding the "vanished" objects. "They are an object in the same sense as the subject; what they put in question is posed as a question that takes on meaning only by way of interpretation, through an interpretive act." Haas, p. 36.
5. Kafka, letter of June 19, 1913, in *Letters to Felice*, p. 282.
6. Kafka, letter of April 3, 1914, ibid., p. 375.
7. Kafka, letter of October 31, 1912, ibid., p. 20.
8. Elias, p. 153 (referring to Kafka's dream): "The sheets are folded two times a day and they fold themselves to comply with the request that one has to answer (two times a day) as if the issue were to establish *at the same time* a continuum, a total communication, and the multiplication of the gesture of the cut."
9. Brod, *Tagebuch*, p. 18: "Da glaubt ich schon in meinem Grab zu sein, / Im Sarg unter der Erde, / Und warte auf die Stimme dein, / Daß ich erlöst und lebend werde" (I thought myself already in my grave, / In a coffin below the earth, / And waited on that voice of yours, / That I be saved and live once more).
10. Kafka, letter of November 9, 1912, in *Letters to Felice*, pp. 33–34.
11. For Brod's sparse remarks about his existence as a postal official, see Brod, "Kafka und Brod," p. 147; and Brod, *Streitbares Leben*, p. 151. That Brod's career encompassed telephone skills is documented in one of Kafka's letters: "Yesterday I completely forgot one principal item—our telephone. You cannot imagine how urgently we need it." Kafka, letter of autumn 1912, in *Letters to Friends, Family, and Editors*, p. 91.
12. Kafka, letter of November 14, 1912, in *Letters to Felice*, p. 38.
13. Kafka, letter of January 22–23, 1913, ibid., p. 166.
14. See "The Logistics of the Poet's Dream," above.
15. Serres, e.g., p. 230.
16. Shannon, "Communication in the Presence of Noise," p. 166.
17. Neumann, "Nachrichten," p. 116.
18. Pott, pp. 19–20.
19. Franz Grillparzer, "An Ovid," quoted in Pott, p. 19: "den in wilde, unwirtbare Wüsten, / wo nie ein Glücklicher sich schauen ließ, / auf Pontus ferne meerumtobte Küsten, / der Grimm von Romas tückschem Herrscher stieß."
20. Renard, "Der Mann und die Muschel," quoted in Kittler, *Gramophone, Film, Typewriter*, p. 53.
21. Ibid., p. 54.
22. Ibid.

23. Rilke, *New Poems*, p. 147.

24. Silence and noise were one and the same after Wilhelm Preyer's research. *On the Perception of Silence* had led him to conclude in 1877 that even complete silence was nothing other than the entotic perception of noise, which the *nervus acusticus* still sent to the brain even when the eardrum no longer received anything at all. Preyer thus came to the conclusion that "at the same time, all or most of the nerves receptive to sound are stimulated by extremely low intensity." Preyer, p. 67.

25. Kafka, letter of January 17–18, 1913, in *Letters to Felice*, p. 253. Translation modified.

26. Anonymous, "Der Musiktelegraph," p. 808.

27. Reis, pp. 208–12. See also Berliner, pp. 6–9; and Feyerabend, p. 14.

28. Kafka, *The Castle*, pp. 93–94.

29. Ibid., p. 27.

30. Shannon, *The Mathematical Theory of Communication*, p. 3.

31. Kafka, *The Castle*, p. 94.

32. Shannon, *The Mathematical Theory of Communication*, p. 39, emphasis in original.

33. Shannon, "Communication Theory of Secrecy Systems," p. 128.

34. Shannon, "Communication in the Presence of Noise," p. 168.

35. Shannon, *The Mathematical Theory of Communication*, p. 39; see also Shannon, "Communication in the Presence of Noise," p. 166.

36. Shannon, "Communication in the Presence of Noise," p. 166.

37. Kafka, letter of January 22–23, 1913, in *Letters to Felice*, p. 167.

38. Ibid., p. 168

39. Neumann, "Nachrichten," p. 116.

40. Hagemeyer, p. 225.

41. Ibid., p. 369.

42. Primarily by Goodall with the collaboration of Shannon and others in the Research Department, as well as Edson and Black in the Systems Development Department.

43. Fagen, 2: 316.

44. On the "basic principles" of PCM, see Hartley et al., pp. 5–13.

45. Goodall, p. 396.

46. Oliver, Pierce, and Shannon, p. 1324.

47. Goodall, p. 397.

48. Heath, p. 83. In order to make it possible to encode twice as many symbols, Baudot nonetheless implemented a type wheel containing 2 x 29 type characters—the letters of the alphabet in one row, numerals and punctuation in the other—and a "shift function" encoded by the thirty-first "code group" that made it possible to shift from one row to the other. Aschoff, "Aus der Geschichte der Telegraphen-Codes," pp. 31–32.

49. Goodall, p. 397.

50. Bennett, "History of PCM. Bell Laboratories Memo," February 23, 1976, quoted in Hagemeyer, p. 384.

51. Hagemeyer, p. 384.

52. Ibid., p. 385.

53. Shannon, *The Mathematical Theory of Communication*, p. 49.

54. Shannon, "Communication in the Presence of Noise," p. 171.

55. Hölzler and Thierbach, p. 78.

56. Lochmann, p. 52.

57. Oliver, Pierce, and Shannon, p. 1327.

58. Lochmann, p. 48.

59. Goodall, p. 400.

60. Shannon, "Communication Theory of Secrecy Systems," p. 113.

61. Schreiber, "Word-Engineering," p. 291.

62. Shannon, "Communication in the Presence of Noise," p. 166; *The Mathematical Theory of Communication*, pp. 82–83.

63. Shannon, "Communication Theory of Secrecy Systems," p. 127.

64. F. Kittler, "There Is No Software," p. 84.

65. Ibid., pp. 83–84.

66. Musil, p. 292.

BIBLIOGRAPHY

"Abbildung und Beschreibung des Telegraphen oder der neuerfundenen Fern-schreibemaschine in Paris und ihres inneren Mechanismus. Von einem Au-genzeugen" (anonymous). Reprint of the 1795 publication in Frithjof Skupin, ed., *Abhandlungen von der Telegraphie*, pp. 25–45. East Berlin, 1986.

Abbot, Scott. "'Des Maurers Wandeln / Es gleicht dem Leben': The Free Masonic Ritual Route in *Wilhelm Meisters Wanderjahre*." *DVjs* 58 (1984): 146–207.

Abramson, Albert. "110 Jahre Fernsehen. 'Visionen vom Fern-Sehen.'" In *Vom Verschwinden der Ferne: Telekommunikation und Kunst*, ed. Edith Decker and Peter Weibel, pp. 146–207. Cologne, 1990.

Adalbertus Samaritanus. *Praecepta dictaminum*. Ed. F.-J. Schmale. Weimar, 1961.

Alewyn, Richard. "Klopstocks Leser." In *Festschrift für Rainer Gruenter*, ed. Bernhard Fabian, pp. 100–21. Heidelberg, 1978.

Allgemeine Deutsche Biographie. Ed. Historische Commission bei der König-lichen Akademie (Munich). Berlin, 1967.

Appel, Kenneth, and Wolfgang Haken. "The Four-Color-Problem." In *Mathematics Today: Twelve Informal Essays*, ed. Lynn Arthur Steen, pp. 153–80. New York, 1978.

Arnim, Bettina von. "Clemens Brentanos Frühlingskranz." In *Werke und Briefe*, vol. 1. Ed. Gustav Konrad. Cologne, 1959.

———. *Goethe's Correspondence with a Child*. Boston, n.d.

"Ars Dictandi Aurelianensis." In Rockinger, part 1, pp. 93–114.

Aschenborn, M. *Das Gesetz über das Postwesen des Deutschen Reichs vom 28. Oktober 1871*. Berlin, 1908.

Aschoff, Volker. *Aus der Geschichte der Nachrichtentechnik*. Opladen, 1974.

———. "Aus der Geschichte der Telegraphen-Codes." *Rheinisch-Westfälische Akademie der Wissenschaften. Natur-, Ingenieur- und Wirtschaftswissen-schaften. Vorträge* N 297 (1981): 7–35.

———. "Drei Vorschläge für nichtelektrisches Fernsprechen aus der Wende vom 18. zum 19. Jahrhundert." *Deutsches Museum. Abhandlungen und Berichte* 49, no. 3 (1981): 1–42.

———. "Von Abel Burja bis zum Fächer 'à la Telegraph': Ein Beitrag zur Historiographie der Nachrichtentechnik." *Archiv für deutsche Postgeschichte* (1981), no. 1: 106–23.

Avé-Lallemant, Friedrich Christian Benedikt. *Die Geheimschreibekunst in ihrer Anwendung auf die Reichspostkarten: Eine praktische Anleitung zur Erlernung der Chiffrirschrift.* Special impression from the illustrated family magazine *Der Hausfreund.* Leipzig, 1875.

Bartholdy, Martin. *Der Generalpostmeister Heinrich von Stephan.* Berlin, 1937.

Bäuml, Michael. "Staatspolitik, Presse und Post: Die Bedeutung des Postzwangs und Postzeitungsdebits für die Staatspolitik und Presse in Deutschland." *Archiv für Postgeschichte in Bayern* 8, no. 1 (1932): 1–23.

Bebel, August. *Die Frau und der Sozialismus.* Frankfurt am Main, 1977.

Behringer, Wolfgang. *Thurn und Taxis: Die Geschichte ihrer Post und ihrer Unternehmen.* Munich and Zurich, 1990.

Bell, Mabel Gardiner. *The Story of the Rise of the Oral Method in America, as Told in the Writings of the Late Hon. Gardiner G. Hubbard.* Washington D.C., 1898.

Benjamin, Walter. "Charles Baudelaire. Ein Lyriker im Zeitalter des Hochkapitalismus." In *Gesammelte Schriften*, ed. Rolf Tiedemann and Hermann Schweppenhäuser, pp. 471–508. Frankfurt am Main, 1980.

———. "The Work of Art in the Age of Mechanical Reproduction." In *Illuminations*, ed. Hannah Arendt, trans. Harry Zohn, pp. 217–51. New York, 1955.

Bentham, Jeremy. "Panopticon; or, The Inspection House." In *The Works of Jeremy Bentham*, vol. 4, ed. John Bowring, pp. 37–66. New York, 1962.

Benveniste, Émile. *Problems in General Linguistics.* Trans. Mary Elizabeth Meek. Coral Gables, Florida, 1971.

Bergius, Johann Heinrich Ludwig, ed. *Policey- und Cameral-Magazin in welchem nach alphabetischer Ordnung die vornehmsten und wichtigsten bey dem Policey- und Cameralwesen vorkommende Materien nach richtigen und vernünftigen Grundsätzen practisch abgehandelt und durch landesherrliche Gesetze und hin und wieder wirklich gemachte Einrichtungen erläutert werden.* Vol. 7. Frankfurt am Main, 1773.

Berliner, S. *Der Erfinder des sprechenden Telephons.* Hannover and Leipzig, 1909.

Beyrer, Klaus. *Die Postkutschenreise.* Tübingen, 1985.

Biedermann, Woldemar Freiherr von. "Goethe als Freimaurer." In Biedermann, *Goethe-Forschungen: Neue Folge*, pp. 296–302. Leipzig, 1886.

Binder, Hartmut. *Kafka-Handbuch.* 2 vols. Stuttgart, 1979.

———. *Kafka-Kommentar zu sämtliche Erzählungen.* 3d edition. Munich, 1982.

Birkenhauer, Klaus. *Kleist.* Tübingen, 1977.

Blake, Clarence John. "Auswahl von Worten zur Prüfung der Hörschärfe in Bezug auf ihren logographischen Werth." *Zeitschrift für Ohrenheilkunde* 11 (1882): 29–31.

———. "Ueber die Verwerthung der Membrana tympani als Phonautograph und

Logograph." *Archiv für Augen und Ohrenheilkunde* 5 (1876): 434–39, and *Zeitschrift für Ohrenheilkunde* 8 (1879): 5–12.

Bohrer, Karl Heinz. *Der romantische Brief: Die Entstehung ästhetischer Subjektivität.* Frankfurt am Main, 1989.

Bolz, Norbert. "Die Schrift des Films." In *Diskursanalysen I: Medien,* ed. Friedrich A. Kittler, Manfred Schneider, and Samuel Weber, pp. 26–34. Opladen, 1987.

Bolza, Albrecht. "Friedrich König, der Erfinder der Druckmaschine, ein Pionier der deutschen Maschinenindustrie." *Deutsches Museum. Abhandlungen und Berichte* 5, no. 1 (1933): 1–30.

Borges, Jorge Luis. "The Garden of Forking Paths." In *Labyrinths: Selected Stories and Other Writings,* ed. Donald A. Yates and James E. Irby, pp. 19–29. New York, 1962.

Bosse, Heinrich. *Autorschaft ist Werkherrschaft: Über die Entstehung des Urheberrechts aus dem Geist der Goethezeit.* Munich and Zurich, 1981.

———. "Dichter kann man nicht bilden: Zur Veränderung der Schulrhetorik nach 1779." In *Jahrbuch für Internationale Germanistik* 10 (1978): 80–125.

Braun, Franz. "'Die Frau im Staatsdienst,' dargestellt an den Verhältnissen bei der Reichs-Post- und Telegraphen-Verwaltung." Dissertation. Würzburg, 1912.

Breithaupt, Heinrich. "War Heinrich von Kleist tatsächlich der Bewerber um französische Postdienste in Westfalen?" *Archiv für deutsche Postgeschichte* 2 (1966): 48–51.

Brod, Max. *Franz Kafka: A Biography.* 2d enlarged edition. Trans. G. Humphrey Roberts and Richard Winston. New York, 1960.

———. "Franz Kafka und Max Brod in ihren Doppelberufen." *Die literarische Welt* 4, no. 18 (1928): 3–4.

———. *Streitbares Leben: Autobiographie.* Munich, 1960.

———. *Tagebuch in Versen.* Berlin, 1910.

———. "Zwei Welten." *Der Jude* 2 (1917–18): 47–51.

Brod, Max, and Hugo Borst. "Über das Taylorsystem." *Der Jude* 2 (1917–18): 493–94.

Browning, Elizabeth Barrett. *Sonnets from the Portuguese.* In *The Complete Works of Elizabeth Barrett Browning.* Vol. 3. New York, 1900.

Bruce, Robert V. *Bell: Alexander Graham Bell and the Conquest of Solitude.* London, 1973.

Buchbender, Ortwin. *Das tönende Erz: Deutsche Propaganda gegen die Rote Armee im Zweiten Weltkrieg.* Stuttgart, 1978.

Burckas, Leo. "Eigentumsrecht, Urheberrecht und Persönlichkeitsrecht an Briefen." Dissertation. Leipzig, 1907.

Bürgel, Peter. "Der Privatbrief. Entwurf eines heuristischen Modells." *DVjs* 50 (1976): 581–97.

Bürgerliches Gesetzbuch. 11th edition. Ed. O. Fischer and W. von Henle. Munich, 1921.

Campe, Rüdiger. *Affekt und Ausdruck: Zur Umwandlung der literarischen Rede im 17. und 18. Jahrhundert.* Tübingen, 1990.

Canetti, Elias. "Kafka's Other Trial: The Letters to Felice." In *The Conscience of Words.* Trans. Joachim Neugroschel. New York, 1979.

Chalmers, Patrick. *James Chalmers: Inventeur du Timbre-poste adhésif.* Nouvelles Recherches sur le Projet de Sir Rowland Hill. London, 1889.

Clark, Ronald William. *Edison: The Man Who Made the Future.* London, 1977.

Conrad, Joseph. *Heart of Darkness.* Harmondworth, Middlesex, 1985.

Corpus iuris civilis, vols. 1–3. Ed. Paul Krueger, Theodor Mommsen, and Rudolf Schoell. Dublin and Zurich, 1967–70.

Cournot, Michel. "Toi qui as de si grandes dentes. . . . " *Le Nouvel Observateur* (April 17, 1972): 59–61.

Cronbach, E. "Die Beschäftigungsneurose der Telegraphisten." *Archiv für Psychiatrie* 37 (1903): 242–93.

Curtius, Ernst Robert. *European Literature and the Latin Middle Ages.* Trans. Willard R. Task. New York, 1953.

Dallmeier, Martin. *Quellen zur Geschichte des europäischen Postwesens, 1501–1806.* Parts 1 and 3. Kallmünz, 1977.

Dambach. *Das Gesetz über das Postwesen des Deutschen Reiches.* Berlin, 1901.

Daunton, Martin J. *Royal Mail: The Post Office Since 1840.* Dover, New Hampshire, 1985.

De Luna, Frederick A. *The French Republic under Cavaignac, 1848.* Princeton, 1969.

De Man, Hendrik. *Vermassung und Kulturverfall: Eine Diagnose unserer Zeit.* Munich, 1951.

Deleuze, Gilles. *Foucault.* Ed. and trans. Seán Hand. London, 1988.

Deleuze, Gilles, and Félix Guattari. *Kafka: Toward a Minor Literature.* Trans. Dana Polan. Minneapolis, 1986.

Derrida, Jacques. "Cogito and the History of Madness." In *Writing and Difference.* Trans. Alan Bass. Chicago, 1978.

———. *Of Grammatology.* Trans. Gayatri Chakravorty Spivak. Baltimore, 1974.

———. *The Post Card: From Socrates to Freud and Beyond.* Trans. Alan Bass. Chicago, 1987.

———. "Signature Event Context." In *Margins of Philosophy.* Trans. Alan Bass, 1982.

———. "Titel (noch zu bestimmen)." In *Austreibung des Geistes aus den Geisteswissenschaften,* ed. Friedrich A. Kittler, pp. 15–37. Paderborn, 1980.

———. *Ulysse gramophone, deux mots pour Joyce.* Paris, 1987.

Deutschbaltisches Biographisches Lexikon. Ed. U. Welding. Cologne, 1970.

"Der deutsche Postverein" (anonymous). In Hüttner, vol. 4 (1850), pp. 145–66.

Dopf, Karl. "Der Briefkasten erzählt seine Geschichte." *Archiv für deutsche Postgeschichte* 2 (1965): 63–64.

Doyle, Sir Arthur Conan. "The Five Orange Pips." In *The Complete Sherlock Holmes*, pp. 217–29. Garden City, New York, 1927.

———. "A Study in Scarlet." In *The Complete Sherlock Holmes*, pp. 15–86.

Drogge, Horst. "Die Entwicklung der optischen Telegraphie in Preußen und ihre Wegbereiter." *Archiv für deutsche Postgeschichte* 2 (1982): 5–26.

Du Bois-Reymond, Emil. "Zur Kentniss des Telephons." *Archiv für Physiologie* 1 (1877): 573, 582.

Eaves, T. C. Duncan, and Ben D. Kimpel. *Samuel Richardson: A Biography*. Oxford, 1971.

Ekschmitt, Werner. *Das Gedächtnis der Völker: Hieroglyphen, Schrift und Schriftfunde auf Tontafeln, Papyri und Pergamenten*. Berlin, 1964.

Elias, Jean-Marc. "Le parlographe: La représentation d'une voix." *Revue des Sciences Humaine* 195, no. 3 (1984): 151–66.

"Entstehung und Entwickelung des Post-Zustellungswesens, 1794–1894" (anonymous). *Archiv für Post und Telegraphie* 23, no. 4 (1895): 97–118.

Erasmus of Rotterdam, Desiderius. "On the Writing of Letters / *De conscribendis epistolis*." Trans. Charles Fantazzi. In *Collected Works of Erasmus*, vol. 25. Ed. J. K. Sowards. Buffalo, 1985.

Eribon, Didier. *Michel Foucault (1926–1984)*. Paris, 1989.

Eulenberg, Herbert. *Schattenbilder: Eine Fibel für Kulturbedürftige in Deutschland*. 9th edition. Berlin, 1912.

Fagen, M. D, ed. *A History of Engineering and Science in the Bell System*. Volume 1. *The Early Years (1875–1925)*. Prepared by Members of the Technical Staff. Bell Telephone Laboratories. New York, 1975.

———. *A History of Engineering and Science in the Bell System*. Volume 2. *National Service in War and Peace (1925–1975)*. Prepared by Members of the Technical Staff. Bell Telephone Laboratories. New York, 1978.

Faulstich-Wieland, Hannelore, and Marianne Horstkemper. *Der Weg zur modernen Bürokommunikation: Historische Aspekte des Verhältnisses von Frauen und neuen Technologien*. Bielefeld, 1987.

Feyerabend, Ernst. "An der Wiege des elektrischen Telegraphen." *Deutsches Museum Abhandlungen und Berichte* 5, no. 5 (1933): 143–74.

———. "August von Etzel, ein Pionier der Telegraphie in Deutschland." *Deutsche Postgeschichte* 11 (1937): 80–84.

———. *50 Jahre Fernsprecher in Deutschland 1877–1927*. Berlin, 1927.

Fichte, Johann Gottlieb. *The Science of Rights*. Trans. A. E. Kroeger. London, 1889.

Figl, A. *Systeme des Chiffrierens*. Graz, 1926.

Fischer, Paul David. *Post und Telegraphie im Weltverkehr: Eine Skizze*. Berlin, 1879.

Fletcher, Harvey. "The Nature of Speech and Its Interpretation." *Journal of the Franklin Institute* 193, no. 6 (1922): 729–47.

Fontius, Martin. "Post und Brief." In *Materialität der Kommunikation*, ed. Hans Ulrich Gumbrecht and Karl Ludwig Pfeiffer, pp. 267–79. Frankfurt am Main, 1988.

Foucault, Michel. *The Archeology of Knowledge and The Discourse on Language*. Trans. A. M. Sheridan Smith. New York, 1972.

————. *Discipline and Punish: The Birth of the Prison*. Trans. Alan Sheridan. New York, 1979.

————. "The Discourse on Language." In The *Archeology of Knowledge*, pp. 215–37.

————. "Für eine Kritik der Politischen Vernunft." *Lettre international* 1 (Summer 1988): 58–66.

————. "La gouvernementalité." *magazine littéraire* 269 (1989): 97–103.

————. *The History of Sexuality: Volume 1. An Introduction*. Trans. Robert Hurley. New York, 1978.

————. "Language to Infinity." In *Language, Counter-Memory, Practice: Selected Essays and Interviews*. Ed. Donald F. Bouchard. Trans. Donald F. Bouchard and Sherry Simon. Ithaca, New York, 1977.

————. "The Life of Infamous Men." In *Power, Truth, Strategy*. Ed. Meaghan Morris and Paul Patton. Sydney, 1979.

————. *Madness and Civilization: A History of Insanity in the Age of Reason*. Trans. Richard Howard. New York, 1965.

————. "Mon corps, ce papier, ce feu." Second epilogue in *Histoire de la folie à l'âge classique*. 2d edition. Paris, 1972.

————. *The Order of Things: An Archeology of the Human Sciences*. Trans. R. D. Laing. New York, 1973.

————. *Die Ordnung des Diskurses*. Inauguralvorlesung am Collège de France, December 2, 1970. Frankfurt am Main, 1977.

————. *Résumé des cours*. Paris, 1989.

————. "What is an Author?" In *Language, Counter-Memory, Practice*, pp. 113–38.

Frank, Manfred. *What is Neostructuralism?* Trans. Sabine Wilke and Richard Gray. Minneapolis, 1989.

Frederick II, King of Prussia. *Posthumous Works*. Vol. 12. London, 1789.

Freiesleben, Hans Christian. *Goethe als Freimaurer: Seine Bedeutung für die Königliche Kunst*. Hamburg, 1949.

Freud, Sigmund. "Beyond the Pleasure Principle." In *Beyond the Pleasure Principle, Group Psychology, and Other Works*, ed. and trans. James Strachey, with Anna Freud, Alix Strachey, and Alan Tyson, pp. 7–66. London, 1955.

————. *New Introductory Lectures on Psycho-Analysis*. Trans. W. J. H. Sprott. New York, 1933.

————. "On the Sexual Theories of Children." In *Jensen's "Gravida" and Other*

Works, ed. and trans. James Strachey, with Anna Freud, Alix Strachey, and Alan Tyson, pp. 209–26. London, 1959.

———. *The Psychopathology of Everyday Life*. Ed. and trans. James Strachey. London, 1960.

Frey-Schlesinger, Anna. "Die volkswirtschaftliche Bedeutung der habsburgischen Post im 16. Jahrhundert." *Vierteljahresschrift für Sozial- und Wirtschaftsgeschichte* 15, no. 3–4 (1920): 399–45.

Friedlaender, Adolph. "Die Verletzung des Briefgeheimnisses." *Zeitschrift für die gesamte Strafrechtswissenschaft* 16 (1896): 756–89.

Frobenius, Herman. *Geschichte des preußischen Ingenieur- und Pionier-Korps von der Mitte des 19. Jahrhunderts bis zum Jahre 1886, vol. 1: Die Zeit von 1848 bis 1869*. Berlin, 1906.

Fussell, Paul. *The Great War and Modern Memory*. New York, 1977.

Geistbeck, Michael. *Der Weltverkehr: Seeschiffahrt und Eisenbahnen, Post und Telegraphie in ihrer Entwicklung dargestellt*. 1895; reprint, Hildesheim, 1986.

Gellert, Christian Fürchtegott. "Briefe, nebst einer praktischen Abhandlung von dem guten Geschmacke in Briefen." In *Die epistolographischen Schriften*. Stuttgart, 1971.

———. "Gedanken von einem guten deutschen Briefe." In *Die epistolographischen Schriften*. Stuttgart, 1971.

———. *Gellerts Briefwechsel*. Vols. 1–2. Ed. John F. Reynolds. New York, 1983–87.

Genth, Renate, and Joseph Hoppe. *Telephon! Der Draht, an dem wir hängen*. Berlin, 1986.

Giehrl, Hermann. *Der Feldherr Napoleon als Organisator: Betrachtungen über seine Verkehrs- und Nachrichtenmittel, seine Arbeits- und Befehlsweise*. Berlin, 1911.

Ginzburg, Carlo. *Myths, Emblems, Clues*. Trans. John Tedeschi and Anne C. Tedeschi. London, 1986.

Goethe, Johann Wolfgang von. *Annals*. Trans. Charles Nisbet. In *Truth and Poetry: From My Own Life together with His Annals*. London, 1894.

———. *From My Life: Poetry and Truth*. Ed. Thomas P. Saine and Jeffrey L. Sammons. Trans. Robert R. Heitner. New York: Suhrkamp Publishers, 1987.

———. *Goethes Briefe*. In *Goethes Werke*. Part 4. Weimar, 1905.

———. *Goethes Briefe: Hamburger Ausgabe*. Vols. 1–4. Ed. Karl Robert Mandelkow. Hamburg, 1962–1967.

———. *Goethes Gespräche: Eine Sammlung zeitgenössischer Berichte aus seinem Umgang auf Grund der Ausgabe und des Nachlasses von Flodoard Freiherrn von Biedermann*. Ed. Wolfgang Herwig. Zurich and Stuttgart, 1969.

———. *The Sorrows of Young Werther*. In *The Sorrows of Young Werther, Elective Affinities, and Novella*. Ed. David E. Wellbery. Trans. Victor Lange and Judith Ryan. New York, 1988.

————. "A Symbol." In *Poetical Works*, ed. Nathan Haskell Dole, pp. 296–97. Boston, 1902.

————. *Wilhelm Meister's Apprenticeship*. Ed. and trans. Eric A. Blackall, with Victor Lange. New York, 1989.

————. *Wilhelm Meister's Journeyman Years*. Trans. Krishna Winston. In *Conversations of German Refugees and Wilhelm Meister's Journeyman Years, or The Renunciations*. Ed. Jane K. Brown. New York, 1989.

————. "Winckelmann." In *Goethes Sämtliche Werke: Jubiläums-Ausgabe*, vol. 34. Ed. Eduard von der Hellen. Stuttgart and Berlin, 1904–5.

Goodall, W. M. "Telephony by Pulse Code Modulation." *The Bell System Technical Journal* 26, no. 3 (1947): 395–409.

Görlitz, Walter. *Kleine Geschichte des deutschen Generalstabes*. Berlin, 1967.

Goux, Jean-Joseph. *Symbolic Economies: After Marx and Freud*. Trans. Jennifer Curtiss Gage. Ithaca, New York, 1990.

Groß. "Die modernen technischen Mittel des militärischen Nachrichtenwesens, insbesondere für die Befehlsübermittlung." *Beihefte zum Militär-Wochenblatt* 6 (1896): 203–30.

Grosse. "Beitrage zur Geschichte der Postkarte." In *Archiv für Post und Telegraphie* 24, no. 21: 667–89.

Grosz, Anton Wenzel. "Aufzeichnungen 1913/14." In *Grosz/Jung/Grosz*, ed. Günter Bose and Erich Brinkmann, pp. 11–71. Berlin, 1980.

Gutzkow, Karl. "Die Kurstauben." In *Gutzkows Werke: Auswahl in 12 Teilen*, ed. Reinhold Gensel, part 5, pp. 147–78. Berlin and Stuttgart, n. d.

Gutzmann, Hermann. "Untersuchungen über die Grenzen der sprachlichen Perzeptionen." *Zeitschrift für klinische Medizin* 60 (1906): 233–66.

Haas, Norbert. "Fort/Da als Modell." In *ZETA 02: Mit Lacan*, ed. Dieter Hombach, pp. 29–46. Berlin, 1982.

Haase, Frank. *Kleists Nachrichtentechnik: Eine diskursanalytische Untersuchung*. Opladen, 1986.

————. "Nachrichtentechnik vs. Romantische Autorschaft in E. T. A. Hoffmanns Novelle Rat Krespel." In *Diskursanalysen I: Medien*, ed. Kittler, Schneider, and Weber, pp. 55–67.

Hagemeyer, Friedrich-Wilhelm. "Die Entstehung von Informationskonzepten in der Nachrichtentechnik. Eine Fallstudie zur Theoriebildung in der Technik in Industrie- und Kriegsforschung." Dissertation. Berlin, 1979.

Hagen, Wolfgang. "Der Radioruf. Zu Diskurs und Geschichte des Hörfunks." In *HardWar/SoftWar*, ed. Martin Stingelin and Wolfgang Scherer, pp. 243–73. Munich, 1991.

Haller, Albrecht von. *Die Alpen*. Ed. Harold T. Betteridge. Berlin, 1959.

————. *Tagebuch seiner Beobachtungen über Schriftsteller und über sich selbst*. Vol. 2. Ed. Johann Georg Heinzmann. Frankfurt am Main, 1971.

Harsdörffer, Georg Philipp. *Der Teutsche Secretarius*. Part 1. New York, 1971.

Hartley, G. C., P. Mornet, F. Ralph, and D. J. Tarran. *Techniques of Pulse-Code Modulation in Communication Networks.* Cambridge, 1967.

Hartmann, Heinrich. "Ueber schwarze Kabinette und ihren Zusammenhang mit der Taxisschen Post in Bayern." *Archiv für Postgeschichte in Bayern* 1, no. 2 (1925): 68–78.

Haslam, John. *Illustrations of Madness.* Reprint, New York, 1988.

Heath, F. G. "Origins of the Binary Code." *Scientific American* 227, no. 2 (1972): 76–83.

Hegel, Georg Wilhelm Friedrich. *Briefe von und an Hegel.* Ed. Johannes Hoffmeister. Hamburg, 1952.

———. *Phenomenology of Spirit.* Ed. J. N. Findlay. Trans. A. V. Miller. Oxford, 1977.

———. *Encyclopedia of the Philosophical Sciences in Outline.* Trans. A. V. Miller. In *Encyclopedia of the Philosophical Sciences in Outline and Critical Writings.* Ed. Ernst Behler. New York, 1990.

Heidegger, Martin. *On the Way to Language.* Trans. Peter D. Hertz. San Francisco, 1971.

———. *On Time and Being.* Trans. Joan Stambaugh. San Francisco, 1972.

———. "The Origin of the Work of Art." Trans. Albert Hofstadter. In *Basic Writings from Being and Time to the Task of Thinking*, ed. David Farrell Krell, pp. 139–212. San Francisco, 1993.

———. *The Principle of Reason.* Trans. Reginald Lilly. Indianapolis, 1991.

Helmholtz, Hermann von. *On the Sensations of Tone as a Physiological Basis for the Theory of Music.* Trans. Alexander J. Ellis. New York, 1954.

———. "Telephon und Klangfarbe." *Monatsberichte der Königlich Preußischen Akademie der Wissenschaften zu Berlin* (1878): 488–89.

Hennig, Richard. *Die älteste Entwickelung der Telegraphie und Telephonie.* Leipzig, 1908.

Herbarth, Dieter. *Die Entwicklung der optischen Telegraphie in Preußen.* Cologne, 1978.

Hermann, Ludomar. "Über physiologische Beziehungen des Telephons." *Vierteljahresschrift der Naturforschenden Gesellschaft in Zürich* 23 (1878): 98–99.

———. "Die Uebertragung der Vocale durch das Telephon und das Microphon." *Archiv für das gesamte Physiologie des Menschen und der Thiere* 44 (1891): 543–74.

Herzog, H. "Die Anfänge der Taxisschen Posten." *Archiv für Post und Telegraphie* 44 (1916): 298–305.

Hill, Sir Rowland, and George Birkbeck Hill. *The Life of Sir Rowland Hill and the History of Penny Postage.* 2 vols. London, 1880.

Hirschfeld, Otto. "Die agentes in rebus." *Sitzungsberichte der Königlich Preussischen Akademie der Wissenschaften* 2 (1893): 421–41.

Hoerner, Ludwig. "Zur Geschichte der fotographischen Ansichtspostkarten." *Fotogeschichte* 7, no. 26 (1987): 29–44.

Hoffmann, Ernst Theodor Amadeus. "Die Automate." In *Die Serapions-Brüder*, ed. Walter Müller-Seidel, pp. 328–54. Darmstadt, 1985.

Holmberg, Erik J. "Zur Geschichte des cursus publicus." Dissertation. Uppsala, 1933.

Holmes, Oliver Wendell. "Das Stereoskop und der Stereograph." In Wolfgang Kemp, ed., *Theorie der Fotographie I: 1839–1912*. Munich, 1980, pp. 114–21.

Hölzler, E. and Thierbach, D., eds. *Nachrichtenübertragung: Grundlagen der Technik*. New York, 1966.

Hubbard, Geoffrey. *Cooke and Wheatstone and the Invention of the Electric Telegraph*. London, 1965.

Hudemann, E. E. *Geschichte des römischen Postwesens während der Kaiserzeit*. Wiesbaden, 1966.

Hyman, Anthony. *Charles Babbage: Pioneer of the Computer*. Princeton, 1982.

Innis, Harold A. *Empire and Communications*. Buffalo, 1972.

Jacobs, Jürgen. *Wilhelm Meister und seine Brüder: Untersuchungen zum deutschen Bildungsroman*. Munich, 1972.

Joost, Ulrich. "'Briefe an Jedermann.' Lichtenberg als Briefschreiber." *Freiburger Universitätsblätter* 23, no. 84 (1984): 53–65.

———. *Lichtenberg—der Briefschreiber*. Lichtenberg-Studien 5. Göttingen, 1993.

Joyce, James. *Finnegans Wake*. Boston, 1975.

———. *Ulysses: The Corrected Text*. Eds. Hans Walter Gasbler, with Wolfhard Steppe and Claus Melchior. New York, 1986.

Julien, Rose. "Unsere Telephonistinnen." *Daheim* 41, no. 20 (1905): 7.

Jung, J. *Der Weltpostverein und sein Einfluß auf den Weltverkehr und die Weltwirtschaft: Ein Vortrag gehalten in der Gesellschaft für Erdkunde und Kolonialwesen zu Straßburg*. Strasbourg, 1903.

Justi, Johann Heinrich Gottlob von. *Die Grundfeste zu der Macht und Glückseligkeit der Staaten oder ausführliche Vorstellung der gesamten Polizeiwissenschaft. In zwei Bänden*. Vol. 1. Aalen, 1965.

———. *Grundsätze der Policeywissenschaft, in einem vernünftigen, auf den Endzweck der Polizey gegründeten Zusammenhang; zum Gebrauch akademischer Vorlesungen*. 3d edition. Göttingen, 1782.

———. *System des Finanzwesens*. Aalen, 1969.

Kaes, Anton, ed. *Kino-Debatte: Texte zum Verhältnis von Literatur und Film, 1909–1929*. Tübingen, 1978.

———, ed. *Weimarer Republik: Manifeste und Dokumente zur deutschen Literatur, 1918–1933*. Stuttgart, 1983.

Kafka, Franz. *The Castle*. Trans. Willa Muir and Edwin Muir, revised by Eithne Williams and Ernst Kaiser. New York, 1969.

———. "Description of a Struggle." Trans. Tania Stern and James Stern. In *Franz

Kafka: The Complete Stories, ed. Nahum N. Glatzer, pp. 9–51. New York, 1983.

———. *The Diaries of Franz Kafka, 1910–1913*. Ed. Max Brod. Trans. Joseph Kresh. New York, 1948.

———. *The Diaries of Franz Kafka 1914–1923*. Ed. Max Brod. Trans. Martin Greenberg, with Hannah Arendt. New York, 1949.

———. "The Eight Octovo Note-Books." In *Wedding Preparations in the Country and Other Posthumous Prose Writings*, ed. Max Brod, trans. Ernst Kaiser and Eithne Wilkins, pp. 54–156. London, 1954.

———. "The Judgment." Trans. Willa Muir and Edwin Muir. In *Franz Kafka: The Complete Stories*, pp. 77–88.

———. *Letters to Felice*. Ed. Erich Heller and Jürgen Born. Trans. James Stern and Elisabeth Duckworth. New York, 1973.

———. *Letters to Friends, Family, and Editors*. Trans. Richard and Clara Winston. New York, 1977.

———. *Letters to Milena*. Ed. Willi Haas, trans. Tania Stern and James Stern. New York, 1953.

———. "Wedding Preparations in the Country." In *Wedding Preparations*, pp. 7–37.

Kalckhoff, F. *Die Erfindung der Postkarte und die Korrespondenzkarten der Norddeutschen Bundespost*. Leipzig, 1911.

Kämmerer, Ludwig. *Johann von Herrfeldt und die Idee des Weltpostvereins*. Hamburg, 1963.

Kant, Immanuel. *Critique of Pure Reason*. Trans. Norman Kemp Smith. New York, 1965.

Karras, Theodor. *Geschichte der Telegraphie*. Part 1. Braunschweig, 1909.

Keller, Gottfried. *Gesammelte Briefe*. 4 vols. Ed. Carl Helbling. Bern, 1951.

———. *Die Leute von Seldwyla*. Preface to Part 2. In *Sämtliche Werke und ausgewählte Briefe*, ed. Clemens Heselhaus, pp. 251–53. Darmstadt, 1963.

———. "The Misused Love Letters." In *The Misused Love Letters and Regula Amrain and Her Youngest Son*, trans. Michael Bullock, pp. 13–94. New York, 1974.

Kennedy, Paul M. "Imperial Cable Communications and Strategy, 1870–1914." In *The War Plans of the Great Powers, 1880–1914*, ed. Paul Kennedy, pp. 75–99. London, 1979.

Kieve, Jeffrey L. *The Electric Telegraph: A Social and Economic History*. Newton Abbott, Devon, 1973.

Kipling, Rudyard. "The Deep-Sea Cables." In *Rudyard Kipling's Verse: Definitive Edition*, p. 174. London, 1969.

Kittler, Friedrich A. "Carlos als Carlsschüler: 'Ein Familiengemälde in einem fürstlichen Hause.'" In *Unser Commercium: Goethes und Schillers Literaturpolitik*, ed. W. Barner, E. Lämmert, and N. Oellers, pp. 241–73. Stuttgart, 1984.

———. *Dichter, Mutter, Kind*. Munich, 1991.

———. *Discourse Networks, 1800/1900*. Trans. Michael Metteer, with Chris Cullens. Stanford, Ca., 1990.

———. "Flechsig/Schreiber/Freud: Ein Nachrichtennetzwerk der Jahrhundertwende." *Der Wunderblock: Zeitschrift für Psychoanalyse* 11/12 (1984): 56–58.

———. *Gramophone, Film, Typewriter*. Trans. Geoffrey Winthrop-Young and Michael Wutz. Stanford, Ca., 1999.

———. "Die heilige Schrift." In *Das Heilige: Seine Spur in der Moderne*, ed. Dietmar Kamper and Christoph Wulf, pp. 154–62. Frankfurt am Main, 1987.

———. "Im Telegrammstil." In *Stil Geschichten und Funktionen eines literaturwissenschaftlichen Diskurses*, ed. Hans Ulrich Gumbrecht and Karl Ludwig Pfeiffer, pp. 358–70. Frankfurt am Main, 1986.

———. "Lullaby of Birdland." *Der Wunderblock: Zeitschrift für Psychoanalyse* 3 (Summer 1979): 5–19.

———. "Das Subjekt als Beamter." In *Die Frage nach dem Subjekt*, ed. Manfred Frank, Gérard Raulet, and Willem van Reijen, pp. 401–20. Frankfurt am Main, 1988.

———. "There Is No Software." *Stanford Literature Review* 9, no. 1 (Spring 1992): 81–90.

———. "Über die Sozialisation Wilhelm Meisters." In *Dichtung als Sozialisationsspiel: Studien zu Goethe und Gottfried Keller*, ed. Gerhard Kaiser and Friedrich Kittler, pp. 13–24. Göttingen, 1978.

———. "Writing into the Wind, Bettina." *Glyph: Textual Studies* 7 (1980): 32–69.

Kittler, Wolf. "Brief oder Blick. Die Schreibsituation der frühen Texte von Franz Kafka." In *Der junge Kafka*, ed. Gerhard Kurz, pp. 40–67. Frankfurt am Main, 1984.

———. *Die Geburt des Partisanen aus dem Geist der Poesie: Heinrich von Kleist und die Strategie der Befreiungskriege*. Freiburg in Breislau, 1987.

———. "Schreibmaschinen, Sprechmaschinen: Effekte technischer Medien im Werk Franz Kafkas." In *Franz Kafka: Schriftverkehr*, ed. Wolf Kittler and Gerhard Neumann, pp. 75–163. Freiburg in Breislau, 1990.

———. *Der Turmbau zu Babel und das Schweigen der Sirenen: Über das Reden, das Schweigen, die Stimme und die Schrift in vier Texten von Franz Kafka*. Erlangen, 1985.

Klaus, Georg, and Heinz Liebscher, eds. *Wörterbuch der Kybernetik*. East Berlin, 1976.

Kleemann, Gustav Heinrich Kurt. "Die Sozialpolitik der Reichs-Post- und Telegraphen-Verwaltung gegenüber ihren Beamten, Unterbeamten und Arbeitern." Dissertation, Jena, 1914.

Kleist, Heinrich von. *An Abyss Deep Enough: Letters of Heinrich von Kleist, with a Selection of Essays and Anecdotes.* Ed. and trans. Philip B. Miller. New York, 1982.

———. *Geschichte meiner Seele: Das Lebenszeugnis der Briefe.* Ed. Helmut Sembdner. Frankfurt am Main, 1980.

———. *Die Hermannschlacht: Ein Drama.* In *Sämtliche Werke und Briefe,* ed. Hemut Sembdner, 1: 533–628. Frankfurt am Main, 1985.

———. "Project for a Cannonball Postal Service." In *An Abyss Deep Enough,* pp. 245–46.

Klüber, Johann Ludwig. *Patriotische Wünsche das Postwesen in Teutschland betreffend.* Weimar, 1814.

———. *Das Postwesen in Teutschland, wie es war, ist, und seyn könnte.* Erlangen, 1811.

Knies, Karl. *Der Telegraph als Verkehrsmittel: Mit Erörterungen über den Nachrichtenverkehr überhaupt.* Tübingen, 1857.

Koch, Alfred. "Die deutschen Postverwaltungen im Zeitalter Napoleons I: Der Kampf um das Postregal in Deutschland und die Politik Napoleons I, (1798–1815)." *Archiv für deutsche Postgeschichte* 2 (1967): 1–38.

König, Bruno Emil. *Schwarze Cabinette: Eine Geschichte der Briefgeheimniß-Entheiligungen, Perlustrationen und Brieflogen, des postalischen Secretdienstes, des "kleinen Cabinets," der "Briefrevisionsbureaus" und sonstiger Briefgeheimnisverletzungen.* Berlin and Leipzig, 1899.

Korella, Gottfried. "Die Leiter der preußischen und deutschen Telegrafie bis zum Jahre 1876." *Archiv für deutsche Postgeschichte* 2 (1969): 18–27.

Koselleck, Reinhart. *Critique and Crisis: Enlightenment and the Pathogenesis of Modern Society.* New York, 1988.

Kunert, Arthur. *Telegraphen-Landkabel einschließlich der Flußkabel: Geschichte der deutschen Fernmeldekabel.* Part 1. Ed. P. Craemer. Berlin, 1940.

———. *Telegraphen-Seekabel: Geschichte der deutschen Fernmeldekabel.* Part 2. Ed. Deutsch-atlantische Telegraphengesellschaft Köln and the Norddeutsche Seekabelwerk A.-G. Nordenham. Cologne and Mülheim, 1962.

Küpfmüller, Karl, and Paul Storch. "Fernsprechen und Fernschreiben." *Europäischer Fernsprechdienst: Zeitschrift für den internationalen Nachrichtenverkehr* 51 (1939): 1–18.

Lacan, Jacques. "The Agency of the Letter in the Unconscious or Reason since Freud." In *Écrits: A Selection,* trans. Alan Sheridan, pp. 146–78. New York, 1977.

———. "The Direction of the Treatment and the Principles of Its Power." In *Écrits: A Selection,* trans. Alan Sheridan, pp. 226–80. New York, 1977.

———. *Encore: Le séminaire livre XX.* Paris, 1975.

———. *The Four Fundamental Concepts of Psycho-Analysis.* Ed. Jacques-Alain Miller. Trans. Alan Sheridan. New York, 1978.

———. "Le séminaire sur 'La Lettre volée.'" In *Écrits* (Paris, 1966), pp. 11–61.

Leclerc, Herbert. "Das 'Frollein vom Amt'—kleine Skizzen zu einem großen Thema." *Archiv für deutsche Postgeschichte* 1 (1977): 138–48.

———. "Kleine Zeittafel zur Geschichte des Briefkastens." *Archiv für deutsche Postgeschichte* 2 (1974): 58–59.

———. "Post- und Personenbeförderung in Preußen zur Zeit des Deutschen Bundes." In *Deutsche Postgeschichte: Essays und Bilder*, ed. Wolfgang Lotz, pp. 171–88. Berlin, 1989.

Ledât. "Zur Geschichte der Postkarte." *Archiv für Post und Telegraphie* 39, no. 22 (1911): 674–80.

Lerg, Winfried. *Rundfunkpolitik in der Weimarer Republik.* Munich, 1980.

Lichtenberg, Georg Christoph. *Sudelbücher*, vol. 1. In *Schriften und Briefe.* Ed. Wolfgang Promies. Frankfurt am Main, 1994.

Liebrucks, Bruno. "Sprache und Kunst." In *bewußt sein: Gerhard Funke zu eigen*, pp. 401–26. Bonn, 1975.

Lindner, Rudolf. "Untersuchungen, die Lautsprache auf elektrischem Wege fühlbar zu machen." *Berichte über die Verhandlungen der Königlich Sächsischen Gesellschaft der Wissenschaften zu Leipzig, math.-physische Klasse* 65 (1913): 82–109.

Lochmann, Dietmar. *Digitale Nachrichtentechnik.* Vol. 1. *Digitale Modulation und Signalverarbeitung.* Berlin, 1990.

Locke, John. *An Essay Concerning Human Understanding.* 2 vols. Ed. Alexander Campbell Fraser. New York, 1959.

Luhmann, Niklas. "How Can the Mind Participate in Communication?" In *Materialities of Communication*, ed. Hans Ulrich Gumbrecht and K. Ludwig Pfeiffer, pp. 371–87. Stanford, Ca., 1994.

McLuhan, Marshall. *Understanding Media: The Extensions of Man.* New York, 1964.

Maddox, Brenda. "Woman and the Switchboard." In *The Social Impact of the Telephone*, ed. Ithiel de Sola Pool, pp. 262–80. Cambridge, Mass., 1977.

Maier, Ernst. "Zum 25jährigen Jubiläum der deutschen Postkarte." *Die Postwertzeichenkunde* 8 (1897): 92–93.

Martin, Ernst. *Die Schreibmaschine und ihre Entwicklungsgeschichte.* 2 vols. Aachen, 1949.

Martineau, Harriet. *Harriet Martineau's Autobiography: With Memorials by Maria Weston Chapman*, vol. 3. London, 1877.

Martini, Fritz. "Der Bildungsroman: Zur Geschichte des Wortes und der Theorie." *DVjs* 35 (1961): 44–63.

Maxwell, J. Clerk. "On Governors." *Proceedings of the London Royal Society* 16 (1868): 270–83.

Meier, Hans. "Die Weltpostkarte." In Paikert, Gasser, and Oldenburg, pp. 262–65.

Melville, Herman. "Bartleby, the Scrivener. A Story of Wall-Street." In *The Piazza*

Tales and Other Prose Pieces 1839–1860. Ed. Harrison Hayford, et al., pp. 13–45. Chicago, 1987.

Meyer, Ulfilas. "Über die Frequenz der Fernsprechströme." *Mitteilungen aus dem Telegraphentechnischen Reichsamt* 9 (1921): 169–70.

Muir, Douglas N. "Post Office Reform." *Gibbons Stamp Monthly* 17, no. 18 (1987): 38–39.

"Der Musiktelegraph" (anonymous). *Gartenlaube* 51 (1963): 807–9.

Musil, Robert. "Die Amsel." In *Prosa und Stücke, Kleine Prosa, Aphorismen, Autobiographisches, Essays, und Reden, Kritik,* ed. Adolf Frisé, pp. 548–62. Reinbek bei Hamburg, 1978.

Nabokov, Vladimir. *Look at the Harlequins!* San Francisco, 1974.

Die Nerven der Armee: Aus dem Kriegstagebuch eines Telegraphisten. Berlin, 1916.

Neumann, Gerhard. *Franz Kafka: "Das Urteil." Text, Materialien, Kommentar.* Munich and Vienna, 1981.

———. "Nachrichten vom 'Pontus.'" Das Problem der Kunst im Werk Franz Kafkas." In *Franz Kafka Symposium 1983,* ed. Wilhelm Emrich and Bernd Goldmann, pp. 101–57. Mainz, 1985.

———. "Umkehrung und Ablenkung: Franz Kafkas 'Gleitendes Paradox.'" In *Franz Kafka,* ed. Heinz Politzer, pp. 459–515. Darmstadt, 1973.

Nietzsche, Friedrich. *Briefwechsel: Kritische Ausgabe.* Ed. Georgio Colli and Mazzino Montinari. Berlin, 1975–84.

———. *On The Genealogy of Morals.* In *On the Genealogy of Morals and Ecce Homo,* trans. Walter Kaufmann, pp. 15–163. New York, 1967.

North, Gottfried. "Die geschichtliche Entwicklung des Post- und Fernmeldewesens." *Archiv für deutsche Postgeschichte* 2 (1974): 6–25.

Novalis (Friedrich von Hardenberg). "Dialogen und Monolog." In *Werke, Tagebücher und Briefe Friedrich von Hardenbergs,* ed. Hans Joachim Mähl and Richard Samuel, 2: 425–39. Munich and Vienna, 1978.

———. "Glauben und Liebe, oder Der König und die Königin." In *Werke,* 2: 290–304.

———. *Henry von Ofterdingen.* Trans. Palmer Hilty. New York, 1964.

Oberliesen, Rolf. *Information, Daten und Signale: Geschichte technischer Informationsverarbeitung.* Reinbek bei Hamburg, 1982.

Obermeit, Werner. *"Das unsichtbare Ding, das Seele heißt": Die Entdeckung der Psyche im bürgerlichen Zeitalter.* Frankfurt am Main, 1980.

Ohmann, Fritz. *Die Anfänge des Postwesens und die Taxis.* Leipzig, 1909.

Oliver, B. M., J. R. Pierce, and C. E. Shannon. "The Philosophy of PCM." *Proceedings of the Institute of Royal Engineers* 36, no. 11 (1948): 1324–31.

Osborn, Albert S. "Schreibmaschinenschrift als Beweismittel." *Archiv für geschichtliche Schriftuntersuchungen und verwandte Gebiete* 1, no. 4 (1908–9): 388–407.

Ott, Hugo. *Martin Heidegger: A Political Life*. Trans. Allan Blunden. London, 1993.

"Das österreichische Post- und Telegraphenwesen im Jahre 1914" (anonymous). *Archiv für Post und Telegraphie* 44 (1916): 293–98.

Paikert, Hans, Arnim Gasser, and Dietrich Oldenburg. *Die UPU-Studie: Philatelistische Belege zum Thema Weltpostverein*. Ed. UNOP. Cologne, 1979.

Pestalozzi, Johann Heinrich. "Über den Sinn des Gehörs in Hinsicht auf Menschenbildung durch Ton und Sprache." In *Ausgewählte Schriften*, ed. Wilhelm Flitner, pp. 246–70. Frankfurt am Main, 1983.

Piendl, Max. *Thurn und Taxis, 1517–1867: Zur Geschichte des fürstlichen Hauses und der Thurn und Taxisschen Post*. Frankfurt am Main, 1967.

Pieper, Hans. "Aus der Geschichte der optischen Telegraphie und die Anfänge der elektro-magnetischen Telegraphen." *Archiv für deutsche Postgeschichte* 2 (1967): 39–55.

Politzer, Heinz. "Franz Kafkas vollendeter Roman: Zur Typologie seiner Briefe an Felice." In *Das Nachleben der Romantik in der modernen deutschen Literatur*, ed. Wolfgang Paulsen, pp. 192–211. Heidelberg, 1969.

Popp, Ernst. "Postgeschichte." In *Post- und Telegraphen-Museum: Jubiläumsführer 1889/1959*, pp. 5–20. Vienna, 1959.

"Post, Telegraphie und Fernsprechwesen während der ersten 25 Regierungsjahre unseres Kaisers" (anonymous). *Archiv für Post und Telegraphie* 41 (1913): 549–69.

"Die Postkarte" (anonymous). *Archiv für Post und Telegraphie* 22, no. 11 (1894): 343–45.

Posthandbuch "Der kleine Stephan." Ed. Fritz Ulrich. 18th edition. Dresden, 1911–12.

Pott, Hans-Georg. "Franz Grillparzer zum 200. Geburtstag." *Gustav Freytag Blätter* 49 (1991): 12–21.

Preyer, Wilhelm. "Über die Grenzen der Tonwahrnehmung." In *Sammlung Physiologischer Abhandlungen*, ed. Wilhelm Preyer, 1: 1–72. Jena, 1877.

Priesdorff, Kurt von, ed. *Soldatisches Führertum*. Parts 1–5. Hamburg, 1937.

Pynchon, Thomas. *The Crying of Lot 49*. New York, 1967.

———. *Gravity's Rainbow*. New York, 1973.

Raabe, Heinrich August. *Die Postgeheimnisse oder die hauptsächlichsten Regeln, welche man beim Reisen und bei Versendungen mit der Post beobachten muß um Verdruß und Verlust zu vermeiden*. Leipzig, 1803.

"Rationes dictandi." In Rockinger, part 1, pp. 9–28.

Reichardt, Wolf. "Das Recht an Briefen." Dissertation. Leipzig, 1905.

Reiners, Ludwig. *Friedrich: Das Leben des Preußenkönigs*. Munich, 1986.

Reis, Philipp. "Über Telephonie durch den Galvanischen Strom." In *50 Jahre Fernsprecher in Deutschland 1877–1927*, ed. Ernst Feyerabend, pp. 208–212. Berlin, 1927.

Renard, Maurice. "La Mort et le Coquillage." In *L'invitation à la peur*, pp. 67–72. Paris, 1970.

Richter, Bruno. "Der Brief und seine Stellung in der Erziehung seit Gellert." Dissertation. Leipzig, 1900.

Riepl, Wolfgang. *Das Nachrichtenwesen des Altertums: Mit besonderer Rücksicht auf die Römer*. Darmstadt, 1972.

Rilke, Rainer Maria. *Neue Gedichte: New Poems*. Trans. John Bayley. Manchester, 1992.

———. *The Notebooks of Malte Laurids Brigge*. Trans M. D. Herter Norton. In *Rainer Maria Rilke: Prose and Poetry*, ed. Egon Schwarz, pp. 3–153. New York, 1984.

Risch, Friedrich Adolf. *Heinrich von Stephan: Die Idee der Weltpost*. Hamburg, 1948.

Rockinger, Ludwig. *Briefsteller und formelbücher des eilften bis vierzehnten jahrhunderts*. Part 1. Reprint, Aalen, 1969.

Rogozinski, Dolorès. "La levée de la lettre." *Revue des Sciences Humaine* 195, no. 3 (1984): 131–50.

Rothschild, Arthur de. *Histoire de la poste aux lettres et du timbre-poste depuis leurs origines jusqu'à nos jours*. Geneva and Paris, 1984.

Rübsam, Joseph. *Johann Baptista von Taxis: Ein Staatsmann und Militär unter Philipp II. und Philipp III., 1530–1610*. Freiburg in Breislau, 1889.

Salvá, Francisco. "Memoria sobre la electricidad applicada á la telegrafia." *Memoria de la Real Academia de ciencias naturales y artes de Barcelona (secunda épocha)* 1 (1878): 1–60.

Sautter, Karl. *Geschichte der Deutschen Reichspost 1871–1945*. Frankfurt am Main, 1951.

Scherer, Wolfgang. "Klaviaturen, Visible Speech und Phonographie: Marginalien zur technischen Entstellung der Sinne im 19. Jahrhundert." In Kittler, Schneider, and Weber, pp. 37–54.

Schiller, Friedrich von. *Wallenstein: A Dramatic Poem*. In *The Robbers: Wallenstein*, trans. F. J. Lamport, pp. 161–472. New York, 1977.

Schlegel, Friedrich. "Über Goethes Meister." In *Schriften zur Literatur*, ed. Wolfdietrich Rasch, pp. 260–78. Munich, 1985.

———. "Über die Philosophie. An Dorothea." In *Kritische Friedrich-Schlegel-Ausgabe*, ed. Ernst Behler, 8: 41–62. Munich, 1975.

———. "Vom Wesen der Kritik." In *Schriften*, pp. 250–59.

Schmiedecke, Hugo. *Die Verkehrsmittel im Kriege*. Berlin, 1906.

Schmitt, Carl. *Land und Meer: Eine weltgeschichtliche Betrachtung*. Cologne, 1981.

Schneider, Manfred. *Die erkaltete Herzensschrift: Der autobiographische Text im 20. Jahrhundert*. Munich, 1986.

———. "Kafkas Lockung: Hochzeitsvorbereitung auf unbrauchbaren Blättern."

In *Das Subjekt der Dichtung: Festschrift für Gerhard Kaiser*, ed. Gerhard Buhr, Friedrich A. Kittler, and Host Turk, pp. 99–117. Würzburg, 1990.

———. "Nachrichten aus dem Unbewußten. Richard Wagners letzter Traum." *Jahrbuch der Bayerischen Staatsoper*, 1990–91: 69–80.

Schöne, Albrecht. "Über Goethes Brief an Behrisch vom 10. November 1767." In *Festschrift für Richard Alewyn*, ed. Herbert Singer and Benno von Wiese, pp. 193–229. Cologne, 1967.

Schottelius, Justus Georg. *Der schreckliche Sprachkrieg: Horrendum bellum grammaticale Teutonum antiquissimorum.* Ed. Friedrich A. Kittler and Stefan Rieger. Leipzig, 1991.

Schöttle, Gustav. *Der Telegraph in administrativer und finanzieller Hinsicht.* Stuttgart, 1883.

Schrader, Hans-Jürgen. "Unsägliche Liebesbriefe. Heinrich von Kleist an Wilhelmine von Zenge." In *Kleist-Jahrbuch 1981/82*, ed. Hans Joachim Kreutzer, pp. 86–96. Berlin, 1983.

Schramm, Percy Ernst, ed. *Kriegstagebuch des Oberkommandos der Wehrmacht (Wehrmachtführungsstab) 1940–1945.* Vol. 4, part 2. Herrsching, 1982.

Schreiber, Jens. *Das Symptom des Schreibens: Roman und absolutes Buch in der Frühromantik (Novalis/Schlegel).* New York, 1983.

———. "Word-Engineering: Informationstechnologie und Dichtung." In *Das schnelle Altern der neuesten Literatur*, ed. Jochen Hörisch and Hubert Winkels, pp. 287–305. Düsseldorf, 1985.

Schultze, Alfred. "Zur Geschichte der Ansichtpostkarte." *Vossische Zeitung*, no. 3367 (August 8, 1903).

Searle, John R. *Speech Acts: An Essay in the Philosophy of Language.* New York, 1969.

Sembdner, Helmut, ed. *Heinrich von Kleists Lebensspuren: Dokumente und Berichte der Zeitgenossen.* Revised and expanded edition. Frankfurt am Main, 1977.

Serres, Michel. *The Parasite.* Trans. Lawrence R. Schehr. Baltimore, 1982.

Shannon, Claude Elwood, and Warren Weaver. "Communication in the Presence of Noise." In *Claude Elwood Shannon: Collected Papers*, ed. N. J. A. Sloane and Aaron D. Wyner, pp. 160–72. New York, 1992.

———. "Communication Theory of Secrecy Systems." In *Collected Papers*, pp. 84–143.

———. *The Mathematical Theory of Communication.* Urbana, 1962.

Showalter, Dennis. "Soldiers into Postmasters? The Electric Telegraph as an Instrument of Command in the Prussian Army." *Military Affairs—The Journal of Military History, Including Theory and Technology* 37, no. 1 (1973): 48 n. 52.

Siebenkees, Johann Christian. *Über das Geheimniß der Posten.* Frankfurt and Leipzig, 1788.

Siegert, Bernhard. "Denunziationen. Über Briefkästen und die Erfindung des permanenten Kontakts." In *Technopathologien*, ed. Bernhard Dotzler, pp. 87–109. Munich, 1991.

———. "Gehörgänge ins Jenseits: Zur Geschichte der Einrichtung telephonischer Kommunikation in der Psychoanalyse." *FRAGMENTE: Schriftenreihe zur Psychoanalyse* 35–36 (1991): 51–69.

———. "'Hold me in your arms, Ma Bell': Telefonie und Literatur." In *Telefon und Gesellschaft: Beiträge zu einer Soziologie der Telekommunikation*, ed. U. Lange and Klaus Beck, pp. 330–47. Berlin, 1989.

———. "Netzwerke der Regimentalität. Harsdörfers *Teutscher Secretarius* und die Schicklichkeit der Briefe im 17. Jahrhundert." *Modern Language Notes: German Issue* 109 (April 1990): 536–62.

———. "Switchboards and Sex: The Nut(t) Case." In *Inscribing Science: Scientific Texts and the Materiality of Communication*, ed. Timothy Lenoir, pp. 78–90. Stanford, Ca., 1998.

Siemens, Werner von. *Lebenserinnerungen*. 16th edition. Munich, 1956.

———. "Über Telephonie." *Monatsberichte der Königlich Preußischen Akademie der Wissenschaften* (1878): 38–53.

Smolak, Kurt. "Einleitung." In Erasmus of Rotterdam, "De conscribendis epistolis," in *Ausgewählte Schriften*, ed. W. Welzig, 8: ix–lxxxvi. Darmstadt, 1980.

Snyder, Charles. "Clarence John Blake and Alexander Graham Bell: Otology and the Telephone." In *The Annals of Otology, Rhinology & Laryngology*, supplement 13, 83, no. 4, part 2 (July–August 1974): 3–32.

Soemmerring, Samuel Thomas. "Über einen elektrischen Telegraphen." *Denkschriften der Königlichen Akademie der Wissenschaften zu München* (1809–10): 401–14.

Staff, Frank. *The Penny Post, 1680–1918*. London, 1964.

Steig, Reinhold. "Bettina." *Deutsche Rundschau* 57 (1892): 262–74.

Steinhausen, Georg. *Geschichte des deutschen Briefes*. Parts 1 and 2. Berlin, 1889–91.

Stephan, Heinrich von. *Geschichte der Preußischen Post*. Berlin, 1928.

———. *Weltpost und Luftschifffahrt: Ein Vortrag im wissenschaftlichen Verein zu Berlin*. Berlin, 1874.

Stifter, Adalbert. *Indian Summer*. Trans. Wendell Frye. New York, 1985.

———. "Die Wiener Stadtpost." In *Gesammelte Werke*. Vol. 6. *Kleine Schriften*, pp. 125–30. Wiesbaden, 1959.

Stingelin, Martin. "Gehirntelegraphie: Die Rede der Paranoia von der Macht der Medien. Falldarstellungen." In *Arsenale der Seele: Literatur- und Medienanalyse seit 1870*, ed. Friedrich A. Kittler and Georg Christoph Tholen, pp. 51–69. Munich, 1989.

Stix, Franz. "Zur Geschichte und Organisation der Wiener Geheimen Ziffernkanzlei (von ihren Anfängen bis zum Jahre 1848)." *Mitteilungen des Österreichischen Instituts für Geschichtsforschung* 51 (1937): 131–60.

Stössel, Wilhelm. "Zur Entwicklung der Briefmarke." *Archiv für deutsche Post-geschichte* 2 (1974): 54–57.

Stramm, August. "Historische, Kritische und Finanzpolitische Untersuchungen über die Briefpostgebührensätze des Welpostvereins und ihre Grundlagen." Dissertation. Halle, 1909.

———. *Das Werk*. Ed. René Radrizzani. Wiesbaden, 1963.

Stumpf, Carl. "Über die Tonlage der Konsonanten und die für das Sprachver-ständnis entscheidende Gegend des Tonreiches." *Sitzungsberichte der Preuß-ischen Akademie der Wissenschaften* 2 (1921): 636–40.

Tarchanow, J. "Das Telephon im Gebiete der thierischen Elektrizität." *St. Peters-burger medicinische Wochenschrift* 4, no. 11 (1879): 93–95.

Tieck, Ludwig. *Franz Sternbalds Wanderungen: Eine altdeutsche Geschichte*. Stuttgart, 1979.

———. *William Lovell*. Stuttgart, 1986.

Todorov, Tzvetan. "Poétique." In Oswald Ducrot, Tzvetan Todorov, Dan Sperber, Moustafa Safouan, and Francis Wahl, *Qu'est-ce que le structuralisme?* pp. 99–166. Paris, 1968.

Turing, Alan. "Intelligente Maschinen, eine häretische Theorie." In *Intelligence Service: Schriften*, ed. Bernhard Dotzler and Friedrich Kittler, pp. 7–15. Berlin, 1987.

Vaillé, Eugène. *Histoire générale des postes françaises*. Vol. 1. *Des origines à la fin du moyen âge*. Paris, 1947.

Van Creveld, Martin. *Command in War*. Cambridge, Mass., 1985.

Vélayer. "Instrvction povr cevx Qui voudront escrire d'vn quartier de Paris en vn autre, & auoir responce promptement deux & trois fois le iour." In Roth-schild, pp. 100–101.

Veredarius, O. (Ferdinand Hennicke). *Das Buch von der Weltpost: Entwickelung und Wirken der Post und Telegraphie im Weltverkehr*. Heidelberg, 1984.

Virilio, Paul. "Fahrzeug." In *Fahren, fahren, fahren* (Berlin, 1978), pp. 19–50.

———. *L'horizon négatif: Essai de dromoscopie*. Paris, 1984.

———. *Speed and Politics*. Trans. Mark Polizzotti. New York, 1986.

Vogt, Martin. "Die Post im Kaiserreich: Heinrich (von) Stephan und seine Nach-folger." In *Deutsche Postgeschichte: Essays und Bilder*, ed. Wolfgang Lotz, pp. 203–39. Berlin, 1989.

Vögtle, Fritz. *Thomas Alva Edison in Selbstzeugnissen und Bilddokumenten*. Reinbek bei Hamburg, 1982.

Voigt, Fritz. *Die Entwicklung des Verkehrssystems*. Vol. 2.2 of his *Verkehr*. Ber-lin, 1965.

———. *Die Theorie der Verkehrswirtschaft*. Vol. 1.1 of his *Verkehr*. Berlin, 1973.

Wagenbach, Klaus. *Franz Kafka: Bilder aus seinem Leben*. Berlin, 1983.

Wagenknecht, Christian J. "Goethes 'Ehrfurchten' und die Symbolik der Loge." *Zeitschrift für deutsche Philologie* 84 (1965): 490–97.

Wagner, Karl Willy. "Der Frequenzbereich von Sprache und Musik." *Elektrotechnische Zeitschrift* 45 (1924): 451–56.

Wagner, Oskar. "Die Frau im Dienste der Reichs-Post- und Telegraphenverwaltung." Dissertation. Halle, 1913.

Walden, Herwarth. *Einblick in Kunst: Expressionismus, Futurismus, Kubismus.* Berlin, 1924.

Weber, Wilhelm. *Geschichte der Lithographie.* Munich, 1964.

Weigert, Franz. "Die Geschichte der Drucksache." *Archiv für deutsche Postgeschichte* 2 (1978): 19–61.

Weiß, Ernst. "Lebensfragen des Theaters." In *Prager Theaterbuch*, ed. Carl Schluderpacher, pp. 97–100. Prague, 1924.

Weithase, Hugo. "Geschichte des Weltpostvereins." Dissertation. Strasbourg, 1895.

Wellershoff, Dieter. *Die Sirene: Eine Novelle.* Frankfurt am Main, 1982.

Wernekke, Hugo. *Goethe und die Königliche Kunst.* Leipzig, 1905.

Wessel, Horst A. *Die Entwicklung des elektrischen Nachrichtenwesens in Deutschland und die rheinische Industrie.* Wiesbaden, 1983.

Wilson, W. Daniel. *Geheimräte gegen Geheimbünde: Ein unbekanntes Kapitel der klassisch-romantischen Geschichte Weimars.* Stuttgart, 1991.

Wordsworth, Ann. "Derrida and Foucault: Writing the History of Historicity." In *Post-Structuralism and the Question of History*, ed. Derek Attridge, Geoffrey Bennington, and Robert Young, pp. 116–25. Cambridge, 1987.

"Zur Geschichte des englischen Postwesens" (anonymous). In G. F. Hüttner, *Beiträge zur Kenntniß des Postwesens*, vol. 4 (1850), pp. 145–56.

Library of Congress Cataloging-in-Publication Data

Siegert, Bernhard.
  [Relais.   English]
  Relays : literature as an epoch of the postal system / Bernhard
Siegert ; translated by Kevin Repp.
    p.   cm. — (Writing science)
  Includes bibliographical references and index.
    ISBN 0-8047-3236-1 (cloth : alk. paper). — ISBN 0-8047-3238-8
(pbk. : alk. paper)
    1. Literature, Modern—History and criticism.   2. Postal Service—
History   I. Title.   II. Series.
PN98.S46S5413   1999
836.009—dc21   99-21523

⊗ This book is printed on acid-free, recycled paper.

Original printing 1999

Last figure below indicates year of this printing:
08   07   06   05   04   03   02   01   00   99

Designed by Janet Wood
Typeset by James P. Brommer in 10/14 Sabon
and Helvetica Black display